A History of
Poland

A History of
Poland

New edition

O. Halecki

*With additional material
by A. Polansky
and Thaddeus V. Grommada*

BARNES
&NOBLE
BOOKS
NEW YORK

This edition published by Barnes & Noble, Inc.

1993 Barnes & Noble Books

ISBN 0-88029-858-8

Printed and bound in the United States of America

M 9 8 7 6 5

Contents

Foreword to the 1992 edition   vii

Introduction   ix

PART I

THE FORMATION OF THE STATE AND OF THE NATION

1	Early Origins	3
2	The First Kings	11
3	The Disintegration of the Kingdom	21
4	The German Colonization and the Mongol Invasion	31
5	The Reconstruction of the Kingdom	41
6	Casimir the Great	52

PART II

THE CENTURIES OF POLAND'S GREATNESS

7	Jadwiga of Anjou	65
8	Grunwald and Horodlo	75
9	Varna and Danzig	85
10	The Zenith of a Dynasty	95
11	The Epoch of the First Congress of Vienna	106
12	The Union of Lublin	117

PART III

THE EXPERIMENT OF THE ROYAL REPUBLIC

13	John Zamoyski	131
14	The Last Great Designs	142
15	The Deluge	153
16	John Sobieski	165
17	The Decay	176
18	The Regeneration	189
19	The Partitions	202

PART IV

THE ORDEAL

20	Napoleonic Poland	217
21	Romantic Poland: The Insurrections	229
22	Romantic Poland: Her Poets	242
23	Organic Work	252
24	Waiting for Freedom	263

PART V

NEW POLAND'S TRAGEDY

25	Resurrection	275
26	Reconstruction	290
27	Destruction	307
28	Ten Years of Trial	326
29	The Rise and Fall of Gomulka	345
30	Poland under Gierek: The Failure of Consumer Communism	374
31	From Kania to Jaruzelski	400

PART VI

TOWARD THE "GRAND FAILURE" OF COMMUNISM IN POLAND

32	Poland under Jaruzelski	429
33	Gorbachev's Impact	437
34	Post-Communist Poland: Mazowiecki's Government	445
	Postscript	455
	Index	457

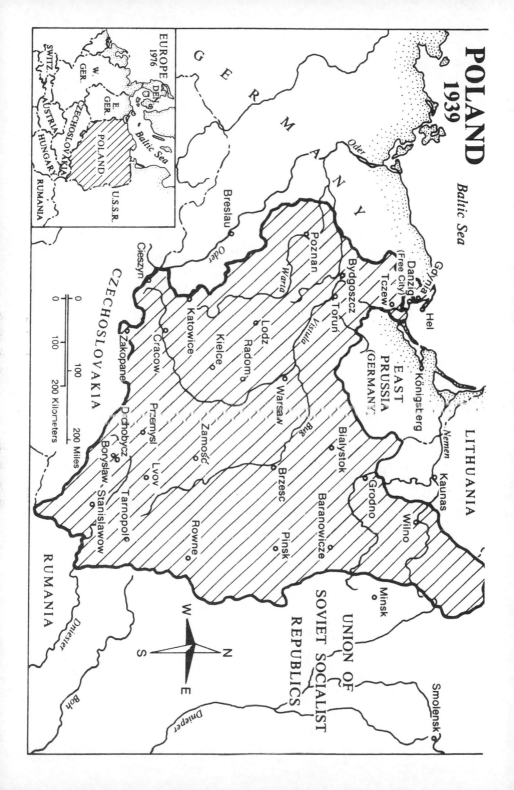

POLAND
1939

EUROPE
1976

SWITZ.
W. GER.
DEN.
E. GER.
CZECHOSLOVAKIA
AUSTRIA
HUNGARY
RUMANIA
POLAND
U.S.S.R.
Baltic Sea

Baltic Sea

G E R M A N Y

Oder

Gdynia
Hel
Danzig
(Free City)
Tczew
Königsberg

EAST
PRUSSIA
(GERMANY)

LITHUANIA

Kaunas
Nemen

Breslau
Oder
Warta
Poznan
Bydgoszcz
Toruń

Cieszyn

Katowice
Cracow
Zakopane
Drohobycz
Boryslaw
Stanislawow
Tarnopole
Lvov
Przemysl
Kielce
Lodz
Radom
Vistula
Warsaw
Zamość
Rowne

CZECHOSLOVAKIA

Bialystok
Brzesc
Bug
Baranowicze
Grodno
Wilno
Pinsk

UNION OF
SOVIET SOCIALIST
REPUBLICS

Minsk
Smolensk

RUMANIA

Dniester
Boh
Dnieper

0
0
100
100
200 Miles
200 Kilometers

W N
S E

Foreword to the 1992 edition

This edition includes an afterword bringing the sequence of events in Poland up to date from the period of martial law through the "grand failure" of Communism and Lech Walesa's inauguration as President.

Introduction

POLAND, who now has reached her millennium, is often regarded as one of the new States. This oblivion of the Poland of the past is at the root of all the misunderstandings which stand in the way of a correct comprehension of the Poland of to-day. True, Polish history is not entirely unknown to the foreigner. But his mind usually retains only a few isolated facts of a specially striking nature, such as that of the Partitions. Rarely, on the other hand, does he go back to the origin of our historical evolution. More rarely still does he grasp its continuity, which even the Partitions were not able to break. Above all, he scarcely ever realizes the role that Poland has played in the general history of Europe from early times.

To remedy this state of affairs, regrettable not only from the point of view of contemporary Poland, but also from that of historical science, a simple manual of Polish history, more complete and more widely read than those which already exist in universally accessible languages, is not sufficient. What is needed is a philosophy of our national history conceived as an integral part of European history.

This little book sets out with a more modest object. The philosophy of history, even that of an individual history, has nothing chimerical in its nature, as was at one time believed. But to have a truly scientific character its study should be prepared by attempts at a synthesis which, without losing sight of their final object, will not form definite conclusions in advance.

To make the reader reflect on the essential problems of Polish history, and on their relations with the destinies of other countries, perhaps to induce discussions on this subject, and, in any case, to bring forward the general questions presented by our past—these are our aims in the following pages. Strictly based on positive facts, as established by the progress of science, inspired by concern for impartiality and loyalty in regard to every other nation, these pages will, however, not be false to the national conscience or even to the personal opinions of their author.

The personal, therefore subjective, element is inevitable, not only in critical judgments which in our opinion are the right and the duty of the historian, but even in the choice of the facts mentioned and of the problems to be treated in so short a synthesis. Let us, therefore, indicate in advance the principles which have guided this choice.

The importance of an historical event is the greater in proportion to the durable character of its consequences. This reasoning ought to determine the attention we should pay to all facts, even distant ones, which have retained a character of actuality up to our own days. The foreign reader will, moreover, require the Polish author to show him what the particular features of Polish history have been, and the contribution that his people have brought to the common patrimony of European civilization. But, in addition, he will be interested in Poland as a member of that European community, in the manner by which Poland became a part of it, and in the relations which she maintained with other countries. And we do not hesitate to add that in the course of all those works of ours which have preceded and prepared the way for this one, we have examined, often with a passionate interest, everything which has seemed able to enlighten us on the providential mission that Poland has, as well as might be, fulfilled in the general evolution of humanity.

What in any case seems to us indispensable is the necessity of basing every historical synthesis on a division into periods, corresponding as logically as possible to the march of events and to their leading ideas. As regards Polish history, this chronological division is relatively easy; because the generally accepted and apparently conventional periods in reality prove to be the only ones that can satisfy the requirements which we have just formulated.

The period of our first dynasty, that of the Piasts, shaped our State and our nation. The second, the great centuries of the Jagiellonian dynasty, from its outset enlarged the framework of our history into unforeseen dimensions by joining to the country, as the result of a whole series of unions, territories and populations which, until then, had been strangers to it. It left as its legacy a 'Republican Commonwealth,' which, under kings freely chosen from the most varied families, attempted during the third period a great constitutional experiment which finally collapsed. The unparalleled catastrophe of the Partitions by its very nature inaugurated a new period, the fourth, in which Poland offered to the world the tragic spectacle of a nation without a State, divided territorially, but profiting by the experiences of the past to preserve all her traditions until the moment which should restore her independence.

That moment came with the Great War. The period that

then began for Poland, as well as for the whole world, far from being closed, cannot yet be the object of any final, synthetic treatment. But in view of recent and current events, it would be simply impossible to describe Poland's tragic destinies without bringing the narrative up to the present day.

We still owe our readers some words of explanation concerning the proportions we have observed in treating of the periods of Polish history. In our opinion historians have often exaggerated in according a privileged place to the times nearest our own. In the case of Poland this exaggeration seems particularly inopportune, since it attaches a disproportionate importance to the period when our nation was in great measure obliged to play a passive part and when its creative powers had no way of manifesting themselves except in the sphere of thought.

For Poland, as for every other country, the most vital historical traditions are those of her great centuries, even if those centuries should be relatively distant. The fact that they are the least known abroad is an additional reason for dwelling upon them. In doing this we have likewise hoped to avoid the grave mistake, more manifest to-day than ever, of making the Partitions the centre of the whole past history of Poland. This central place belongs rather to the epoch of the Jagiellos, and, even in that of the Piasts—the furthest removed but the longest—we at times find ourselves in the presence of events whose repercussions may be felt in our own days. Hence, each of these four great periods occupies an almost equal place in our story.

*   *   *

Part I

THE FORMATION OF THE STATE
AND OF THE NATION

1

Early Origins

IN ORDER to find an adequate approach to Polish history, it is essential to observe in what epoch and under what conditions Poland passed from the prehistoric stage into history: that is to say, from an isolated and legendary existence to a life related to the life of neighbouring peoples, upon which light is thrown by documentary evidence. In the case of the majority of European nations, with the exception of the Greeks and Romans, this transition was effected either at the moment when they entered into contact with the Graeco-Roman world, or in that of their conversion to Christianity. At times these two moments are almost simultaneous: and this is precisely the case with Poland, where their respective dates are as near to each other as 963 and 966.

These dates are in themselves highly eloquent. They lead us into the midst of the tenth century, which was an epoch of profound transformation for the whole of Europe. It was not only Poland who then made her entry into history. Up to this date only the southern and western part of Europe was well known to history. Henceforth the historic community, so long limited to the ancient territories of the Roman Em-

3

pire and to its sphere of influence, was gradually extended towards the north-east, to the entire Slavonic world, and to the Scandinavian countries.

On the other hand, this same tenth century, which was for many countries a century of chaos, saw the consolidation of the two universal powers which were to preside over the destinies of Europe during the course of the following centuries: the Papacy and the Empire. It was the latter which, after the transitory Carlovingian restoration, was first definitely reconstituted and transferred to the King of Germany. It is worth emphasizing that this important event took place exactly one year before the first Polish-German conflict which inaugurated the political history of Poland. The new Empire, in return for its renovation by the Papacy, assured its protection to the latter, which enabled it to emerge from one of the gravest crises through which the Holy See has passed, and to prepare, together with the reform of the Church, the way for its temporal power. At the same time, the Church of Rome, being leagued with the Empire of the West, alienated the Empire of the East, and although the schism was not yet consummated, the rupture with Byzantium was impending. At the moment, therefore, when Poland accepted the Christian faith she had to choose between the two centres of Christianity, and at the same time between the two increasingly divergent centres of European civilization.

But what was the reason which had retarded the opening of Poland's historical role until the moment when she was faced with such a delicate position? Why had the other western Slavs, indeed, even the eastern Slavs, preceded her in their relations with the external world? This reason is easily to be found in her geographical situation.

This situation, which was to influence but not determine all its historical evolution, soon proved very dangerous to the

Polish State then forming. But, on the other hand, it had been favourable to its first pagan beginning. Dwelling in the centre of the Slav world, removed from the routes of the great migrations and even from the great trade routes, the tribes which were to form the Polish nation only experienced later the grave difficulties and dangers that beset their neighbours. These immediate neighbours, who had sprung from the same race as the Poles, but were separated from them by vast forest frontiers, had to face far earlier the double danger which surrounded the Slavs: on one side, the Germanic danger; on the other, the Asiatic danger.

However, the stubborn resistance that the Slav populations between the Elbe and the Oder offered to the German conquest was nearing its end. Bohemia was gradually entering the orbit of German influence, and Great Moravia had only been an ephemeral power. At the same time the tribes which were to form the different Russias were uniting, thanks to Norse conquerors, in one vast state, extending almost indefinitely its colonization and expansion to the east, but not succeeding in hurling back the Asiatic nomads who were successively occupying the steppes bordering the Black Sea.

Under these conditions the relative security which prehistoric Poland had enjoyed was becoming increasingly precarious. Soon she would no longer be able to keep apart from the struggles which were being waged still outside her frontiers, but which were approaching her own territory in an alarming fashion. Moreover, the limits of that territory were far from being established, and in proportion as the young State consolidated itself it was bound to anticipate numerous territorial disputes even with its Slav neighbours.

We speak of a State in formation, because the beginning of the Polish State goes back to an epoch anterior at the very least by a century and a half to its first contact with the German Empire and to its christianization. Unfortunately, this beginning is lost in prehistoric obscurity out of which the most penetrating archaeological and linguistic researches can disentangle but little of value. Their results compel us to admit that the primitive life of the Polish population in no way differed from that of the other Slav tribes of the same epoch. But this discovery, which was moreover one easily foreseen, tells us nothing that is of particular interest. It is likewise of slight importance from the point of view of general history whether one or another of the Slav chiefs who had chance relations with the Carlovingian Empire can be reasonably held to have been Poles. From this same point of view it is scarcely more important to know whether a small part of the future Poland was really attached, more or less closely, to Great Moravia, because, in any case, even the Christian influences which then seem to have penetrated there under the form of the Slavonic rite had no result.

But, on the other hand, there is another long-disputed problem which is of interest, not only to the erudite specialist and to the Pole curious to learn the condition of his first ancestors. It is the question of ascertaining whether the Polish State was formed by way of conquest, particularly Norse conquest, similar, perhaps, to that which formed Russia.

Now we know as a matter of fact that there was nothing of the sort. No hypothesis put forth to this effect can be maintained. Certainly the union of the different Polish tribes in a single political organism could not have been effected without struggles. But the conquests that these struggles, the details of which are completely unknown, necessarily implied, were only, so to speak, internal conquests, subjecting one tribe to another, and ending in the hegemony of one among them, the Polians, and of its princely dynasty, the

Piasts. These two names hold a place in Polish history which deserves a brief comment.

The Polians, which signifies dwellers in the fields, have left their name, hardly modified, to the whole Polish nation. Their territory, the region of Gniezno, the first capital, and that of Poznan, the seat of the first bishop, became the nucleus of the Polish State. This region was to remain for a long time simply Poland: Poland properly so called, although from a very remote epoch it bore the name of Great Poland, as in our own days.

Among the other tribes that soon became subject to the Polians we must mention at least the Silesians and the Maso- vians. The region of these latter, neighbours of the Baltic peoples, of the ancient Prussians of Lithuanian race, for cen- turies kept a special and somewhat archaic character. We know to-day that the region of the Upper Vistula with Cracow was also, in pagan times, joined to that of the Polians; but it was precisely this region, the future Little Poland, the new Poland often opposed to the ancient Poland, which was gradually to take the first place in the common State where regionalism, based on such old traditions, never ceased to be clearly manifested.

It is likewise in the region of Cracow that these traditions, in regard to the local princes who reigned there before the unification of Poland, are the most explicit. The legends consecrated to the prehistoric memories of this region, in part confirmed by scientific research, have retained great popularity to this day. But they are not of equal importance to the traditions which enlighten us on the origin of the Polish princes, the direct ancestors and immediate prede- cessors of the dukes and kings of historic Poland.

According to the legend this dynasty, which towards the

middle of the ninth century replaced another more ancient, descended from a simple peasant of the name of Piast. This name became that of our only national dynasty, which governed the whole of Poland until 1370, its Masovian branch not being extinguished until 1526, and its Silesian branch only in 1675. In addition, the name of Piast has remained the symbol to the Polish people of their purest ethnical traditions, of the continuity of their race on the soil of their fathers, of their national unity from the king to the labourer.

Was this Piast, whose son was raised to the throne of Gniezno, really a peasant? It is very doubtful. Several hypotheses have been formed around this problem. The most ingenious suggestion is that Piast is not a proper name, but the title of a high functionary, of a master of the palace, whose descendants took the place of their ancient sovereigns. The striking analogy with the almost contemporary origin of the Carlovingians will be observed.

On the other hand, tradition seems trustworthy when it enumerates the three first Polish monarchs of the House of Piast. Their names do not tell us much. What is certain is that one after the other worked at the unification of the Polish tribes, and that they left to the fourth, named Mieszko, an already considerable State.

We are ignorant of the date of his accession, and we know no more of the commencement of his reign than we do of that of his predecessors. This is all the more reason for supposing that their programme of unification was little troubled from outside. It was not until 963 that Mieszko, hitherto scarcely known abroad, saw himself the object of a first attack from the German side.

This was not organized by Germany as such, nor even—at least openly—by the famous margrave Gero, who was using every means to extend his frontiers on the east. It was a simple German count, banished by the Emperor Otto I, who inflicted two defeats on Mieszko of Poland.

The latter realized the danger of seeing his country become, like the other Slav lands, the object of continual invasions which would end in her conquest by Germany. Instead of exhausting himself in fruitless conflicts, he hastened to enter of his own accord into contact with the Emperor himself. It was probably in the same year that he succeeded in concluding a treaty with Otto I which recognized the Duke of Poland as a friend of the Emperor, to whom he promised to pay tribute levied on the western confines of his territory.

Mieszko thereby gave an indisputable proof of his diplomatic talent. At the price of a strictly limited concession to which his agreement was freely given, he made Poland a State officially recognized by the young imperial power and one which could no longer be invaded on any pretext by her German neighbours. But this was not all. If she remained pagan Poland could always be threatened from that direction under the pretext of Christian propaganda, and could not be definitely accepted on a basis of equality among the European nations.

We are ignorant of what were Mieszko's real religious sentiments. In any case, he had understood that it was necessary to adopt immediately and voluntarily the Christian faith, without waiting for pressure on the part of the Germans. It was moreover necessary to avoid accepting it from their hands. The Duke of Poland had no intention of effecting this by addressing himself to distant Byzantium, although the influence of the latter had already made itself felt among its eastern neighbours. He would have thereby escaped all German interference, but at the same time he would have given Poland an orientation that was contrary to his intentions. It was his desire to consolidate his relations with the

Latin West, and fortunately he was able to find another intermediary than Germany. In 965 he married Dubravka, a Bohemian princess, thus allying himself with a Slav neighbour which had been Christian for some time; the following year he was himself baptized, and immediately took in hand the conversion of all his nation.

In this manner he was able to make his people accept the new faith with comparative ease and rapidity; in spite of inevitable reactions of paganism, the new faith soon penetrated into the soul of all Poland, guiding her to a new future. If the hopes which Mieszko had attached to a political alliance with Bohemia were soon deceived, its immediate results, the christianization of Poland, bore all its fruits. Poland took her historic place in Christian Europe.

2

The First Kings

In the dawn of her history Poland experienced an epoch of unquestioned splendour. This splendour was not lasting, but nevertheless that first great century has left an unforgettable memory. Tradition has linked that memory with the personalities of the kings who bore the henceforth illustrious name of Boleslas. But their work was greatly facilitated by the solid foundations which Mieszko I had established. He never wore the royal crown. It is not even known whether he took any sort of steps with the object of obtaining it. Nevertheless, the first Christian Duke of Poland, to whom foreigners sometimes gave the royal title which corresponded to his actual position, deserves a place of honour by the side of her first kings.

Until his death in 992 the policy of Mieszko I was dominated by anxiety to regulate his relations with Germany. In this respect his attitude was extremely well balanced, taking into account the situation in Germany and the policy of the first three Emperors, his contemporaries. Very prudent when faced by Otto I, he was able to repulse the expedition that Otto II led against Poland, but he recognized the suzerainty

of the young Otto III, and even marched with him against
the Slav tribes, still pagan, that then separated Germany from
Poland.

There is no doubt that he hoped thereby to secure for himself a part of their territory; but while avoiding useless conflicts with the Empire he never lost sight of the most important problem, that of Poland's access to the Baltic Sea. In
fact, he succeeded in subjecting to his authority Pomerania,
the inhabitants of which were, moreover, the most nearly
related among all the Slav populations to the Poles. This
success, decisive in the history of Poland, was the more
valuable since Mieszko was obliged to reckon not only with
the rivalry of the Germans on this territory, but also with
that of the Danes, who desired to establish themselves at the
mouth of the Oder, and who had even created a species of
military colony there, a base for the Norse Vikings.

The only charter of Mieszko I which is known to us shows
beyond doubt that Poland then stretched as far as the *longum
mare*. But at the same time it bears witness to another initiative of this prince which proves still more clearly his extraordinary far-sightedness and his anxiety to assure the future of
his State. At an epoch when the Papacy was still far distant
from it future political influence which was to counterbalance
that of the Empire, Mieszko gave all his territory into the
hands of the Holy See, made it part of the patrimony of St
Peter, and thus placed it under pontifical protection.

This act of an only recently converted prince was more
than an act of homage paid to the Church, and the Peter's
pence that Poland was to pay under this understanding more
than a simple symbol. In compensation for his acts of submission to the Empire, Mieszko thus gave his young State the
best possible guarantee for its independence and security.
Centuries later, this close and never-forgotten tie with the

Holy See was to serve Poland as a solid support in the gravest crises through which she passed. Opposed to the imperial pretensions, it was to ensure the integrity of her frontiers, and even her national character. It was to be at the same time the external expression of a principle of the spiritual order which animates the whole of Polish history.

His constant solicitude in regard to German affairs did not lead Mieszko to neglect the development of his relations with other countries, notably with the young Scandinavian kingdoms, always very influential on the Baltic Sea; also with Hungary, who soon herself accepted Christianity, and who was so often to be a valuable ally to Poland. But, his attention being turned essentially to the west, he seems to have neglected the eastern problem, which Poland was never able to escape. Vladimir the Great of Kiev profited by this in 981 to take from the Poles Przemysl on the San, and other strongholds along the Bug.

This fact might seem insignificant in a synthesis like ours. Nevertheless, it calls for our close attention as the starting-point of a long territorial conflict, many times renewed, under the most diverse forms, between the Poles and their Ruthenian neighbours. As, moreover, this same Vladimir, when, like Mieszko, he was converted some years later, turned not to Rome but to Byzantium, this conflict was soon intensified by religious divergence, increased by equally differing cultural influences.

Mieszko's eldest son and successor, Boleslas I, took a keen interest in the eastern problem, despite his preoccupations on the side of the west, which were still more absorbing than those of his father. This, so to speak, parallel interest at once indicates the primary difference between the policy of these two princes, the second of whom far surpassed the example left by the founder of historic Poland. In order to grasp all the new elements that during the thirty-three years of his reign Boleslas introduced into Polish history, it is by no means necessary to describe here the numerous campaigns which led him from the Elbe to the Dnieper, and won for him the surname of the Brave. If tradition has also ascribed to him that of the Great it is for another reason. It is because athwart the epic of his exploits we catch sight of the outlines of a great design which stretched far beyond the ethnical limits of Poland. While following up all the schemes initiated by his father, Boleslas extended them to the scale of a truly European conception.

Two striking events stand out against the background of his immense activity: the Congress of Gniezno in the year 1000, and his coronation in 1025, on the eve of his death. These indicate the first of the objects that Boleslas had proposed to himself, and the one which he fully realized: the complete independence of Poland, recognized by the Empire and perpetuated by the royal crown.

Profiting by a fortuitous circumstance to which we shall have occasion to return, Boleslas, freed from the rivals he had found in the bosom of his family, solemnly received in his capital the Emperor Otto III, the same who, following the example of Otto I, had received Boleslas's father in Germany in the character of a vassal. We know the idealistic and generous conception which, in agreement with Pope Silvester II, young Otto had formed of the imperial power and its universal mission. A free and independent Poland under a king who would collaborate with the Emperor in the restoration of Christian order in the world could easily find her place in this conception, so far removed from the plans of conquest entertained by other German emperors. Otto III, therefore, did not limit himself to sanctioning the independent organization of the Church of Poland with a metropolitan see at

Gniezno and several bishoprics dependent upon it: he did not hesitate to place his own crown on the head of Boleslas and to present him with the lance of St Maurice, a symbol of royalty.

It is difficult to determine the exact significance of this gesture, and in general the political plans adopted in common by the two monarchs. In any case, it was with the consent of the Emperor that Boleslas addressed himself immediately to the Pope, who alone could authorize his consecration. There were, however, several delays in Rome, and during this time Otto III died, to be soon succeeded by Henry II, who, solicitous for the interests of Germany, opposed Boleslas's ambitious projects.

The latter was fully determined not to abandon any one of them. Only, as it had become impossible to realize them in agreement with the Empire, he at first devoted all his energies to the inevitable struggle with the new Emperor. This war lasted, with some interruptions, until 1018. The peace which was at last concluded at Bautzen secured to Poland a great part of the conquests that Boleslas had made since the beginning of his reign in Slav territory between the Oder and the Elbe, advancing one moment as far as the Elster. It is noteworthy that Lusatia then passed to Poland, whose frontiers have never extended further towards the west.

But what is no less significant is the fact that in 1003 Boleslas, profiting by internal troubles in Bohemia, temporarily occupied the throne of Prague, retaining throughout his reign Moravia as well as a good part of Slovakia. On the other hand, closely following Russia's affairs, he immediately made use of the peace of 1018 to make his victorious entry into Kiev. It was from there that he sent his message of triumph and of defiance to the Emperors of the West and the East.

Naturally, Boleslas never intended to annex Bohemia and

Russia to Poland, as he had succeeded in doing with the pagan populations which would otherwise have fallen under the power of Germany. He returned from Kiev, contenting himself with having strengthened Polish influence there and recovered the adjacent territory that had been wrested from his father. His Czech and Ruthenian policy is chiefly explainable as a consequence of his conflict with Henry II, who was anxious to have a docile vassal in Prague and an ally against Poland in Kiev. Poland was thus threatened by a league of her principal neighbours and, above all, as so often was to happen in the future, by a simultaneous attack from the west and the east. To avert this danger Boleslas probably thought of grouping all the Slavs of the north in a large political community which would have taken its independent place in the European system between the two divisions of the Christian world, one of which was subject to the preponderance of Germany, the other to that of Byzantium.

This idea was, without any doubt, premature. The part of Europe which Boleslas would have wished to organize in this manner was certainly not ripe for such a co-operation, and Poland was not ready to take upon herself its direction. Yet this idea, which impresses us by its magnitude, will reappear in another period of Polish history, thus creating a link between Poland of the eleventh and Poland of the fifteenth century.

It was likewise under Boleslas the Great that another idea appeared; one, moreover, connected with the former, and which also was to be fully realized in the Poland of the Jagiellos. What attracted Otto III, that great Christian Emperor, to Gniezno was the desire to visit the tomb of St Adalbert, formerly Bishop of Prague, who, encouraged by Boleslas, had departed to preach the faith to the Prussians, and had recently found a martyr's death among them. St Bruno also, who was a German, but who reproached Henry II for his alliances with pagans against Poland, found at the court of Boleslas a starting-point and support for his missionary activities, which reached even the Petchenegs and finished with his death in the borderlands of Lithuania and Ruthenia. And when Boleslas married his daughter to a grand duke of Kiev he sent his Bishop of Pomerania there on a mission that was at once diplomatic and ecclesiastical. From these facts there emerges the vision of a vast movement of Christian propaganda, a propaganda at the same time of Latin civilization, organized by a Poland who herself had only very recently been converted.

Furthermore, all this bears witness to the efforts that in the midst of all his wars Boleslas the Brave was able to devote to the internal organization of his country and to the raising of her culture. The royal crown, obtained at last with the assent of the Holy See, was his well merited reward, and also became the symbol which, in spite of the premature death of the first king, prevented destruction of his work in the future.

This destruction was never so threatening as it became almost immediately after 1025. Boleslas I had left his heritage to his younger son, Mieszko II, who was at once able to inaugurate his reign by the ceremony of consecration as king for which his father had so long waited. The new king was by no means the puppet that legend has imagined. On the contrary, what destroyed him was his rash attack upon the Emperor Conrad II. The war he thereby provoked was the more inopportune as Mieszko II was threatened by the pretensions of a disinherited elder brother, who was able to find supporters both in the country itself, including the royal family, and among Poland's neighbours. Humiliated by Germany, and only maintaining the unity for his state with great difficulty, Mieszko perished in 1034 in tragic circumstances, like his brothers and shortly afterwards his eldest son. In the

chaos which followed these catastrophes the work of the first
Piasts seemed as if it must founder. Christianity itself was
rudely shaken in Poland by a revolution of the masses of the
people who, in certain regions, were still pagans, and who at
the same time recalled their primitive particularism. The
Czech invasion of 1038 consummated the ruin of the country,
including the capital.

That Poland was able to rise from this ruin at the end of
only a few years, and to resume a little later the part which
she had played under Boleslas I, is undoubtedly the best proof
of her vitality. But this is also owing to two princes, one of
whom recalls the memory of Mieszko I, the other that of his
great successor.

Casimir I, to whom the title of the Restorer has justly been
given, the youngest son of Mieszko II, had taken refuge in
Germany. He returned to Poland with the support of the
Emperor himself, the latter being disquieted by the anarchy
on the German frontier and by the unexpected success of his
Bohemian vassal. With equal moderation and patience the
new Duke of Poland—he prudently abstained from aspiring
to the royal crown—resumed his great-grandfather's work of
organization. Recognizing the suzerainty of Conrad II and of
Henry III, his successor, he likewise profited by the Ruthenian alliance to crush the centre of revolt which was maintained in Masovia. Passing over irreparable losses beyond the
ethnical boundaries of Poland, such as those of Lusatia and
Moravia, he obtained the return of Silesia, which the Czechs
had temporarily occupied. Finally, he reorganized the religious life of his country, from that time making a return to
paganism impossible.

It was thus a well consolidated state that Casimir left in
1058 to his eldest son, Boleslas II, called the Bold, with the result that the latter was at once able to resume the great policy

of the first King of Poland. There are very pronounced analogies between the activities of the two Boleslases. Like his glorious ancestor, Boleslas the Bold made Poland completely independent of the Empire. Following his example, he made an adventurous expedition to Kiev to intervene in favour of princes who were his allies. Like Boleslas the Brave he had himself crowned King of Poland at the Christmas of 1076.

Let us, however, note certain differences between the policies of the two kings. The capital of restored Poland being now at Cracow, Boleslas II made less effort to extend her western frontiers. On the other hand, he exercised a considerable influence on the affairs of Hungary. Together with that country, where he supported the party that was hostile to the Empire, he took a lively interest in the quarrel over investitures which then divided the Christian world. Closely bound to the Holy See, Boleslas, like his Hungarian ally, adhered to the side of Gregory VII, and the support that he found from the great Pope enabled him to give his policy a genuinely European expansion. The opposition of Poland to the pretensions of Henry IV, an opposition which, moreover, was not unconnected with that of the Saxons in the interior of Germany, was greatly facilitated by her close understanding with Rome, which was strengthened on the actual eve of Canossa. The policy of the King and that of the Pope were closely bound together even in Russia, since the pretender to the throne of Kiev, supported by Poland, was at the same time protected by Gregory VII as a partisan of union with the Roman Church. It goes without saying that the definite regulation of the ecclesiastical questions which concerned Poland herself was carried out in full accord with the Pope and his legates, in the spirit of the Gregorian reforms.

We might have supposed that under these conditions the kingdom of the Piasts would have advanced towards a stable

and prosperous future as an increasingly important and active
member of the Christian community. It was not the case. This
great impulse was abruptly interrupted in 1079 by a catastrophe far more difficult to explain than that which had so
closely followed the death of Boleslas I. On his return from
Kiev, Boleslas II, whose character seems to have been passionate and vindictive, put the Bishop of Cracow, Stanislas, to
death.

The motive of this act of violence was an accusation of high
treason. But none of the numerous hypotheses built up
around this perplexing enigma have been able to show why
and with whom the bishop would have betrayed his king. The
martyrdom of the man who later became the patron saint of
Poland and the symbol of her national unity provoked an
immediate reaction against Boleslas the Bold. Supported by
some of the powerful families of the land, his younger
brother, Ladislas Herman, took the opportunity of seizing the
royal power. Boleslas II died in exile, and his legendary tomb
is shown in an old monastery in distant Carinthia, where he
is said to have expiated his crime.

3

The Disintegration of the Kingdom

THE epoch of the dismemberment of the kingdom of the first Piasts has generally been held to have only begun at a date posterior by nearly sixty years to the fall of Boleslas II. The disintegration of his heritage did not, in fact, take place at once, and before it became final Poland once more recovered herself under a monarch of worth, a third Boleslas, glorified by his chronicler—most probably a Frenchman by birth— and resembling in certain respects the great kings whose name he bore.

But neither he nor the immediate successor of Boleslas II dared to claim the royal crown, and we shall see that the dynastic troubles, in spite of an attempt made to allay them by dividing the national territory, began in the reign of Ladis- las Herman, to the detriment of Poland's external situation.

The details of this troubled epoch are of little concern to general history, but its essential character is worthy of atten- tion inasmuch as it corresponds in a certain measure to the feudal parcelling out of the western kingdoms. Feudalism proper was never known in the social evolution of Poland. The formation of a privileged class which, moreover, always ignored the feudal hierarchy, as well as the recrudescence of regional particularisms, were more a consequence than a cause of the internal crisis from which Poland suffered for more than two centuries, and which retarded her national development. The true cause of this crisis was of a dynastic character.

In the epoch of the first Piasts the want of a regulating principle that would have legally fixed the order of succession, as well as, on the other hand, the right each member of the dynasty possessed to a territorial apanage, had at different intervals created great difficulties. If we have not dwelt upon this, it is because these difficulties had then been surmounted by the energy or the prudence of the inheritor of the throne. Ladislas Herman, who occupied, thanks to favourable circumstances, the throne of Boleslas II, and who succeeded in keeping it from the son of the vanquished king, unfortunately possessed neither of these qualities.

His reign of twenty-three years, signalized by its weakness, was indisputably a period of decadence. In her external relations we witness a surprising change of Poland's policy, in turning from the Pope to the Emperor: a policy contrary to her traditions and to her interests, and one which soon condemned her to an increasingly insignificant and passive role. As regards her internal policy, the duke became the instrument of one of the great lords to whom he owed his accession to power, the Palatine Sieciech, with whom the prototype appears in Polish history of the magnate with inordinate ambitions, solicitous beyond all else for his private interests, and leader of a faction combated by a no less violent opposition.

The opposition against the Palatine was directed by the duke's two sons: Zbigniew, the elder, whose legitimacy was disputed, and Boleslas, the younger, who aspired to occupy the first place. Ladislas Herman was obliged during his lifetime to grant vast territories to each, thus inaugurating the disintegration of the ancient kingdom. After the fall of Sieciech and the death of Ladislas in 1102 a fratricidal struggle soon began. Zbigniew, driven into exile, took refuge in Germany, and committed the imprudence of asking Henry V for help. The Emperor profited by this to march against Poland. The year 1109 is memorable for the heroic defence of Silesia organized by Boleslas. The imperial army suffered such severe defeats under the walls of Glogow and before Breslau that it was forced to retreat, leaving Boleslas III, called the Crooked-mouthed, master of the whole of Poland. He even recalled his brother, but suspecting him of treason had his eyes put out, which brought about Zbigniew's death.

Was this crime, of which Boleslas afterwards repented bitterly, counterbalanced by the merits of his foreign policy? His principal anxiety was to recover Pomerania, which in spite of its ethnical ties with Poland had emancipated itself under local dynasts and remained stubbornly opposed to Christianity. By a series of obstinate campaigns that extended over more than twenty years Boleslas III did, in fact, reestablish Polish supremacy there. He likewise encouraged the definite conversion of the Pomeranians by pacific missions. But coming into collision with German influences in the political domain as well as in that of ecclesiastical organization, the Duke of Poland had to resign himself in 1135 to accept Pomerania with the island of Rugen in fief to the Empire. Thus he became the vassal of Lothair II. Under these conditions Poland's domination in Pomerania, which was only strongly established in the south and east of the country, was precarious, and Polish independence, so energetically defended in 1109, was again compromised.

However, Boleslas III's most pressing anxiety towards the

end of his life was to prevent internal troubles, the easier to foresee from the fact that he had several sons. A new division of the former kingdom seemed to him inevitable, but he endeavoured to regulate it systematically and once for all. In his will—a real organic statute of the Polish monarchy, the unity of which he maintained in principle—Boleslas apportioned four territories as hereditary duchies. His eldest son, Ladislas, received Silesia; the second, Boleslas, Masovia; the third, Mieszko, the principal part of Great Poland; the fourth, Henry, the region of Sandomierz, to the east of Cracow. We must add that after Henry's premature death in 1166 the fifth brother, Casimir, probably a posthumous child, for whom no portion had been provided, inherited this latter duchy. But what is more important is that the throne of Cracow, with all the central part of Polish territory and the suzerainty over Pomerania, was henceforth always to belong to the eldest of all the dynasty, thus passing in rotation to the representatives of the different branches.

This system might have seemed ingenious. In practice it gave rise to endless disputes. Each prince installed in Cracow inevitably ended by wishing to transmit the supreme power to his direct descendants. Inevitably also this tendency was bound to disturb the other dukes, dissatisfied at the prerogatives reserved to the elder and impatient to see their turn arrive. On the other hand the different hereditary duchies, corresponding approximately to the territories of the prehistoric tribes and situated at the boundaries of Poland, soon became accustomed to entrench themselves in their individual interests, and to pursue their own policy, which was often incompatible with the common good. Moreover, this by no means prevented further divisions in the interior of each duchy, and it was in this manner that in proportion to the ramifications of the dynasty certain parts of Poland split, little by little, into minute principalities. Finally, a powerful aristocracy which was in process of formation, headed by the high clergy and the chief functionaries, and which became accustomed to play a decisive role in the struggles between the princes, profited by all these dynastic rivalries.

These struggles that Boleslas III had intended to avert began almost immediately after his death in 1138. In 1146 his eldest son, against whom all his younger brothers had combined, was driven not only from the throne of Cracow, but even from his own duchy of Silesia. Married to a German princess, sister-in-law to Conrad III, he was led to seek the most dangerous of supporters, the Emperor, who immediately undertook an expedition against Poland. Terminated by a compromise and followed by pontifical intervention, the German attack was repeated in 1157 under Frederick Barbarossa. The second son of Boleslas III, who bore his father's name, could not defend himself as well as his predecessors in similar circumstances, and was obliged to humiliate himself as no other Polish prince had done before the Emperor. It is true that he was able to keep the supreme power in Poland, but on conditions which clearly demonstrated the imperial suzerainty. After a second campaign by Frederick II, he was obliged, in 1163, to consent definitely to the establishment of the sons of Ladislas in Silesia, which thus remained the apanage of the elder branch of the Piasts.

When he died in 1173 Boleslas IV left his only son under the tutelage of the young Casimir, who was the most gifted of Boleslas the Crooked-mouthed's sons. The latter, for his part, was awaiting in his duchy of Sandomierz the moment for mounting his father's throne. This moment arrived far sooner than the dynastic law had foreseen, because Mieszko, Duke of Great Poland, who as third heir should have reigned at Cracow until his death in 1202, soon lost the sympathies of

the barons of Little Poland on account of his hard and im-
perious character. In 1177 Mieszko the Old—as he was called
later, when he was making attempts which only ended with
his life to take the position which had legally fallen to him—
was driven from Cracow, where Casimir immediately installed himself. After having inherited, as he had hoped, the
duchy of Masovia, this prince united in his hands all the
centre and east of Poland.

Surnamed the Just and, like his father, glorified in a contemporary chronicle, written this time by a Pole, Casimir
really governed in a manner which distinguished him among
the Polish princes of his generation. From a general point of
view his reign of seventeen years claims our attention for two
different reasons.

Let us first observe that, thanks to his spirit of initiative,
Poland at last resumed a more active foreign policy. Given
the geographical situation of the provinces directly subject to
Casimir the Just, the orientation of this policy could only be
towards the east. It was, moreover, dictated by two exterior
circumstances. One was the result of the powerful movement in favour of the Crusades, which for a hundred years
had been sweeping through Europe. Before Casimir II's
reign the Polish princes, unable to embark for the Holy Land,
had already been desirous of at least combating the infidels
in their immediate vicinity, but they did it without a precise
plan or positive success. Contrary to their own interests, they
at times helped the Germans to subjugate the last of the Slav
tribes remaining on the west of the Oder. More frequently
they marched against the Prussians, who were not threatening them seriously, but who, when attacked, offered a decided resistance, and at times inflicted on them severe defeats.
Casimir turned upon the Baltic tribe which had advanced
the furthest towards the south, namely the Yatvegians, who,

in the region of the Bug, constituted a real danger to Poland. He succeeded in subjugating at least a part of the country, which later was called Podlasia, and was to be colonized by the Masovians.

This crusade was not without its connection with his Ruthenian policy. The Russia of the first Ruriks had disintegrated still more rapidly and irremediably than the Poland of the first Piasts. Kiev, passing from hand to hand, and cruelly devastated, had kept nothing more than the faint reflection of its ancient power. Two new political centres had appeared: one in the north-east, where the Slavonic colonization of the basin of the Volga was preparing the future role of Moscow, the other in the south-east, in the principalities of Volhynia and Halicz, in the borderlands of Poland. It was precisely here that Casimir the Just desired to reestablish the Polish influence that had been obtained at the time of the first kings. His interventions were not always fortunate, but they accustomed the Ruthenian princes who were disputing for power there to reckon with Poland, and paved the way for Casimir's successors.

They had likewise their repercussion in the internal life of Poland, where different political parties had come into existence. Casimir the Just, desiring to consolidate his position and that of his descendants, could not neglect these. A younger son, raised to the throne in violation of the statute laid down by his father, in 1180 Casimir convoked at Lenczyca the lords of his territories, as well as the bishops of the whole of Poland, and made them recognize that Cracow and the supreme power were to be henceforth hereditary in his house. This reform, sanctioned by the Pope and the Emperor, was naturally always contested by the other branches of the Piasts. Therefore Casimir endeavoured to gain the permanent support of the clergy, to whom, as well as to the great aristocratic families, he forthwith granted a first charter of privileges.

These families constituted, as it were, clans, powerful on account of their landed property and their political solidarity. They were descended either from old tribal chiefs or from foreign knights who had settled in Poland, or, finally, from the most influential members of that numerous military class which had been formed as a result of the wars of the first Piasts, and which at times gathered round the great lords like the *ministeriales* of the western countries. These clans, which subsequently formed the Polish nobility, were in process of adopting war cries which were to furnish them with names, as well as the coats-of-arms that symbolized their unity. Their role proved decisive for the first time during the course of the dynastic struggles which followed the sudden death of Casimir the Just in 1194.

The lords of Little Poland, headed by the Palatine of Cracow, Nicholas, who disposed of the throne as he pleased, for the most part favoured the eldest son of the dead ruler, the young Prince Leszek, whose younger brother Conrad received the Duchy of Masovia. It was not, however, until after eight years of struggle with Mieszko the Old and his son that Leszek, surnamed the White, was able to install himself at Cracow, where he reigned, not without a temporary interruption, for a quarter of a century.

A contemporary of Innocent III, he placed Poland in 1207 under the protection of the Holy See. This act had a more immediate result than the somewhat analogous one of Mieszko I, because this time Poland entered wholly into the system of the vassal kingdoms of the Church which the great Pope opposed to the imperial power. In adopting this attitude, which redeemed the acts of submission to the Empire imposed upon his predecessors, Leszek was led to collaborate closely with the clergy, and notably with the archbishop Henry Kietlicz, who then introduced into Poland the reforms elaborated by Innocent III.

This collaboration of Leszek with the Holy See made itself felt also in his Ruthenian policy, which continued that of his father, but with far more ambitious designs. After the death of Roman of Volhynia and Halicz, a powerful prince who, first supported by Poland, perished in 1205 in a somewhat mysterious conflict with Leszek, the latter allied himself with Hungary to create in these Ruthenian regions a Catholic kingdom under a Hungarian prince, married to a daughter of the Polish duke. This plan which, towards 1214, appeared to be on the point of being realized, soon completely collapsed. Roman's eldest son, Daniel, finally secured his succession to his father, and Leszek, who had hoped to keep for Poland at least the boundaries that had been disputed since 981, was obliged to abandon all his plans of eastern expansion.

He was no happier in his Pomeranian policy. In this direction the Duke of Cracow once again acted as sovereign of all Poland in the interest of all the duchies of which it was composed. Western Pomerania with the mouth of the Oder having been definitely lost, to the gain of the Empire, it was now necessary to obtain at least the submission of that Pomeranian prince who possessed the eastern part of the country with the mouth of the Vistula. But this prince, of the name of Swientopelk, profited by the disputes among the Piasts, and it was with the complicity of one of them that he killed Leszek, when the latter in 1227 attempted to force him to render the homage he refused.

The throne of Cracow again became the object of dynastic struggles, which this time were so prolonged that the downfall of the ancient kingdom might have seemed a certainty.

But it is precisely in the course of these sterile struggles that the idea of returning to the royal traditions of the first Piasts reappeared in the eminent personality of one of the competitors. We must examine more closely the conditions under which this project came to birth, soon to founder in a new crisis. The two essential problems which are about to present themselves will retain their capital importance for the whole future of Poland.

4

The German Colonization and
the Mongol Invasion

A T THE moment when Leszek the White succumbed to his
enemies his only son Boleslas was scarcely two years old. It
was an excellent opportunity to dispute his inheritance and,
above all, the throne of Cracow, if only under the pretext of
tutelage. The conflicts which followed, with the participation, more or less direct, of all the Piasts and principal families of the Polish knighthood, lasted in successive stages for
nearly sixteen years. It was not till after a decisive victory had
been gained in 1243 that Boleslas V, surnamed the Chaste,
became for a long period the uncontested master of Little
Poland. But, in spite of the long duration and extension of
these struggles, their details are of no greater interest to us
than those of other dynastic conflicts of that epoch. On the
other hand, it is the personalities of the two principal competitors that throw most light upon their real significance:
Conrad of Masovia, uncle of the young prince, and Henry of
Silesia, surnamed the Bearded, representing the elder line of
the Piasts.

Before, however, placing them in their opposite camps, a
preliminary question must be determined. Why did Ger-

many, who formerly had profited by every similar opportunity to reduce Poland to the role of a vassal state, not interfere in this crisis, the most serious of all? The answer is easily found. At the end of Frederick Barbarossa's reign and that of Henry VI, the Empire was absorbed in the question of Italy and in the Crusades, as well as in fresh conflicts with the Papacy. It was the same during the long reign of Frederick II, which followed the internal troubles in Germany at the opening of the thirteenth century, and which ended in a permanent weakening of the imperial power.

But during this time German influence did not cease to penetrate into Poland under another form. Although Poland, anxious to strengthen her links with Latin culture, had from the outset entertained relations with all the west, including the Latin nations, France and Italy, these links were naturally particularly close with Germany, her immediate neighbour. The Polish clergy counted among its members many foreigners, of whom a great part were Germans, especially in the principal monasteries. We know, moreover, that German colonization had begun in certain parts of Poland at the end of the twelfth century, and had developed increasingly during all the thirteenth. It is true that the villages which were founded in such great numbers by the dukes, the bishops, and the lords, often obtained only the franchises of German law, although the majority of the settlers were Polish. It is equally true that the origin of urban life, which was then organized in a definite manner in Poland, was not so exclusively German as has been supposed. Nevertheless, we do not attempt to deny the very great importance of the role that the German elements then played in these different spheres.

It would be equally absurd to deny its advantages. These advantages, tangible even in the intellectual life of a country which was relatively a young one in the Christian community and removed from the regions where western civilization had its first roots, were valuable, especially in the sphere of material culture, of economic and commercial life, and of the social organization of the municipal and rural community. In this respect German law was of itself a powerful factor of progress. Nevertheless, this German influence, although seemingly of a purely pacific order, represented a danger scarcely less grave for Poland than the military expeditions of the Emperors. It was, in fact, a case of foreign infiltration, doubly menacing in a divided State and in a population whose national consciousness was scarcely in process of formation. The towns with their essentially German inhabitants, and the monasteries, which sometimes did not even admit Poles among their religious, while being important focuses of culture, were at the same time so many foreign islands in the very heart of Poland. And the country districts, too readily abandoned to German settlers, and to institutions of Germanic character, could only too easily detach themselves, little by little, from Poland, especially those which were situated in the neighbourhood of her frontiers.

This danger continued to increase in proportion as the drive of Germany's political expansion to the east took a new impulse. From the first half of the thirteenth century it gave rise to anxiety. Therefore this grave problem must not be overlooked when we compare the methods and results of the policy of the two princes who were disputing for the first place in Poland.

The Duchy of Masovia, which served as a base for Conrad's conquests, somewhat isolated to the north-east of the state of the Piasts, was scarcely touched by German influences. Conrad, therefore, might have seemed the representative of the purely Polish element. And we likewise know that this prince was by no means an adventurer, extending his dominion through pure greed, as has been long imagined. It was he, however, who, while labouring to reunite a large part of Polish territory, committed in his relations with Germany the most disastrous mistake to be found in Polish history, a mistake the consequences of which are influencing general history even to our own day. At the very moment when he was attempting to assume the sovereignty in Cracow, Conrad of Masovia introduced the first members of the Teutonic Order into Poland.

The war with the Prussians was continuing without intermission along the northern frontiers of Conrad's duchy. In spite of interesting attempts at co-operation with the other Polish princes he did not succeed in extending these frontiers, nor even in protecting them against Prussian incursions. Also the Christian mission in Prussia, although organized with the concurrence of the Polish bishops at the Lateran Council, made but slow progress. In despair of the situation, Conrad then appealed in the beginning of 1226 to one of the great orders of chivalry, which were founded in the Holy Land to fight the infidels. Hermann von Salza, Grand Master of the Teutonic Order, accepted his offers the more readily because the project of establishing that Order on the borders of Hungary had just fallen through, the real intentions of the German Knights having been discovered in time. Conrad was less prudent and less discerning. In 1230 members of the Order planted themselves in considerable numbers on the bank of the Vistula, and soon founded the stronghold of Thorn, cr, in Polish, Torun.

The question, so much debated, of the authenticity of the first charters which regulated the legal situation of the Teutonic Order in its new field of action matters little here. What is certain is that the intentions of the two contracting parties differed completely. Conrad, while offering the territory of

Chelmno to the new arrivals, fully intended to keep entire sovereignty over it. The future conquests of the Order in Prussian territory were likewise to be subject to the ducal authority. The Grand Master's conception was wholly different. According to him, the base of operations provided by Conrad, as well as the whole of Prussia, was destined to form a new State of ecclesiastical character, governed by the Teutonic Order: a State completely independent of Poland, and recognizing only the authority of the Holy See and that of the Empire. Frederick II hastened to confer upon the Order an imperial charter, in which this point of view found its first confirmation.

The conquest of Prussia took the Teutonic Knights more than fifty years. They had to break the resistance of each tribe one after the other, and subsequently organize a completely new life. A vast German colony was thereby created from the mouth of the Vistula to that of the Niemen, where a German population, crowding in from all parts of the Empire, superimposed themselves upon the natives, and even replaced the latter, who were either enslaved or exterminated. They finished by usurping the very name of the former Prussians.

However, this 'new Germany,' as it was called later, remained geographically separated from the Empire by Danzig Pomerania, which was still independent. The duke of this Pomerania, the fiery Swientopelk, whom we saw resisting the Piasts, speedily understood that a far greater danger was beginning to threaten him. But the war that he carried on for ten years against his new German neighbours changed nothing in the situation. When he began it in 1242 it was already too late. In 1233 the Order had inflicted a decisive defeat upon the Prussians so that their insurrection, encouraged by the Duke of Pomerania, had no chance of success. Moreover, in 1237 the Teutonic Knights had federated with another German Order, that of the Sword Bearers, who had founded a somewhat similar colony at the mouth of the Dvina in Livonia. Lithuania and Samogitia, situated in the centre of the Baltic populations, thus found themselves, like Pomerania, surrounded on two sides by Germanic conquests.

All these events seem to have aroused no anxiety whatever in Conrad of Masovia, to whom this German colony of a political character owed its striking success. One can still understand that he helped the Order at the outset of the campaign in Prussia, as other Polish princes and Swientopelk himself had also done. But, misunderstanding Poland's real interests, Conrad, with his sons, also supported the Teutonic Knights against the Duke of Pomerania.

We can feel no surprise that a prince who showed so little political foresight did not succeed in removing from the throne of Cracow a rival as energetic and as prudent as Henry the Bearded. The Duke of Breslau, the grandson, son, and husband of German princesses, also encouraged the German colonization. But he did it in a very different fashion. He profited by it to raise the general level of culture in his duchy, which included the greater part of Silesia, and to give his authority a solid economic basis.

This authority rapidly extended beyond the Silesian frontier. Henry, before securing in 1229 the sovereignty in Cracow, had made no less persevering efforts to bring Great Poland also under his dominion. From the beginning of the thirteenth century he had not ceased to intervene in the disputes which were carried on between the descendants of Mieszko the Old. At last, in 1234, a good half of that province was formally ceded to him. But he aimed higher. This Silesian prince not only intended, like Conrad of Masovia, to enlarge his possessions: he proposed to make them the nucleus of a restored kingdom of Poland.

The royal crown, almost forgotten since the fall of Boleslas II, was destined by him for his eldest son, whom he associated in his rule towards the end of his life. This Henry II, who succeeded his father in 1238, was, in fact, entirely worthy of the heritage of the first Piasts. Pursuing the very able policy of Henry the Bearded, his son, surnamed the Pious, was, moreover, able to obtain the support of the clergy, with whom his father had had frequent disagreements. Following the old tradition of his race, he placed himself under the protection of the Holy See, with which he also allied himself against Frederick II. In spite of all his German connections, Henry the Pious would, therefore, assuredly have maintained the independence and the prestige of the kingdom if all his plans had not been annihilated by an unforeseen catastrophe. In 1241 he died as a Christian hero in the battle of Lignica, in which he was attempting to arrest the Mongolian invasion. In his little army Poles and Germans fought bravely side by side against the barbarians who were invading Europe.

Poland, so often during three centuries threatened from the west, had never yet suffered so directly and so brutally an assault from the east. For the first time she had to fill the splendid, if ungrateful, part of the front bastion of Christendom. All the Russias, first the new Russia, established in Finnish territory, then the old Russia, with her glorious metropolis Kiev, had been devastated and conquered by the Tartars between 1237 and 1240. The following year Batu Khan hurled himself upon Poland, and after crushing the knights of Little Poland in the battle of Chmielnik, triumphed equally at Lignica. But this victory was to be the last, at least in those regions. Together with rumoured events in Asia the desperate resistance of Poland contributed to make the Mongolian hordes retreat. Europe was saved.

For Poland also the sacrifice of Henry the Pious was not in vain. She escaped for ever from the Tartar yoke. Her frontier became that of free Europe and of triumphant Christianity. But she had suffered cruelly from the passage of the enemy; and for long centuries she remained exposed to the perpetual danger of a new Tartar invasion, of which the next was perpetrated in 1259, and to the terrible neighbourhood of the Khans of Kipchak, the masters of the whole European east.

It is true that they were not immediate neighbours. The power of the Khans, residing at Sarai on the lower Volga, weighed heavily on eastern Russia, where the historic role of Moscow was then beginning, but was less felt in the Ruthenian principalities bordering on Poland. Daniel, the son of Roman, the former adversary of Leszek the White, was still reigning in Halicz and Volhynia. Wishing to liberate himself from the Tartars, he turned spontaneously to the side of the Catholic west. Ready for religious union with Rome, he entered into negotiations with Innocent IV, who was deeply interested in all aspects of the eastern question. In 1253 he received the royal crown from the hands of a papal legate. The Pope had just conferred the same dignity on a Lithuanian prince, Mendog, who had accepted Catholicism in order to escape from the political aggression of the Teutonic Order. He, too, put up an energetic resistance to the Tartars and, by attaching the Ruthenian lands which surrounded her on the south-east to Lithuania, he put a limit to the Mongolian conquests.

The consolidation of these two new Catholic kingdoms was to the interest of all Europe, and more especially Poland. But for the moment both needed to be supported by efficacious help. Unfortunately, the west was too absorbed in the conflict between the Papacy and the Empire to be able to intervene in these distant regions. The Teutonic Order's only concern was to wrest territorial concessions from Mendog, and as regards Poland, she was too divided and too enfeebled to undertake common action with the two kings.

The Polish clergy alone endeavoured to make use of a situation so favourable to Catholic propaganda in the Lithuanian and Ruthenian lands. The princes of the House of Piast played the part of intermediaries between the Holy See and Daniel. It fell to their lot to collaborate with the latter against the Yatvegians who separated them from Mendog's Lithuanian kingdom. But that was all. Under these conditions Daniel, obtaining no help from the west, was obliged to humble himself again before the Tartars, and even to provide them with reinforcements against Poland. Mendog, carried away by a violent pagan reaction, not only recommenced his struggles with the Germans, but also his incursions into Poland.

The latter did not at that time possess a monarch who understood the needs of the hour, and who had at his disposal the necessary authority to place himself at the head of all the Piasts. Henry the Pious, who alone could have played that part, was no more. His sons, who were disputing his heritage, proved themselves completely unequal to it. Their influence no longer extended beyond Silesia. Conrad of Masovia took this opportunity to occupy Cracow for the last time, from 1241 to 1243, but he could not hold out there and died shortly after, dividing his duchy between his sons. Boleslas the Chaste, at last established on his father's throne, was not lacking in good qualities, but possessing only Cracow and Sandomierz, and dependent on the great noble families, he was incapable of imposing the supremacy that had reverted to him upon the other Polish princes.

He allowed himself to be led with them to take part in a war which was entirely foreign to the interests of Poland.

Hungary, where Boleslas had found a remarkable wife, and
Bohemia, which under Ottakar II had attained to great
power, were disputing with each other for the Austrian heritage of the Babenbergs, and we see the princes of Poland
fighting for twenty years to no purpose in the two opposite
camps. Ottakar II, who gained a great hearing, above all in
Silesia, made an appeal to Slav solidarity so as to associate all
the Piasts with himself on the eve of his decisive campaign
against Rudolf of Hapsburg in 1278. But, in point of fact,
only the Germans, notably the margraves of Brandenburg,
made any profit out of this long disorientation of Polish policy. All along the Oder and the Warta they wrested important
territories from the Piasts of Silesia and Great Poland, extending their influence into Pomerania. With this new German advance, a new danger had, therefore, come to menace
Poland, who seemed condemned to an increasingly passive
role both in the west and in the east.

Her princes of the next generation, however, succeeded
in finding the remedy.

5

The Reconstruction of the Kingdom

THE thirteenth century, which in the west was the century of St Louis and of a brilliant efflorescence of medieval culture, was an epoch of trouble and undeniable weakness in Polish history. After the new successes of the German colonization, which was assuming an increasingly political aspect, and after the glorious but disastrous day of Lignica, the dissolution of the ancient kingdom of the Piasts seemed final.

Nevertheless, the first of our modern historians to have drawn a synthetic picture of this confused epoch has been led to maintain that the general impression is not so discouraging as might have been expected, and that in the midst of an apparent decadence an early regeneration was preparing. Moreover, the great historian of Polish law and Polish institutions, who has studied this regeneration of the kingdom of Poland in the fourteenth century with particular care, has found strong elements of unity in the preceding century which ensured the continuity of our historical evolution.

Taking these elements of unity, let us begin by considering that one among them which, in spite of everything, the old national dynasty represented. True, it was this dynasty itself which had made Polish history a veritable mosaic of duchies whose number increased unceasingly. But this divided Poland of the thirteenth century still remained the common patrimony of only one family, whose members, even while fighting each other, were still conscious of their ties of close relationship. In spite of their individual titles, they all, including the Silesian princes, who were the most numerous, remained dukes 'of Poland.'

If that subdivided Poland did not at that time disappear from the map of Europe, as she did after the partitions between foreign powers at the end of the eighteenth century, this is also due to another circumstance. Medieval Poland was not only a political conception: she was also an ecclesiastical province. Being at different periods the subject of the Holy See, she kept for that reason a unity in the whole extent of her territory that was recognized by the highest authority of the Christian world. In Rome even the provinces lost by the Piasts were always regarded as forming part of the Poland which belonged, in all its entirety, to the patrimony of the Church and which paid Peter's pence. At the same time the clergy of the whole of Poland, headed by the archbishops of Gniezno and the bishops of Cracow, several of whom particularly distinguished themselves in the thirteenth century, remained closely united by the links of ecclesiastical organization, and this of itself formed a further link between the different duchies.

We can say almost the same of the great families of the future Polish nobility, despite the heavy responsibility which they incurred by the part they took in the struggles between the princes. They often helped to prolong, indeed to embitter, these fratricidal struggles, and to weaken the authority of the dukes whom they changed so easily. But, on the other hand, as nearly all of them had residences in several duchies

at the same time, and some—the most powerful—were scattered over every part of Poland, these strongly united families
created a whole network of permanent connections between
the different regions that were separated politically.

To these positive facts another and more intangible one
was added: the national consciousness which, little by little,
became more pronounced. Born of the ancient community of
language and of customs, that consciousness was asserted in
the reaction against Germanism. In the second half of the
thirteenth century, the clergy, the great majority of whom
were now recruited from among the Poles, protested against
the German exclusiveness of certain religious orders, and
constituted themselves the defenders of the rights of the national language in the churches and in the schools dependent
upon them. At the same epoch the Polish knighthood showed
its indignation against those princes who were too much disposed to surround themselves with foreigners. And if the
antagonism between knights and citizens had also social
causes, yet it was inspired in the first place by displeasure at
seeing the German element dominating the towns.

Yet a real and deep national feeling cannot be developed in
a negative sense alone, by opposition to another nation. The
Polish nation has been formed, above all, by the cult of a
common past, by that sense of tradition—let us even say by
that historic sense—which she manifested from a very ancient
epoch. The glory of the first century of Polish history seemed
to gain in splendour by its contrast with an increasingly painful present. And precisely in the midst of her greatest straits,
in 1253, an act which had doubtless been considered for a
long time played its part in recalling the glories of the past,
in explaining their eclipse, in symbolizing a mystic faith in
their return. Stanislas, Bishop of Cracow, the victim of Boleslas the Bold, was canonized. The following year the ceremony

of the exposition of his remains on the altar of the Vavel Cathedral at Cracow gathered together the princes of the whole of Poland. On the part of the dynasty this was an act of expiation. As for the nation, she saw in it the guarantee that the reparation of the crime would soon efface its consequences, and that the divisions of their torn country would.be reunited. Thus the religious element which we find at the base of Polish patriotism in every epoch fostered its early growth.

The canonization of St Stanislas recalled at the same time the traditional role of Cracow. Hence the new attempts to reconstruct the unity of Poland sprang from the intention of giving the ancient capital the strongest possible monarch, who would reunite to Little Poland other important parts of the old kingdom. From this standpoint, the nomination of the successor of Boleslas V, who had no children and who died in 1279, was by no means a happy one. Leszek the Black, the eldest of Conrad of Masovia's grandsons, belonged to the branch which had divided between them the central provinces of Poland, Kujavia and the territories of Lenczyca and Sieradz; he joined only this last and unimportant duchy to Little Poland. The new duke was looked upon coldly by a powerful party who favoured the candidature of a prince of the younger branch that had remained in Masovia proper, and it actually revolted on two different occasions against Leszek. The latter, who died in 1288, likewise childless, was more ingenious in the choice of his successor. Passing over his brother of Kujavia and his cousins of Masovia, he nominated Henry IV of Breslau, grandson of the hero of Lignica.

It is true that Silesia was submitting more and more to the influence of German culture and to the political influence of the kingdom of Bohemia. But did not this constitute all the greater reason for renewing its ties with Cracow? It is true that Henry IV himself, famed as a poet in the German language, had committed the imprudence of submitting the duchy of Breslau to the suzerainty of Rudolf of Hapsburg and promising the succession to Venceslas II of Bohemia. But after he was raised to the throne of Cracow he not only proved his excellence as an administrator: he resumed the Polish policy of his ancestors, a policy that aimed at the reconstruction of the kingdom of the Piasts. He immediately began to take steps in Rome towards obtaining the royal crown. His premature death in 1290 prevented the realization of this plan, but the Duke ol Cracow and Breslau was still able to communicate his last desire to the prelates and lords who surrounded him.

Henry IV left Little Poland to Przemysl II, Duke of Great Poland, and the duchy of Breslau, not to Bohemia, but to his cousin, Henry of Glogow. It was probably understood that the latter would subsequently also inherit the possessions of Przemysl, who had no son. Three-fourths of the kingdom would have then been united in his hand. But the fact alone of an immediate reunion of Little and Great Poland under a monarch of great promise stood for progress of the first order. Great Poland, so rich in national traditions, long torn by internal strife, had for thirty years again been playing an often decisive role, mainly owing to Przemysl's uncle, Boleslas the Pious, the indefatigable defender of the Polish frontiers on the side of Brandenburg and Pomerania. After the death of Boleslas in 1279, his nephew had not only reunited Gniezno and Poznan, but in 1282 he had been nominated as heir by the Duke of Danzig Pomerania, son of the famous Swientopelk. We cannot sufficiently insist on the significance of this success, which restored Poland's access to the sea, arrested German expansion, and allowed Przemysl to resume the traditions of the first Piasts.

He was installed at Cracow immediately after Henry IV's

death; but he found himself faced by two equally dangerous rivals. On one side, the nearest kindred of Leszek the Black had never renounced his heritage; even in Henry of Breslau's lifetime one of them, Ladislas the Short of Kujavia, Leszek's younger brother, forestalling all the others, had made attempts which, pursued with unparalleled tenacity, ended by making him the real renovator of the kingdom of Poland. On the other side, Venceslas of Bohemia, availing himself of the Duke of Breslau's former promises and of Rudolf of Hapsburg's support, also put forward his own pretensions to the throne of Cracow. Several Polish princes of Upper Silesia having become vassals of the King of Bohemia, the latter was enabled to march straight on Cracow with such considerable forces that Przemysl and soon Ladislas were compelled to yield the town to him.

However, neither of them was discouraged. Moreover, all those who, constantly increasing in numbers, desired to hasten at all costs the restoration of the Polish royalty, considered that even the occupation of Cracow by a foreign monarch should not prevent their design from being effected. The first plan had been to begin by uniting the greater part of the Polish territories round the capital and then to obtain the crown for the prince who was to reign there. But could they not proceed in the reverse order: crown the Polish prince who seemed the most worthy and use the prestige of royalty to draw the other regions of Poland to this monarch? This seems to have been the idea of the Archbishop of Gniezno, James Swinka, the principal promoter of the restoration of the kingdom. With the approbation of the Holy See he crowned Przemysl King of Poland on 26th June 1295. The Vavel being still inaccessible, this long delayed ceremony took place in the cathedral of Gniezno.

the religious capital of the whole of Poland. The opinion has been expressed that Przemysl's kingdom was only the kingdom of Great Poland, and essentially differed from that of of the first Piasts. This hypothesis seems to us untenable, but what it contains of truth is the fact that from this moment Great Poland, proud and jealous of the first place, once more acquired after so many centuries, was often to oppose the preponderance of Little Poland, although the latter soon resumed her central role in Polish history.

On the eve of his consecration, Przemysl also had the great satisfaction of entering into actual possession of Pomerania after the death of the duke who had bequeathed it to him. But the following year he was assassinated, the victim of a plot hatched between the margraves of Brandenburg and some discontented lords of the young king, who, therefore, was never able to rise to his full capacity. The crisis which followed this catastrophe took a fatal course. While Ladislas the Short and Henry of Glogow mutually disputed the succession to Przemysl, it was Venceslas of Bohemia who profited. Master of Little Poland, he occupied Great Poland in 1300, and the same archbishop, who five years earlier had been instrumental in the triumph of the national idea, was compelled to place the crown of the Piasts on the head of a foreigner.

The renovation of the kingdom of Poland had thus become pure fiction, because the kingdom appeared to be nothing more than an annexe to that of Bohemia, together with which it would have been easily incorporated in the German Empire. Fortunately this situation did not last. Ladislas the Short, exile as he was, did not waste his time. He succeeded in gaining, on one hand, the moral support of the Pope, Boniface VIII; on the other, the help of the Hungarians. In

1305 he reappeared in Little Poland. The following year he occupied Cracow. In 1314 he became the master also of Great Poland.

This success of the national candidate, obtained in spite of the opposition of the German burghers, who went so far as to revolt against him, was due, in great measure, to the indefatigable perseverance with which he worked for his aim, to the experience acquired in the course of so many years of desperate efforts, and to the sympathy of the population which he at last succeeded in gaining. It is also true that Ladislas was aided by circumstances. Venceslas III, who had succeeded his father in 1305, and who at once marched against his rival, was assassinated the following year. The dynasty of the Premyslides expiring with him, Bohemia herself became the object of a prolonged rivalry between the candidates for the throne. In 1309 Henry of Glogow also died, and his sons proved incapable of maintaining themselves in Great Poland against the partisans of Ladislas the Short. Finally, taking advantage of the dynastic quarrels in Germany, and of the goodwill that he still found at the Curia, in Avignon as formerly in Rome, Ladislas had himself crowned King of Poland in 1320 at Cracow itself.

This time the restoration of the kingdom of the Piasts was definite. But it was not their integral inheritance that passed into the hands of the new king. In the course of his contests, of which we have only been able to trace the chief stages, he had lost one province of the greatest value, Pomerania. In 1307 the treachery of the powerful Swienca family had almost let it fall into the power of the margraves of Brandenburg. It was then that the Poles made an appeal to the Teutonic Order, installed at the frontiers of Pomerania by the king's grandfather. The Knights did, in fact, check the advance of the Brandenburgs, but only to seize the disputed province for themselves, beginning with Danzig, where, in 1308, they massacred the royal garrison and a great part of the population. In 1309 the whole country was subjugated by them and, determined never to loose their hold, they transferred the seat of their Grand Master to the recently constructed castle of Marienburg.

Ladislas never resigned himself to abandoning this ancient Polish province to them, indispensable to the kingdom as its only access to the sea. He only waited for his coronation to direct all his efforts towards the scarcely less important object of regaining Pomerania, without even waiting for the reunion of all the other duchies of the Piasts. In 1320 he requested the Holy See to nominate a tribunal which, as the result of a canonical process, recognized the rights of Poland over Pomerania. In the same year he confirmed his alliance with Hungary by marrying his daughter Elizabeth to the successor of the Arpads, Charles Robert of Anjou. Five years later he allied himself with Lithuania, whose power had considerably increased, thanks to the Grand Duke Gedymin, the inflexible defender of his country against the Teutonic Order. But the collaboration with a still pagan Lithuania ceased in 1331, not without having, at times, compromised the King of Poland in the eyes of the Catholic west; and in the midst of such complicated conflicts as were then agitating that west, Ladislas did not always succeed in choosing the most efficacious diplomatic course.

He was to be found, generally speaking, among the partisans of John XXII in the struggle of that Pope with the Emperor Louis the Bavarian. He was the more justified in taking this side inasmuch as the House of Bavaria, having succeeded the former margraves of Brandenburg, was carrying on their policy, which was a very dangerous one for Poland. But Ladislas even approached the Wittelsbachs when it was a case of finding support against another neighbour, a particularly menacing one since he energetically abetted the Teutonic Order. This was John of Luxemburg, the new King of Bohemia, who by reason of this title put forward claims to the crown of Poland. These claims were not particularly serious in themselves, and John preferred to employ another means of extending the influence of Bohemia to the detriment of the 'King of Cracow.' He was well aware that among the princes of the House of Piast only those of Kujavia, the nearest relations of Ladislas, recognized the latter's authority and collaborated with him. The King of Bohemia, on the other hand, succeeded in exacting homage in 1327 and 1329 from nearly all the Silesian princes, and even from one of the dukes of Masovia who, like himself, had ranged themselves on the side of the Teutonic Order.

Taking advantage of this diversion in the quarter of Bohemia, the Order no longer hesitated to enter into open war against Ladislas. The Teutonic invasions of 1331 and 1332 were most disastrous. It is true that during the first the Poles gained a victory, albeit incomplete, over the Teutonic Knights at Plowce. But on two occasions all the north-west of the kingdom was terribly devastated and, what was still more serious, Kujavia, including Ladislas's own patrimony, remained, together with the territory of Dobrzyn, in the hands of the enemy.

At his death in the following year the king therefore left to his only son a Poland that was mutilated and menaced, enfeebled and impoverished, the more so because, absorbed by his innumerable campaigns, Ladislas had been obliged to neglect the needs of the country's internal life. This prince, short of stature, as his untranslatable surname *Lokietek* witnesses, seemed in no wise predestined to the amazing role which he played, and the opening of his career had been signalized by many checks and sterile adventures; nevertheless, this prince, heroic in his defeats, had accomplished the task which, during more than two centuries, Poland had in vain awaited from her dynasty. The vast territories that he had definitely united, at the same time restoring to them the henceforth undisputed rank of an independent kingdom, offered a solid basis for the remarkable work which his successor was to undertake, completing in every respect that of his father.

6

Casimir the Great

It was more than six hundred years ago that the son of Ladislas the Short, succeeding his father without difficulty, was crowned King of Poland. But to this day Casimir the Great has remained for the Polish nation the ideal of a sovereign; and whenever the historian would grasp the origin of any problem concerning the subsequent development of Poland he must return to that epoch. Let us point out in advance King Casimir's two chief titles to greatness. On the one hand, it is the universal nature of his genius, which, in his external policy, recalls Boleslas the Great, and which remains without an equal in all that concerns the regulation of internal questions. On the other hand, it is the excellent method, one of skilled wisdom and patient moderation, which he applied to the solution of the numerous problems that awaited him.

As only the chief of these can be considered here, let us begin with his settlement of a political situation which was seriously compromising the security of Poland. Seeing that he could not remedy it by a new war which offered no chance of success, as it would have to be carried on simultaneously against both the Teutonic Order and Bohemia, Casimir decided to negotiate a compromise. The terms were fixed in 1335 at the Congress of Visegrad in Hungary, where he went to meet his father's implacable adversary, John of Luxemburg, at the court of his brother-in-law, Charles Robert. Taking into account the actual situation created before his accession, young Casimir recognized the suzerainty of the King of Bohemia over the Silesian Piasts who had rendered him homage. It was at this price that John at last renounced his pretensions to the throne of Poland.

Having thus isolated the Teutonic Order, the king could realize, on that side at least, the minimum of his programme: the securing of Kujavia with Dobrzyn at the price of a temporary renunciation of Pomerania and Chelmno. This was obtained in 1343 by the Treaty of Kalisz. We have said 'temporary renunciation,' because Casimir enveloped this surrender with ingenious reservations, and lost no subsequent occasion of preparing for the return of these regions to Poland. He had clearly indicated this ultimate intention in the course of the preliminary negotiations. In 1339 he organized a new canonical process in Warsaw against the Order, which recalls that organized in the time of Ladislas the Short. But this time it was no longer the Polish bishops who were nominated as judges. Desiring to give the tribunal an impartial character, he summoned to Poland, as representatives of the Holy See, two eminent French prelates, one of whom was the Nuncio, Gailhard de Carces. And this time it was no longer some twenty persons, but a hundred and twenty-six representatives of all classes of the population, who were cited as witnesses to answer a long interrogation investigating the whole relations between Poland and the Teutonic Knights.

The judgment which accorded to Poland all the disputed territories, including Danzig Pomerania, as well as large reparations for the losses she had suffered, was unconditionally rejected by the Order. But all the same the judgment retained all its moral force, and thanks to this initiative the whole Polish nation—princes and knights, clergy and functionaries, citizens and peasants—emerges for the first time as conscious of her unity and rights.

Silesia likewise had not been abandoned without reservations, and Casimir seized every occasion of formulating all the claims that could prevent the rupture of the traditional ties between the kingdom of Poland and that province, where he supported the last independent Piasts. Moreover, if the great king had not been able to regain all the territories that his country had lost on the western side, he immediately found large compensations on the eastern side, where he opened almost unlimited vistas to Poland. This constitutes the second problem which dominated his foreign policy.

Let us first state the facts. Ten years before Casimir's accession the last Ruthenian princes of Halicz and Volhynia, descendants of King Daniel, had perished in their struggles against the Tartars, and it was a Piast of Masovia who as their nephew had succeeded them. This Polish prince died by poison in 1340, and Casimir, whom he had probably appointed his heir, at once claimed the succession. In his first campaigns he came into collision with the hostility of the Tartars, and with the rivalry of a Lithuanian prince, the son of Gedymin, who based his claims on ties of relationship with the ancient Ruthenian dynasty. After a victorious advance by the King of Poland in 1349 the Lithuanians recaptured Volhynia from him, and the truce of 1352 left him only the region of Halicz with the increasingly flourishing town of Lwow. It was not until after new Polish victories in 1366 that a treaty with the Lithuanian princes ensured western Volhynia also to Casimir and extended his influence over the descendants of Gedymin, established in the east of that province, as well as in Podolia.

All these important acquisitions were subject to the royal crown of Poland. This was not, however, an annexation pure and simple. Although part of these regions had been Polish in the time of the first Piasts, the boundaries of the kingdom now exceeded the territory of ethnographical Poland. Casimir scrupulously respected the traditions, institutions, and cus- toms of his new Ruthenian subjects, and even while preparing the organization of a Catholic hierarchy in their country he appealed to the Greek patriarch of Constantinople to reestablish the ancient Orthodox metropolis at Halicz. The king even secured the collaboration of some of the princes of Lithuanian origin by attaching them as vassals to his crown. He thus inaugurated that supple and liberal method which enabled vast new territories, inhabited by the most diverse populations, to be united to the kingdom of Poland under different constitutional forms.

At the same time, in spite of repeated conflicts, he inaugurated a policy of closer intercourse with Lithuania. For, in addition to a common antagonism against the Teutonic Order, there was now the urgent necessity of regulating by a common agreement the political situation of the Ruthenian territories, from which the Poles and Lithuanians were successively thrusting back the Tartars. Therefore Casimir also encouraged every project of at last winning Lithuania over to the Christian faith, not by the sword of the German Knights, but by pacific means with the active participation of Polish missionaries and clergy.

It was thus that the extension of the frontiers, and of Polish influence in eastern Europe, became one of general importance for the Christian world. Louis of Hungary, who had succeeded his father, Charles Robert, in 1342, assisted his Polish uncle in several of his campaigns, not, however, forgetting the old Hungarian pretensions to the 'kingdom of Galicia.' Charles of Luxemburg, King of Bohemia since his father's death at Crecy, and at the same time Emperor of the Romans, took a lively interest in the plan of converting pagan Lithuania, and associated himself with Casimir's efforts.

For Casimir, while basing his external policy on an increasingly close alliance with Hungary, succeeded, as soon as circumstances permitted, in establishing relations with the House of Luxemburg. He thus placed his relations with both Bohemia and the Empire on a peaceful footing, while at the same time he fixed the western frontiers of Poland, which were to undergo no modification until the epoch of the Partitions, except from the side of the Teutonic Order. He also made Poland participate in the policy of the whole of central Europe, displaying a diplomatic talent of the first order, and gradually gaining an undisputed authority among all the great contemporary monarchs.

To illustrate the extent of his political relations, it is enough to emphasize that Polish embassies succeeded each other at Avignon without intermission; that Casimir sent reinforcements to the Pope in the Italian wars; that he allied himself with Valdemar Atterdag of Denmark; that together with the Scandinavian kings he had himself named protector of the archbishops of Riga; that finally he intervened in the affairs of the young principality of Moldavia. But nothing is a better proof of the change that had been effected in Poland's international position during the reign of Casimir the Great than the political congress which assembled at Cracow towards the end of his reign in September 1364, that 'moult grand parlement,' which a French poet of the epoch, Guillaume de Machault, describes with magniloquence.

This congress had been convoked to facilitate the propa-

ganda of the King of Cyprus, Pierre de Lusignan, in favour of
a new Crusade. In the capital of Poland he found, as guests of
her king, renowned for his campaigns against the infidels, the
Emperor Charles IV, who had just married a granddaughter
of Casimir, the Kings of Hungary and Denmark, as well as
many other princes, naturally including those of the House of
Piast. The receptions were sumptuous and, in addition to the
discussions devoted to the eastern question, which was considered no longer possible to treat without the co-operation
of Poland, Casimir, in the character of arbitrator, decided the
differences between Louis of Anjou and Charles of Luxemburg. What a difference when we remember the Congress of
Visegrad at the outset of his reign!

But what a difference also between the Poland which his
father had left to him, and that which he had succeeded in
creating during thirty years! Among the Piasts who surrounded the head of the dynasty, even the duke of that
Masovia which had nearly become a Czech fief, and which,
thanks to Casimir's patient efforts, had again become an integral part of the kingdom of Poland, was not absent. But we
have said enough of political questions. The congress of 1364
coincided with the foundation of the University of Cracow.
The creation of this first Polish university—following that of
Prague, the second to be opened in the whole of central Europe—bears witness both to the high level of culture which
Poland had reached, and to Casimir's desire to raise it higher
still.

It was in his mind that the new school, organized on the
model of the Italian universities, should primarily cultivate
the study of law; for the king, who severely repressed all
disorders and who condemned to death a Palatine guilty of
fomenting troubles in Great Poland, was, above all, distinguished as a legislator. We are indebted to him for a remark-

able work of codification, his celebrated statutes at which he laboured for over twenty years.

Glancing over their numerous articles, chiefly devoted to penal law, we are struck by the merciful spirit they disclose. In vain do we search this very humane code for the atrocious penalties enjoined by other legislations of that epoch. These statutes were, moreover, dictated by respect for national traditions, being not only largely based on common law, but also drawn up originally in two different versions, one for Great, and the other for Little, Poland. The king said justly that he aimed at establishing a uniform law for all the kingdom; but this great unifier, who had nothing of the brutal centralist in him, took into account the individualities of the different parts of his state.

Finally, let us emphasize that Casimir's statutes, as well as his other legislative acts, show a great care for equity for all the social classes. Certainly, the nobility which, grouping together the descendants of the old clans of Polish chivalry, had definitely taken shape, appears in the foreground in the full possession of its rights that were already guaranteed by many individual charters. The king even began to associate the nobles with himself in the most important political decisions for the country's future. But he likewise extended his protection to the Polish towns, for which he created a special tribunal and whose commercial interests he carefully safeguarded. He was also deservedly given the name of 'the King of the Peasants,' whom he protected against all ill treatment and succoured during famines. And the Jews, persecuted in other countries, took refuge in Poland to a greater extent than they had ever done before his reign, certain of finding there favourable conditions of existence.

These characteristic features of his government are in strict accord with his desire to develop economic life. Casimir was as interested in the salt mines of Wieliczka as he was in the commercial routes to the Black Sea which he had opened to his country. He covered this country, even in the forests of the Carpathians, with new villages to which he granted extensive liberties. And, a great constructor, he built, besides numerous churches, solid fortresses designed to protect the frontiers.

When we contemplate this very varied activity we ask ourselves who were this powerful personality's collaborators. It was among the higher clergy that Casimir seems to have found the most faithful servants, the best interpreters of his ideas, such as the archbishop Jaroslaw Bogorja, or his nephew John Suchywilk. This is not surprising, considering the profound piety of the king, who lived in constant and confidential relations with the Holy See. But it is also explainable by the fact that Casimir, himself highly cultured, rivalling the brilliant courts of Prague and Buda, chose to surround himself by these prelates of fine intelligence, graduates of foreign universities. Naturally, he also utilized the talents which he found among the knighthood, choosing by preference the less powerful families upon whom he bestowed the highest offices. He was careful to perfect these talents, with the result that many of the politicians who were to distinguish themselves after his death had been trained in his school.

Unfortunately, providence withheld from him that collaborator whom he most ardently desired to continue his work. Although he married three times, Casimir had no son. He was haunted for a long time before his death by his anxiety to find a successor. No one among the Piasts of the collateral lines seemed to him worthy of the crown. He therefore destined it for his nephew, Louis of Hungary, and this promise of the succession, often formally stated, was, at the same time, the price of the Hungarian alliance. But Casimir was counting very reasonably upon the eventuality of Louis also leaving no son. He therefore considered in advance what would happen after the Polish-Hungarian union, which he foresaw would be temporary. He had a favourite grandson who bore his name, born of the marriage of one of his daughters to a prince of western Pomerania. This part of Pomerania round Stettin, subject to the Empire, still kept its Slav character under a local dynasty. By a slight, but important, modi fication of the frontier, Casimir established an immediate contact between this duchy and his kingdom, at the same time separating the New March, an annexe of Brandenburg, from eastern Pomerania, occupied by the Teutonic Order. A glance at the map is enough to enable us to grasp what the elevation of a prince of western Pomerania to the throne of Poland would have brought about. Casimir the Great intended to pave the way for it by adopting Casimir of Stettin and by bequeathing to him in his will the Polish provinces adjacent to the two Pomeranias, as well as vast territories in the very centre of the kingdom.

Immediately after the death of the king, who in 1370 succumbed prematurely to a hunting accident, Louis of Hungary took care to frustrate these plans. Thus the ingenious project of Casimir the Great concerning his succession was not realized. He left, however, a far more important legacy to Poland. We see it in the positive results of his reign and still more in the course that he marked out for the future development of Poland. He had made her a state as powerful and influential as that of the first Piasts, but infinitely more solid, thanks to the relations established with nearly all the countries of Europe, thanks to her excellent internal organization, and, above all, thanks to the fact that the fate of this state no longer depended exclusively upon the personality of her king.

For the real successor of Casimir the Great, that last king of the national dynasty, was the whole Polish nation, which

after the ordeal of so many dynastic crises had been prepared
by Casimir's clear-sighted guidance to shape its future lot
by itself. The last Piast likewise prepared the Polish nation
to collaborate with other nations in the framework of a common state, even were it under a king of foreign origin. This
explains how the end of the epoch of the Piasts was, at the
same time, the starting-point of the epoch of the Jagiellos.

Part II

THE CENTURIES OF POLAND'S
GREATNESS

7

Jadwiga of Anjou

Poland's great centuries are inaugurated by the remarkable history of a princess of the fleur-de-lis, who was raised to the throne of the Piasts when scarcely eleven years of age, and died fifteen years later in the odour of sanctity. This life, so short, but entirely devoted to a great cause, marks, like the life of Joan of Arc in the history of France and the west, the most decisive turning-point in the destiny of Poland and eastern Europe.

Fourteen years passed between the death of Casimir the Great and the arrival of Jadwiga of Anjou. They have been described to us with a number of picturesque details by a former vice-chancellor of the dead king, who was filled with admiration for his master's glorious reign, which he contrasts with the decadence that set in under his successor. This tendency, expressive of the author's personal rancour, is so evident that the historian cannot utilize without reserve these first memoirs to be written by a Pole. It is none the less true that under Louis of Anjou, who in Hungary was Louis the Great, the general situation of Poland underwent a very marked retrogression, as the whole policy of these last years of his life was dictated by only one concern, that of ensuring to his daughters the succession to his kingdoms, including, if possible, that of Naples.

As regards Poland, the agreements concluded in the time of Casimir the Great only recognized this right of succession as accruing to the eventual sons of Louis, sons for whom, like his uncle, he waited in vain. It was necessary, therefore, to make the Polish nobility accept a modification of these contracts. Assisted by his mother, Casimir's sister, as well as by the faithful partisans he possessed in Little Poland, Louis at last triumphed over opposition.

In 1374, the Polish representatives, summoned to Koszyce in Hungary, found themselves obliged to guarantee the crown of the Piasts to whichever daughter of Louis should be named by the king. In return, the latter granted them a charter of great importance which, for the first time, guaranteed all the rights of the Polish nobility, while considerably extending them. Among other privileges it was freed from all imposts with the exception of an infinitesimal tax, more of a symbolic nature, levied upon its landed property.

Louis's first idea was to leave Poland to his eldest daughter Catherine, and as she was betrothed to a son of Charles V of France, the future Louis of Orleans, the latter seemed destined at one moment to become the presumptive successor of the Piasts. But Catherine died before her father, who then destined Poland for his second daughter, Maria, betrothed to Sigismund of Luxemburg, son of the Emperor Charles IV. However, this project also was not realized. Immediately after the death of Louis the Great in 1382, Maria was raised to the throne of Hungary, and as the Poles would have no further personal union between the two kingdoms and had no liking whatever for Sigismund, then Margrave of Brandenburg, the queen mother, Elizabeth of Bosnia, proposed to them her youngest daughter, Jadwiga.

It was, therefore, against every expectation that this princess, who was to have reigned in Hungary, gathered round her all the Poles who desired to respect the promises made to her father. The great majority of the Polish nobility was in full agreement upon this point, and even desired to hasten Jadwiga's arrival so as to put an end to the troubles of the interregnum. But this same majority was wholly opposed to the fiancé whom Louis had given to his third daughter, William of Hapsburg, son of Leopold III of Austria. There was no wish to see a German prince reign in Poland; and, moreover, this candidate was apparently not powerful enough to bring any advantage to the kingdom. It was equally in vain that a Piast, Ziemovit of Masovia, who was supported for some time by a party of the nobility, especially in Great Poland, aspired to Jadwiga's hand in order to gain with it the throne of his ancestors. Even before the arrival of the little princess in October 1384 a far more influential party had decided her fate. The chief aristocratic families of Little Poland, such as the lords of Tenczyn of the House of Starza, the lords of Tarnow and Melsztyn of the House of Leliwa, and with them a whole group of politicians, who succeeded in sparing the kingdom the grave dangers of a prolonged chaotic situation, also succeeded in finding a candidate to the throne who represented a whole programme for the future, worthy of the traditions of Casimir the Great. This candidate was Jagiello, Grand Duke of Lithuania.

Since Gedymin's reign Lithuania had again enjoyed years of power under his son Olgierd, who had closely associated with himself his brother Kiejstut. Dividing the rule between them, they succeeded in defending themselves against the invasions of the Teutonic Order, and at the same time in extending their state in Ruthenian territory, where it reached Kiev and approached the Black Sea. But the frail nature of their work appeared after Olgierd's death in 1377. His son Jagiello, to whom he left the supreme power, soon became embroiled with Kiejstut. The latter, vanquished after the long vicissitudes of a civil war of which the Germans made skilful use, perished in 1382 in the prison where Jagiello had thrown this last hero of pagan Lithuania. But the position of the conqueror became still more precarious. A son of Kiejstut, Vitold, having taken refuge in Prussia and been converted to Catholicism, provided the Order with an excellent instrument with which to conquer Lithuania, under the pretext of restoring his patrimony to the exile. Possibly Jagiello could have resisted had he been able to dispose of all the forces of a consolidated state. But that state, one of the vastest in Europe, still remained the patrimony of the very numerous descendants of Gedymin, each of whom, master of an autonomous principality, followed his individual policy. Those who governed the vast Ruthenian lands that were grouped round the Lithuanian nucleus had joined the Orthodox Church on their own account, and were gravitating towards the new Great Russian and Orthodox state of Moscow, the inflexible rival of Lithuania, which Olgierd had fought against in vain. Moscow was, on the one hand, shaking off the yoke of the Tartars, and, on the other hand, was still itself deeply penetrated by Mongolian influence. And on the horizon there was already appearing the new menace of the Asiatic orient incarnated in the terrible Tamerlane.

It was not only in his personal interest, but to save the existence of Lithuania, to give her at last an integral part in the Christian world, that Jagiello, if he did not instigate them, readily accepted the Polish proposals. In the beginning of 1385 his ambassadors appeared at Cracow and Buda to ask the hand of Jadwiga, meeting, at her mother's court, the French ambassadors who were asking the hand of Maria of Hungary for Louis of Orleans. This latter project failed, and the civil war in Hungary ended two years later with the triumph of Sigismund of Luxemburg, who married his fiancée. William of Austria was less fortunate. It was in vain that he betook himself to Cracow without even waiting for Jadwiga to reach marriageable age. The Polish lords would not allow him to establish himself in the Vavel, and at the same time, on 14th August 1385, their envoys concluded, at Krewo in Lithuania, the most important treaty in the whole of Polish history.

Jadwiga at first rebelled. It was her wish to rejoin her childhood's companion, who, a veritable Prince Charming, had re-appeared to save her from the 'barbarian' whom stern reasons of state destined for her husband. But this generous child of the race of St Louis soon understood that the project, whose realization now depended on her alone, was far more than a mere political combination like so many others. At Krewo, Jagiello had promised that he would unite his Lithuanian and Ruthenian lands to the crown of Poland forever.

A great state was thereby formed, capable of resisting both Germanism and the East, those two perils which since the dawn of history had threatened the nations that were henceforth to be federated. Sinking, once for all, their mutual differences, these nations could ensure for themselves a common access to two seas—the Baltic and the Black Sea. They thus resumed the designs of the great Piasts, the realization of which was beyond the strength of Poland alone, as well as the designs of Mendog and Daniel, who separately had each in vain attempted to make the Lithuanians and Ruthenians enter into the system of western civilization. Jagiello also promised, more sincerely than the first King of Lithuania, to convert his dynasty and all his nation, the last pagan people in Europe, to Catholicism, and this was the article of the treaty which was bound to make the deepest impression upon

Queen Jadwiga. The cross, at the foot of which she accepted her own cross, is still shown in the cathedral of Cracow.

As soon as Jadwiga had reached the age of twelve Jagiello came to Poland with several of his brothers and his cousin Vitold, with whom he had been reconciled. Immediately after his baptism, at which he received the name of Ladislas, on 18th February 1386, he married Jadwiga, and a fortnight later his coronation was celebrated. William, who had returned to Vienna, could take no action, as his father was at war with the Swiss and soon fell at Sempach. It was the Teutonic Order which took upon itself the task of opposing the events which, if once Lithuania were converted, would have deprived it of its own reason for existence. In agreement with a brother of Jagiello, hostile to the king, and with the Grand Duke of Smolensk, who oscillated between Moscow and Lithuania, the German Knights invaded the latter at the moment when her princes were being baptized in Cracow. But Jagiello's other brothers, returning in haste, repulsed the aggressors, and at Christmas time he went back himself to his native country to carry out his promises.

In the month of February 1387 Catholicism was officially introduced into Lithuania; a first bishopric, founded at Wilno, at once received privileges analogous to those of the Church of Poland, and a first charter of privileges was simultaneously granted to the Lithuanian boyars. It proclaimed the principle by which the latter were to obtain all the rights enjoyed by the Polish nobility; this grant was the best means of introducing into Lithuania the essential elements of the new social order that was to replace the arbitrary absolutism of the pagan epoch in that country. The Ruthenian provinces of the Grand Duchy with their Orthodox population kept their traditional autonomy; the princes of the House of Gedymin, who governed these territories, were only asked to swear fidelity to the King and Queen of Poland.

Jadwiga was never set aside, and, young as she was, she inaugurated from that moment her political role at the side of a husband who submitted to the ascendancy of her character and intelligence and that of her high culture. Jagiello, who, on his side, was remarkably gifted and who seems to have undergone a profound moral transformation after his baptism and marriage, was certainly not a simple prince consort; but Jadwiga, who herself, in 1384, had been crowned 'king,' became, after 1386, a co-ruler whose influence increased with her years.

At the moment when King Ladislas was drawing up the new statute of Lithuania, Jadwiga, at the head of an expedition which scarcely required to have recourse to arms, restored to Poland the regions of Lwow and Halicz that Louis of Anjou had detached from his Polish kingdom and where he had left Hungarian governors. The influence of the new state was so considerable that the Voivode of Moldavia soon paid homage to the crown of Poland, while at the other extremity of the territory subject to Ladislas Jagiello, the rich republic of Novgorod showed itself willing to receive one of his brothers, who was to become its 'governor.' The whole of ancient Russia, whose links with the west had never been entirely broken, would thus have been withdrawn from the influence of the new Muscovite Russia, as well as from that of the Tartars, and on the side of Livonia the German expansion in the basin of the Baltic would have been arrested.

But in the midst of all these almost dazzling successes Jagiello committed one mistake that had serious consequences. Even after his accession to the throne of Cracow, he had hesitated to give his cousin Vitold the privileged position in Lithuania to which the latter always aspired. His political talent of the highest order distinguished him among all the members of the dynasty, and yet he only received a modest apanage, while one of Jagiello's brothers replaced the king at

Wilno as well as at Troki, the patrimony of the line of
Kiejstut. After having attempted in vain to modify this state
of affairs, in the beginning of 1390 Vitold took refuge a second time in Prussia, compromising in the gravest manner the
interests of his country.

For again the Teutonic Order seized the opportunity to
organize with him 'crusades' against Lithuania, calling her
conversion in question and imposing upon the good faith of
many western knights who came, even from France and England, to fight beneath its banners. For two years the situation
remained extremely critical. Only the reinforcements sent
from Poland saved Lithuania, and notably Wilno, which was
twice besieged. At last Jagiello decided to seek the only possible solution. Through the intermediation of the Piasts of
Masovia, whom he had rapidly conciliated, he offered such
important concessions to Vitold that the latter once more
abandoned his German protectors. In 1392 he was reconciled
with the king and queen at Ostrow, and the administration of
Lithuania was conferred upon him, including the Ruthenian
provinces of the former Grand Duchy. Authorized by
Jagiello, he soon even rid himself of all the local dynasts,
without excepting the brothers of the king, whose provinces
were mediatized, one after the other. The close collaboration
of the two cousins, full of promise for the future, had begun.

This beginning of their common work was frequently benefited by intervention on the part of Queen Jadwiga, inspired
by her anxiety for peace and her spirit of moderation. We see
her, for example, appear as mediator when Vitold's policy of
unification came into collision with the interests of the other
Lithuanian princes. But the authority that the young queen
wielded in every sphere, her prudence and moderation, were
still more indispensable in the nation's relations with the
Teutonic Order. The latter was aware that the agreement between Jagiello and Vitold put an end to all possibility of con-

quering a Lithuania supported by Poland. It could only take
its revenge by acting directly against the latter. To effect this
the Grand Master entered into negotiations with Sigismund
of Hungary, who had in the past been humiliated by the failure of his candidature to the Polish throne, as well as with a
Silesian Piast, Ladislas of Opole, who was afraid of losing under the new regime the fiefs that he had obtained in Poland
in the time of Louis of Anjou. They went so far as to speak of
a partition of Poland, which was a chimera. But Ladislas of
Opole did, in fact, pawn his most important fief to the Order,
that same territory of Dobrzyn which the Teutonic Knights
had so long coveted. In order to prove that this transaction
was illegal, Jadwiga, in 1397, went in person to a meeting
with the Grand Master. She did not gain the case, but she
averted an armed conflict which was abhorrent to her and for
which Poland was not prepared.

In the meanwhile, Polish diplomacy, which, thanks again
to the queen, Sigismund's sister-in-law, was successful enough
in regard to Luxemburg, in vain attempted to bring about a
coalition of all the other Baltic Powers against the Order. On
the other side, the Teutonic Knights, while branding Vitold's
'treacheries,' succeeded in again approaching that prince, and
even in imposing upon him a separate peace in 1398. For Vitold was then dreaming of the vast conquests that he was pursuing on the side of the east, where he had occupied Smolensk
and, while fighting the Tartars, had established his domination over the shore of the Black Sea. These were undeniable
successes. But Jadwiga very wisely dissuaded him against enterprises of too ambitious a nature designed to make all eastern Europe subject to him, but which, in fact, led him in 1399
to a disastrous defeat at the battle of the Worskla, impru-
dently launched against the Tartars under Tamerlane's protection.

Moreover, the queen, anxious for the interests of Poland,

while her husband's thoughts were frequently given in preference to those of his dynasty, was uneasy at seeing Vitold arbitrarily exceeding his functions as administrator of the Grand
Duchy. He had certainly no intention of breaking the union
with Poland, the advantages of which were too evident; but
he aspired to the royal crown and, in any case, to a complete
liberty of action. Jadwiga assisted in finding an equitable
compromise in a very delicate situation, which served as the
basis of the acts of union signed shortly after her death.

Before her death she again impressed upon those around
her that the Polish-Lithuanian union must be built up not
merely on constitutional charters, but, above all, on a true
spiritual fellowship. The university of Casimir the Great having fallen into a state of decay, she prepared its renovation;
the Sorbonne, with its brilliant theological department, was
this time taken as its model, because the University of Cracow
was to serve as a centre of faith and civilization for Lithuania,
from which country the queen also sent students as far as
Prague, as well as for the Ruthenian provinces, where new
projects of religious union with the Roman Church were in
preparation.

Dying in 1399, immediately after the death of her only and
new-born child, Jadwiga of Anjou did not see the opening of
the university, which was restored the following year. Nor
did she behold the increasingly fruitful results of all her personal sacrifices. But her contemporaries knew what they owed
to this queen, whose work in history had been a more
astounding miracle than those which soon glorified her tomb.
These brought about the inception of the process of her
canonization in the beginning of the fifteenth century, and to
bring it to a successful conclusion would be an honour to the
Poland of to-day.

8

Grunwald and Horodlo

ALTHOUGH he married again three times, Ladislas Jagiello never forgot his first wife, and during all the rest of his reign, which lasted until 1434, he loyally strove to develop the work he had undertaken with her. Moreover, his cousin Vitold remained his valuable and faithful collaborator for nearly thirty years. It was only on the eve of the latter's death, which preceded by four years that of the king, that an unfortunate misunderstanding came near to embroiling the two cousins, whose good relations had for so long been well known throughout Europe. The consequences of this crisis troubled Jagiello's last years, but they could not compromise the essential results that had been attained in common.

We may best judge what these very important results were if we group them round two events which symbolize, even to this day, a whole epoch of Polish history. Evoking the memory of Grunwald and Horodlo, we see, on one side, a great military success which terminated in serious political disappointments, but which kept throughout the ages all its moral value. And we see, on the other side, a purely pacific work which immediately bore full fruit, and in which, at the same time, the purest spirit of immortal Poland is incarnate.

The great war between Poland and the Teutonic Order, crowned by the victory of 1410, narrowly missed breaking out immediately after the death of Queen Jadwiga. The question of Samogitia, a Lithuanian province which touched the Baltic Sea and separated the two German colonies of Prussia and Livonia, had been added to that of Dobrzyn. Unable to subject the whole of Lithuania, the Order was determined to wrest from her at least this province, and thus to unite the two parts of the Teutonic territory. It was evident that here was a question as vital for Lithuania as that of Pomerania for Poland. Unfortunately, the Lithuanian princes had not always understood this, and in 1398 Vitold had even believed he was definitely conciliating his dangerous neighbours by yielding the whole of Samogitia to them. He soon saw his mistake. The Order again began to insinuate itself into the internal affairs of Lithuania by supporting a pretender to the throne who was hostile to Vitold, and it established so harsh a rule in Samogitia that the enslaved population turned in desperation to the prince who had abandoned them.

However, the situation which, on the threshold of the fifteenth century, was extremely strained, appeared to calm down in 1404 as the result of a treaty by the terms of which Jagiello and Vitold once more renounced Samogitia. On the other hand, the Order restored the territory of Dobrzyn to Poland, insisting on payment of the great sum for which Ladislas of Opole had pledged it. To collect this sum the King of Poland was obliged to convoke, for the first time, assemblies of the nobility in all his provinces, the regional Diets which voted extraordinary taxes. But it was only putting off the evil day. Too many disputed questions remained unsettled, including that never-forgotten one of Pomerania; too

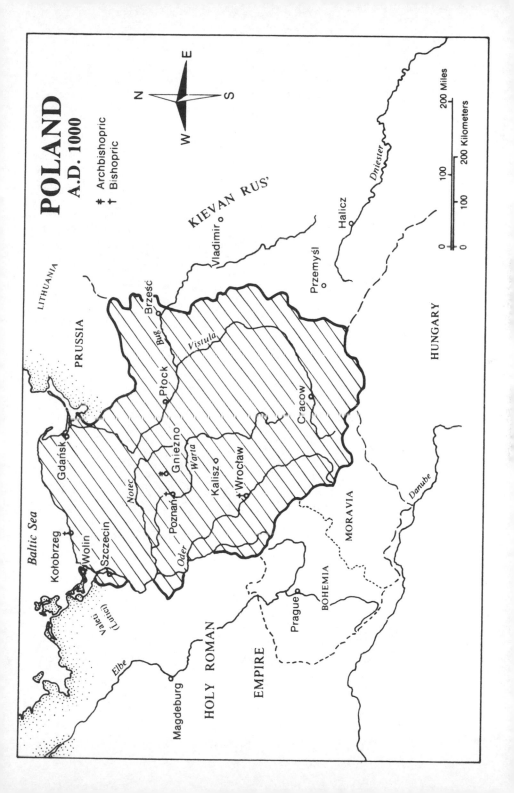

POLAND
A.D. 1000

✠ Archbishopric
✝ Bishopric

N E
S
W

200 Miles
100
200 Kilometers
100
0
0

KIEVAN RUS'

LITHUANIA

PRUSSIA

Baltic Sea

Vladimir

Halicz

Dniester

Brześć

Bug

Vistula

Płock

Przemyśl

HUNGARY

Gdańsk

Notec

Warta

Gniezno

Kalisz

Cracow

Poznań

Wrocław

Oder

Kołobrzeg

Wolin

Szczecin

Vale (Lutici)

Elbe

Magdeburg

HOLY ROMAN

EMPIRE

Prague

BOHEMIA

MORAVIA

Danube

many fresh disputes arose along the frontiers; finally, the whole policy of the Order remained too clearly directed against that Polish-Lithuanian union with which its projects of expansion clashed.

The rupture was provoked in 1409 by a general revolt in Samogitia, where the yoke of the Order had become intolerable. The warlike Grand Master, Ulric von Jungingen, was not mistaken when he accused Vitold of complicity with the insurgents. For the Grand Duke had at last realized that he could not sacrifice an essential part of his country and his people. All depended now on the attitude of Poland. She declared her entire solidarity with Lithuania and refused to abandon her. Under these conditions the Grand Master preferred a direct attack upon the kingdom, and soon the territory of Dobrzyn, only just redeemed, saw itself again invaded.

The campaign of 1410, which was foreseen to be a decisive one, was carefully prepared on both sides. Jagiello and Vitold, convinced that the very existence of the federated state was at stake, had assembled all their forces, Polish, Lithuanian, and Ruthenian. They had also Czech and Tartar reinforcements, but the importance of the latter was greatly exaggerated by the enemy in order to scandalize European opinion. The Order, on its side, had proceeded to a general mobilization, and for the last time many knights from all the western countries believed it their duty to fight with the Order against the 'infidels' and their allies. Its army, somewhat inferior in numbers, had the advantage of an indisputable technical superiority.

We know all the vicissitudes of the battle fought on 15th July 1410 between Grunwald and Tannenberg. The strategic talent of the King of Poland, as well as the gallantry of his cousin, were worthy of admiration. Nevertheless, at the outset, the Lithuanian wing of their army was routed by the German Knights. But in the second phase of the battle the latter were crushed in their turn by the Polish nobility, who on that day achieved its most brilliant victory.

The Order, whose Grand Master and chief dignitaries fell on the field of honour, seemed lost. In Pomerania, as in Prussia proper, one town after another and entire districts surrendered to the victors. A partition of the whole state between Poland, who hoped to recover the mouth of the Vistula, and Lithaania, who would have secured the mouth of the Niemen, was regarded as certain. Nothing of the kind took place. On their side also their forces were exhausted, and, in addition, serious strategical mistakes had been committed. They were obliged to raise the siege of Marienburg, valiantly defended by Henry von Plauen, under whose command the Order rallied and regained possession of all its territory. Therefore, the peace concluded at Torun in 1411 in no way corresponded with the hopes of Grunwald. Poland contented herself with insignificant concessions, and the question of Samogitia was regulated in an absurd manner. Jagiello and Vitold were to be its masters until their death, but then it was to return to the Order. After the treaty was signed each party began to accuse the other of not respecting its stipulations. The struggle was resumed three times. These by no means glorious wars offer little that is of interest. They ended in 1422 in a new treaty of peace which obliged the Order definitely to renounce Samogitia.

But the essential point was that after Grunwald all the prestige of the Order had disappeared. Its proceedings could still disquiet Poland and Lithuania, but it had ceased to be a danger to them. It still kept the whole of Prussia, with Danzig Pomerania and the district of Chelmno; but opposition to its rule was daily increasing in the very heart of its state. It still posed as the defender of the faith against the barbarians; but the keen interest that so violent and prolonged a conflict had evoked in all Europe finished by enlightening impartial opinion on the true state of affairs. On the eve and the morrow of Grunwald the two sides had carried out an intense propaganda to justify their cause. This propaganda was resumed at the Council of Constance, before which the whole problem was officially laid. The Polish contention was expounded in an exceedingly eloquent manner in the treatises of Paul, the son of Vladimir, rector and delegate of the University of Cracow. He affirmed the right of all nations, even should they be pagans, to their territorial independence; he openly proclaimed that the doctrine of Christ should be spread by methods compatible with charity; he showed that the Teutonic Order in the pursuit of its conquests had taken no account of the conditions of a just war, established by Christian traditions. The Order, on its side, replied by an infamous pamphlet, the conclusions of which were inspired by the theme of tyrannicide, which was defended at the same time by the famous Jean Petit in the interests of the Duke of Burgundy. This coincidence gained for the Poles the support of the representatives of the King of France and of the University of Paris.

What, however, most deeply impressed the whole of the Council was what it saw before its eyes of the positive results of the Polish-Lithuanian union. A delegation from distant Samogitia came there to prove that even that only recently regained province, following the example of the whole of Lithuania which the Order had never been able to christianize by force of arms, was in process of being converted spontaneously. And a Ruthenian delegation, with the Metropolitan of Kiev at its head, assured Pope Martin V, whose election had just put an end to the schism of the west, that the schism of the east could on its side be liquidated, thanks to the efforts of Jagiello and Vitold.

These pacific efforts met with the warm approbation of the Pope and the Council, even though it was impossible for them to settle the political side of the conflict with the Order. Parallel with this armed conflict the development of closer relations between the nations united since 1386, and called upon to extend in common the boundaries of Christian civilization, was carried on without a pause. To gain this end it was necessary, in the first place, to regulate the union from the constitutional standpoint. The compromise to which the way had been opened by Queen Jadwiga avoided the primitive idea of an incorporation, pure and simple, of the Lithuanian and Ruthenian territories with the kingdom of Poland. In 1401 Jagiello delegated his grand-ducal power to Vitold, and a statute of autonomy was granted to all Lithuania with her Ruthenian provinces, while at the same time she remained bound to Poland by feudal ties.

This principle was enforced in 1413, when Poles and Lithuanians met at Horodlo on the Bug to sign new articles of union. These articles, dated the 2nd of October, guaranteed to Lithuania that she should have her own Grand Duke, even after Vitold's death, it being understood that this Grand Duke would be nominated by the King of Poland in agreement with the qualified representatives of the two countries. Similarly the throne of Poland could not be filled in the future without the agreement of the Grand Duke and the Lithuanians. Invoking the common interests of the two parties, the principle of absolute solidarity in foreign policy was once more stressed. But what distinguishes the Union of Horodlo from all the other Polish-Lithuanian agreements is the idea of perpetuating it by a tie higher and more intimate than that of legal settlements: the *élite* of the two nations were to form one single, united family, thanks to that 'mystery of charity' which the document drawn up by the Polish nobility extols as the fundamental element of public life.

With this object the representatives of forty-seven houses of that nobility adopted at Horodlo the same number of Lithuanian boyars, granting them, as well as their kindred, the right of bearing the coats of arms of the families into whose bosoms they were thus admitted. These coats of arms symbolized the close solidarity which for centuries had united the clans of the Polish knighthood, and which was now to extend to the newly adopted fraternity of Lithuanian origin. Under the inspiration of this principle it was at once decided that delegates of the two countries, such as had assembled in 1401 and in 1413, should henceforth regularly hold 'conventions and parliaments,' so that the parliamentary institutions which were in course of being developed in Poland could soon be formed in Lithuania likewise. Other articles inserted in the Act of Union granted new liberties and privileges on the Polish model to the inhabitants of the Grand Duchy, completing those which they had obtained in 1387.

The initiative taken at Horodlo proved exceedingly fruitful in results. The Polish-Lithuanian union definitely ceased to be an affair negotiated between the dynasty of Gedymin and a few lords of Cracow: the two nations were thereby associated, assimilated into one another, and growing accustomed to treat together all the questions that concerned them. Increasing numbers of Lithuanians came to Poland. either in the entourage of the king or to go through their university studies there, while Poles crowded into Lithuania to take their part in the Grand Duke's military campaigns and to serve in his court or his chancellery.

For Vitold, solicitous as he was for the prestige of his

Grand Duchy, and for the extension of its administrative limits in the federated State, favoured, none the less, the entrance of Polish civilization into all the territories subject to him and into every domain of life. He exercised at the same time considerable personal influence even in purely Polish affairs. It is true that he followed more particularly the eastern questions by maintaining the ancient Lithuanian pretensions to the republic of Novgorod in rivalry with Moscow, where, moreover, a grandson of Vitold, subject to his tutelage, had been reigning since 1425, and by intervening as arbitrator in the interminable conflicts between the Tartar khans. But he also appeared at the side of the King of Poland in their relations with Hungary and Bohemia, with Brandenburg and Denmark, even with France and England. It was then, in the course of the fifteen years that followed Grunwald and Horodlo, that the collaboration of the two princes, who each complemented the other in an extraordinary manner, gave all the hoped-for results.

The authority which they enjoyed in Europe and even with the emperors of the Greeks and the Turks, an authority which increased, above all, after the Council of Constance, seemed to be manifested with the greatest splendour at the congress which assembled at Luck in Volhynia in the beginning of 1429. There, surrounded by their eastern vassals, Jagiello and Vitold solemnly received, together with a papal legate, the Emperor Sigismund of Luxemburg, who some years since had added the crowns of Germany and Bohemia to that of Hungary. Despite treaties of alliance renewed on several occasions, Sigismund's attitude in respect to Poland had always remained equivocal. An ally of the Order at the time of Grunwald, he had subsequently attempted to arbitrate in its conflict with Jagiello and Vitold. But these two soon had occasion to learn the Emperor's partiality. In return they profited by the embarrassments that the Hussite movement caused him, to intervene in the affairs of Bohemia. The sympathy which they found in the Czech opposition, which had even offered them the crown, naturally disquieted Sigismund. A strong reaction against the doctrines of Huss, condemned by the Church, had certainly arisen in Poland, but the two Slav nations remained in close contact, and the Pope even considered entrusting to the King of Poland that pacification of Bohemia which was not succeeding under Sigismund. This was precisely what the latter wished to prevent at all costs; and this explains why he profited by the Congress of Luck to create a serious internal embarrassment for Poland herself by attempting to break the solidarity of that country with Lithuania and her Grand Duke.

Clearly perceiving that Vitold's official position did not correspond either to the role that he was actually playing or to his ambition, he suggested raising him to the dignity of King of Lithuania. It was easy to foresee that the Poles would oppose this by invoking the articles of the Union which considered the Grand Duchy as an integral part of the kingdom of Poland. In fact, they entered immediately into irritating discussions on the interpretation of these articles, and a want of tact on the part of the Polish chancellery exasperated Vitold, who, at the outset, had himself hesitated before so delicate a proposition. Jagiello's attitude complicated the situation. As the sons who were at last borne to him by his fourth wife, a Lithuanian princess, had no hereditary right to the crown of Poland and were obliged to be elected to it by the nobility, the old king was, in principle, favourable to the creation of a Lithuanian kingdom which his sons should inherit after the death of Vitold, who had no sons. In this case, their election by the Poles, who had no intention of breaking the union of the two countries, would be a pure formality. Consequently, while trying to avoid an imperial intervention dangerous for the Polish-Lithuanian union, Jagiello was quite ready to authorize the coronation of Vitold, but the latter died on 27th October 1430.

The conflict which then broke out seems to us the best proof of the merits of that Grand Duke, who, in spite of inevitable collisions, had so well known how to reconcile the individual interests of Lithuania with the principle of her highly advantageous union with Poland. As his successor, Jagiello appointed one of his own brothers, the only one still living—the turbulent Swidrygiello. The latter was immediately possessed by the idea of modifying the legal conditions of the Polish-Lithuanian union; the Poles on their part claimed the cession of Podolia and Volhynia, holding that these provinces had only been administered by Vitold in virtue of a personal right. In the civil war that ensued grave mistakes were committed on both sides. Swidrygiello allied himself with the Teutonic Order, which broke the peace treaty of 1422 and invaded Poland: the latter opposed another Grand Duke to him in the person of Sigismund, Vitold's brother, so that Lithuania found herself divided into two hostile camps. Despite a final victory that was compared, very erroneously, to that of Grunwald, and despite the renewal of the Union of Horodlo by the Grand Duke Sigismund, these fratricidal struggles were prolonged in a deplorable fashion and were still going on when Jagiello died on 1st June 1434. He had not succeeded in checking them, but this failure on the part of the old king did not prevent the following generations from rendering homage to a reign of nearly half a century which, in spite of a violent final shock, had definitely created a new Poland, the great Jagiellonian Poland.

9

Varna and Danzig

THE founder of the Jagiello dynasty, a king of alien origin desirous of gaining the confidence of the Polish nobility, had granted to it new privileges, in a whole series of charters, including the famous guarantee that no one should be imprisoned without a trial. The nobility, however, had only accepted these charters with the explicit reservation that it was free to choose the successors of the king. Legally, therefore, the Polish throne was henceforth elective. In point of fact, there had never been any doubt that Jagiello's eldest son, who, like his father, was called Ladislas, would become king after him.

In 1434 the future hero of Varna was only ten years old. It was, therefore, necessary to institute a regency. There was hardly room for doubt that the real power would fall to the eminent Zbigniew Olesnicki, the Bishop of Cracow, who had succeeded in counterbalancing even the influence of a Vitold. To this day we see nearly the whole of the Polish history of this epoch through the eyes of this great statesman, because the illustrious contemporary historian, John Dlugosz, was his disciple and passionate admirer. And he was not wrong. We may even add that the imposing figure of the first Polish cardinal belongs indisputably to general history. In the first place, Olesnicki was a distinguished humanist, admired by the future Pius II. This in no wise prevented him from being an exemplary prelate, of perfect integrity and piety. And this European of the Renaissance epoch, this prince of the Church, possessed of a universal outlook, was at the same time a great Polish patriot who embodied the national consciousness of all his generation. But he had one great defect, more serious than that of a restless ambition which only became disquieting towards the end of his career: he was a doctrinaire. He proved it in the vital question of Poland's relations with Lithuania, desiring as he did to observe to the letter clauses which no longer corresponded to the actual situation. He proved it in the conflict between the Pope and the Council, a conflict which had such a strong repercussion on Polish affairs, when, together with the great majority of the Polish clergy, whose representatives had played a considerable role at Constance and Basle, he remained attached to the extreme limits of the conciliar doctrine in spite of his country's official neutrality.

This twofold attitude was later to create serious difficulties for Jagiello's two sons. During their minority, Olesnicki and his collaborators, among whom were several members of his family, had, in any case, the merit of putting an end to the civil war which had been raging since the death of Vitold, and which was, at the same time, a new war with the Teutonic Order. At the end of 1435 the latter was obliged to sign a 'perpetual' peace, guaranteed by its own subjects in Prussia, who thus began to play a part, soon to be a decisive one, in the Order's relations with Poland. At the same time, the Order abandoned Swidrygiello, who had suffered an irreparable defeat, but who still held out in the Ruthenian territories. At one moment it could even seem as if the Jagiellonian State would become a tripartite federation, which would not have been without certain advantages. However, the Ruthenian question was settled otherwise, following the principle recognized on the eve of Jagiello's death. The Ruthenian provinces, whose autonomy, in fact, deprived them of the privileges which both Poland and Lithuania proper successively obtained, were granted, some of them the Polish law which they had long demanded, others an equal standing in the provinces of the Grand Duchy. The Grand Duchy then obtained a first charter which was no longer limited to Lithuania proper, and no longer drew any distinction between Catholics and Orthodox.

Having seen the different parts of the Grand Duchy gradually united and pacified, at least to outward appearance, under the rule of Vitold's brother, Olesnicki turned to the grave problems by which Poland was then faced. Sigismund of Luxemburg having died in 1437, his son-in-law, Albrecht of Austria, was to have succeeded him not only in Germany but also in Bohemia and Hungary. The Poles, however, knew very well that the accession of the Hapsburgs was not looked upon with favourable eyes by the national parties in these two kingdoms. They therefore aimed at gaining at least one of these crowns for their own dynasty. A Jagiellonian candidature to the throne of Bohemia, already considered in the time of Jagiello and Vitold, seemed particularly opportune, the more so as ties with Silesia could thus be renewed. This project suited, above all, a fairly considerable group of the Polish nobility which had allowed itself to be gained over by Hussite influences. For Olesnicki, on the contrary, this was precisely a reason for opposing it, and although the younger brother of King Ladislas, young Casimir, had been sent to Bohemia to join his partisans there, his candidature was not seriously advanced, and completely failed.

Soon, however, in 1439, Albrecht of Austria died in his

turn without leaving a direct heir, and this time Olesnicki, who had triumphed over his adversaries within the State, decided to place Ladislas himself on the throne of Hungary. It was not only a case of re-establishing the union with that purely Catholic country in conditions more favourable to Poland than in the time of Louis of Anjou; the Bishop of Cracow intended to go farther. Neither Sigismund nor Albrecht had succeeded in repulsing the Turkish danger, which, after the conquest of the Balkans, was looming ever more menacingly on the frontiers of Hungary to the apprehension of the Christian world. What glory for Poland should her king place himself at the head of a new Crusade, save Hungary, deliver the southern Slavs, and go to the help of Constantinople! The Greeks themselves could then be won over to the Roman Church in a more efficacious manner than by the Union of Florence, which won little sympathy from Olesnicki, because it was concluded by Eugenius IV in opposition to the Council of Basle.

No one could reproach the Polish statesman for his large vision, and for having dreamt of so great a mission for his country and his king. But, on the one hand, he had no conception of the difficulties that awaited Ladislas in Hungary itself, and, on the other hand, he had failed to understand that it was not the Council of Basle with its antipope, but the legitimate Pontiff alone, possessing a true comprehension of the eastern question, who could efficaciously encourage the projected Crusade. In Hungary the King of Poland had first of all been elected without dispute; but the Queen Dowager Elizabeth of Luxemburg, after having given birth to a posthumous son of Albrecht of Austria, like his rival named Ladislas, showed herself firmly resolved to secure for him the whole of his paternal heritage. From 1440 to 1442 Hungary was therefore torn by a civil war between the two

Ladislases, both crowned and each supported by his own
party. And when at last an agreement, at least provisional,
ensured the sovereignty to the Jagiello and allowed him to
turn against the Turks, Poland, after so much time and
money wasted, had lost patience, and Olesnicki was ill pleased
at the compromise with the Hapsburgs having been concluded under the auspices of a legate of Eugenius IV who
formed the league against the infidels.

Instead, then, of fresh reinforcements from Poland, the
king only received reiterated appeals demanding his return.
But he himself remained faithful to the idea that had led
him to Hungary. Having come to an understanding with the
Pope, and pronounced in favour of the Union of Florence
which he considered useful for his Ruthenian provinces, he
counted on the support of the Catholic Powers of the west.
During his first Balkan campaign in 1443, this support was
entirely lacking. Nevertheless, with his Hungarian army led
by John Hunyadi, as well as with the group of Polish knights
who had remained attached to his cause, he achieved extraordinary successes, such as the Christian world, assailed by
the Ottomans, had never known, and was for centuries not
to know again. As a victor he crossed Serbia, penetrated into
Bulgaria, and only the advanced season forced him to a return which was marked by new exploits. The following year
the Turks offered him a ten years' truce. But at Szeged Ladislas refused to ratify the treaty and proclaimed that he
would take up the struggle again until the Turks were driven
out of Europe. For the king and the legate, Julian Cesarini, had just been informed that the Christian fleet, provided by Eugenius IV, his Venetian fellow citizens, and
Philip of Burgundy, had set out to occupy the Straits and to
prevent Murad II from transporting the bulk of his troops
from Asia to Europe. Unfortunately, this fleet failed in its

task, and it was near Varna on the shores of the Black Sea
that Ladislas flung himself into a hopeless battle. In a heroic
charge recalling that of the French at Nikopoli, this twenty-
year-old king died with the greater part of his Polish comrades, as well as the papal legate. Hungary was saved from
destruction by Hunyadi, but the fate of the Balkans, including Constantinople, whose emperor had sent despairing appeals to the Jagiello king, was sealed for hundreds of years.

For long, men refused to believe in the death of the hero
of Varna. In Poland, however, where the absence of the king
had been severely felt, there was the wish to replace him as
quickly as possible. Yet it was not until three years later, in
1447, that his younger brother, Casimir, was crowned in the
Vavel cathedral of Cracow. From the beginning he had been
the only serious candidate, though there had been talk of
Frederick of Brandenburg and Boleslas of Masovia in order
to hasten the decision of the Grand Duke of Lithuania. For
Casimir had governed the country of his ancestors since 1440,
the Grand Duke Sigismund having been assassinated by the
leaders of an aristocracy which he had oppressed. This Lithuanian aristocracy, whose influence had increased during the
civil war and Casimir's minority, was not willing that he
should accept the throne of Poland without having received
a guarantee that the Grand Duchy should no longer be sub-
ordinate to the kingdom, and that the disputed provinces
of Volhynia and Podolia should belong to Lithuania.

When Casimir at last reached Poland he had made the two
parties accept a provisional compromise which he succeeded,
after six years of persevering efforts, in making final. The
new king had none of his brother's mystic and confident
enthusiasm. Destined, like his father, to reign for half a century, like him he distinguished himself by his long patience,
while at the same time surpassing him by his energy and the

clearness of his political conceptions. Resolved to avoid, at all costs, a new internal conflict, he saw clearly that the consequences of that which had followed the death of Vitold could only be effaced by an essential change in the conditions of the Polish-Lithuanian union. He attached little importance to the process of signing new documents as his predecessor Sigismund had done, dissembling a doubtful loyalty. He simply gave the Poles to understand that Lithuania, christianized and organized on the basis of western civilization, was now fit to be placed on a completely equal footing. He made the Lithuanians renounce the institution of a Grand Duke of their own, whose personal ambitions could provoke new dissensions between the two countries. To which of these countries certain disputed territories should belong was, in reality, a question regarded with great indifference by their common monarch, as long as arms were not taken up to contest it. Finally, he admitted the established *status quo*, which, in fact, stood for an equitable division, the chief part of Volhynia remaining with the Lithuanians, and Podolia, with the exception of her eastern borders, with the Poles.

In order to reach this satisfactory result Casimir had been obliged to isolate the irreconcilables on both sides, who were displeased at seeing the king restrain their inordinate influence. In Poland, the oligarchy of Little Poland in general, including Olesnicki, despite the Roman purple which he had obtained not without difficulties, were gradually put aside for the benefit of the gentry and the representatives of Great Poland. In Lithuania the Palatine of Wilno, John Gasztold, who had abused his power during Casimir's minority, now in vain stood forward as the chief of an opposition of which one member after another rallied to the partisans of the king.

But the latter was well aware that nothing could better

cement the Polish-Lithuanian union than a great task undertaken in common and responding to the hopes of Krewo.
The realization of these could not be effected without the
redintegration of the territories lost in the past by the two
nations, and the extension of the federated State to its natural limits: the Baltic and the Black Sea. As regards the latter,
the disaster of Varna, the consequences of which were soon
to be manifest in the political situation of Poland and Lithuania, did not encourage the resumption of any projects of so
risky a nature. Moreover, for the moment, the seaboard between the mouths of the Dniester and the Dnieper remained
beyond dispute subject to Casimir, as formerly to Vitold.
On the other hand, the Baltic was only accessible by a small
corner of Samogitia, as long as the Teutonic Order still kept
the mouths of the Vistula and the Niemen.

Casimir, therefore, closely followed the internal crisis
through which the State of that Order was then passing. The
discontent that was increasing among its subjects had led
them to create a Prussian League, which began by defending
the rights of the nobility and the towns and which finished
by open revolt. Having seized nearly all the strongholds of
the country, the insurgents had recourse, in the beginning of
1454, to the King of Poland, spontaneously placing the whole
of Prussia, naturally including what had once been Polish
Pomerania, under his sovereignty. Casimir, who had just
regulated Polish-Lithuanian relations, did not hesitate to
accept so tempting an offer. True, this time it was Poland
who was breaking the latest treaty of peace, but she did it at
the request of the populations concerned, who turned to her,
attracted by liberties unknown under the rule of the Order.
And no one foresaw that the resistance of the latter was to
impose upon Poland a war of thirteen years, the result of
which was to fall far short of its initial hopes.

Neither the Prussian League nor the Poles had sufficiently

reckoned with the international relations and the material resources which were still at the disposal of the Teutonic Knights. A victory that was almost unexpected, gained over the Polish nobility at Chojnice at the outset of hostilities, enabled the Order to gain time and organize its defence. On the other hand, King Casimir at once experienced a severe disappointment in the discovery that the Lithuanians, misjudging their own interests, did not intend to bring in all their forces. The Samogitians alone attacked Memel and cut the communications between Prussia and Livonia from which the Order was trying in vain to draw reinforcements. The army of the Order was composed chiefly of mercenaries, better disciplined and more accustomed to prolonged operations than the mass of the Polish gentry whom, following tradition, the king had chosen to use. However, Casimir was soon obliged to have recourse, on his side, to mercenary troops or to gain over those whom the Order could no longer pay regularly and who, in 1457, sold the capital, Marienburg, to Poland. Even then the war was far from being decided. Dreary and ruinous, it no longer had the character of a conflict between two nations as at the time of Grunwald. The German element predominated in the Prussian League which was particularly enraged against the Order, and the town of Danzig, in which the majority of the population was at this epoch already German, rendered the most signal services to the king by providing him with large sums of money, and by successfully undertaking the naval war against Denmark, the ally of the Order.

At last, from about 1462, Poland redoubled her efforts, both military and diplomatic. Her troops, better commanded, gained successes which effaced the deplorable impression of the battle of Chojnice, and thrust back the troops of the Order towards East Prussia. Laborious negotiations, in the course of which one European Power after another

attempted to play the part of mediator, prepared the compromise which served as the basis of the treaty of 1466. This
second Peace of Torun was infinitely more advantageous for
Poland than the first in 1411. This time Danzig Pomerania,
with the territory of Chelmno, was after a century and a half
of alienation restored to her, together with a part of Prussia
proper, including the port of Elbing, Marienburg, and the
bishopric of Varmia or Ermeland. All this territory, which
secured the kingdom extensive access to the sea, and was
called henceforth Western or Royal Prussia, remained in the
possession of Poland until the first partition.

But the rest of Prussia, with Königsberg as its new capital,
remained under the rule of the Order, which Casimir vainly
endeavoured to tranfer to the Turkish or Tartar borderlands
where it could have resumed its original vocation. However,
this East Prussia was no longer to be an independent state
but a fief of Poland. According to the treaty each Grand
Master was to pay homage to the king and provide him with
reinforcements in case of necessity. In addition, the Order
was to renounce its exclusively Teutonic character. It undertook to receive Polish knights to the number of half of its
members.

The whole question now was whether this treaty would be
strictly respected in the future. And in the last resort this
again depended on the extent of authority and power at the
disposal of the Jagiellonian State. In any case, and in spite
of the disquieting concessions which he had been obliged to
make, Casimir could be proud of the results obtained. One
of the essential objects of the Polish-Lithuanian union, foreseen, perhaps, in part, by Casimir the Great, pursued in vain
by Ladislas Jagiello, was attained by one of his sons, whose
kingdom now stretched literally from one sea to the other.

10

The Zenith of a Dynasty

Historians are unanimous in paying homage to all that Casimir Jagiello effected during the first half of his long reign. They are far less so as regards the second part of that reign. It has, in fact, been observed that the policy of the king, at the outset dictated only by the vital interests of his people, subsequently became an essential dynastic policy. But this is no matter for surprise. The Jagiello king only followed the example of the other monarchs of his time. All the great states which were then being created in Europe owe their foundation in a large measure to dynastic interests. As regards Casimir, they were the more natural inasmuch as he had thirteen children, six of whom were growing sons, all born of his marriage with Elizabeth of Austria, a marriage that was concluded on the eve of the Prussian war.

This 'mother of the Jagiellos' was the sister of the hero of Varna's former rival, Ladislas the Posthumous, who, since 1444, had been the undisputed sovereign of Hungary as well as of Bohemia. After his premature death in 1457 his Austrian possessions naturally returned to the younger line of the Hapsburgs, whose head was then the Emperor Frederick

III. But the two kingdoms which Ladislas had inherited through his mother could now be considered as the heritage of his sister, the Queen of Poland, and her children. Such was the principle invoked at the outset by Casimir, who only awaited the opportune moment to avail himself of it, and thus to resume, with a new legal basis, former projects which consisted in establishing the Polish-Lithuanian dynasty either in Bohemia or in Hungary, or even in both countries at once.

Before taking any steps in this direction Casimir was naturally obliged to wait for the end of the thirteen years' war against the Order. He therefore did not oppose the elections which, carried out in Hungary and Bohemia after the death of his father-in-law, summoned native kings to the throne: Matthias Corvinus, son of John Hunyadi, and George of Podiebrad.

The King of Poland even allied himself with the latter in 1462, and he also interested himself in the vast design of perpetual peace and European organization that the King of Bohemia propagated with his French collaborator, Antoine Marini. George of Podiebrad's religious attitude, which favoured the moderate Hussitism of the Utraquists, despite his project of a league against the infidel, greatly disquieted the Holy See. Urged by Casimir to confirm the Peace of Torun, Paul II demanded of him in return that he should advance against the Hussite king. But it was not by force of arms directed against the national King of Bohemia that the Jagiello sovereign aimed at obtaining his throne. It was through Podiebrad himself, whom he supported by overtures of conciliation, that he won the promise that the King of Poland's eldest son Ladislas should succeed him at Prague. This prince was, in fact, elected King of Bohemia when George died in 1471. But there was also another candidate

in the person of Matthias of Hungary, who, in contradistinction to Casimir, had become the instrument of the pontifical
policy directed against George, and now claimed the price
of his efforts.

The King of Poland attempted to prevent his intervention
in Bohemia by sending into Hungary another of his sons,
young Casimir, whom a party hostile to Matthias promised
to raise to the throne. But the Hungarian expedition of the
future saint was a complete failure, and only exasperated
Corvinus against the Jagiellos. In the dispute for the crown
of Bohemia he carried out a war against them which ended
in 1478 with a very precarious compromise: Casimir's eldest
son kept Bohemia proper, but Silesia and Moravia remained
in the hands of Matthias of Hungary, who, on his part,
claimed the title of King of Bohemia. This equivocal situation lasted until the death of Corvinus in 1490. The King of
Poland then profited by the disappearance of his adversary
to claim again the throne of Hungary for one of his sons.
This time he obtained his object, but after a prolonged
struggle between two Jagiello brothers: John Albert, originally supported by his father, and Ladislas of Bohemia, who
won and thus united the two kingdoms, also restoring to
Bohemia the provinces which had been detached from her.

This brief account of the essential facts will suffice to show
both the advantages and disadvantages of Casimir's dynastic
plan, completely realized on the eve of his death in 1492.
The triumph of his house was manifest. It had united under
its rule so extensive a territory—from the gates of Moscow
to the waters of the Adriatic—as to surpass by far that of any
other European Power. This immense Jagiellonian federation seemed a valuable element of equilibrium and peace in
Europe, as none of the Jagiellos dreamt of war, unless it were
to oppose the advance of the infidel, against whom an appar-

ently insurmountable barrier was now raised. This federal
system, heightening the prestige of each of the states that
composed it, did not suppress the independence of any of
them: because the Jagiellos respected their national traditions and the liberties they had acquired, while their strict
solidarity removed any possibility of conflict among these
states.

Naturally, Poland, together with the other federated states,
profited on her side by the advantages of this situation; as
it was her king who had created it she became, in conformity, moreover, with geographical conditions, the centre of
what might be called the Jagiellonian system. But also it was
Poland who had been the first to suffer from the complications that the dynastic policy of Casimir had brought in its
train. Thus, during the Bohemian war, Matthias Corvinus
allied himself with the Teutonic Order, which considered
that the opportunity of breaking the Peace of Torun had
now arrived. The agreement of 1478 forced the Grand Master to pay that homage to the King of Poland which had been
for long withheld; but once the conditions of 1466 were
called into question, the Prussian problem again became the
source of troubles liable to open again at any moment.

This was all the more disquieting inasmuch as the Order
was now regaining the support of the Empire. The House of
Hapsburg, which had held the imperial power since 1437,
had never regarded the success of the Jagiellos in Bohemia
and Hungary with favour, and Maximilian I, far more energetic than his father, Frederick III, had also presented himself as a candidate for the succession to Corvinus. Unwilling
definitely to renounce it, he entered into relations with the
adversaries of the Jagiellos and, like Matthias, he did not
limit himself to the greatly enfeebled Teutonic Order, but
also took into consideration a more formidable enemy who
was threatening Casimir from the east.

We have, in fact, reached the moment to emphasize that it is precisely on that side, indisputably neglected for years together, that the great king, absorbed in the affairs of central Europe, had allowed the growth of a twofold danger, soon to become overwhelming.

Let us begin with that one of the two which was presented by the ally whom Matthias Corvinus and after him the Hapsburgs believed they had found in the borderlands, hitherto almost unknown, between Europe and Asia. We know that since the fourteenth century Lithuania had met with a rival in the rapidly growing power of Moscow. A certain equilibrium of their opposing forces was gradually established. In 1449 a treaty concluded between Casimir Jagiello and the Grand Duke Basil II fixed the spheres of their respective influence. But Basil, who had exhausted himself in long internal struggles from which a strongly centralized state at last emerged, was in 1462 succeeded by his son Ivan the Severe, who soon married the heiress of the Palaeologi, and who was determined to extend the domination of Moscow— a third Rome—over all the Russias. A few years, the same that Casimir had devoted to the Bohemian war, were sufficient for Ivan III to put an end to the independence of the Republic of Novgorod, which, after having counted in vain on Lithuanian help, was crushed and annexed by Moscow. This was a first warning to Casimir which drove him to seek the most varied alliances against so inconvenient a neighbour. But he was not able to prevent fresh successes on the part of Ivan, who, towards the end of Casimir's reign, when the latter was preoccupied with the Hungarian question, began in time of peace to appropriate one after another of the Lithuanian Grand Duchy's frontier districts.

However, these losses, humiliating, but, so far, not very appreciable, disquieted the king far less than a complete change of the political situation which was taking place in

the direction of the Black Sea. Here also warnings had not
been wanting. Following in his youth Vitold's example, Casimir had established good relations with the Tartar khanate
that was the nearest to his frontiers, that of the Crimea where
the Gherai family reigned, benefiting by the support of the
Jagiellos and, in general, remaining faithful and devoted to
them. Moreover, the rich commercial city of Kaffa, an old
Genoese colony in the Crimea, had placed itself under the
protection of the King of Poland. This protection did not
prevent the Turks from taking possession of that town in
1475, and the Khan Mengli Gherai, whom they had made
prisoner, soon returned to the Crimea as vassal of the Sultan.
Neither was Moldavia, which had many times recognized the
suzerainty of Poland, supported in the desperate struggles
that she waged against the Ottoman power, especially since
the accession of Stephen the Great. In 1484 the Turks tore
from her two ports of great importance: Kilia, at the mouth
of the Danube, and Akkerman, at the mouth of the Dniester.
Thus they had reached as far as the frontiers of the Polish-
Lithuanian State which was almost imperceptibly losing its
access to the Black Sea, the steppes between the Dniester and
the Dnieper having become the field of action for the Tartars of the Crimea, in subjection to Turkey. Their invasions
were becoming, at the same time, a perpetual scourge to the
Ruthenian lands of Poland and of Lithuania; the latter even
entered the risky path of an entente with the Tartars of the
Volga, the old Golden Horde, rendered discontented by the
emancipation of the Horde of the Crimea.

Without neglecting this method, which could serve
equally against Moscow, Casimir was too far-sighted not to
be aware that other means were needed to deal with a situation which was seriously compromising the security of all the
Jagiellonian states. He knew also that nothing could more

effectively heighten their prestige in Europe than victories over the infidels, victories which would avenge the memory of his brother. But while organizing the defence of the Polish-Lithuanian frontiers, the king, now grown old, bequeathed the great task which confronted his dynasty to his sons and successors. He envisaged this task as common to Ladislas, in respect of his title as King of Hungary, to John Albert, whose election he recommended to the Poles, and to Alexander, who was to inherit Lithuania. Lithuania, the most directly threatened by Moscow, was to have her own Grand Duke again; but the latter, while occupying himself more especially with his relations with Ivan III, naturally was also to collaborate in the solution of the Turco-Tartar problem.

Moreover, Casimir had prepared for his sons an excellent team of collaborators in Poland and Lithuania, chosen from the flower of the two nations whom he left closely united with each other. The generation of the Olesnickis and the Gasztolds had long since disappeared. In the kingdom new aristocratic families were grouped around the throne, but it was, above all, the gentry favoured by the king that were coming into power. At the side of the Senate formed by the ancient royal council, the deputies elected by the provincial dietines assembled in a second Chamber, which, together with the Senate, constituted the Polish Diet. Its composition was fixed before its functioning powers, but the determination of these could not be long delayed, since the dietines, of which the Diet was the emanation and the central organ, had to be consulted by the king according to the statutes of 1454 on all important questions of public life. In the Grand Duchy, on the contrary, the general Diets had so far only a very restricted role, and the dietines were non-existent. The Council of the Grand Duke alone limited his power, which fact Alexander officially recognized at his accession, and which left the door open to the rival influences of a few powerful ducal and aristocratic families. We may name at least one, the Radziwills, who were henceforth always to occupy one of the first places—if not the first—in Lithuania.

This constitutional development, fertile in consequences for all the future, enables us to understand better the critical years which followed the death of Casimir in 1492. Not only Ladislas, whose excessive weakness in regard to the States of Bohemia and Hungary has become proverbial, but also his brothers were not entirely free to make their own decisions. Even John Albert, arbitrary though he was, perhaps the only one of the Jagiellos who dreamt of absolute rule, had to begin his reign by conciliating the Diets of 1493 and 1496—the first Diets we know much about—by means of new concessions to the nobility and gentry which were to the detriment of the other social classes. Alexander, who succeeded him in Poland in 1501, thus re-establishing the personal union with Lithuania, hesitated, up to his death in 1506, between the interests of his dynasty and the pressure that was exercised upon him either by the Senate of the kingdom, or by the parties who were fighting each other in the bosom of the Grand Ducal Council, or, finally, by the Polish gentry who, in 1505, compelled him to recognize the legislative power of the Diet.

All this did not prevent the members of the dynasty from at times preparing their common political action in secret meetings—such as a family congress held in Hungary in 1494. This is why the definite result of that action, the expedition to the Black Sea undertaken in 1497, remains enveloped in a mystery which historical research attempts in vain to pierce. After having proclaimed that he was marching against the Turks to recapture Akkerman, Kilia, and perhaps even Kaffa, John Albert suddenly turned upon Stephen the Great of Moldavia. We are ignorant how far this fatal decision was justified by the voivode's action. Be that as it may, the latter inflicted a. sanguinary defeat on the Polish nobility in the forests of Bukovina. His success was aided by the Turks, who in the following year penetrated far into Polish territory, and by the connivance of the Hungarians, who, in spite of dynastic ties and a friendship that elsewhere was traditional, were always Poland's rivals on the soil of Moldavia. It was only Alexander of Lithuania, advancing at the same time towards the Black Sea, who achieved some successes over the Tartars and prevented a complete collapse of John Albert's army. Ladislas of Hungary had to confine himself to subsequently reconciling Stephen the Great with the Jagiellos.

The latter had, in any case, suffered a defeat which put an end to their active policy in the eastern question. This defeat was, in addition, followed immediately by another which most directly affected Lithuania. Alexander, attacked by Ivan on the morrow of his father's death, had hoped to appease his neighbour by marrying the latter's daughter. But this marriage only provided the Grand Duke of Moscow with fresh pretexts to recommence a war, the aim of which was to wrest from Lithuania all her Ruthenian provinces. His victorious campaign in 1500 enabled Ivan to conquer by one blow a substantial third part of these. The frontier of the two states which formerly approached Moscow was thrust back to the gates of Kiev. With the intention of repairing these losses, Alexander allied himself on one side with Livonia, and on the other with the last khan of the Golden Horde; but he was not able to support at the opportune moment the efforts of his allies, the second of whom was crushed by Mengli Gherai of the Crimea, the ally of Ivan of Moscow.

A truce concluded in 1503 ratified, at least provisionally, the situation created by the aggressor.

Even after the death of Ivan, Alexander did not succeed in his retaliation, and before he himself died in the following year he had to content himself with seeing one of the most dangerous invasions by the Khan of the Crimea repulsed. It goes without saying that this decline of the power of the Jagiellos on the eastern side encouraged at the same time their western adversaries. In order the more efficaciously to react against the Peace of Torun, the Teutonic Order had elected a prince of the Empire, Frederick of Saxony, as Grand Master; and neither John Albert nor Alexander succeeded in making him pay the vassal's homage which was due to them. But, in spite of all these sinister facts, the crisis which had followed so close upon the zenith of the Jagiellonian dynasty was not irreparable. In 1500 the three brothers had concluded an alliance with France which crowned the diplomatic relations that had been already knit in the course of the fifteenth century with their first tangible result, and which could become a very valuable instrument in their rivalry with the House of Hapsburg. The King of England himself did not fail to appeal to them when projecting a new league against the Turks.

Moreover, we must not forget that John Albert, who died shortly after the disaster of Bukovina, Alexander, the least gifted of all the Jagiellos, and the indolent Ladislas, the eldest who survived them, were not the only representatives of the family. It is true that their brother Casimir had died young, giving his glorious family a saint, for he was soon canonized by the Church. It is also true that another brother, Frederick, archbishop and cardinal, had passed away in 1503 without having rendered the services that were expected of him. But the youngest of the six princes, Sigismund, who had long waited for a position equal to that of his brothers, had matured in the course of these years; and his high qualities, which showed themselves on several occasions, made him, with good reason, the hope of his dynasty and of Poland.

11

The Epoch of the First Congress of Vienna

DESPITE all the splendour of the fifteenth century, it is the following century that national tradition considers Poland's 'golden century.' It is, therefore, peculiarly instructive to study its essential elements in order to penetrate into the significance of our history, and to realize the manner in which its spirit has been interpreted by succeeding generations.

Nearly half of this sixteenth century, to the memorials of which Poland attaches so much value, was filled by the reign of Sigismund I—from 1506 to 1548. No chronicle comparable with that of Dlugosz has drawn an adequate picture of it. Fortunately, a discerning and well documented contemporary has left us an immense collection of diplomatic papers and even confidential letters, whose texts, written in the beautiful Latin of the Renaissance, evoke before our eyes all the incidents of this epoch. Above all, they show us the fundamental principle of the whole of Sigismund I's policy and of that of his collaborators, which was the constant desire of ensuring to Poland the peace and security indispensable to her internal development. Such was, in fact, the perma-

nent anxiety of the king, to whom, more by way of character-
izing his wisdom, prudence, and noble moderation than to
record his age, the surname of Old was given. Such was, in
equal measure, the preoccupation of the remarkable states-
men who surrounded him. Among these two groups are dis-
tinguishable which at times appeared to be hostile parties.
The one, which had the Archbishop John Laski and his family at its head, certainly held bolder ideas than the other, led
by the Chancellor Christopher Szydlowiecki and his friend,
the Vice-Chancellor Peter Tomicki. But if these groups differed in temperament, and often, also, in the orientation of
their foreign relations, it would be an exaggeration to look
for an opposition of principle between them at the outset. It
was, however, the second, which always inclined to the most
nicely balanced solutions, indeed, to compromises and to
half measures, which finally came uppermost and to which
the king rallied.

The best method of comprehending the diverse and complex problems of the king's foreign policy is to group them
in their mutual relations against the background of an international congress which dealt with all of them. This
congress, which closed in Vienna three hundred years before
another better-known congress that aimed at determining the
composition of modern Europe, did not meet until 1515.
But the principal events of the first nine years of Sigismund I's
reign seem to converge to its deliberations. First elected
Grand Duke of Lithuania, then King of Poland, he at once
occupied himself on parallel lines with the two capital questions for each of these countries, the Muscovite danger and
the situation in Prussia.

In the east it was necessary to put a final stop to the conquests of a neighbour who, in Alexander's time, had been
able to advance almost with impunity. A first war, under

taken by Sigismund in 1507 under sufficiently favourable
conditions, was complicated by the rebellion of Prince Michael Glinski, who, complaining, not without reason, of having lost his old influence, ranged himself on Basil of
Moscow's side, although this Catholic magnate of Tartar origin cannot be considered as representative of the Orthodox
Ruthenians of Lithuania. The peace of 1508 was broken
four years later by the Grand Duke Basil with the very
definite object of seizing Smolensk. The first attacks directed
against that extremely important stronghold were repulsed,
but in 1514 it fell into the hands of the enemy, and the brilliant victory achieved by Sigismund's army at the battle of
Orsza did not affect this disastrous loss.

The Lithuanians, commanded by Prince Constantine
Ostrogski, himself Orthodox and Ruthenian, had enjoyed
the benefit of very considerable Polish reinforcements; but,
generally speaking, Poland was absorbed in interminable efforts to force the Teutonic Order at last to put into execution the stipulations of the Peace of Torun. After the death
of the Grand Master Frederick of Saxony, who had to the
end refused to pay homage as a vassal, the Order, in 1511,
nominated as his successor another prince of the Empire, Albert of Brandenburg, of the younger line of the Hohenzol-
lern-Ansbachs. Although his mother was the daughter of
Casimir Jagiello, the new Grand Master followed in regard
to the king, his uncle, the fundamentally hostile policy of his
predecessor, bringing to nothing the projects of agreement
that were under negotiation at frequent intervals, and, more
serious still, entering into relations with Sigismund's other
adversary, Basil of Moscow.

But there was yet another political link between these two
enemies of Poland and Lithuania. They were both encouraged in their uncompromising attitude by the Emperor Max-

imilian I. In regard to the question of Prussia, he constituted himself the defender of the long since obsolete rights of the Empire; but why, in the critical year of 1514, did he send an ambassador to Moscow who allowed himself to be won over to an alliance against the Jagiellos? It was because the Hapsburgs never forgot their pretensions to the crowns of Bohemia and Hungary, and if the Emperor now exercised such a strong pressure upon Sigismund, it was to make him abandon the interests of his dynasty, and to secure to the House of Austria the right of succeeding his brother Ladislas.

Always closely united, the two Jagiellos in these circumstances decided on a meeting, first with the Emperor's plenipotentiaries who came to Pressburg, then with Maximilian I himself. The Treaty of Vienna, signed in the summer of 1515, did not recognize any formal right of the Hapsburgs to the succession in Bohemia and Hungary. But the double marriage contracted on this occasion between the children of Ladislas and the grandchildren of Maximilian naturally gave a new basis to Austrian influence in the two coveted kingdoms, and to the pretensions that Ferdinand I raised eleven years later. However, the negotiators at Vienna could not have foreseen that the only son of Ladislas was to die so early, leaving no children, and in 1515 the reconciliation with the Emperor brought to the Jagiellos, and, above all, to Sigismund, indisputable advantages. For Maximilian loyally kept his promise no longer to support the Grand Master in his opposition to Poland and to undertake nothing with Moscow against Lithuania.

It is true that the change which resulted held nothing decisive, the more so as the Emperor died in 1519, and the Jagiellos did not succeed in exercising a definite influence at the time of the election of his successor. In the conflict between Sigismund and Basil, Charles V, like Maximilian I, made attempts at mediation, but the question of Smolensk prevented any lasting peace. The truce, concluded in 1522, and periodically prolonged, was interrupted after the death of Basil in 1533, and during the minority of his son, the future Ivan the Terrible, by a third war which restored only an insignificant part of her lost territories to Lithuania. All that Sigismund the Old could obtain on that side was the organization of a serious resistance against any new aggression, and the establishment of an equilibrium between the two rival powers.

As concerns the Order, the Grand Master Albert had no intention of yielding, even when abandoned by the Emperor; the armed intervention upon which Sigismund, losing patience, decided in 1519, resulted in no solution. The one which was at last found in 1525 was of a nature to evoke the greatest astonishment throughout the whole of Europe: Albert accepted Poland's conditions, but it was no longer the Grand Master of the Teutonic Order who knelt in his person in the great square of Cracow to pay homage to the king. It was the secular and hereditary prince, the first Duke of Prussia. For he had adopted the doctrines of Luther, and the Order, whose religious mission had for long been pure fiction, was secularized. With it an implacable enemy, who, even though weakened, had remained a veritable nightmare to Poland, disappeared from her vicinity. As had been the case at the Congress of Vienna, it was difficult to foresee the distant consequences of the new state of affairs. It is true that East Prussia thereby became the apanage of a German dynasty, but the right of succession was strictly limited to the direct descendants of Albert and of his brothers, so that the elder line of the Hohenzollerns, that of the Electors of Brandenburg, found itself excluded. As for Albert himself, placed under the ban of the Empire, with which he seemed to have definitely broken, he found the best guarantee of his power in the suzerainty of Poland, where he soon attempted to gain friends and to extend his personal influence.

This solution was in reality little liked by Sigismund I, since it offended the religious feelings of this profoundly Catholic king, who was, at the moment, repressing the beginning of the Lutheran movement in the territory of western Polish Prussia, and notably in Danzig. If, notwithstanding, he decided on the agreement made at Cracow, it was because he was becoming increasingly uneasy in regard to the situation of his young nephew Louis, who had succeeded Ladislas on the thrones of Bohemia and Hungary. The latter country was more than ever threatened by the Ottoman power, and while the King of Poland was counselling it to avoid, at all costs, a new war with Soliman the Magnificent, the influence of Austria was impelling the Hungarians to the conflict which ended in the catastrophe of Mohacs. In 1526, as in 1444, it was a Jagiello prince who died in vain, abandoned by the Christian Europe which he was defending, and the Hungarian army, to which Sigismund had only been able to send very feeble reinforcements, was annihilated. At the same time, the question of the succession once more came forward both in Hungary and in Bohemia. We know that the treaty of 1515 had not prejudged it. But the King of Poland, who had felt sufficiently strong to ensure for himself the succession to the last Piasts of Masovia and at length to incorporate this old Polish province in the kingdom, hesitated before the crushing task of assuming power in the two great countries which were escaping his dynasty. Therefore, Ferdinand of Austria met with no opposition on the Polish side when he was elected, first, King of Bohemia, and then also of Hungary.

In Hungary, however, the Hapsburg was the candidate of

only one party, while another party had previously elected
the national candidate, John Zapolya. The latter, whose
sister had been Sigismund's first wife, counted on the sup
port of Poland, where he had won many sympathies. But, officially, the Polish policy remained strictly neutral, in spite
of the checks with which several attempts at mediation had
met. Not having succeeded before the battle of Mohacs in
allying himself with the King of France against the House of
Austria, Sigismund hesitated still further before now making common cause with the new adversary of the Hapsburgs,
who was openly protected by the Sultan. An extremely delicate situation resulted for Poland, which was prolonged for
many years and was further aggravated towards the end of
the old king's reign. For, although he had given his daughter
in marriage to John Zapolya, he could neither definitely
reconcile the two parties who were contending for Hungary,
nor prevent the Turks from occupying Buda in 1541, shortly
after King John's death, under the pretext of supporting his
son, who was a minor and, at the same time, the grandson of
the King of Poland.

In order to judge fairly the attitude of Sigismund in the
face of these serious complications, we must take into account one circumstance that was almost without intermission paralysing Poland's forces, above all when it was a
question of taking up her position in regard to the Turks.
We must not forget that, side by side with the great political
problems which we have just passed under review, the king
was obliged to ensure the permanent defence of his Ruthenian provinces against the Tartars of the Crimea. It is true
that he had succeeded before the Congress of Vienna in putting an end to their regular co-operation with Moscow, and
even in allying himself with the Khan. But this alliance,
frequently renewed, remained a very precarious one, in spite

of the 'gifts' that he sent each year to the Crimea. It constituted no guarantee against sudden invasions, justified after
the event by some kind of pretext, but more often dictated
by the will of the Sultan, to whom the khanate of the Gherais
was always subject. To this perpetual danger another was
added from the side of Moldavia, who in spite of several
Polish victories, as that carried off in 1531 by the great captain John Tarnowski, profited by an interminable disagreement over frontiers to disturb the borderlands of Poland,
and fell eventually under the Ottoman suzerainty.

Under these conditions it is indisputably to the credit of
King Sigismund that he organized, in a far more efficacious
manner than his predecessors had done, the defence of those
vast and threatened borderlands. It was not his fault if the
Polish troops who mounted ceaseless guard at the extreme
boundaries of European civilization were not always as numerous as they should have been. Since his accession Sigismund had maintained that the military and financial means
at the disposal of a King of Poland were in obvious dispro-
portion to the size of the state and the place it held in
Europe. From 1510 projects of reform were brought before
successive Diets as well as dietines, to ensure a permanent
army to the kingdom, destined exclusively, however, to the
defence of the south-eastern frontiers, as well as a treasury
sufficient to maintain it. And, if it were necessary to justify
the concessions made at the Congress of Vienna, it is enough
to point out that it was precisely at this epoch that the fate of
these projects was decided. Unfortunately they were met by
the opposition of the nobility and gentry, and had to be ad-
journed, so that the king was obliged to make a fresh demand from each particular Diet for the most indispensable
taxes.

However, new efforts at reform, launched by the court, reappear in the second half of his reign. But then the initiative emanated less from the king himself than from his second wife, the beautiful Milanese princess Bona Sforza, whom he had married in 1518 by the advice of the Emperor. Recent researches have brought to light the truly superior intelligence and prodigious activity of this queen, whose ideas, dictated by the interests of the dynasty, also agreed in great measure with the interests of Poland. Nevertheless, we remain convinced that the methods applied by Bona, doubtless in conformity with the political doctrines of the Renaissance, departed in a deplorable manner from the Jagiellonian traditions. In contradistinction to the king, who always respected the existing laws, his wife, whose influence was always on the increase, cared little for the legality of the means chosen, even stooping to corruption, and when, towards 1531, the tried collaborators of Sigismund began to disappear, she saw to it that her docile but often unworthy protégés were nominated to the highest offices. The grievances which accumulated against the court were, therefore, in great part justified, and in 1537 the king himself had to acknowledge it after violent discussions with the nobility, whom he had inopportunely mobilized. From that time it was evident that any constitutional reform had, for the moment, become impossible.

In this respect, therefore, the reign of Sigismund the Old, whose authority emerged impaired from this internal crisis, marks a decided halt in the historical evolution of Poland. But by a happy compensation this same reign constitutes one of the most brilliant stages in the development of our civilization. At the Congress of Vienna Maximilian I was struck by finding in his rival as distinguished a humanist as himself, and the prelates and lords who surrounded the king, whatever may have been their political leanings, were, without exception, penetrated with that Renaissance culture which was then taking possession of all Poland and appearing even in far-off Lithuania.

Naturally, the Italian queen, by intensifying the relations of Poland with the land of her birth, contributed on her part to this movement. But when she arrived in Cracow the royal castle was already being restored under the direction of eminent Italian architects, and she could admire in the Vavel cathedral the first monuments sculptured in the new style, which was gradually replacing that of the Gothic epoch. An analogous transformation was making itself felt in intellectual life. In Poland, as elsewhere, it was effected more particularly outside the university curriculum; but the University of Cracow still retained its prestige of the preceding century, and soon its most illustrious pupil, Nicolas Copernicus, covered with glory the school where his genius had been formed.

On the other hand, numerous distinguished members of the nation frequented the foreign universities, subsequently to return in diplomatic missions to the western countries, the culture of which always inspired them with a lively and sympathetic interest. The example of John Dantiscus, who spent many years at the court of Charles V, is particularly significant, because that diplomat and humanist has left us not only circumstantial reports but also fine poetry. On their return to Poland these men of refined culture delighted in the role of Maecenas, encouraging artists who adorned even small provincial spots with works of real talent, as well as poets whom they sent at their own expense beyond the Alps.

Side by side with a literature of Polish inspiration but Latin in language, the first small works to be written in the language of the country were also emerging from our first printing presses. But they were still as rare as the Polish texts that we find among the official documents of the epoch of Sigismund I. It is only towards the end of his reign—the date 1543 is usually cited—that we can record, on the one hand, the birth of a political literature, full of new ideas, and on the other, that of a literary production which at last expressed in Polish, whether in verse or prose, the deepest feelings of our race. And it is only under the son and successor of Sigismund the Old, who was the support of his father in the decline of his life and continued his work, that Latin civilization, so rapidly assimilated by Renaissance Poland, became at the same time a national civilization in that country.

12

The Union of Lublin

Sigismund Augustus, the only son of Sigismund I and Bona Sforza, born in 1520, did not succeed his father until 1548; but, theoretically at least, from 1530 Poland had two kings at the same time, the young prince having been elected and crowned during his father's lifetime. Those acts, by which it was the queen's intention to make the right of the nobility to the free election of the King of Poland an empty illusion, had been preceded in 1522 and 1529 by analogous acts, thanks to which Sigismund Augustus had first become Grand Duke of Lithuania. As on the occasion of his father's accession in 1506, the dynasty had been careful to stress his hereditary right to the Grand Duchy, even though the acts of union, signed in 1501, had stipulated that a common election of the sovereign was to guarantee the lasting bond between the two nations. The opposition between the dynastic interests of the Jagiellos, and the necessity of giving a more solid base to the Polish-Lithuanian union, was again accentuated when Sigismund Augustus was entrusted, in 1544, with the administration of Lithuania, who thus had, for four years, her own Grand Duke. He married there, as his second wife, Barbara

Radziwill, widow of the last of the Gasztolds, sister and cousin of the two Radziwills, Nicholas the Black and Nicholas the Red, princes of the Holy Empire, who directed the opposition of the high Lithuanian aristocracy against every tightening of the constitutional link with Poland.

At the first Diet convoked in Poland by the new king after his father's death, the Polish nobility openly manifested its hostility against the queen, whom a premature death soon tore from Sigismund Augustus's side, but who remained the only love of his sad and solitary life. The Diet of 1548–9 was succeeded by many others of which the detailed reports enable us to follow, day by day, the dissensions between the king and the Chamber of Deputies, who desired to impose upon him their programme of so-called 'execution,' pressed for in vain since the latter half of Sigismund the Old's reign. Under these conditions, at the first glance it seems surprising that Sigismund Augustus should have rallied to this programme from 1562, devoting the following Diets to its realization until that of 1569, held in Lublin, where the final union with Lithuania was concluded. This termination only becomes comprehensible when we take into account that the great work accomplished at Lublin, scarcely three years before the king's death, was the logical conclusion of the whole of his foreign policy, and, at the same time, the natural consequence of the internal transformations, at once constitutional and intellectual, which took place during his reign both in Poland and in Lithuania.

In his external relations Sigismund Augustus seems in many respects to have been inspired by the example of his father. Like him, he only intervened in the conflicts between the Hapsburgs and the Zapolyas—his sister and his nephew —as mediator, without, however, losing his concern with what went on in Hungary and, above all, in Transylvania. Also like Sigismund I, he remained determined to avoid a rupture with Turkey; and this is why he hesitated every time that the troubles of Moldavia seemed as though they would permit influences of the past, even Polish suzerainty, to be re-established there. Finally, like his father, he attached a capital importance to the defence of his Ruthenian provinces against the Tartar invasions, which he effectually succeeded in making of more rare occurrence. But the second Sigismund undoubtedly surpassed the first by his diplomatic talent and his spirit of initiative, and he proved it, above all, in the grave problems of his eastern policy, to which with good reason he attached the greatest importance.

Sigismund Augustus had no love for the family of his first and his third wife, the Hapsburgs, whom he accused of wishing to dominate the whole world. He mistrusted his cousin Albert of Prussia, whose ambitious intrigues he divined. But the real enemy, to whom he indignantly refused his sister's hand, was, in his eyes, Ivan the Terrible of Moscow. It is, in fact, impossible to imagine a more absolute contrast than that between the last Jagiello, thoughtful and refined, who held all violence in horror, and the first tsar, a despot with revolutionary tendencies, who drew up in cold blood the list of the victims of his pathological cruelty. But it was a case of much more than personal antipathies. In spite of a continual exchange of embassies, which wasted their time in discussing official formulas, the threat of a new Muscovite invasion weighed incessantly upon the Ruthenian provinces of Lithuania, which, despite their common Orthodox faith and all their racial affinities, had no desire to exchange the benevolent rule of the Jagiellos for the tyranny of an Ivan.

Sigismund Augustus soon perceived with anxiety that the dreaded attack this time could come not only from the east, but also from the north. On this side, Lithuania had as her neighbour Livonia, where the Order of the Sword Bearers, formerly affiliated to the Teutonic Order, still held out. Fallen into decadence, like the latter, the Livonian Order was no longer capable of resisting the tsar, who was determined to cut a free access for himself through its country to the Baltic Sea. His threats, followed by cruel invasions, forced the unhappy country to seek efficacious help, which only Sigismund Augustus could provide. He began, in 1557, by settling on his own account without striking a blow the differences there had been between himself and the Knights. Two years later he entered into his first agreements in regard to protection against Moscow. Finally, in 1561, the last Master of Livonia, Gothard Kettler, ceded the entire country to the king, contenting himself with the duchy of Courland which he received in fief. The secularization of the Order was followed by that of the archbishopric of Riga, and that town also placed itself under the royal protection, obtaining, moreover, like the whole of Livonia, privileges which guaranteed the autonomy of the new province.

It is superfluous to insist upon the importance of this acquisition, which made the Jagiellonian Federation a great Baltic Power. But this was the very reason why it at once provoked the rivalry of all the other interested Powers. The House of Brandenburg had hoped to profit by the secularization of Livonia, as it had formerly done by that of Prussia, the more so as a brother of Albert had been the last Archbishop of Riga. Sigismund Augustus succeeded in dismissing these pretensions, but at the price of a concession that the future proved to be disastrous: he extended the right of succession in East Prussia to the elder, electoral line of the Hohenzollerns.

This was, however, the only mistake with which his policy

can be reproached amidst all the complications of the first 'war of the north,' which broke out soon after the submission of Livonia and lasted until the Congress of Stettin in 1570. The inopportune intervention of the Scandinavian kingdoms, which wished to divide between them the inheritance of the Order, did not prevent Sigismund II from allying himself, first in 1563 with Denmark, then in 1568 with Sweden, who had taken Estonia from him, but where his brother-in-law John had succeeded Eric XIV, the ally of Ivan the Terrible. It was against the latter that Sigismund Augustus concentrated all his forces, creating the first Polish fleet in the Baltic to cut the tsar's communications with the west, sending reinforcements to the Livonians, and on several occasions mobilizing the Lithuanian army to defend the White Ruthenian borderlands. In spite of it all he could not prevent Ivan from taking the town of Polock in 1563, a loss even more grievous than that of Smolensk, and from occupying a great part of Livonian territory.

The precarious situation that resulted, and which the truce of 1570 only prolonged, is explained by the fact that until then only one of the Jagiellonian States was directly and fully engaged in the struggle. As always in similar cases, Lithuania obtained valuable Polish reinforcements; but so long as the regulation of the Union remained in suspense Poland declined all responsibility in an affair which seemed to have no connection with her own interests. It was not only the common sovereign who then understood the absolute necessity of creating a more intimate communion between the two countries. The great mass of the Lithuanian gentry, which an oligarchy jealous of power kept outside public affairs, but which had to support all the weight of continual military and financial efforts, began to raise its voice, claiming a closer collaboration with its 'Polish brothers.'

This wish, very clearly formulated in 1562, with a complete programme of union which anticipated the settlement of 1569, was also dictated by the desire of at last enjoying the same 'good, free, and Christian' rights, of which the Polish gentry had so long reaped the benefits. The problem of an integral constitutional assimilation was still awaiting the solution that had been promised at the beginning of the Union. The highest offices were invariably held by a few great aristocratic families who combined them with judicial power and imposed their will upon the Lithuanian Diets. The first Lithuanian statute, a fine work of codification which in 1529 had accompanied the elevation of Sigismund Augustus to the grand-ducal throne, needed a fundamental revision in this respect. The last Jagiello long put it off on account of the attitude of the Radziwills, and meanwhile proceeded with a vast agrarian reform, the utility of which no one could dispute. It was not until 1564–6 that a new drawing up of the statute satisfied the demands of the Lithuanian gentry, introducing in the Grand Duchy tribunals and dietines, district by district, on the model of the kingdom. By law the Lithuanians now possessed a parliamentary system as democratic ·as that of the Poles. But, in practice, the deputies elected by the dietines found themselves reduced to a very modest role, as long as the Lithuanian Diet met separately under the effective direction of the Grand-Ducal Council, always exclusively aristocratic. The gentry went further and demanded the fusion of the two Diets, Polish and Lithuanian, into one common Parliament, which, together with the common election of the sovereign, was, in fact, the essential condition of a lasting union.

Such was likewise the desire of the Polish gentry, which had long made it a capital point of its programme of 'execution of the laws.' This expression of a conservative character should not mislead us. It is true that there was no question in Poland of such fundamental reforms as in Lithuania. But, nevertheless, inveterate abuses called for a remedy. Among the ancient laws, the execution of which left much to be desired, there was, above all, that of 1504 which forbade the king to mortgage estates without the consent of the Diet. Now, contrary to this provision, a very large part of the crown domains had, little by little, passed into the hands of the aristocratic families who were enriching themselves inordinately, while the king, lacking revenues, was obliged to demand from the Diets extraordinary taxes. On this point also Sigismund Augustus in 1562 rallied to the programme of the party of 'execution.' The revision of the mortgaged estates, carried out with care by the Diet of 1563–4, did not result in their restitution, but, at least, it was decided that a quarter of their revenues should henceforth be devoted to the defence of the south-eastern frontiers. Thus Poland obtained a public treasury especially destined to ensure the maintenance of permanent armed forces, as Sigismund I had desired.

The Diets of his son were never able to concentrate all their attention on this, the most positive, aspect of the 'execution.' Under the pretext of also carrying into execution the laws concerning the relations between ecclesiastics and laity, these Diets at the same time discussed the whole problem of religious reform, the most absorbing of the epoch. The edicts of Sigismund the Old, severe but scarcely ever applied, had not been able to check the progress of Lutheran propaganda. After his death Poland became a veritable 'shelter for heretics.' The Bohemian Brethren, a survival of the Hussites, driven out of Bohemia, established themselves in Great Poland, competing with the Lutherans. Calvin and the other Swiss reformers exercised a predominating influence in Lit-

tle Poland and Lithuania. But the disciples of their adversaries, the anti-Trinitarians of all shades, including the most
radical, together with the Anabaptists, also found here an almost unlimited refuge and field of action. Encouraged by the
sympathy of the great aristocratic families, as well as by the
indolence of the greater part of the clergy, this movement became so powerful that it was feared in Rome that the whole of
Poland would abandon the Catholic faith.

These apprehensions were by no·means justified. It is true
that for some twenty years the Reformation seemed to be
attracting the *élite* of the nation. By the side of those who
made use of it mainly to rid themselves of tithes and ecclesiastical tribunals, there were also in Poland reformers inspired
by very serious religious convictions, such as John Laski the
younger, nephew of the former archbishop, renowned all
over Europe, as well as several promoters of the Polish 'Ari-
anism,' who also preached very advanced social doctrines.
But in reality all these ideas imported from abroad never
took deep root in Poland. Without touching the masses they
acted exclusively on the urban population and on the nobility, which was jealous of every liberty, including, therefore,
the liberty of conscience, and was curious of every novelty, in
which it desired to experiment, passing from one creed to another. The mutitude of these creeds which, profiting by Polish tolerance, competed with one another, was one of the
chief weaknesses of the Protestant party, which only in 1570
succeeded in creating a species of very superficial union between its adherents, excluding, however, the Arians. The
bishops who were the most devoted to Rome, with in the first
rank Cardinal Hosius, who had been very active at the Council of Trent, made use of this to confront their adversaries
with the unity of the Church, defined with precision, and al-

ready defended towards the end of Sigismund Augustus's reign by the first Jesuits.

As regards the king himself, the Protestants hoped in vain to win him to their cause. He was interested in their ideas, and, above all, he was hostile to all religious persecution. The papal nuncios could only count upon him so long as they gave evidence of great moderation and diplomatic tact. But in spite of his desire to divorce his third wife, Catherine of Austria, he remained firmly attached to Catholic tradition, and was perturbed to perceive how greatly vain discussions on matters of faith were retarding the political work of the Diets.

In this respect the movement set on foot by the Reformation unquestionably had regrettable consequences, even though Poland never knew the horrors of religious wars. It is likewise regrettable that minds of the first order, to cite only Andrew Frycz Modrzewski, whose political writings do honour to Poland and abound in happy and generous suggestions from the social point of view, should have subsequently devoted themselves to sterile theological discussions. But on the other hand these discussions, from which, moreover, Polish Catholicism emerged strengthened, had stimulated and enriched the thought of our golden century, and in Poland, as elsewhere, the Reformation spread the use of the national language and contributed to the development of literature.

Polish literature, in fact, experienced under Sigismund Augustus a first efflorescence which produced works of art of enduring value, like those of Nicholas Rey, a Protestant gentleman who has perpetuated his ideal of the 'honest man,' and, above all, those of John Kochanowski, the Catholic humanist, the Polish Ronsard, who for long centuries remained our greatest lyric poet. The growth of Polish culture was re-

flected in Lithuania and the Ruthenian regions in a still
more striking manner than the constitutional evolution of
the kingdom. This explains the progress made there by the
Polonization, entirely spontaneous and almost instinctive, of
the most cultivated classes of the population. And in its turn
it is this assimilation in the sphere of thought, language, even
the customs of daily life, which, together with the considerations of a political order that we have pointed out, explains
the success of the negotiations in the affair of the Polish-
Lithuanian union.

These negotiations, broached in preceding Diets, exacted
at that of Lublin half a year more of work before the memorable Acts could be signed on 1st July 1569, which created
the Republican Commonwealth, and gave it the constitutional basis destined to endure until the Partitions. The principal credit falls to Sigismund Augustus, who, after having
transmitted his hereditary rights over Lithuania to the crown
of Poland, appeased with as much patience as skill the extremists on both sides—the radical party of the Polish Chamber of Deputies which wished, purely and simply, to incorporate the whole of Lithuania, and the Lithuanian oligarchy
which was averse to the project of creating a common Diet.

To put an end to the resistance of this little group of magnates which was exercising so strong a pressure on the other
representatives of the Grand Duchy that for a time they left
Lublin, the king assigned to Poland the long disputed provinces of Podlasia and Volhynia. The first was only a narrow
intermediate territory between Masovia and Lithuania. The
second brought with it the vast regions of Kiev and Braclaw,
so that all the Little Russian provinces—Ukrainian, following the terminology of to-day—found themselves gathered
within the boundaries of the kingdom of Poland, immediately obtaining a large autonomy. By this action the king-

dom assumed the whole charge of defence against the Tartars, and henceforth shared with the Grand Duchy the still heavier responsibility of facing the territory of Moscow; the more so as Livonia became, from that time, a common province of the two component parts of the federated State.

In this State, called the Republican Commonwealth, one and indivisible, Lithuania proper, together with the White Ruthenian provinces, retained all the prerogatives of a grand duchy placed on an equal footing with the kingdom. She therefore kept her own administration, army, treasury, and law. The power of legislation alone was to be shared in common, which guaranteed the unity of the general policy, in the same way as the common election of the sovereign was to guarantee the perpetual duration of the Union.

This solution, which responded to the desire of the great majority of the Lithuanians, was the more urgent, inasmuch as, like the last Piast, Sigismund Augustus waited in vain for an heir. Conscious of having accomplished all his task and of having crowned the work of his dynasty, but full of apprehension in the face of the intrigues of his neighbours, who were aiming at securing the throne after his death for themselves, the last Jagiello could only recommend in his will that the two nations he had united should remain faithful 'to that reciprocal charity and concord which their ancestors had called by the Latin name of union.'

Part III

THE EXPERIMENT OF THE
ROYAL REPUBLIC

13

John Zamoyski

THE last Jagiello died on 7th July 1572, before the two Diets
that had met after that of Lublin had regulated the multiple
questions that the election of his successor presented. We
know that by law the throne of Poland had become elective
since the distant epoch of the founder of the Jagiellonian
dynasty. But, as long as this dynasty had lasted, nobody seriously considered electing a king outside it. It is, therefore, not
without reason that tradition only regards our kings as freely
elected from the time of 'the first interregnum' that followed
the death of Sigismund Augustus. And it is only from this
moment that the dangerous consequences of the right of a
free election made themselves really felt.

We must not exaggerate these dangers. The Polish nobility,
matured by a long and active participation in public life, in
1572 succeeded in fixing the principles which ruled that life
during the interregnums, and, in fact, they asked nothing
more than to find a new dynasty which, under the form of
successive uncontested elections, would, in practice, become
hereditary like that of the Jagiellos. This was, indeed, the case
with the Vasas, who, since the election of Sigismund III in

1587, occupied the throne for eighty-one years until the ab-
dication of the last descendant of their Polish branch. The
election of the young Prince of Sweden, who, moreover, was
descended through his mother from the never-to-be-forgotten
Jagiellos, was preceded by two others, those of Henri de Valois in 1573 and Stephen Bathory in 1575, neither of which
could give us a durable dynasty, since the first of these kings
left Poland for France after only a few months, while the
second died without leaving children.

In spite of these rapid changes and in spite of the troubles
of the second and third interregnums, during each of which
an Austrian candidate, elected by the partisans of the Hapsburgs, had first of all to be put aside, the end of the sixteenth
century still constitutes a very brilliant epoch in our past and
is a worthy close to that 'golden century.' We can best be convinced of this fact by following as a guiding line the activities
of a personality of the very highest order, who laid the basis
of the definitive organization of the Republic, decided the
result of the first three elections, and did not lose his active
influence until the eve of his death on the threshold of the
following century. We allude to John Zamoyski, the faithful
collaborator of the greatest of the three kings of this epoch, a
typical representative of that nobility which had just taken
the direction of the State into its hands and was identifying itself with the whole of the nation, a politician whose career
seems to symbolize, in one brief epitome, the destiny of modern Poland.

No essential transformation, however, distinguished this
new Poland from that of the Jagiellos, which also had, with
increasing frequency, been designated by the name of Republic in the Latin and very general sense of that term. Yet
we see the 'republican,' or rather the democratic, character of
the State immediately emphasized, even though it had not

ceased to have a king at its head. For on the one hand it was admitted during the first interregnum that every man of noble birth had the right to take a personal share in the election, and even to be elected himself. And on the other hand, the traditional parliamentary institutions were then surrounded with new guarantees, completing these general rules by special conditions imposed since the time of Henri de Valois on every candidate elected: the famous *pacta conventa*.

All this system, which lasted to the eve of the Partitions, was in great measure the work of John Zamoyski, who played the part of a veritable 'tribune of the noble plebs.' This comparison is a very apt indication that the young statesman who then emerged from the ranks of the lesser nobility was inspired, not only by the national traditions of which he had a remarkable knowledge, but also by those of the ancient Roman Republic, with which the Polish Republic at the time of the Renaissance was frequently compared. The general tendency of these regulations was inspired by the fear of seeing a liberty, acquired at the cost of long efforts, violated by a king following the example of the other sovereigns of an epoch when absolutism was making such rapid progress in the rest of Europe. This fear was by no means a delusion. Given the absence of a serious national candidature, the elected king would, of necessity, be a foreign prince, and among these candidates there were, on one side, representatives of the House of Austria, which had so rapidly liquidated the ancient liberties of Bohemia and Hungary, and on the other—strange paradox!—Ivan the Terrible himself.

But the French candidature which triumphed at the first unanimous election could also inspire similar apprehensions. St Bartholomew's Day was but of yesterday; the accounts of which alarmed not only the Protestants in Poland, but all those who, by the terms of the celebrated Confederation of

Warsaw in 1573, had reciprocally guaranteed a general religious peace in spite of all their disagreements on the subject of their faith. Nevertheless, the idea of a lasting *rapprochement* with France, an idea which was born in the time of the Jagiellos, and which seemed now as though it would resolve in the most efficacious manner all the difficulties of the political situation, emerged victorious over these hesitations. A Polish embassy went to Paris to fetch the brother of the King of France, and on 21st February 1574 he was crowned in the Vavel.

Unfortunately, before Henri de Valois was able to familiarize himself with his new surroundings, on receiving the news of the death of Charles IX he fled precipitately from Cracow, thereby inflicting a sharp blow upon Franco-Polish sympathies. Faced with the evidence that, having inherited France, he had no intention of ever returning to Poland, the Poles were obliged to declare the throne vacant; and disconcerted by a first discouraging experience, on this occasion they offered Europe the dismal spectacle of two conflicting elections: that of the Emperor Maximilian II, the candidate of the aristocratic party, and that of his Hungarian adversary, the Prince of Transylvania, to whom it was decided to marry the last Jagiello's sister. This candidate of the majority came with haste to Poland in the beginning of 1576, and soon the death of his rival made his election unanimous.

Stephen Bathory justly ranks among the most glorious of our kings. He first broke the resistance of Danzig which, under the pretext of remaining faithful to the party of Maximilian II, had attempted to acquire a semi-independent position. He then completed the political work of Sigismund Augustus by at last repulsing Ivan the Terrible, and ensuring to the Republic the undisputed possession of the whole of Livonia which the tsar, profiting by the troubles at Danzig, had once more invaded. Of his campaigns, which were organized with all Stephen's strategic talent, the first, that of 1579, recaptured the town and the region of Polock. The two following, in 1580 and 1581, penetrated into Muscovite territory, where the tsar himself was menaced and the town of Pskov besieged. The treaty of 1582 restored to Lithuania her frontier prior to 1563 and enabled the king to organize the administration of Livonia on a durable basis.

The Holy See, which had entrusted the Jesuit Antonio Possevino with negotiating the peace between Stephen Bathory and Ivan the Terrible, hoped in vain to win Moscow to the union of the Churches. Soon, however, its attention was turned by the King of Poland to a project of capital importance for Christendom. Contrary to the last Jagiellos, who remained sceptical in regard to plans for a league against the Turks, Bathory, anxious to save his native Hungary, conceived his own similar plan. On the death of the tsar in 1584 it was his intention to subject Moscow to his sovereignty; but he saw this only as a means of organizing an expedition against Turkey which would have banded all eastern Europe in a coalition.

In these ambitious projects, the realization of which was prevented by Stephen's premature death, the personal initiative of the king is evident. It seems to have been less exclusive in the campaigns against Ivan the Terrible, where it is difficult to distinguish between the merits of the king and those of John Zamoyski, the Grand Hetman of Poland. On the other hand, the latter, loaded with honours, married to a cousin of Bathory, was also Grand Chancellor, and his influence was still more considerable in politics than in military questions. There was, however, complete agreement between the king and his minister. In their diplomatic relations they both remained resolute adversaries of the Hapsburgs. In their

internal policy they applied one and the same method with
the object of settling the problems that Sigismund Augustus
had left open.

In religious affairs they were like Sigismund, partisans of a
prudent tolerance. They were none the less attached to the
Catholic faith and anxious for a good understanding with
Rome. It was in Bathory's time that the decrees of the Council
of Trent were introduced into Poland and that the activity
of the Jesuits developed: the latter's college at Wilno was
even raised in 1579 to the rank of a university. But the most
delicate internal problem was that of establishing a just equilibrium between the principle of liberty on which the whole
Polish constitution rested and that of the royal authority,
more and more limited since the Jagiellonian epoch. King
Stephen, of foreign, and comparatively speaking, modest
origin, was, nevertheless, firmly determined to exercise his
power in an effective manner, and he found unreserved support in John Zamoyski. For the latter saw clearly that the
Royal Republic, such as he had conceived of it from the beginning of his career, had more need than an absolute monarchy of a scrupulous respect for the laws and a solidly established internal order.

At the beginning of the reign great progress was realized in
this direction by the creation of tribunals, or rather courts of
appeal, in 1578 for Great and Little Poland, and in 1581 for
Lithuania. Hitherto the king himself had been the supreme
judge; but naturally he could not give his personal attention
in the time required to all the affairs which had not been settled by the district tribunals, and his authority suffered
thereby as much as the public order. Henceforth, the nobility
itself could elect the judges of the new central tribunals, and
it hailed with satisfaction a reform which guaranteed the
more rapid and regular conduct of justice.

But the good relations between the court and the nobility were soon troubled by the unfortunate affair of the Zborowskis. This powerful family had largely contributed to the election of the Prince of Transylvania, and was now highly displeased at seeing Zamoyski occupying a quite exceptional position. Incapable of competing with him, the Zborowskis entered into very suspicious foreign relations, notably with the House of Austria, and then believed themselves strong enough to brave openly the king and the chancellor. After Samuel Zborowski was executed in 1584, in conformity with the law but with an unusual harshness in its application, the one thought of his brothers was to avenge him, and they appealed to all the nobility. The proceedings which were instituted against them ended with a severe sentence upon the one most guilty among them. But a minority of the deputies then broke up the Diet of 1585 in a manner which was at that epoch still exceptional, and in spite of all his energy the king, in the end, suffered great discouragement. Hence, in spite of all the brilliant successes of this reign of ten years, the kingdom was profoundly divided when he died in the following year.

The consequences of this division made themselves felt during the third interregnum. In opposition to John Zamoyski, under whose influence a strong majority had elected Sigismund of Sweden, the Zborowskis succeeded in getting the Austrian candidate, the Archduke Maximilian, brother of the Emperor Rudolf II, proclaimed as king. Passions were so excited that it was necessary to have recourse to·arms. It was not till the beginning of 1588 that the victory of Byczyna, won by Zamoyski over Maximilian and his partisans, assured the throne to the Vasa.

His reign, which lasted till 1632, thus began under gloomy auspices. And the most serious of these was that the new king soon deceived the hopes of those who had put forward and defended his candidature, in particular those of John Zamoyski. Generally speaking, historians have been inclined to be severe towards Sigismund III, whom it is, in fact, difficult to compare with his predecessor and the great Jagiellos whose memory he evoked. To-day, however, we are beginning to find out that the reproaches made against him have often been exaggerated; and, in any case, we must distinguish between the two parts of his long reign: before and after the critical events of 1605–6.

John Zamoyski, who, in fact, died in 1605 after having played in the last period of his life the role of a leader of the opposition, reproached Sigismund above all else for his increasingly intimate relations with the Hapsburgs. The chancellor, who had always combated their influence and who had wished to exclude them for ever from the throne of Poland, was indignant when he saw that the new king retained no resentment against the dynasty which had contended with him for the crown. But what most disquieted him was Sigismund III's clandestine negotiations with a brother of Maximilian, the Archduke Ernest, who was attempting to get Poland spontaneously ceded to him by the Vasa. At the Diet of 1592, called the 'Diet of Investigation,' the king protested his loyalty, but he had no intention of abandoning his policy of drawing close to Austria.

No doubt Zamoyski went too far in considering that this policy was, under every circumstance, incompatible with the interests of Poland. There was, in reality, no cause of conflict at that time between the two Powers, which were, moreover, both threatened by the advance of the Turks. If Sigismund gave a favourable reception to the projects of an anti-Ottoman league which Austria, in agreement with Rome, proposed to him, he was only taking up Stephen Bathory's plans again under another form. And Zamoyski, who, towards the end of the sixteenth century, intervened with success in the affairs of Moldavia and even of Walachia, himself came near to a rupture with the Porte, although he attempted at all costs to avert it.

To explain Sigismund III's Austrian sympathies historians are accustomed to insist upon his religious sentiments. It is true that he was unreservedly devoted to the Catholic Church, and that he never forgot this in his general policy. But, in our opinion, he by no means deserves the reproach of fanaticism, for which he has become almost a byword in public opinion. Certainly he made a mistake in not having repressed with sufficient energy the 'tumults' which broke out from time to time in the large towns, when the mobs, hostile to the 'heretics,' attacked their places of worship. Yet, in spite of these regrettable incidents, it would be absurd to speak of a religious persecution comparable to what was then going on in other countries. The king even confided the highest offices to Protestants, although these latter only constituted a small minority, spontaneous returns to Catholicism having multiplied during the last ten years.

As regards the far more numerous members of the Orthodox Church, Sigismund III showed himself favourable to the project of religious union with Rome, realized in 1596 at the Synod of Brzesc. But in thus acting in agreement, moreover, with John Zamoyski, he was only encouraging a movement which had originated among the Ruthenians themselves and the flower of their clergy. This return to the traditions of the Union of Florence, which had here survived the fall of Constantinople, raised the intellectual and moral level of the Ruthenian Church, withdrew it from the influences of Stambul and Moscow, and completed the political union concluded at Lublin. It is true that a party of the Ruthenians, led

for personal motives by Prince Constantine Ostrogski, rejected the Union, so that it gave rise to dangerous divisions.
However, the first revolts of the Ukrainian Cossacks, which
broke out about the same epoch, and to the consequences of
which we shall have to return, had nothing in common with
this religious problem. Hence it stands indisputably to the
credit of the king and his collaborators that they worked for
its solution on lines in conformity with the interests of the
Church, as well as with those of the Republic and her Ruthenian population.

We can more truly reproach him with not having followed
this up with sufficient consistency, preoccupied as he was with
a problem which turned his attention in a completely different direction. Since the death of his father, John III, in 1592,
Sigismund III was king of both Poland and Sweden. When
he was raised to the throne of the Jagiellos, this personal
union between the two Baltic Powers, or, at least, their close
co-operation, such as had been prepared by Sigismund Augustus, was counted upon in advance. Here, again, the Vasa's
electors experienced a great deception. Sigismund met with
a far stronger opposition in Sweden than in Poland, dictated
by the hostility of a fundamentally Protestant nation and by
the ambition of his uncle, Charles of Sudermania, who ended
by usurping the crown in 1600. Hence, instead of a Polish-
Swedish alliance there was a war between the Vasas of Poland
and those of Sweden which was to last sixty years. Sigismund
III succeeded in interesting the Republic in this war by con-
ferring Estonia, the object of disputes between the two countries, upon her, and Zamoyski distinguished himself once
more in the conflict that began to rage in Livonia. Another
military leader, younger than he, to whom he subsequently
confided the defence of that province, John Charles Chodkiewicz, won a great victory in 1605 at Kirkholm. If neither

Poland nor Sigismund was able to profit by it, this was because a new conflict more serious than all the others was already preparing between the king and the nation.

After having suspected Sigismund of foreign intrigues, Zamoyski now accused him of intending to violate constitutional liberties and make Poland an absolute monarchy. The chancellor, who under Bathory had upheld the royal authority against the elements of disorder, considered it his duty to defend the traditional institutions of his country against a sovereign whom he never ceased to distrust. The reforms of which Sigismund dreamt were, in the main, useful. They corresponded to the ideas that the great preacher of the epoch, the Jesuit Peter Skarga, had developed with such eloquence in his celebrated political sermons. But, as in the time of Sigismund I and Bona Sforza, they were compromised by the manner in which the court wished to impose them. Fearing a *coup d'état* on the part of the king, Zamoyski profited by the Diet of 1605 to set forth his defence of his own conception of the Republic, based on the principle of liberty. His opposition, however, remained within legal limits, and consequently his death, which followed close upon this dissolved Diet, was an irreparable loss to Poland.

In spite of his grievances against the king, he had wished to avert the disaster of a civil war, and at the same time he placed the Polish nobility on its guard against a policy of adventure that a turbulent aristocracy was preparing in respect to Moscow. He departed without having been able to prevent either of these disastrous errors; and with him there departed not only an eminent statesman, but also a great humanist, the founder of a university in his own town Zamosc, a protector of letters and of arts; in a word, the most worthy representative of the last generation to know a wholly sound and prosperous Poland.

14

The Last Great Designs

THE project for the organization of Europe, known under the name of 'Henry IV's great design,' a project so characteristic of the political situation of the first half of the seventeenth century, gave a very honourable place to Poland. Among the three towns where the supreme Council of the 'most Christian Republic' was to sit, we find by the side of Paris and Trent our ancient capital Cracow, where our kings were always crowned and buried, even though their residence was now in Warsaw, the city where the elections and Diets were held. And Poland was considered as the 'bulwark and rampart' against Turks, Tartars, and Muscovites; in virtue of this title it was worthy of exceptional advantages.

In fact, until the date of 1648, as decisive in Polish as in general history, the Poland of Sigismund III and of his son Ladislas IV indisputably stood in the rank of a great Power which the whole of Europe regarded very seriously. Her role as the bulwark of Christendom even became more marked than ever, owing to the glorious battles then fought by the Polish armies, and the frontiers of the Republic had never been more extensive. It is not surprising that in Poland herself truly 'great designs' then made their appearance, which if they had been realized would have changed the destinies of eastern Europe, as the Polish-Lithuanian union had done in the past. Even the level of our culture, that had stood so high at the end of the sixteenth century, only declined slowly and imperceptibly; and if the Polish literature of the seventeenth century no longer equalled that of the 'golden century,' it does not, in reality, deserve the sharp criticism of which it has at times been the object.

Nevertheless, in the beginning of this new epoch of Polish history two events, so to speak, deflected the normal evolution of the Republic, creating evil precedents and grave menaces for the future. One of them disturbed the internal state of Poland, the other disorientated her foreign policy.

We have said that, until now, the historic evolution of Poland had been normal, and this applies equally to her constitution, which has been so much decried. The institution of a Royal Republic, sustained by a democracy of nobles, opposing a genuine cult for liberty to the absolutist rule of its neighbours, had certainly been, from the outset, a bold experiment which created a peculiar position, difficult and delicate, for Poland among the other states. But, in spite of the critical and pessimistic voices which were raised in our country in the sixteenth century—as, in fact, in every country and in every epoch—nothing foretold a fatal issue to this experiment, so long as a certain practical equilibrium was maintained between the royal authority and the rights of the nobility, and so long as the latter remained conscious of its duties and responsibilities.

In spite of the mistakes which he may have committed towards the end of his career, John Zamoyski had always admirably understood this. After his death two men, formed under his influence, believed themselves destined to continue his work. One of them, Nicholas Zebrzydowski, Palatine of Cracow, desired, like Zamoyski, to defend the liberties of the Republic. But, lacking the talent and prudence of his model, in 1606 he provoked a civil war, unhappily famous under the name of Zebrzydowski's rebellion. Starting from an interpretation of the Polish constitution according to which a king, accused of having violated that constitution, had no right to the obedience of the citizens, the Palatine gathered all the malcontents round him. A very devout Catholic, he allied himself with the leaders of the Protestants, who were only too eager to denounce obedience to the protector of the Jesuits and the ally of Austria. The revolt was crushed in 1607 in a fratricidal battle by Stanislas Zolkiewski, then Vice-Hetman of Poland. It is in this second personage that we see the man who really carried on the policy of John Zamoyski. He did not attempt to shut his eyes to the faults committed by the court, and his opinions differed in many respects from those of Sigismund III. But this great patriot nevertheless held it his duty to defend the lawful sovereign and to put an end to a scandalous rebellion, which, however, did not prevent him from subsequently recommending a general amnesty, voted, in fact, in the Diet of 1609.

In spite of this peaceable conclusion this first rebellion in Polish history had sinister consequences. Royalty lost, to a great extent, the moral prestige it had enjoyed in the time of the Jagiellos, which alone could compensate for all the constitutional limitations of its power. The insurgents, even though vanquished and compelled to implore pardon from Sigismund III, nevertheless gained their cause; for the Polish constitution was henceforth regarded as sacrosanct and the king had to renounce not only the idea of making any far-reaching changes in it, but even any reform which, without touching its principles, would have improved the functioning of parliament and ensured to the Republic the financial and military measures that were necessary to her.

This was the more serious, as in the course of these highly disturbed years Poland had become engaged in a vast enterprise, contrary to the pacific and prudent traditions of the Jagiellos, contrary even to the bolder but always definite and clear ideas of a Stephen Bathory. In the conflict with Moscow, a conflict which since the Union of Lublin had concerned the whole of the Republic, the aggressions until now had been on the part of her eastern neighbour, against whom Poland attempted nothing further than to recapture the territories which the other had seized. But this time an impostor found encouragement in Poland which enabled him to inaugurate a period of troubles in Moscow, in the course of which the Poles overran the whole of Russia without being able to agree among themselves upon the object of this intervention.

The lamentable history of the false Demetrius is well known. In 1598 the Tsar Feodor, son of Ivan the Terrible and the last of the line of the Ruriks, was succeeded by a simple boyar, Boris Godunov, who was suspected of having caused the death of another of Ivan's sons, Demetrius. Some years later a Russian of obscure origin appeared in Poland, asserting that he was this Demetrius who had escaped from the assassins and demanding assistance to ascend the throne of his fathers. Like Zamoyski, who lived to see the beginning of this affair, Sigismund III was distrustful, and all official support was refused to the pretender. Nevertheless, the latter won the co-operation of some Polish lords, notably George Mniszech, whose daughter he promised to marry as soon as he had overthrown Godunov. This came about in 1605, and with Demetrius and his wife Polish influences of every kind penetrated into Moscow. The following year this new regime was, in its turn, overthrown, and Prince Basil Shuiski took posses-

sion of the crown. But scarcely had the first false Demetrius
perished when a new pretender presented himself whose im-
posture was still more evident. This did not prevent the ambitious Marina Mniszech from acknowledging him as her husband, and a great number of Poles, for the most part former
combatants in Zebrzydowski's revolt, from supporting him
against Tsar Basil. The latter allied himself in 1609 with
Charles of Sweden, Sigismund III's chief adversary, thus
hastening the official rupture with Poland.

It is useless to follow all the vicissitudes of the war. What
concerns us is the project of submitting all Russia to Polish
domination, a project which soon assumed two different forms.
The king dreamt of a conquest of Moscow, which would
accept him as tsar and be converted to Catholicism. Stanislas
Zolkiewski, whose fame as a military leader was always on the
increase, regarded this as a dangerous chimera. He covered
himself with glory, winning in 1610 the battle of Kluszyn,
and bringing Tsar Shuiski and his brothers to Warsaw as
prisoners of war. But he would have preferred to gain Moscow by a freely conceded union, like that formerly concluded
with Lithuania. Thanks to his spirit of conciliation, the son
of the King of Poland, young Prince Ladislas, was elected tsar
by the boyars, to whom Zolkiewski guaranteed that their Orthodox faith should be respected. However, this project, more
in conformity with the Jagiellonian traditions, proved as impossible of realization as the other. Sigismund III only accepted it with reservations which discouraged his son's partisans, and, moreover, the differences between the two countries, which the Poles desired to unite by perpetual bonds,
went far too deep not to provoke a violent reaction in Moscow
against any foreign appropriation. After the second false Demetrius had been assassinated, this reaction turned exclusively against the Poles, whom the Russians saw occupying the

Kremlin. In 1613, after the election of another tsar in the person of Michael Romanov, the founder of a second national dynasty, the projects of the king, as well as those of Zolkiewski, were doomed to certain failure.

The only positive result of a whole series of campaigns was the capture of Smolensk, which surrendered in 1611, after a siege of nearly two years, and which was yielded by Russia under the terms of the truce of 1618, as well as Czernihow, which had been formerly torn from Lithuania before the loss of Smolensk. After the death of Sigismund III, Ladislas, who still continued to claim the title of tsar, delivered that hotly contested town from a fresh Muscovite siege, and it was not until 1634 that a treaty of peace confirmed the territorial clauses of 1618. But Russia, humiliated in the epoch of disturbances and invasions, only awaited the moment to take her revenge, and thus the memories and the distant consequences of all this war, which was prolonged by designs of too ambitious a nature, were to affect the relations between the two neighbours in a deplorable manner.

The latent danger for the Republic which resulted from this was the more serious because, even while avoiding a direct participation in the Thirty Years War, she saw her conflict with Sweden aggravated and the dreaded war with Turkey at last break out. Her relations with the latter had already been marred during the Moscow campaigns. Since 1612 the inopportune interventions of some Polish nobles, notably of the increasingly influential Potocki family, in the affairs of Moldavia where they supported their cousins the Moghilas, as well as the maritime expeditions of the Ukrainian Cossacks who penetrated up to Trebizond, had threatened to bring about a rupture with the Ottoman State. Zolkiewski succeeded in delaying this by the treaty of 1617; but on the one hand, the Cossacks did not attempt to respect the pledges given by the Government, and on the other, despite the similar pledges of the Porte, the Tartars, who depended on the latter, continued to stir up the Ukraine. Poland, therefore, found herself faced with a veritable vicious circle, and in the borderlands of the Republic with a chaotic situation which could not last.

The catastrophe was precipitated by the attitude taken by Sigismund III at the outset of the Thirty Years War. Without heeding a strong current of opinion hostile to the Hapsburgs, and hesitating to profit by their difficulties to recapture Silesia, the king sent the Emperor reinforcements against the Hungarian Protestants who, under Gabriel Bethlen of Transylvania, were threatening Vienna. The Sultan Osman, whose help was invoked by Bethlen, readily profited by this pretext to launch a long-meditated attack against Poland. Zolkiewski, who saw his prudent policy fall to the ground, had only very insufficient forces with which to defend the frontiers of the Republic against the Mussulman invasion that had been foreseen for more than a hundred years, and that now became a terrible reality. Abandoned by the Cossacks, whose undisciplined forays had greatly contributed to provoke the Porte, the old Hetman died heroically in the autumn of 1620, during a disastrous defeat in the vicinity of Cecora. This defeat was redeemed the following year by a not less courageous and more effective resistance that the Poles, commanded by John Chodkiewicz and this time assisted by the Cossacks, opposed to the sultan himself at the battle of Chocim.

Peace was restored on this side; but in the same year, 1621, Gustavus Adolphus, who had succeeded King Charles in Sweden, profited by Poland's struggles against the enemy of Christendom to invade Livonia. He took possession of Riga, and subsequently occupied in succession the chief ports of Prussia. East Prussia, Poland's vassal duchy, was as much a victim as Royal Prussia; but the situation on the side of the

Baltic was the more complicated for Poland inasmuch as, after the death of the son and last heir of Albert of Prussia, his duchy had passed into the hands of the Elector of Brandenburg in conformity with the concessions made to the Hohenzollerns since the reign of Sigismund Augustus. As Duke of Prussia the Elector paid homage to the King of Poland in the critical year of 1621; but the fact that Königsberg and Berlin, separated from each other by Polish territory, now belonged to the same prince naturally held great danger for the future.

The war against the Swedes, carried on by land and sea, was signalized by several victories, owing, chiefly, to Stanislas Koniecpolski, one of the great leaders in whom Poland at that epoch was not lacking, owing also to the Polish fleet which was organized by his advice. Nevertheless, the treaty concluded at Altmark in 1629 left provisionally to Gustavus Adolphus all his conquests on the south coast of the Baltic, and enabled him to turn upon the Emperor.

Thus the alliance with the House of Austria had brought about disastrous results, which explains why Ladislas IV, who was elected without any difficulty after the death of his father in 1632, attempted also to approach France. The latter, seeing that the Hapsburgs alone profited by the hostility between Poland and Sweden, had, since the days of Henry IV, played the part of mediator between those two Powers several times. The truce of 1635, like that of 1629, was concluded with the co-operation of French diplomacy. It restored to Poland the towns of Prussia that were occupied by the Swedes, but the latter kept Livonia as far as the Dvina, and the dynastic question, which was the basis of the whole conflict, remained in suspense. The son of Sigismund III was no more willing than his father to renounce his rights to the throne of Sweden, whose Diet had definitely disinherited the Polish line of the Vasas.

The new king was far more popular in Poland than his father, who was always looked upon as a foreigner. In fact, Ladislas IV ensured one last period of peace and prosperity to the Republic. He was full of initiative and remarkably gifted; nor was he lacking in vast projects which, if they had succeeded, could have given back to Poland her old power, which had been so manifestly shaken since the first years of the seventeenth century.

Within the state, the king, conscious of the dangers presented at this epoch by religious dissensions, attempted to pacify the minds of his subjects by a policy of wide tolerance. In view of the fact that a great part of the Ruthenian population remained opposed to union with the Roman Church, Ladislas IV, at his accession, sanctioned the re-establishment of an Orthodox hierarchy side by side with that of the Uniats. An Orthodox college, founded at Kiev by the eminent Metropolitan Peter Moghila, a native of Moldavia, became an important centre of culture, open to western influences, and at the same time shedding its light beyond the eastern frontiers of the Republic. Uneasy also at the attitude of the Protestant minority, the king cherished the hope of re-establishing religious unity by means of amicable discussions, by the famous *Colloquium Charitativum*, which was held at Torun in 1645.

The atmosphere of the Thirty Years War, which was still raging in the vicinity of Poland, was by no means favourable to such a project. It failed completely. But, and this was more serious, the king was no more successful in fixing the guiding line of his foreign policy in the conflict which continued to ravage central Europe. Without sufficiently taking into account the inflexible rivalry which Richelieu's policy then opposed to that of Ferdinand II, Ladislas IV oscillated between France and Austria, avoiding a decision, although he was even given a hint of the possibility of obtaining the imperial crown. In 1637 he even preferred to return to the alliance with the Hapsburgs, forgetful of his father's unfortunate experiences. He, too, in his turn married an archduchess, and hastened to conclude a treaty with the new Emperor Ferdinand III to help him to conquer Sweden. It was not till 1645 that his second marriage to Louise Marie de Gonzague, Princesse de Nevers, marked a revision of his policy and a new friendliness with France, encouraged by the most eminent of Ladislas IV's collaborators, the Chancellor George Ossolinski.

About this time it seemed as though the last of the king's great projects was to be realized. Deceived in his hope of re-establishing the domination of the Vasas in the country of their origin, he decided to turn his whole strength against the Mussulmans. The beginning of this project, prepared by Ladislas IV in agreement with Ossolinski and Koniecpolski, dates, in fact, back to the first years of his reign. Here, again, we maintain that his policy was not so fundamentally different from that of his father as has been long supposed. His plan of an anti-Ottoman league was, however, distinct from that which had been formerly considered by Sigismund III. This time it was not a question of an Austrian initiative with which Poland was to be closely associated. In accord with the Holy See the king intended to take command of this new crusade upon himself, ensuring the support of Venice and even that of Moscow. Antagonism against the latter was to have given way before a common action against the Tartars of the Crimea, while the King of Poland, avenging the hero of Varna whose memory his name recalled, would not only have restored to the Republic her access to the Black Sea, but also delivered the Balkan populations, possibly even driven the Turks out of Europe, and given the Holy Land back to Christendom.

It is easy to perceive all the grandeur but also all the Uto-

pian features of this plan. Where the Jagiellos in the period
of their greatest power had failed, the Poland of the seventeenth century, still great but weakened and menaced on every
side, could have no real success. And Europe, such as we see it
on the eve of the Treaty of Westphalia, was far less disposed
to lend Poland effective support than even Renaissance Europe. On the other hand, it is true that the project of Ladislas
IV had some chance of success as regards its direct and immediate object, the establishment of order and security in the
southeastern borderlands of Poland, but under the condition
of obtaining the adherence of the whole nation, which would
have had to accept very heavy sacrifices. But the king, foreseeing some resistance, fell into the mistake which had caused
so many equally happy initiatives of his predecessors to mis-
carry: he attempted to impose his plan in an arbitrary manner, disregarding the consent of the Diet, and overstepping
his constitutional authority. The opposition which inevitably
followed ended by discouraging Ladislas himself, who was,
moreover, mourning the death of his only son, and weakened
by a mortal sickness.

But what contributed the decisive factor was that public
opinion had not grasped the chief positive advantage which
the crusade dreamt of by the king could have ensured to
Poland. The nation was not yet aware of all the gravity that
the Cossack problem was assuming, a problem which would
have found a natural solution if all the Ukrainian Cossacks
had been mobilized against the Moslem world. The abandonment of Ladislas IV's great design had as its immediate
consequence a Cossack insurrection, infinitely more violent
than all those preceding it, and which, breaking out on the
eve of the king's death in the spring of 1648, was to destroy
the work of all his life, at the same time inflicting an irreparable blow to the prestige of Poland.

15

The Deluge

THE most penetrating historical intuition has found only the one significant word 'deluge' with which to characterize the series of catastrophes which, from 1648 onwards, shook the foundations of the Polish State. Thanks to the vital forces of the Polish nation the Republic emerged therefrom battered and mutilated, but independent and capable of prolonging her existence for more than a century. But if, as there was every reason to fear, she had succumbed in the middle of the seventeenth century to the enemies who were invading her and were prepared to partition her, the cause of her fall would have been easy to name: Poland would have been blotted out from the map of Europe because she had been unable to solve the problem of the Ukrainian Cossacks. It is, therefore, all the more necessary to explain who these Cossacks, of whom we have spoken with increasing frequency in the preceding pages, really were.

Since the end of the fifteenth century this name of Tartar origin was given to a class, difficult to define, of the population which gradually formed in the 'Ukraine,' that is to say, on the borders of the Jagiellonian State, under the exceptional

conditions which were created there by the perpetual danger
of the neighbourhood of the Tartars. Remaining outside the
normal organization of society and of its traditional classes,
rebellious against all authority, recruited among the Ruthenian inhabitants of the border provinces, but also among the
newcomers of every social class, these Cossacks had only one
means of livelihood: that of fighting the Mongolian invaders
while at the same time imitating their proceedings, and, in
return, making adventurous inroads as far as the Crimea and
the Ottoman strongholds on the shores of the Black Sea. Disciplined and organized, they could have rendered service to
the Republic, the more valuable since the defence of the
frontiers, entrusted to the armies of the State, always left
something to be desired. Hence projects of utilizing this
heterogeneous element, which was concentrated in the steppes
beyond the rapids of the Dnieper, make their appearance in
the middle of the sixteenth century. Sigismund Augustus and
Stephen Bathory had attempted to make part of the Cossacks,
enrolled into regiments and subject to the military authorities, into a species of army corps charged with the defence of
the frontiers. But it was impossible to admit into this organization the whole of a social group which, in peace time, had
no motive for existence; so that even the enrolled Cossacks
paid little heed to the official treaties with Turks and Tartars,
and instigated new invasions on their own account.

Naturally, no State could tolerate such a situation, which
perpetuated the disorder that reigned in the Ukraine: an ap-
pellation which more particularly signified the Palatinates of
Kiev and Braclaw. But to remedy it, the Republic, on the one
hand, would have had to guarantee to these provinces adequate security from the Tartar side, and, on the other, gradually to assimilate the Cossacks with the thousands of members
of the gentry, with whom their military occupations formed

a bond, as had been done by progressive stages with the old Ruthenian boyars. Hesitating between risky concessions and severe repressions with the object of converting the majority of the Cossacks into peasant serfs, Poland saw the repetition from the end of the sixteenth century onwards of increasingly frequent and savage insurrections. They were all the more dangerous as they inflamed provinces which differed in faith and the ethnical origin of their inhabitants from Poland proper. This explains why the social character of the problem was increased twofold by a religious or even national aspect, i.e. why the Cossacks, who were highly indifferent to the ecclesiastical point of view, became defenders of Orthodoxy, and why, at a given moment, a purely separatist movement was capable of arising in the Ukraine.

This moment arrived in 1648 when the Cossacks had found a leader of the first rank in the person of Bohdan Chmielnicki, who was himself a member of the gentry, but was anxious to avenge personal wrongs he had suffered, and when the Polish armies, hitherto generally victorious in their battles with the insurgents, experienced several shameful defeats. It was at this precise moment that Ladislas IV, who enjoyed a great reputation among the Cossacks, died, and of his two brothers, the only serious candidates for the crown, the elder, the weak and undecided John Casimir—he had first embraced an ecclesiastical career—became King of Poland.

The new monarch was won over by the Chancellor Ossolinski to a programme of compromise with the revolt. But it was too late for a policy of concessions. Chmielnicki himself would no longer have been able to master the movement that he had unchained. The masses of the people, carried along by the Cossacks, would have nothing more to do with the nobility, the clergy, or the Jews, whom they included in one same passion of hatred; and in the midst of a social revclution, the more sanguinary inasmuch as Chmielnicki had allied himself with the Khan of the Crimea, a programme of national independence was born, which placed the Orthodox Ruthenians in opposition to the Polish Republic, and which broke with the long traditions of a common life.

The aristocracy of the revolting provinces, in great part itself of Ruthenian origin, as was notably its undisputed head, Prince Jeremy Wisniowiecki, was therefore not mistaken when it remained sceptical in regard to equivocal negotiations with Chmielnicki. The atrocities committed by the Cossacks and their allies were retaliated by hardly less cruel reprisals, and soon the richest regions of the Republic were in ruins. Wisniowiecki, whose strategic talent far surpassed that of the commanders nominated by the king, distinguished himself by the heroic defense of Zbaraz, where a small Polish garrison resisted the assaults of many thousands of Cossacks and Tartars during six weeks of Homeric combat. The royal army, which at last advanced, allowed itself to be caught in a position from which there was no exit. It was therefore necessary to conclude, in 1649, an agreement of doubtful worth, which granted considerable concessions to the Cossacks, without, however, satisfying the ambitions of their chief or the appetites of the masses he had mobilized.

The most disquieting factor was that this agreement had been negotiated with the help of the Tartars, who, as it appeared, had passed over to the side of the Poles. In reality, the whole Moslem world had resolved to profit by the civil war in the Ukraine to crush the last rampart of Christendom. The battle of Beresteczko, which lasted three days, from the 28th to the 30th June 1651, was, therefore, of decisive importance for the whole of Europe. The king, who had at last succeeded in assembling a new army, gained a brilliant victory over Chmielnicki, who with his Turkish and Tartar reinforcements commanded forces three times superior in number. But, like so many other Polish victories, this military success had no sequel. Neither the king nor the nobility, divided by factious rivalries, showed sufficient perseverance and energy to put an end to the chaos which continued to reign in the Ukraine.

At last, in 1654, Chmielnicki, who, on the eve of Beresteczko, had not hesitated to place himself under the suzerainty of the sultan, took a decision still more serious for the future of his people. By the terms of the Treaty of Perejaslaw he placed the Ukraine under the suzerainty of Alexis, the Tsar of Moscow, who promised it a large autonomy. This promise was not kept. On the contrary, Great Russia took advantage of this rash act of the Cossack leader to attach the Little Russia of Kiev as closely as possible to herself and to resume her old programme of aggression against her western neighbour. In the same year the Muscovite invasion, a tardy retaliation for the Polish intervention at the beginning of the seventeenth century, tore Lithuania's White Ruthenian borderlands from her, including Smolensk, and the following year, in the summer of 1655, Wilno itself fell into the hands of the enemy.

Some ten days after the sanguinary sack of the capital of the Grand Duchy, Princes Janusz and Boguslas Radziwill, instead of defending Lithuania, treacherously handed her over to another invader. For the tsar had not been the only one to profit by the misfortunes of the Republic. Charles Gustavus, Palatine of Zweibrucken, who had been King of Sweden since 1654, had without scruple broken the truce with Poland so as to ensure his share in a partition that seemed imminent. Aiming, above all, at the occupation of Prussia in order to secure all the Baltic coast for Sweden, Charles Gustavus was helped at the outset by the policy of the Elector, Frederick William, who was determined to take this unique opportunity of freeing himself from the bond of vassalage which united East Prussia to Poland. But, what was far worse, the treachery which, declaring itself in Lithuania, intended to replace the Jagiellonian union by an improvised union with Sweden, also delivered Poland proper to the new aggressor.

A magnate who had fallen out with the king, the Vice-Chancellor Radziejowski, had encouraged Charles Gustavus to take the field. Another, the Palatine Opalinski, after having sought the Elector's protection, brought about the capitulation of the whole of Great Poland to the Swedish army. The veterans of the Thirty Years War took Warsaw on 8th September 1655; a few weeks later Cracow, in its turn, was obliged to surrender. The lawful king, abandoned and discouraged, took refuge on the borders of Silesia, and all the provinces, one after another, rendered homage to Charles Gustavus. Only a miracle could save the Republic.

At the height of the disaster this miracle was effected. Like a Noah's ark in the midst of the deluge, the monastery of Czestochowa resisted the enemy. The prior, Augustine Kordecki, gathered a handful of soldiers round the picture, venerated for centuries, of the Black Madonna; and after a forty days' siege the Swedes were, for the first time, forced to beat a retreat. This was on the day after Christmas. Faced with this unheard-of fact, which seemed like a legendary tale, the nation recovered itself. It mattered little now that in the beginning of 1656 the Great Elector, consummating his disloyalty, allied himself with the King of Sweden and declared himself his vassal in his capacity of Duke of Prussia. Some days later the Confederation of Tyszowce united the immense majority of the Polish nobility and gentry round John Casimir, who had returned from exile, and the whole country in a unanimous outburst of reviving patriotism rose against the foreigner. The chief traitors disappeared, struck by death that seemed a judgment of heaven, and courageous and disinterested leaders, Stephen Czarniecki in Poland, Paul Sapieha in Lithuania, placed themselves at the head of the movement of liberation.

The king himself, mediocre as he was, then lived the great hours of his life. He, too, yielded to the inspiration of religious enthusiasm which had rekindled love for a native land, and to the exalted moral convictions which called the nation to the expiation of inveterate faults. When he reached Lwow, that ever faithful city which had just repulsed Cossacks, Tartars, and Muscovites, John Casimir solemnly made a double vow.

In the name of the whole nation he first proclaimed that the Blessed Virgin should henceforth be venerated as 'Queen of the Crown of Poland.' The Polish nation was never to be false to that promise. The cult of Our Lady remained its supreme consolation through epochs the anguish of which surpassed that of 1655.

At the same time John Casimir swore that when once his native land was freed, the peasant population should in its turn be liberated from the serfdom by which it was oppressed. This serfdom was no heavier in Poland than in other contemporary States, including her neighbours. But in a country which boasted of being a land of liberty it was peculiarly unjust to limit that liberty to a single class which identified itself with the nation. This identification was now more than ever arbitrary, considering that the nobility had so ill fulfilled the task of defending the country, which mission was the only justification of its privileges. Moreover, in a country where the bourgeoisie had never had the same importance as in the west, and was being increasingly effaced, it was all the more regrettable that the peasants who constituted the immense majority of the population should be deprived of all

their rights. And even when they saw their position growing
steadily worse since the economic transformations of the sixteenth century that were felt in Poland as elsewhere, the
Polish peasants never reacted by revolts, so frequent in other
countries. It was in vain that the Cossacks attempted to gain
them over to the civil war directed against the nobility. Their
propaganda won only insignificant results in the purely Polish
provinces, whose rural population distinguished itself, on the
contrary, in the nation's struggles against foreign conquerors,
above all against the Swedes.

In spite of all this, this second promise of John Casimir's
was unfortunately not respected. Nothing was done all
through the following century to ameliorate the lot of the
Polish peasant. And this may be the basic reason why the war
of liberation did not realize its initial hopes, and did not
mark a real regeneration of the Republic.

This war, moreover, dragged on for several years, during
the course of which each success was followed by a fresh reverse of fortune. Charles Gustavus, threatened in the spring of
1656 with total defeat, escaped with the bulk of his army. On
the 30th June Warsaw was liberated, but a month later an
unsuccessful three days' battle caused her to fall once more for
several weeks into the enemy's hands. The alliance concluded
with Austria ensured indispensable reinforcements to Poland,
and so ameliorated her diplomatic situation that she was able
to gain another ally in Denmark. But this did not prevent
the King of Sweden from building up new plans for the partition of the Republic, and even a prince with as little power
as George Rakoczy, of Transylvania, believed he could attack
her with impunity in order to claim his share. He was defeated, and ended by losing his own principality, and soon the
Elector of Brandenburg, kept in play by the Hapsburgs, found
it convenient to become reconciled with John Casimir. But

his alliance with Poland had to be paid for by the Treaty of Wehlau, on the 19th September 1657, which put an end to Polish suzerainty over East Prussia, with the result that a veritable foreign wedge dependent on Berlin was established between Polish West Prussia and the Grand Duchy of Lithuania.

In 1658 and 1659 the war with the Swedes, of which so many romantic details have been described for us in the celebrated memoirs of John Chrysostom Pasek, was obviously drawing to its end. But in these same years the last project of agreement with the Cossacks collapsed. Since the death of Bohdan Chmielnicki in 1657, the moderate element, disposed to enter into an understanding with Poland, seemed to be uppermost in the Ukraine, and John Wyhowski, having secured the rule during the minority of Bohdan's son, concluded a very important treaty with the representatives of the king, the Union of Hadziacz, ratified by the Diet of 1659. This union ought to have happily completed that of Lublin by creating a Ruthenian duchy similar to the Grand Duchy of Lithuania, and, like it, placed on an equal footing with the Republic of Poland. It was to be limited to the Ukraine proper, that is to say, the Palatinates of Kiev, Braclaw, and Czernihow; but this solution was, in any case, far more favourable to the Cossacks and the Ruthenians in general than their subjection to Moscow had been. Unfortunately, this treaty could not take effect in an atmosphere of reciprocal distrust. Among the Cossacks, themselves divided, the party of young George Chmielnicki proved itself the strongest. The tsar, whose support he sought, imposed conditions upon the Ukraine that were of great danger to her autonomy, and once more attempted to conquer Lithuania also, from which country he had been driven back during the course of the preceding years.

The year 1660 at last brought the greatly needed peace with

Sweden, and on tolerable conditions. It was only a case of renouncing Livonia on the north of the Dvina, which since the
days of Gustavus Adolphus had been practically lost. The
work of the Congress of Oliva which reconciled the two nations was placed under the guarantee of Louis XIV, who, like
his predecessors, had played the part of mediator between
Pole and Swede. In this same year appreciable defeats were
inflicted on the armies of the tsar and George Chmielnicki,
but the hostilities on that side were indefinitely protracted.
Tartars and Turks again threatened to profit by the struggles
that were tearing the Ukraine, and finally Poland and Russia,
signing in 1667 the Truce of Andruszow, divided between
them the country which had dreamt of a more or less complete independence. The Republic was forced to abandon to
the tsar, with Smolensk and Czernihow, all the territories beyond the Dnieper, and even the greatly coveted town of Kiev
on its right bank. The latter was only yielded provisionally
for two years, but it was easy to foresee that it would not be
given back to Poland.

As a final result, it was thus that the Ukraine and the national aspirations of the Ruthenian people were ruined by
the movement started by Bohdan Chmielnicki. Poland was
saved, but at the price of desperate efforts and sinister concessions which she was obliged to make to the gain of Berlin and
Moscow. These concessions were the more inevitable because,
without waiting for the end of the war on the eastern boundaries of the Republic, a new internal conflict had broken out.
The history of this conflict offers striking analogies with the
constitutional crises that we have encountered in the course
of the preceding years. The project of a reform, more than
ever necessary, but propagated by the court in an inopportune manner, again provoked a violent reaction which, as
under Sigismund III, reached civil war.

The most deplorable abuse to have deformed Polish parliamentarism was, beyond all doubt, the too famous *liberum veto,* which permitted any deputy to dissolve the Diet, even annulling the decisions taken before his intervention. This absurd consequence of the principle of unanimity, a principle long applied in a reasonable fashion, had developed as time went on, and it is not accurate to date it from the Diet of 1652, dissolved by the deputy Sicinski. But the application of the *liberum veto* had never before been of so revolting a nature. Neither had it ever been so clear that the member of the gentry who put himself forward as the champion of democratic liberty, was only the miserable instrument of one of the great lords who, in spite of the dogma of absolute equality among the nobility, in reality exercised an increasingly dominating influence on their less fortunate 'brothers.'

To the project of remedying this vice of parliamentary life, that was ceaselessly discussed since the darkest days of the Deluge, there was added, in the same epoch, the often renewed plan of avoiding the troubles of a 'free' election after the death of a childless king by nominating his successor during his lifetime. This plan especially appealed to the queen, that same French princess Louise Marie who, soon after the death of her first husband, Ladislas IV, had married his brother, gaining an extraordinary influence over John Casimir. It goes without saying that she wished to give him a French successor and, in agreement with Cardinal Mazarin, she chose the Duc d'Enghien, son of the Great Condé.

The opposition which arose against this project, and which had the Grand Marshal of Poland, George Lubomirski, at its head, exasperated the queen to the point of resorting to corruption, to conspiracies, and even to a *coup d'état,* which she prepared in secret. On the other side, Lubomirski had not hesitated to encourage a purely revolutionary movement among the disbanded troops, who were in vain demanding their pay. At the Diet of 1664, the defender of the threatened liberties found himself sternly condemned under the influence of the court, and it was then that, imitating Zebrzydowski, he placed himself at the head of a second rebellion, which ended in 1666, in exactly the same way as the first. After fratricidal combats, a mournful epilogue to the Deluge, Lubomirski asked pardon of the king, who, on his side, was obliged to renounce all his plans of reform, including the idea of altering the law of free election.

Yet the election of John Casimir's successor took place before his death. For, disillusioned and worn out by his many trials, and foreseeing the future partitions of the Republic, the last Vasa only waited for his wife's death to abdicate the following year, in September 1668. Four years later he died in France, where he had retired to the abbey of Nevers; and his heart, which during his life had never known rest, found it at last under the aisles of the church of Saint-Germain-des-Prés.

16

John Sobieski

At the election of 1669 all the foreign candidates, representing the most diverse dynasties, presented themselves in vain. This time the recent memory of the many invasions and the many intrigues at the court of the last Vasa brought about the realization of an idea which had been discussed since the first free election: that of raising to the throne a compatriot belonging to the ranks of the Polish nobility, a new 'Piast.'

Unfortunately, the unanimous choice fell upon a completely insignificant personage, a young man who had nothing to recommend him to the electors except his father's name. Michael Wisniowiecki was the only son of that Prince Jeremy who had covered himself with glory by opposing almost alone the mounting flood of the Cossack insurrection, and who had died prematurely. But King Michael bore no sort of resemblance to this much admired hero. Neither the tradition which maintained that his family was descended from a brother of Jagiello, nor his marriage with a sister of the Emperor Leopold I, could enhance his authority. As regards internal affairs, he showed himself incapable of controlling the scandalous rivalries between the partisans of France

and those of Austria. He was still more feeble in the face of
the sanguinary troubles which were perpetual in the Ukraine
and which, at last, provoked the most dangerous intervention
of the epoch, that of the Sultan Mahomet IV, to whose
suzerainty the Cossack leader Doroszenko had submitted. In
1672 the fortress of Kamieniec in Podolia was taken by the
Turks, to whom an ignominious peace surrendered the whole
of that province as well as all that was still left to Poland of
the Ukraine.

But at the side of an indolent king there stood the great
figure of a leader in war who had already distinguished himself under John Casimir in battle with the Mussulmans. It
was he who the following year carried off the second victory
of Chocim, a more brilliant one than the first, which in 1621
had avenged the death of Stanislas Zolkiewski. John Sobieski,
who was, moreover, a great-grandson of the hero of Cecora,
thereby saved Poland from a new Ottoman invasion, and at
the same time gained the royal crown. For Michael Wisniowiecki died on the eve of this victory, and when the
triumphant victor appeared at the election of 1674 he was
elected in an outburst of general enthusiasm.

This time no better choice could have been made. The
noble who accepted the succession to the Piasts and the
Jagiellos was entirely worthy of it. In the whole history of the
ancient Republic there is no name more popular in Poland,
better known abroad, than that of Sobieski. And we know
to-day that the traditional prestige which had not ceased to
surround his memory is fully justified in the light of critical
research.

He was not only a great military commander. Like the
most eminent of his predecessors, he concerned himself as
much with the eastern problems which had a passionate interest for him as the defender of Christendom, as with the

political possibilities which an alliance with the France of Louis XIV opened to him in the west and on the Baltic. This alliance was concluded in 1675 by the new king of Poland, who had married a Frenchwoman of Queen Louise Marie's court, the beautiful and tenderly loved Marie Casimire de la Grange d'Arquien. This Franco-Polish alliance was directed, in the first place, against the Great Elector, Frederick William of Brandenburg, with the definite object of recapturing East Prussia, which was, in fact, very discontented under the absolutism of Berlin. This plan, which would have redeemed a long series of Polish political mistakes reaching as far back as that of Conrad of Masovia, preoccupied John III for several years. In 1677 he concluded a new alliance to this effect with Sweden by a treaty signed at Danzig. But soon a complete and sudden change seemed to come over the king's foreign policy. The king, who had supported the Hungarian insurgents against Austria and had even thought of reclaiming Silesia which had so long been lost, gradually approached the Emperor, and instead of pursuing the project of a coalition against the Elector of Brandenburg he took the initiative in forming a Christian league against the Turks. This new policy, which began in the Diet of 1678–9, ended in 1683 with the memorable campaign which was to save the capital of the Hapsburgs.

The relief of Vienna holds so considerable a place in universal history that it is necessary to grasp, as clearly as we can, the complex reasons which determined this unlooked-for orientation of Polish policy. For it was by no means the result of a lack of firm decision on Sobieski's part any more than of the caprices of his wife, of which so much has been said. On the contrary, this change of attitude is to be explained, not so much by the diplomatic adaptability of the king as by his qualities as a clear-sighted statesman who, in addition, perfectly understood the nation who had entrusted him with power.

John III's original plans could not have succeeded unless they had been unreservedly supported by Louis XIV. Now the latter never came to the point of ensuring that security to Poland on the Turkish side which was indispensable before she could undertake an action of wide scope on the coast of the Baltic. The efforts at conciliation attempted by French diplomacy did not prevent new Ottoman attacks in 1674 and 1675, attacks which were only repulsed owing to new victories on the part of the king, and which, in spite of his brilliant defence of the city of Lwow, were repeated in 1676. This time French mediation contributed to the signing of the preliminaries of peace, which, however, were unsatisfactory for Poland since they left the greater part of Podolia with Kamieniec to the Turks. The co-operation with Moscow on which Sobieski had for a time counted proved to be still more illusory, inasmuch as the new Tsar Feodor soon concluded a long truce with the Porte. Under these conditions the Mussulman danger took precedence for the moment over all others.

Sobieski was aware that the danger from the side of the Hohenzollerns might in the future become still more disquieting. But the Great Elector succeeded, in 1679, in himself forming an alliance with Louis XIV, and found French diplomats to help him in upholding the opposition directed in Poland against the king. This opposition was composed chiefly of partisans of Austria and conducted by magnates jealous of Sobieski's elevation and unscrupulous as to the means they employed. It had, from the outset, created innumerable difficulties for the king and paralysed the work of the Diets, so that every bolder initiative in foreign relations became a risk. At one moment John III had wished to march against Brandenburg without waiting for the approval of the

Diet, and to take possession of East Prussia for his family as the basis of a dynastic policy. But, unwilling to alienate the sympathies of his people, he renounced the idea, and looked for some object that he could pursue with the support of the nation.

It goes without saying that the alliance with Austria was only a means to an end. Sobieski was not ignorant of the fact that if thereby he tranquillized the partisans of the Hapsburgs, at the same time he created a new opposition, composed of the partisans of France. But, very skilful in his relations with the great lords, whose susceptibilities he knew how to spare, and of whom only one, the Grand Treasurer Morsztyn, went so far as treason, John III aimed, above all, at rallying to himself the great majority of the gentry and rekindling the enthusiasm which had decided his election. This enthusiasm, evoked in 1674 by the victorious defence of the Republic against the Mussulman invasion, could only be reawakened in the presence of an equally great reason. A war designed to occupy East Prussia would have had the appearance, at least, of a war of aggression and conquest, and consequently would never have gathered the whole nation, which had little knowledge of Berlin's diplomatic intrigues, round the king. On the contrary, every member of the Polish gentry understood the nature of the situation, both humiliating and perilous, which the Mussulman advance created for his country. An appeal for the defence of the Republic and Christendom, in conformity with age-long traditions, was sure to meet again with a universal response.

Moreover, the king had no intention of a co-operation only with Austria. The Peace of Nimeguen, concluded in the beginning of 1679, appeared to remove the obstacles which had opposed the formation of a league of all the Christian Powers against the common enemy. To realize this project that

Sobieski had had in consideration for several years, Polish ambassadors went not only to Vienna, Venice, and Rome, but also to France, England, and the Low Countries. It was, however, easy to foresee that, apart from the Holy See, only the Emperor would receive the Polish initiative favourably, as he also was directly threatened by the Ottoman power. This menace became all the greater when, in 1682, Tököly, the leader of the Hungarian opposition, made his submission to the Turks. John III's negotiations with Leopold I, there-fore, ended in a complete agreement. All that remained to be done was to gain over the Polish Diet to a treaty of al-liance with Austria, which especially provided that, in the case of an attack directed against the capital of one of the contracting parties, the other would go immediately to its help; a clause evidently dictated by Vienna's dangerous situ-ation.

It was then that Sobieski exercised all his energy and all his skill to obtain unanimity of public opinion. He succeeded admirably. On 31st March 1683, the Diet authorized the sig-nature of the treaty, which demanded of Poland, exhausted by many wars, an extraordinary effort; and the whole country showed a readiness which shrank from no sacrifice and which recalled the best hours of the past. Poland once more rose to her feet, conscious of a historic mission to fulfil.

In the July of the same year the case provided for in the alliance, that had hardly been as yet concluded, became fact. One hundred and thirty-eight thousand Turks, commanded by the Vizier Kara Mustafa, laid siege to Vienna, the fate of which seemed desperate. Responding to the appeal of the Pope and the Emperor, the King of Poland immediately pro-ceeded to mobilize, and rapidly led an army of thirty thou-sand men into Austria. The Austrians had also obtained rein-forcements from most of the princes of the Empire, with the exception of the Elector of Brandenburg. Their forces, which numbered forty-six thousand soldiers, were commanded by Prince Charles of Lorraine, who a short time previously had considered contending with John Sobieski for the Polish crown. Happily, no personal rancour hindered the collaboration of the two leaders, and by unanimous agreement the supreme command was entrusted to the king, who with his own hand drew up the plan of campaign. The unique experience he had acquired in the course of his glorious battles with Turks and Tartars secured unreserved acceptance of his orders, and this same experience made the presence of the flower of the Polish knighthood doubly valuable.

It was, in fact, the latter which decided the great battle of the 12th of September 1683. Descending from the heights of the Wienerwald, its terrible charge broke the furious resistance that the enemy was opposing to the German troops. By the evening, the immense Ottoman army was in flight, and amidst the enthusiastic acclamations of a population delivered after great sufferings, the King of Poland entered the walls of Vienna as its saviour. The victims of Varna and Mohacs were avenged, the advance of Islam arrested for ever, and before the eyes of the whole Christian world a last ray of glory shone upon the twilight of the Republic.

In the face of such a spectacle we almost hesitate to reckon up in cold blood the advantages that Poland reaped from this campaign. It has sometimes been regarded as an act of useless generosity, even dangerous in its consequences, since it served the interests of a State which a hundred years later shared in the partitions of the Republic. The most competent of our historians have refuted this superficial and narrow point of view. We know to-day that Sobieski's decision, generous as it was, was also justified by the circumstances, and by the fact that the fall of Vienna would have had for Poland also incal-

culable consequences. Independently, besides, of any immediate advantage, the victory of 1683 had a moral bearing of
the first order and of lasting value. It recalled the traditional
role of Poland in the history of Christian Europe; it showed
that the Republic, in spite of all her weaknesses, was still
capable of worthily filling that role; it became a symbolic
memory whose value increased with the misfortunes which
were again to fall upon our country.

We have all the more reason to ask ourselves another question, more disturbing and more difficult to determine. Why
did not the second half of the reign of John III, which followed that unparalleled but short-lived triumph, realize any
of the hopes of 1683? Why, on the contrary, did it know only
lamentable failures, inaugurating the period of the deepest
decadence of the Royal Republic? This turn of events is the
more surprising as Sobieski cannot be reproached with the
want of perseverance and consistency which prevented so
many other Polish victories from being turned to good account. Without being discouraged by the cold and haughty
reception to which Leopold I, on his return to his capital,
treated him, the king, before he went back to Poland, took
part also in the beginning of the campaign in Hungary, faced
new dangers there, and distinguished himself by new feats of
arms; and the following year, on 5th March 1684, he formed
with Austria, the Holy See, and Venice, that 'Holy League,'
whose obligations never ceased to direct all his foreign policy.
But the reproach commonly levelled against him is precisely
that of having made himself, so to speak, the slave of that policy of the league, of having continued to serve only the
interests of his allies, exhausting the Polish forces in sterile
undertakings.

In our opinion, the problem has been badly stated. To
make the Republic benefit by the *beau geste* of 1683, it was
indispensable to pursue the war against the Turks, and this it

was quite impossible to carry out otherwise than by co-operation with Austria and the other western Powers with which even France seemed ready to associate herself. It was no less natural that, leaving the Austrians to recapture Hungary from the Ottoman Porte, the King of Poland should have started his subsequent campaigns from Podolia, where Kamieniec still remained in the enemy's hands, and that he should have directed them towards the Black Sea so as to restore access thereto to the Republic. But he seems to us to have committed a serious mistake in his choice of the route which was to lead him to that sea, as well as of the territories which were to be the reward of his efforts. From 1684 to 1691, Sobieski incessantly renewed his attempts to conquer Moldavia and even Walachia, and thus to reach the lower Danube and its mouth. To gain this object he was obliged to fight, not only the Turks, but also a Christian population, hostile to his intervention, and at the same time he impaired his relations with the Hapsburgs, who desired to re-establish the former Hungarian influence in these regions. Devoting all his forces to a series of expeditions fully as unfortunate as many other Polish campaigns in Moldavia—it is enough to recall that of 1497—losing his prestige of an invincible leader, the king at the same time lost sight of the essential problem which presented itself to Poland from the side of the Black Sea: that of re-establishing her domination over the steppes between the Dniester and the Dnieper, reaching the coast between their mouths, and putting an end to the continual invasions of the Tartars of the Crimea.

John III, who knew how to treat the remaining Cossacks with such wise moderation, and who made the work of the union of the Churches progress peacefully, seemed admirably qualified to solve the question of the Ukraine and to repair the errors of the past there. Unfortunately, he re signed himself to concluding the treaty of peace with Mos-

cow in 1686 which perpetuated the surrenders of the truce
of 1667, including that of Kiev, in the hope that the tsar
would, on his side, give his support to the Holy League, and
would, in particular, take upon himself the struggle with the
Tartars. This illusion was no less deplorable than that which
at one moment led the king to seek the alliance of the Khan
of the Crimea himself, whose hordes were ceaselessly penetrating into the very heart of Polish territory, again threatening Lwow. The opportunity of making Poland benefit
from that enfeebling of the Ottoman power to which her
king had contributed in so decisive a manner, was thus definitely lost.

The plan of conquering Moldavia which for so long en-
grossed John III is chiefly explained by his desire to make of
it a sovereign principality for his son. Is this dynastic motive
an additional reason to criticize the project? We think not.
From the outset of his reign Sobieski had cherished the ambition of founding a dynasty. This ambition was not only
justified by the desire of sparing the Republic the danger of
a new interregnum after his death; it was also the essential
point of a whole programme of constitutional reforms envisaged by the king. Here, again, he proceeded with a good
deal of prudence, and while doubtless inspired by the example of Louis XIV, he had no intention of imposing an
absolute monarchy on the Polish nation, but rather of gradually eliminating the abuses which had vitiated the parliamentary regime and made the principle of the free election
of the kings one of increasing danger.

Sobieski would, perhaps, have succeeded here had his military glory lasted. Losing the ascendancy which he owed to
his victories, he could not surmount the double obstacle
which presented itself in his path. On the one hand, the
neighbours of Poland, who had every interest in maintaining
internal disorder there, united at this epoch in impeding

every reform capable of consolidating the Royal Republic. Without ignoring the steps that Frederick William of Brandenburg took to this effect, attention should be drawn to the treaty concluded in 1676 between Austria and Russia, who undertook to defend Polish liberties against the projects of the king. On the other hand, it is undeniable that this attitude of foreign Powers could not have embroiled the internal life of the Republic had it not been that those Powers found blind instruments in the persons of many of the great lords, in the pay of foreign courts, who were mutual rivals, but who, above all else, acted in stubborn opposition to John Sobieski. We have seen him triumph over their proceedings on the eve of the Vienna campaign. He was less fortunate in this respect on the eve of his death, the more so because this time the opposition had found particularly violent leaders in the Sapieha family.

But what gave the finishing stroke to the ageing king's discouragement was dissension in the bosom of his own family. The queen was certainly justified in attempting a new *rapprochement* with France, and the treaty that she negotiated with Louis XIV in 1692 seemed to promise Poland a solid support against Austria, Russia, and Prussia combined. Unfortunately, the treaty was never put into force; and, moreover, all Maria Casimira's policy was dictated by her personal ambitions and by her hatred of her eldest son James, who, married to a sister of the Empress, allowed himself to be influenced entirely by the court of Vienna. Under these conditions, although there was some question of the candidature of James's younger brother Alexander, who was more worthy of the crown, it was with no hope of leaving the throne to his descendants that their father died in 1696. The hero of 1683 departed with the mournful presentiment that nothing could now avert the ruin of the Republic.

17

The Decay

ACCORDING to the argument of one of our most distinguished historians, the epoch of Polish independence came to an end in 1696, and the hundred years which preceded the Partitions constitute, with the century that followed them, an epoch of struggle to re-establish that independence. Under a paradoxical appearance this idea contains a good deal of truth. It is, at least, true that the four kings who succeeded John Sobieski were imposed on their electors by foreign Powers. This affected fatally all their foreign policy, and at home the nation was no longer free to proceed with the most indispensable reforms, because its neighbours saw in these an obstacle to their plans of partition. These plans, which we have seen appear at different critical moments of Polish history, became at the end of the seventeenth century an almost permanent spectre, and for long—unhappily, too long —the Poles were unable to find the forces necessary to react against the tragic conclusion which was visibly approaching.

Fortunately, this melancholy story does not apply to the whole of the last century of the Republic. We shall see that the last third of the century repaired many errors. Nothing on the contrary is more depressing than the history of the sixty-six years that the rule of the kings of the House of Saxony lasted in Poland. A great part of the responsibility for this falls, without doubt, on these two kings. But how can we explain the fact that the Polish nation, so jealous of its right of free election, should have twice accepted foreign kings whose candidature had only been upheld by a minority? And, above all, how can we explain the fact that this nation, accustomed for centuries to oppose every abuse, real or apparent, of the royal power, should have tolerated the arbitrary methods, unscrupulous and lacking in greatness, of an Augustus II, as well as the revolting indolence of an Augustus III?

We see here, in the first place, a proof that the part of the king in our former Republic was by no means so insignificant as the text of the constitution would have led us to suppose. But we must also admit that the Polish nation was then passing through the most profound moral crisis that it had ever undergone. The share of responsibility that falls to it was far more the result of a failure of moral sense than of the obstinacy with which it defended its traditional institutions. We have stated that the experiment of the Royal Republic, such as it emerged from the first interregnum, could only succeed if its structure, bold and at the same time delicate, was sustained by moral principles orientating its political life. We have noted on several occasions the signs of a weakening, at least transitory, of the moral forces of the nation, showing itself in the unpardonable faults committed by its leaders. But the reason which eventually led to the breakdown of the forces of a whole people was the long series of almost uninterrupted wars, including those particularly pernicious episodes of civil strife, which filled the Polish seventeenth century.

Far longer, taken altogether, than the Thirty Years War, the consequences of which for Germany are well known, almost recalling the Hundred Years War which came near to destroying France, these wars had internal consequences for Poland still more disastrous than their territorial losses. Fought out in great part on the still very extensive territory which remained to Poland, they ruined her economically. Absorbing the flower of the nation, they made us pay for even our victories, not only by our best blood, but also by a halt, if not a backward step, in the development of our civilization.

The consequences were to be felt even in the religious sphere, from which the source of Poland's life had sprung for centuries. Religious exaltation, so often in the seventeenth century the decisive factor in Poland's struggles with Mussulmans, schismatics, and heretics, could not last. What replaced it was, unhappily, not the sentiment of daily duty, inspired by the Christian understanding of life, but a sentiment which attached itself, above all, to the exterior forms of devotion, and which was too often manifested in a negative way by the ill will which accumulated against all the Dissidents. It was, therefore, incapable of triumphing over another sentiment which appears to have hovered over the whole of this epoch: that of an extreme lassitude which was the basis of the worst weaknesses, and which tolerated the most degrading adventures in public and private life.

Under these conditions the Poland whose regeneration by her own strength John Sobieski had not succeeded in effecting, had imperative need of the support of another state. This support could not come to her from any of the neighbouring countries, which were only too anxious to profit by her weakness. Against this there was another state, very distant, it is true, but united to Poland by ever closer bonds of intellectual affinities and influence, a state which had every interest in making the Royal Republic, duly consolidated, a sure ally in the east of Europe. This was France, who had already so often negotiated with Poland on the subject of such an alliance, and who precisely at this epoch was living the great century of her history. In fact it was a French candidature, put forward in spite of the preceding failures at the election of 1697, the candidature of Prince François Louis de Conti, that seemed this time to have the most chances of success. Among the other candidatures, as usual very numerous, it was the only one that corresponded with the interests of the country, and for which an indisputable majority declared itself. But hardly had the Primate of Poland proclaimed Conti's election when a minority opposed him with a candidate who had appeared nearly at the last moment, Frederick Augustus I, Elector of Saxony, who hastened to have himself crowned King of Poland under the name of Augustus II.

The Poles had never wished for a king of German origin. Accordingly, they had in the past discarded candidates who were worth much more than Augustus the Strong. His despotic ways, which with his physical strength had gained him this surname, were assuredly not of a nature to win the sympathies of the Polish nobility. The descendant of a Protestant dynasty, he had recently embraced Catholicism; but every one knew that this conversion was only inspired by the desire of becoming King of Poland. He was able to secure the throne of Poland thanks only to the unanimous support of the Powers who eventually brought about the Partitions. That of the new tsar was particularly efficacious, as Peter the Great did not content himself with the corruption practised by the other courts: he also applied a method which the tsars and their ambassadors were to follow through the whole of

the eighteenth century, that of intimidation. Nevertheless
two years were needed to break all resistance. The Prince de
Conti even attempted to disembark in Poland, and it was
only when discouraged by the hostility of the Danzigers that
he returned to France. But it was not till the Diet of 1699,
called the Diet of Pacification, that his partisans acknowledged Augustus II as their lawful king.

This same date marks the liquidation of John III's political programme and the inauguration of that of his successor.
The latter began by gathering the tardy fruits of Sobieski's
victories, when the Peace of Karlowitz restored the fortress
of Kamieniec to Poland with the rest of the Podolian borderlands occupied, until then, by the Turks. He then launched
out into an enterprise that was directly contrary to the interests of his new kingdom. Poland had imperative need of
peace. Augustus II dragged her against her will into a new
war, which completed her ruin. She had no more implacable
enemy than Peter the Great; the king made him his intimate
ally. Since the Treaty of Oliva every reason for a conflict
with Sweden had disappeared. The king's project of attacking that country, in concert with Denmark and Russia, rekindled that conflict. The only advantage of an eventual victory would have been the recovery of Livonia; but Augustus
II promised his Russian ally and Frederick I of Prussia, who
was soon to assume the royal title, and even Austria, territorial compensations in advance which were equivalent to as
many projects for the partition of Poland.

The great northern war began, however, in 1700 by a defeat of all the allies, and it was Poland who paid the cost by
becoming the territory where the epic of Charles XII was
enacted. The Poles in vain declared that they were in no way
parties to the aggression that their king had perpetrated
against Sweden. Charles, in his turn, invaded Poland, and in

1702 the greater part of the country, including Warsaw and Cracow, found itself, as in 1655, in the hands of the Swedes. From the outset their young king had laid down as the condition of peace the deposition of Augustus II. In 1704 he, in fact, caused the election of a new King of Poland. The candidate he nominated, after having first considered a son of John Sobieski, was the Palatine of Poznania, Stanislas Leszczynski.

This national king beyond doubt deserved general esteem. His subsequent career, although abounding in disillusions, proved him infinitely more worthy of the crown than Augustus of Saxony. But the first election of Leszczynski was still less legal than that of his rival had been. Its consequence, furthermore, was to divide the nation into two opposite camps, one of which endured all the caprices of the Swedish conqueror, while the other humiliated itself before the Russian despot. After having effected the coronation of Stanislas I, Charles XII, wearying at last of sterile battles in Poland, in the autumn of 1705 turned directly upon Saxony, and in the following year imposed upon Augustus II the Treaty of Altranstadt, which compelled him to renounce the throne.

The King of Sweden had now only one adversary left, but that one was the most formidable of all. As we know, his war with Peter the Great, in which he counted on the support of the Cossacks of Mazeppa, the defender of Ukrainian autonomy, ended, on 8th July 1709, with the catastrophe of Poltava. This battle likewise decided the fate of Poland. Leszczynski naturally had to depart into exile, and Augustus II was re-established. But it has been rightly said that it was the tsar who then became the real master of Poland. It is true that in 1711 he suffered an unexpected check in his campaign against the Turks, with whom Charles XII had taken refuge, and who seemed suddenly to become allies of Poland.

However, all they were in reality intending was to seize the opportunity of recapturing the Polish Ukraine; and, moreover, Peter the Great knew how to extricate himself at very little cost from the blind alley in which he had involved himself. Understanding that as yet it was too soon to dream of the partition of the Ottoman Empire, he preferred to profit by the decline of Poland, not to partition her as the King of Prussia then suggested, but to subject her entirely to his scarcely disguised domination.

The king himself soon offered him an excellent pretext to make his influence decisively felt there. Augustus the Strong believed the moment had come in which to realize the project that had haunted him since his election to the throne of Poland, that of making it by a *coup d'état* the throne of an absolute monarch. This plan, which had not even the merit of involving serious and positive reforms of the Polish constitution, naturally came up against a furious opposition which in 1715 ranged the great majority of the nobility, coalescing in the Confederation of Tarnogrod, against the Saxon army of Field Marshal Flemming. In this conflict between the king and the nation it was the ambassador of the tsar who played the part of arbitrator. The agreement which he negotiated, and which was ratified by the 'Dumb Diet' of 1717, claimed to pacify the Republic. In reality it signified the most profound humiliation for her. It limited her army to the ridiculous figure of twenty-four thousand men, a figure that the provisions relating to the maintenance of the troops did not even permit of its actually attaining. From that moment Poland found herself disarmed in the midst of the military powers who surrounded her on all sides.

Augustus II himself had had enough of his ally by now. The prodigious success of the tsar, who was preparing to assume the imperial title, was, moreover, beginning to arouse considerable uneasiness in Europe. In 1719 the king was consequently enabled to enter into an alliance against him with the Emperor Charles VI and even with England under conditions very favourable for Poland. Considering the indignation which roused the whole of the latter country against the Muscovite design, the hour seemed at last propitious for an understanding between the king and the nation, inspired this time by the vital interests of the Republic.

This moment, unique in the long reign of Augustus II, was unfortunately lost. The king could scarcely be surprised that he met with no confidence, for until now he had done nothing to deserve it. But he was assuredly not wrong in reproaching the Poles for the shameful weakness which in 1720 led them to renounce every effort that could have delivered them from the supremacy of the tsar. The latter, on his part, concluded with Prussia the first treaty directly aimed against the existence of Poland, and designed to prevent in advance any project of recuperation. A year later, in 1721, the Peace of Nystadt, imposed on Sweden soon after the death of Charles XII, ended the northern war to the sole advantage of Peter the Great. Until his own death in 1725 the latter did not cease to work for the ruin of the Republic, and as she no longer counted in the general policy of Europe, he and his successors meddled all the more boldly in her internal life.

During all the rest of Augustus II's reign only one event attracted foreign attention to Poland. But it was of a nature to alienate the sympathies of many from her, and seemed to justify the interference of her neighbours. We know that Polish public opinion, gradually departing from the wise traditions of religious tolerance, had become increasingly hostile to the Dissidents. The most radical sect, that of the Arians, had been expelled in 1658. Later, though without attacking the liberty of conscience of the Protestants and the Orthodox Church, the stage was reached of excluding them from public offices. Yet there had never been a sanguinary persecution for religious opinions in Poland. But in 1724, because the municipal authorities of Torun had not prevented the odious excesses of the mob against the Jesuit College, the mayor of that town and nine other Protestants were condemned to death. The severity of this sentence was so excessive that even the Apostolic Nuncio attempted to intervene in favour of the accused. Nevertheless, the king ordered their execution. This did not add to his popularity in Poland, while in non-Catholic countries a violent propaganda, exaggerating the regrettable but isolated incident, was immediately set on foot against the Polish nation. Russia and Prussia, who had inspired it, soon profited by it to renew their alliance, mutually guaranteeing their right of protecting the religious minorities in Poland.

Augustus II concerned himself little with this growing danger. The 'great design' which preoccupied him towards the end of his life had in reality only one object: that of securing absolute power for himself in Poland as in Saxony, and of transmitting it to his son Frederick Augustus who, like himself, had become a Catholic with a view to his future election to the Polish throne. To effect this, the old king counted, above all, on one of the parties which had formed among the Polish aristocracy, and was briefly entitled 'The Family.' It was led by the Czartoryski princes and their brother-in-law Stanislas Poniatowski, a former partisan of Charles XII, of very modest origin, but who, owing to exceptional qualities, had attained to the highest offices. The other party, gathered round the Potockis, was so fundamentally opposed to the court that there could be no question whatever of gaining it over to the candidature of a second king of the House of Saxony. The opposition had, moreover, a candidate ready in the person of Stanislas Leszczynski, whose chances had become far more favourable since his daughter Maria had, in 1725, married the King of France, Louis XV.

The advantages of his re-election were so evident, and the indignation provoked by the rule of Augustus II so general, that after the latter's death in 1733 the two parties which were directing the whole of the nobility united to exclude every foreign candidate from the throne, and to elect, on 12th September, Leszczynski, who obtained more than thirteen thousand votes. This time the election of Stanislas I was indisputably legal, and to assure his rule he no longer counted on the orders of a foreign conqueror, but on the support that Louis XV would give to his father-in-law and to a Poland desirous of freeing herself from German and Russian influence.

Unhappily, the neighbours of the Republic, who had first had the idea of imposing a Portuguese Infante on her as king, had agreed with each other to uphold, at all costs, the Elector of Saxony. They gained for him a minority of three thousand electors who, protected by Russian cannon, gave their votes, on the 5th October, to the son of Augustus II. Unfortunately also Cardinal Fleury, who was then directing French policy, did not provide the efficacious help to his rival which the latter had anticipated. With the Primate of Poland and the French ambassador, Leszczynski vainly waited for succour from his son-in-law in the town of Danzig, which this time gave a fine example of devotion to the lawful king. The heroism of the Comte de Plelo, who died for the freedom of Poland and the honour of France, did not prevent the capitulation; on 29th May 1734, the king was obliged to take refuge in Prussia.

The war which had resulted from the double Polish election was finally decided, not by the attitude of the immense majority of the nation who in the Confederation of Dzikow had declared themselves in favour of Stanislas I, but by the great European States, among which eighteenth-century Poland no longer held her former place. In 1735 the Peace of Vienna obliged Leszczynski to abdicate and to content himself with the Duchy of Lorraine, while Augustus III definitely remained King of Poland.

He spent the thirty years of his reign almost exclusively in Saxony, abandoning his kingdom to the mercy of his favourites, among whom the Saxon Bruhl and his son-in-law, the Pole Mniszech, acquired an unenviable celebrity. This scandalous hegemony was able to continue, as the apathy of the king, the most unworthy sovereign that Poland has ever had, seemed as though it had taken possession of the whole nation. Under the impression of the dreary monotony which those thirty years reveal, we almost end by asking ourselves whether Poland, condemned to a more and more passive role, had indeed at that time any history of her own worthy of the name.

In any case, she had no longer any foreign policy. Considering that the War of the Polish Succession had been liquidated without the Poles, we are scarcely surprised to see Poland remaining neutral in all the succeeding conflicts which roused the passions of Europe: in the war against the Turks from 1735 to 1739; in the War of the Austrian Succession which broke out the following year, and even in the Seven Years War which synchronized with Augustus III's last seven years. But, which was much worse, the Republic could no longer even make her neutrality respected, and became accustomed to see foreign armies violate her territory. It has been possible to liken the former rampart of Christendom to a roadside inn, serving, above all, the Russian armies which were thus enabled to make their appearance on the battlefields of central Europe.

On the other hand, the great majority of the Poles were not aware of the immense danger that the policy of Frederick the Great represented to their country. His attack directed against Austria in violation of the most solemn engagements should have been a warning, the more serious because it decided the fate of Silesia, formerly Polish, now separating Poland from Saxony, and the annexation of which by Prussia caused all the western provinces of the Republic to be surrounded by that country. Not having known how to profit by those years that had seen Prussia and Russia in two hostile camps, Polish diplomacy hesitated between two equally dangerous alternatives, seeking by turns the support of each of these formidable neighbours against the other. It ended by Poland finding herself faced with a close alliance between these two Powers, an alliance inaugurated by the Tsar Peter III and, in spite of the *coup d'état* that overthrew him in 1762, continued by Catherine II.

We have mentioned Polish diplomacy. Rather we should say the foreign relations maintained by the two factions which, under Augustus III, had recommenced disputing with each other for the highest public offices and the influence they carried with them. This unscrupulous rivalry had the deplorable result that no Diet under this king could carry through its work normally, and that the second half of his reign offers, in this respect, a still more wretched aspect than the first. The 'Family' of the Czartoryskis had, beyond doubt, far more political foresight and a more definite programme than the party of the Potockis. They had even begun by an attempt at collaboration with the court with a view to bringing about a reformation of the internal situation. Having failed in their plans, seeing themselves removed from

power, and finding no serious support from the western
Powers, including France, the Czartoryskis went so far as to
prepare a *coup d'état* in agreement with Catherine II. The
death of the king, on 5th October 1763, released them from
a highly equivocal situation, but it seemed only to aggravate
that of the Republic. In her state of decadence a fresh interregnum was, in fact, only a fresh pretext for interference by
the Empress of Russia and the King of Prussia.

18

The Regeneration

THE epoch of our Saxon kings has been compared to a night which fell upon Poland, and we all know that under their successor this night was followed by the partitions which signified her death. The conclusion might easily be drawn that the crime of these partitions was justified, or, at least, explainable, by the century of incurable decay which had preceded it, and that, in any case, the ruin of the Royal Republic was inevitable. But this opinion, very prevalent among foreigners, in no way corresponds with historical truth.

Since the internal history of Poland under Stanislas Augustus has been thoroughly studied, and the latter's part in the history of Polish culture clarified, it has been necessary to revise the too hasty judgment which had weighed so long on the last of our kings. To-day we know that, in spite of all the failures of his foreign policy, his reign constitutes an epoch of genuine national regeneration, a regeneration which could not avert the final catastrophe, but which forbids us to see in that catastrophe the immediate and fatal consequence of the decay that had preceded it.

But this is not all. The most penetrating analysis of the night of the Saxon epoch enables us to perceive through its darkness the rays of a dawn, which was breaking, rich in promise, on the horizon of the future. Briefly, it is true, the character of that most dreary epoch whose history we have sketched is in keeping with the most striking external facts, but it would remain incomplete and superficial if we did not at the same time endeavour to point out certain signs which then foreshadowed the complete change brought in by Poniatowski's reign.

Moreover, let us not forget that Stanislas Augustus did not only succeed Augustus III, the docile puppet of foreign States, but also Stanislas I, the lawful king who, from his distant residence in Lorraine, never ceased to follow the fortunes of his country. In the papers of this exiled king a vast plan of perpetual peace has recently been found, based on a new organization of Europe, a plan which arouses our admiration for its broad views on international policy, and for its generous ambitions, worthy of the finest traditions of Poland. But what had a more concrete and direct influence was the role which he filled, until his death in 1766, of an educator of the Polish nation, giving his protection to the young compatriots whom he received at his court at Luné-ville, and lifting his authoritative voice in political writings of high value, which indicated the road that should be followed to preserve the liberty of the Republic, once it had been wisely reformed.

This voice had such a hearing in Poland, it found such a lively echo in other publications appearing in the country, that we perceive here in the middle of the eighteenth century the germ of all the salutary ideas which were subsequently to expand and be realized under Poniatowski. What is particularly significant is the fact that the author of a most

remarkable political treatise, Father Stanislas Konarski, of
the Piarist Order, was at the same time a great practical educator, a real reformer of the educational system which was
then in force and the results of which left so much to be
desired. This explains why the political reforms which aimed
at ensuring to Poland a stable government, well ordered finances, and an army comparable with that of her neighbours
—reforms attempted in vain by a group of the best of the generation under Augustus II—could be successfully resumed
by the following generation which, formed by a more adequate education, raised itself to a higher level of culture.

To this new generation belonged the son of that Stanislas
Poniatowski whom we saw raise himself to the rank of the
most powerful aristocrats and marry a Czartoryska. Born
in 1732, Stanislas Augustus shone among his contemporaries
by a refined culture which he owed to innate gifts, a careful
education, and long sojourns in the west. First Vienna, then
chiefly Paris and London, familiarized him with all the currents of eighteenth-century European culture, and prepared
him for his future role of a Maecenas of letters and arts, an
enlightened protector of industry and commerce, and a renovator of the political ideas of the nation. All that was accomplished during his reign in these very diverse spheres
bore the stamp of his initiative, and he had, in addition, the
merit of getting the best minds of his epoch to work together
around his fascinating person. This new epoch of our civilization, recalling in certain respects the golden age of the
Jagiellos, lives in history as that of Stanislas Augustus, whose
name remains linked with the new style of Polish architec-
ture as also with the great constitutional reforms now at last
realized.

Unfortunately, the moral strength, which alone could have
made young Poniatowski the king that Poland needed in the

tragic hours that awaited her, formed no part of that accomplished intellectuality. Supple and benevolent, he was wanting not only in the energy which had assured his father's
amazing career, but, above all, in the moral principles which
were then being reborn in the tormented souls of many other
Poles. This explains why, attracting talents as he did, he
numbered among his adversaries, side by side with the jealous and the reactionaries, the most generous hearts and the
most ardent patriots. Some would remind him of the modest
origin of his family and the quite secondary position from
which he was raised to the throne. Others reproached him
with far better reason for many culpable weaknesses in his
private and public life, beginning with the manner in which
he had gained the crown of the Piasts and the Jagiellos.

At the election of 1764, which was preceded by troubles of
evil augury, and which was unanimous only because of the
armed intervention of Russia, Poniatowski, like his Saxon
predecessors, was imposed on the nation by Poland's worst
enemies, Frederick II of Prussia and Catherine II of Russia.
But what gave a peculiarly disgraceful character to this proceeding was that Stanislas Augustus owed the empress's
decisive support to the notorious fact that during his diplomatic missions in Petersburg he had been her lover. This
scandalous origin of his elevation to the throne lay heavy
on all his reign, and his sentiments of gratitude and attach-
ment to Catherine II warped all his foreign policy. Even the
internal reforms which constitute his chief merit suffered
from the illusion that made him endeavour to carry them
through successfully in agreement with Russia and using her
support.

These reforms, thanks to the initiative of the Czartoryskis,
had been begun at the Diet of Convocation which, according
to usage, preceded that of the election. In amelioration of

the parliamentary regulations, the decision had been reached for the first time to limit the principle of unanimity, the rigour of which, hitherto absolute, had clogged all progress. Modest beginnings of administrative, economic, and social reforms had also taken place. Stanislas was only too willing to carry on this immense work immediately after his coronation, celebrated in Warsaw on 25th November 1764. He at once came up against unlooked-for difficulties. Even the Czartoryskis, who had hoped to obtain the crown for a member of their old princely house, descended from the race of the Jagiellos, showed little alacrity in supporting the nephew who had been so favoured by fortune. On the other hand, the king soon provoked the anger of his protectress by showing himself less docile than she had anticipated, and by even seeking a *rapprochement* with Austria and France, Powers which at the election had favoured the House of Saxony, but whose support now seemed indispensable. Frederick II hastened to notify Catherine II of these plans, so that they had only one result, that of strengthening the understanding between Russia and Prussia, both of whom were firmly resolved to oppose everything that could favour the revival of Poland.

The king had proof of this at the Diet of 1766. He had not thrown away the two years which had passed since his accession. Permanent commissions, genuine ministries, were functioning ever more satisfactorily. A council of ministers, ensuring the continuity of the nation's policy, was in process of being formed. Financial and monetary reforms enabled the budget to be balanced. In collaboration with his cousin, Adam Czartoryski, Stanislas Augustus founded an excellent military school. Assisted by the chancellor, Andrew Zamoyski, he showed great solicitude for the urban population. And he hoped that the first Diet of his reign would develop these beginnings, and, above all, bring in a new limitation of the principle of parliamentary unanimity. But hardly had this delicate problem been approached when the diplomatic representatives of Catherine II and Frederick II protested, going so far as to threaten the Republic with a declaration of war.

On their side they raised the question of the equality of the rights of the religious minorities, Orthodox and Protestant. Under an appearance of liberalism which deceived Europe, this manœuvre was designed to create new internal difficulties for Poland, to exasperate the conservative opposition, and, above all, to embroil the latter definitely with the king, who was ready to compromise in the matter. Prince Repnin, the Russian ambassador, in fact succeeded in thus stopping all the practical work of the Diet, and from this moment it was really this foreign diplomat who, with frank brutality, dictated his will to the Poles.

In 1767 the opposition to the parvenu Poniatowski formed the Confederation of Radom which, deceived and subsequently terrorized by Repnin, requested the Empress of Russia to guarantee the former Polish constitution. At the Diet of this same year, the ambassador had two bishops, a senator, and a deputy, who had dared to protest against these demands, arrested and deported to Russia; and despite certain useful reforms voted by this Diet the independence of Poland now seemed pure fiction.

But it was precisely now that Russia perceived that she was no longer dealing with the decadent Poland of Saxon times. On the 29th February 1768, in the small Podolian town of Bar, a new confederation—and this one was spontaneous—courageously took up the struggle for freedom. This desperate struggle lasted four years until the eve of the first partition, for which it served as a pretext. It recalls the war for independence which had saved Poland at the epoch of the Deluge. Again the nobility took up arms in the name of their threatened faith and country, and again all the provinces of the Republic rallied, one after another, to this movement which saved the honour of Poland.

But why did it not save Poland herself? Why was the sanctuary of Czestochowa, which, as in 1655, served as the rallying-point for the reviving patriotism, finally compelled this time to capitulate? Why do the exploits of these courageous knights of Christ and His Mother resemble, not the campaigns of independent Poland, but rather the future insurrections of partitioned Poland? Their ardour was, indeed, checked in the first year by the atrocities of a popular revolt in the Ukraine, where Russia, although she subsequently assisted in its repression, was not without her share of responsibility for the outbreak. It is also true that the confederates did not find the foreign support on which they had counted. Turkey entered into war with Russia, but was herself beaten, and France only sent Poland a handful of soldiers, who all distinguished themselves, but whose counsels were not always happy ones. But what decided the failure of the movement was the impossibility of securing union among all the Poles, including the king. The latter made at that time serious mistakes which roused the indignation of the confederates, and subsequently caused them to repulse all his overtures. On their side they committed the great error of proclaiming, in 1770, the deposition of Poniatowski, and in the following year going so far as an attempt upon his person. Even if we deplore the spirit of faction which divided the confederates among themselves, still we must render homage to their disinterested leaders, such as the Krasinskis, and, above all, the Pulaskis, the most heroic of whom, Casimir, unable to save the freedom of Poland, died for that of America.

The Confederation of Bar was crushed by the Russians.

The hour, therefore, seemed to have arrived in which to realize the plan of Catherine II and her minister Panin of subjecting the whole of Poland to Russian domination. But Frederick II had his own plan which he had been patiently developing since 1768 and with which he acquainted the empress in 1770. He succeeded in gaining Russia to the idea of a partition of Polish territory, and at the same time he hinted to Austria, who at one moment had seemed to support the confederates, the advantages of a share in this act of violence. It was, indeed, the Austrians who, in spite of Maria Theresa's scruples, were the first to penetrate into Polish territory.

On the 5th August 1772 Poland's three neighbours entered into an agreement, and proceeded immediately to occupy the provinces which they had arrogated to themselves. Russia's share was the most extensive, comprising all that still remained to the Republic beyond the Dvina and Dnieper. Austria appropriated a territory hardly less large with a still more considerable population, the whole of the future Galicia as far as the Vistula; but it was Frederick the Great who secured the most valuable acquisition, obtaining West Prussia which had separated East Prussia from the rest of his possessions, and, if he was obliged to renounce provisionally the towns of Danzig and Torun, he took in return the north of Great Poland.

Exhausted by her preceding struggles, Poland could not prevent these annexations. But the partitioning Powers were, in addition, anxious to obtain their ratification by the Polish Diet. This Diet, assembled in April 1773, did not close its labours until April 1775. It yielded, like the king, to the peremptory argument that in the case of refusal further territories would be detached from Poland. Let us pass over in silence the names of the miserable men who facilitated this blackmail. Rather let us record that of the deputy who protested the most courageously, Thaddeus Reytan.

But the most cheering feature of the story is the fact that this first spoliation was not able to arrest the great movement of national rebirth. Russia, who, like Prussia, saw in the partition of 1772 only the first stage of the project for the integral destruction of Poland, intended on this occasion to impose upon her an internal administration, which would have cut short every attempt at reform, perpetuated the causes of her weakness, and limited still more strictly the royal power by a Permanent Council. Now it was precisely this council that Stanislas Augustus and his collaborators succeeded in making into a highly useful institution. All the administration of the State was concentrated in its five departments, and the king, who presided, secured considerable influence there for himself. Thanks to this stable government, which gained by degrees in authority, a vast work of organization was accomplished in a dozen years. These years are certainly not brilliant in the political history of Poland, and her role in Europe seemed increasingly reduced; but 'in the shadow of the proconsul'—that is to say, of the Russian ambassador Stackelberg—Poniatowski was patiently preparing a better future. Without suffering himself to be discouraged by inevitable failures such as that of the industrial enterprises of the too ambitious grand treasurer, Anthony Tyzenhaus, or by the rejection of the project for a code prepared by the chancellor, Andrew Zamoyski, the king strove above all to raise the intellectual level of the nation by developing reforms in the sphere of education, reforms whose modest beginnings we have pointed out above.

In this respect the lamentable Diet which had been forced to sanction the first partition created in the course of its labours, in 1773, an extremely valuable institution, the celebrated Commission of National Education. The Jesuit Order having been dissolved by Clement XIV, Poland assigned the funds that had thus become at her disposal to the foundation and functioning of this new organization, which has been justly compared to a ministry of public instruction, the first in Europe. The whole of Polish education, from the primary school to the Universities of Cracow and Wilno, was reorganized by this commission with as much competence as moderation and good method. Among the inspirers of this movement we must mention at least the devoted secretary of the commission, the Rev. Gregory Piramowicz.

Moreover, without waiting for the result of his other efforts, Stanislas Augustus succeeded at once in creating what has been called his 'kingdom of Parnassus.' He gathered round him, in particular at his famous 'Thursday dinners,' the flower of Polish intellect who, while still cultivating the sciences and arts, also gave birth to a new period of Polish literature, resuming the fine traditions of the sixteenth century. Among the poets who made his reign illustrious the first place is undoubtedly held by Ignatius Krasicki, a mediocre bishop but an incomparable author of fables and satires. By his side, writers as different as Stanislas Trembecki, a sceptical and satirical courtier, and Francis Karpinski, a sentimental poet of religious and national inspiration, were all distinguished for their high culture and the classical perfection of their language. Contrary to their predecessors of the 'golden century,' they wrote exclusively in Polish, although strongly influenced by French literature. One of them, Bishop Adam Naruszewicz, was also an eminent historian who, assisted by the king, organized vast researches in the archives in order to give a scientific basis to the knowledge of the past. His work remained unfinished, but the documents he gathered together are still used by the Polish historians of to-day, as also is the magnificent library formed shortly before by another bishop, Joseph Andrew Zaluski, one of the deported senators of 1767.

It is impossible to enlarge here upon the beginnings of the Polish theatre and press, which belong to this same epoch. Instead, let us emphasize that the efflorescence of belles-lettres was now accompanied, as in the sixteenth century, by quite as remarkable a development of political literature. And let us note the significant fact that its most illustrious representative, Stanislas Staszic, gave the first of his works, which appeared in 1785, the form of *Observations on the Life of John Zamoyski*. This essentially modern writer, of plebeian origin and liberal tendencies, thus recalled the memory of the founder of the Royal Republic in order to stigmatize the later distortions of his work, and to establish a complete plan of reforms, which were especially bold in the social department. Together with Staszic, it was also Hugo Kollataj, known first as the reorganizer of higher education, who, surrounded by a staff of friends, prepared and stimulated by his writings the work of effective reforms which was at last accomplished by the Four Years Diet, the Polish 'Great Parliament' which sat from 1788 to 1792.

Without entering into details of its activities, let us first point out its immense difficulties. In the midst of political preoccupations, the gravity of which we shall consider later, this Diet had to convert all the wise and generous ideas, which had come to the fore in the course of the preceding years, into legislative acts. These ideas still met with opposition from a turbulent minority which, conducted by a few reactionary magnates, prevented unanimous decisions. The Diet, therefore, constituted itself into a Confederation, which permitted it to abide by the majority of votes. To reinforce its authority it made an appeal in the midst of its labours to the public opinion of the country. Doubling the number of the deputies by new elections it became thereby a genuine national assembly.

Inspired by the tendencies of the French Revolution, and, like it, proclaiming the rights of man and the citizen, our constituent Diet succeeded, however, in avoiding all violence and in following the lines of Poland's historical evolution. Let us, moreover, observe that all the reforms which it adopted exacted considerable sacrifices from those who voted them. The nobility which alone was represented at this assembly was obliged, in the general interest, spontaneously to renounce traditional privileges and many of the principles which were dear to it. It began by decreeing, in 1788, this time unanimously, the creation of an army of a hundred thousand men, which involved heavy financial burdens. It then made important concessions to the 'third estate,' the urban population whose delegates, assembled in Warsaw, were insistent in formulating their claims. At last it accepted, by a crushing majority, the celebrated Constitution of the Third of May 1791, the anniversary of which is still in our days kept as the Polish national feast day.

This constitution ratified the rights accorded to the burghers, giving them access to public offices and to Parliament, and thus breaking down the barrier which had hitherto separated them from the nobility. It placed the peasant population under the protection of the Government, not going so far as to abolish serfdom, but encouraging and guaranteeing individual contracts between the gentry and the peasants, contracts which became more and more frequent and ameliorated the situation of the latter. Perfecting the central administration and the management of the finances, the new constitution resolutely abolished the right of *liberum veto,* as well as that of the 'free' election of the king, a right which had ended by imposing upon the Republic the candidates of foreign Powers. It decreed that after Poniatowski's death the throne should be hereditary in the House of Saxony.

It is easy to criticize the choice of this dynasty. It is equally regrettable that, in view of the protests of a dissatisfied minority, it was considered necessary to have the project of the constitution adopted almost by surprise. This does not affect the fact that from the moment of its promulgation it evoked a refreshing enthusiasm, and that this grand result of a loyal collaboration between the king and the patriotic party, among whom was the Speaker of the Diet, Stanislas Malachowski, permitted the belief that this time the Royal Republic, happily adapted to the needs of the hour, was definitely saved.

19

The Partitions

CONTRARY to all hopes, the Constitution of 1791, eloquent witness to the national rebirth, was followed in 1793 by the second, and in 1795 by the third partition of Poland. These last partitions, which erased our country from the map of Europe, are essentially different from the first, which was, in reality, only a mutilation of our territory. Poland's neighbours who, in 1772, had thought it necessary to justify their annexations by appealing to historical rights—easy, however, to refute—did not even put themselves to the trouble of invoking any kind of right when they proceeded to the complete partition. And while at the first partition they had been able, with a certain show of reason, to denounce the internal troubles which had then been seething for several years in Poland, no such argument could serve them after the reforms accomplished without the slightest disturbance of order by the Four Years Diet. The accusation of Jacobinism, raised against the new Poland, was in such obvious contradiction to the spirit and methods of that Diet, that no one could take it seriously. Under these conditions, even the immediate origin of the partitions of 1793 and 1795 raises highly com-

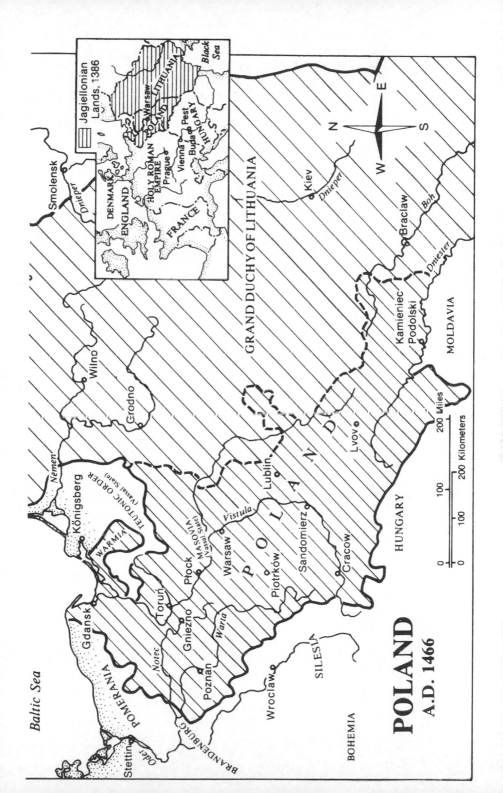

POLAND
A.D. 1466

Baltic Sea

Smolensk

Dnieper

GRAND DUCHY OF LITHUANIA

Kiev

Dnieper

Braclaw

Boh

Dniester

Kamieniec
Podolski

MOLDAVIA

Wilno

Grodno

Nemen

Königsberg

TEUTONIC ORDER
(Vassal State)

WARMIA

Lvov

Lublin

Vistula

P O L A N D

Plock

MASOVIA
(Vassal State)

Warsaw

Piotrków

Sandomierz

Cracow

HUNGARY

Gdansk

Toruń

Gniezno

Warta

Poznań

Notec

POMERANIA

Stettin

Oder

BRANDENBURG

Wroclaw

SILESIA

BOHEMIA

N
E
W
S

200 Miles

200 Kilometers

100

100

0

0

Jagiellonian
Lands, 1386

LITHUANIA

Black
Sea

Warsaw

POLAND

Pest

HUNGARY

Buda

Vienna

HOLY ROMAN
EMPIRE

Prague

DENMARK

ENGLAND

FRANCE

plex problems that we shall attempt to solve before analysing the deep-seated causes of the catastrophe.

During the years of her internal work following the first partition, Poland had sedulously avoided everything that could have provoked a new conflict, either with Prussia, or, above all, with Russia. Stanislas Augustus, always filled with admiration for Catherine II, was all the more convinced of the necessity of a good understanding with the empress because she had lately carried off a fresh success of 1783, by annexing the Crimea and putting an end to the existence of the last Tartar khanate, which had formerly been so dangerous both to Russia and to Poland. In 1787, on the eve of the Great Diet, the two sovereigns met at Kaniow, on the Ukrainian borders of their states, and, in agreement on this point with the most reactionary group of the Polish aristocracy, the king himself showed favour to the project of a Russo-Polish alliance, directed against Turkey.

On the other hand, the alliance between Russia and Prussia, which had had such fatal consequences to Poland, came to an end in 1788, and Frederick William II, who had succeeded Frederick the Great, appeared to be embarked on a policy hostile to the empress. This explains why the Polish patriots, directed by Ignatius Potocki, believed the moment had come to profit by the rupture between the two principal adversaries of Poland. They calculated that, instead of allowing the dominating influence of Russia to be perpetuated over the whole of the territory which still remained to the Republic, it was more advisable to conclude a defensive alliance with Prussia which would guarantee both the integrity of that territory and its complete independence.

Prussia attempted on this occasion to have the greatly coveted towns of Danzig and Torun ceded to her. Her minister, Hertzberg, even foresaw diplomatic combinations which would have restored Austrian Galicia to Poland by way of compensation. These projects turned out to be unrealizable, but the Polish-Prussian alliance was, nevertheless, signed on 29th March 1790, the king having rallied to the foreign policy of the party with whom he was collaborating with a view to constitutional reforms. This alliance provided that in the case of aggression against one of the contracting parties the other would come to its assistance, so that the safety of Poland seemed assured.

This was unhappily a pure illusion. For Prussia this transitory alliance with Poland was merely a tactical move which she was willing enough to use as long as her antagonism with Catherine II lasted, but which she was ready to renounce as soon as a new opportunity presented itself of extending her frontiers to the detriment of Poland. The latter was anxious to gain some years of peace by maintaining a part of passive neutrality, in the hope that the diplomatic support of Prussia would enable her to escape Russian appropriation of her country. But it was easy to foresee that in the event of real danger this support would entirely fail her, and it was still more evident that the empress, indignant at the policy of the Great Diet which had emancipated itself from her tutelage, was only waiting for a pretext to interfere more energetically than ever in Polish affairs.

She was, unfortunately, provided with this pretext scarcely a year after the adoption of the new constitution by a handful of Polish nobles, who, dissatisfied with that reform, did not hesitate to invoke the help of Catherine II against the lawful government of their own country. The empress only waited for the signing of peace with Turkey before she invaded Poland, in response to the appeal of a new confederation which a few traitors had formed at Targowica, after it had been carefully prepared in Petersburg.

At the outset of the campaign of 1792 the Polish army, which, thanks to the recent reforms, numbered more than sixty thousand men, well equipped and disciplined, gained some important successes under the command of two eminent leaders: young Prince Joseph Poniatowski, nephew to the king, and General Thaddeus Kosciuszko, who had distinguished himself in the American War of Independence. But when Prussia flatly refused to keep her engagements and to uphold the independence of Poland, the king, and with him the majority of the most influential politicians, lost courage. Stanislas Augustus, therefore, put a premature end to all military resistance and, believing in the possibility of reconciliation with Russia, he himself adhered to the Confederation of Targowica.

The results of this capitulation surpassed the worst anticipations. Not only did the Russians enter Warsaw and force the abolition of the work of 3rd May 1791, but Prussia, seeing that the whole of Poland was falling into the hands of Catherine II, suggested a new partition, which she had inaugurated by occupying Poznan. This time Austria took no part in the scheme, but neither had she any intention of opposing it, in her desire of securing Prussian collaboration in her war against Republican France. Russia, who the confederates of Targowica had intended should march against Prussia, quickly came to an understanding with the latter, and, in the beginning of 1793, the agreement between these two Powers were effected. The new frontiers that they drew up between them, purely artificial and almost rectangular, assigned to Prussia the whole of Great Poland and part of Masovia as well as Danzig and Torun, and to Russia all the eastern part of the former Grand Duchy of Lithuania and the rest of the Ukraine, including Podolia and a part of Volhynia. The Republic retained no more than a mutilated fragment, incapable of subsisting as an independent State.

As had been the case after the first partition, a Diet, this time assembled at Grodno, the last Diet of the old Poland, was forced to consent to this new spoliation, a far more grievous one than that which had preceded it. It was in vain. that the parliamentary resistance now showed more energy. The Russian ambassador Sievers broke it by violence, and did not desist until he had obtained the ratification of the treaties of partition, first with Russia, then also with Prussia. But, nevertheless, he obtained nothing beyond a desperate silence which a dishonourable deputy interpreted as a un animous consent.

The honour of Poland was saved by the insurrection of the following year. Prepared since the second half of 1793 by conspiracies in Warsaw and by overtures to revolutionary France, which, however, remained without result, this insurrection found a leader, full of devotion and courage, in the person of Thaddeus Kosciuszko. The conditions in which he undertook his task were by no means favourable. For this reason he put off moving until the moment when the Russians proceeded to the compulsory reduction of the Polish army, prescribed by the Diet of Grodno. The resistance that several generals opposed to this disarmament which was dictated by the enemy put an end to all hesitation. On the 24th March 1794, Kosciuszko swore in the great square of Cracow to fight until the end for the liberty, the integrity, and the independence of his native land. It was assuredly no fault of his that this object was not gained.

It is easy to reproach the insurgents with the fact that their action, undertaken without due consideration, merely hastened the third partition, as the Confederation of Bar had accelerated the first. In any case, Kosciuszko has the high merit of having, for the first time, interested all classes of the population in the national cause. Having at the outset only four thousand soldiers at his disposal, this member of the Polish gentry did not hesitate to make his appeal to the peasants, armed only with their scythes. It is thanks to them that, on the 4th April, he won the battle of Raclawice, and a few days later Warsaw was delivered from the Russian occupation by a popular movement, inspired by the shoemaker Kilinski. Kosciuszko then energetically opposed the excesses of the mob, which was beginning to rise against certain magnates suspected of treason. But, convinced that only the participation of the masses could secure victory to the insurrection, he published, on the 7th May, the Manifesto of Polaniec, which proclaimed the principle of the liberty of the peasant and freed immediately from serfdom those who had taken up arms.

Kosciuszko's insurrection, which had begun at Cracow, rapidly gained all the provinces of the Republic. Wilno, led by General Jasinski, rid itself of the Russians as Warsaw had done, and the war for independence, which had repercussions even in Danzig and Courland, was particularly violent in Great Poland, where, directed by John Henry Dabrowski, the general who afterwards became so famous, it caused grave anxiety to the Prussians.

The Prussians had not failed to enter the war against the insurgents, even though the latter had, at the outset, only fought the Russians. The unexpected appearance of a Prussian army decided Kosciuszko's first defeat at the battle of Szczekociny, and it was the Prussians who took Cracow, subsequently to besiege Warsaw side by side with the Russians. The responsibility for the final defeat of Maciejowice has been much discussed. What is certain is that the insurrection was broken by this disastrous battle, as Kosciuszko, seriously wounded, fell into the hands of the Russians. The horrors of the sack of Praga, a suburb of the capital, where Suvorov's army massacred thousands of its inhabitants, brought about the capitulation of Warsaw itself on 5th November 1794.

The only task left for the victors was to fix among themselves the conditions of the final partition of the Republic. As in 1772, Austria hastened to secure her share without having participated directly in the campaign of 1794. On 3rd January 1795, she made an agreement with Russia, obtaining the territory included between the Pilica and the Bug, the prolongation of Galicia towards the north as far as the centre of Poland. But it was Prussia who once more succeeded in securing the best part for herself, gaining, with Warsaw, the very heart of the former Republic by the treaty of 24th October in the same year. Having concluded the Peace of Basle with France, she had her hands free on the eastern side, and even Russia was obliged to reckon with her. However, Catherine II, as usual, obtained the vastest regions: all that was still left of the former Grand Duchy of Lithuania and of Volhynia.

A month later the last king of Poland, who had not known how to take any firm decision in the tragic hours of 1794, was forced to abdicate at Grodno, and departed to die in Russia. The Prussians, when they left Cracow, which had been allotted to Austria, carried away the royal insignia from the Vavel; and, finally, on 26th January 1797, the three partitioning Powers, believing they had liquidated the Polish question forever, completed their territorial settlement by the reciprocal pledge never to use a title which could recall the existence of a kingdom of Poland. After eight centuries of a history, so often a glorious one, the Poland of the Piasts and the Jagiellos had disappeared, and the experiment of the Royal Republic had finished in utter failure.

Having reached this extraordinary break in the historical
evolution of Poland, we think it incumbent on us to recall
what we have emphasized in our introductory remarks: it
would be an exaggeration, especially in our days after the re-
establishment of Polish independence, to envisage all that
evolution from the standpoint of the Partitions, as if for centuries she had been making her fatal way towards that catastrophe, and as if the continuity of our history had been
broken only to be resumed later under entirely different
forms. It is, however, quite reasonable to seek for an explanation of so exceptional, not to say unique, an event in general history. It is true that even in the history of modern
Europe many States have more than once had to face a partition similar to that of Poland; but all, without excepting
Turkey, who has been particularly threatened with such a
revenge on the part of the Christian world, have escaped
total destruction. Why had Poland alone suffered that cruel
fate, the consequences of which she endured for more than
a century?

In regard to the direct and immediate causes which
brought about the solution of 1795, we have just shown how
dangerous was the course in which Poland involved herself
by allying with Prussia in 1790, what illusions induced her
to lay down her arms prematurely in 1792, and, finally, how
full of risks was the renewal of the struggle in 1794. Yet is it
not a certainty that a contrary decision on Poland's part at
each of these critical moments would have had consequences
fully as deplorable for her? In 1790 Russia assuredly was de-
serving of no greater trust than Prussia; a prolonged resistance in 1792 would only have made the defeat of that same
year a more honourable one; a more prudent attitude in
1794 would only have condemned the Republic to a slower

and more ignominious death. But we have had enough of
hypothetical suggestions. It suffices to state the brutal fact
that nothing could then have saved Poland from two adversaries who were firmly resolved to finish her, and who had
each at their separate disposal forces three or four times
superior to those of Poland, thanks to their military and
financial resources.

But how were these two neighbours of Poland thus enabled to abuse their forces, and why did they turn them only
against Poland? When we come herewith to the essential
causes of the partitions, far more interesting and instructive
than the occurrences of her last moments, the answer to the
first of the two questions that we have set ourselves is a very
easy one. Those partitions which later opinion, even that of
the nations responsible, was to stigmatize, at least, in theory,
as crimes against international morality, were calmly accepted by an epoch in which that morality no longer existed
even in theory, and was perpetually violated with impunity
in practice. Together with the last memories of Christian
solidarity, the conceptions of an international society and of
a common good superior to the individual interest of particular states had completely disappeared. The idea of European equilibrium was incapable of replacing them, and in
the case with which we are dealing this idea did nothing beyond adjusting itself to the advantages which the two chief
enemies of Poland were seeking, and encouraging Austria,
who was less directly interested, to demand an equivalent
compensation.

The future was to prove that even the political equilibrium of Europe was far better ensured by the existence of an
independent Poland. In any case, no one has ever been able
to claim that she had threatened that equilibrium and constituted a danger for her neighbours. On the contrary, those

who have been anxious to cast the responsibility for her fate upon herself have never reproached Poland with being too strong, but, on the contrary, with being too weak, and consequently incapable of maintaining her own life. This reproach would have had some show of reason if the destruction of Poland had immediately followed her decadence in the first half of the eighteenth century. It falls to the ground from the fact that the national rebirth had begun before the first partition, which attempted in vain to stop it, and that it was effected before the other two partitions, which did not allow it time to bear all its fruit. Before she perished the Royal Republic provided the proof that the course of constitutional development which she chose in the sixteenth century could result normally, without passing through the hard school of absolutism or through that of revolutionary upheavals, in a government which was as good as that of other contemporary states. A constitution which enabled Poland to remain for so long a great Power, to traverse subsequently a long period of wars and trouble, and, finally, to remedy by law the abuses which had deformed her, such a constitution could not have caused the fall of the Republic, as has long been asserted.

Rather, it is thanks to her institutions that the State, based on the Jagiellonian traditions, was capable of triumphing over the difficulties which might have resulted from the differences of nationality and religion among its inhabitants. On the eve of the partitions the assimilation of the Grand Duchy of Lithuania with the kingdom of Poland had become so complete, that the Four Years Diet could discard the dualism of the central administration, which no longer corresponded with any actual need. This same Diet pacified, with no disturbance and to the general satisfaction, the question of the religious minorities, artificially magnified by foreign interference at the time of the first partition. The Cossack question, once so serious, no longer presented itself at the time when Poland disappeared, as the principal part of the Ukraine already belonged to Russia, who had suppressed the last remnants of its autonomy. Ethnical individualities, therefore, no longer existed in the Republic except among the peasant population, which counted for nothing from the political viewpoint. This fact may be deplored; but, at the same time, we must bear in mind that the lot of that population was infinitely harder in the empire of the tsars and was scarcely beginning to be improved in Austria and Prussia.

Does it follow that Poland had in no wise contributed to her own ruin, and that the covetousness of her neighbours was alone responsible? We claim nothing of the sort. Without renouncing the constitutional principles peculiar to her, Poland could have secured to herself, within their own military organization and on her vast territory, far more considerable forces, and thus have more efficaciously resisted external dangers, if her citizens, rich in privileges as they were, had shown more devotion to the public cause, and if their spirit of sacrifice had not only shown itself at exceptional moments. A still heavier responsibility than this one of a general nature is the individual responsibility of the leaders of political factions who, from the rebels of the seventeenth century to the inspirers of the Confederation of Targowica, at times went as far as high treason.

In both cases it is a question of moral responsibility, and it is on the moral plane that we must, in fact, consider the problem of the partitions—in regard to the Poles as well as their adversaries—if we wish to understand it fundamentally. From this standpoint even the builders of the renascence in the time of Stanislas Augustus, including the king himself, cannot escape bitter reproach. While they revived Polish culture and reformed Polish institutions, they did not arrest the decay of morals, and they were, for the most part, of too feeble character themselves to regenerate the national character.

The Poles of the eighteenth century could not remedy this situation, because they had no longer the deep religious faith which had animated their ancestors when they tried the great experiment of the Royal Republic and defended the frontiers of Christendom. Hence, Providence sent them a great ordeal which was to purify the national soul and give their sons to behold in the humiliation of expiation a new historic mission, worthy of a great past.

Part IV

THE ORDEAL

20

Napoleonic Poland

Poland is still living
While we are alive.

S UCH was the cry of defiance which on the morrow of the Partitions was proudly flung in the name of the Polish nation to those who had recently brought about the disappearance of the Polish State; it was a simple song of the legionaries, contemporary with the *Marseillaise*, and destined to become our national hymn.

This song of victory was composed in Italy, far from the territory of the old Poland. A heavy oppression was then weighing down that territory, and evoking a profound discouragement and an almost general apathy. Under the Prussian and Austrian rule this oppression was the more dangerous inasmuch as it was at the same time a systematic Germanization. Under Catherine II the violence of the conqueror had made itself felt in a still more brutal manner; but the empress only survived the third partition by a year, and under her son Paul, as under Alexander, who succeeded his assassinated father in 1801, the Poles were treated in a far more conciliatory manner. Prince Adam Czartoryski, nephew of the last King of Poland, who had become one of the tsar's ministers, was, therefore, not only able to make the University of Wilno a more powerful centre than ever of Polish culture, but could even envisage the possibility of a reconstruction of the kingdom of Poland by the Emperor of Russia.

If, however, this ambitious illusion was able, twenty years after the last partition, to become a modest and transitory reality, it is because in that interval the Polish question, scarcely as yet condemned to silence, had again risen before the whole of Europe, thanks to the Napoleonic epic. We use this traditional phrase designedly, because the Napoleonic epoch was for Poland, as for France, a veritable epic. It is easy to contend that the relations, which have been so closely studied, between Napoleon and Poland were, at bottom, a long series of deceptions and misunderstandings from which the Poles often suffered cruelly, and which the emperor regretted at St Helena. It is none the less true that the former Republic, now partitioned, was almost immediately replaced by what we can call Napoleonic Poland, a glorious vision which haunted the enslaved nation, disquieted her masters, covered the timid and ephemeral creation of the Duchy of Warsaw with its splendour, and still set its imprint on the 'kingdom' of 1815.

Thanks to Napoleon, Poland, instead of foundering in oblivion, lived years of true grandeur beyond the tomb; and it is this that the Poles will never forget.

In the midst of the sad symptoms of indifference and servility which unhappily were multiplied in the three mutilated sections of Poland, attempts for liberation were certainly not lacking. But they inevitably took the form of conspiracies, often almost puerile, which could have no chance of success. The most clear-sighted patriots had at once understood that only a general overthrow of the European order, of that artificial order based upon the agreement between the partitioning Powers, could create conditions favourable to the resurrection of Poland. When the moment should arrive this overthrow, opening the way to a new era of history, could only come from the side of France, against whom the enemies of Poland were in coalition, who had been enabled to breathe more freely when their attention was concentrated on the problem of the Partitions, and whose tricolour flag seemed to announce the liberation of all oppressed peoples. Hence the Polish emigrants, who from that time gathered together in Paris, were anxious to interest the Directory in the project of forming 'Polish Legions' in the service of France as the nucleus of an allied army.

It was Bonaparte alone who understood the importance of this idea. During the course of his first Italian campaign, in January 1797, he authorized General Dabrowski, the former collaborator of Kosciuszko, the latter of whom was now maintaining a strict reserve, to form these legions in the service of the Lombard Republic. The Poles who enrolled in them hoped that, marching with Napoleon against Austria, they would soon pass from Italy into Poland and would thus be fighting for their own country. They were profoundly disappointed by the Peace of Campo Formio, concluded some months later, as well as by the Peace of Lunéville in 1801; neither the one nor the other touched upon the Polish question, with the result that there seemed no reason for the existence of the legions. In 1802 the First Consul even sent a detachment of them to San Domingo, where these unfortunate Polish soldiers were compelled to fight against the negroes, and perished *en masse*.

However, these first sacrifices were not entirely sterile. The crushing victories that Napoleon achieved from 1805 to 1807 in central Europe broke in succession the forces of the three Powers which had partitioned Poland. A unique opportunity was thus presented of liberating her, an opportunity of which

Dabrowski made use to launch, in 1806, an appeal for a general insurrection. What was left of his legions could at last go to Poland to constitute there the framework of a national army, and the emperor only seemed to be awaiting its definite formation before proclaiming the independence of Poland. Nevertheless, in spite of the considerable part played by the Poles towards the end of the Prussian campaign, the Peace of Tilsit, on 7th July 1807, again deceived their hopes.

Why was Poland, whose re-establishment they expected, reduced to a small buffer state between Russia and Prussia: a state that only included the territories annexed by Prussia on the occasion of the two last partitions—without Danzig, which was established as a free city—and that received the artificial title of Duchy of Warsaw? The reason is very simple. Napoleon was then anxious to enter into an understanding with Alexander I in order to divide his adversaries, and the Polish question had consequently become a subject of barter between the two emperors. Inevitably the result was a compromise of which the Poles had to pay the price.

Nevertheless, the creation of the new duchy was still a first and very important step towards the restoration of Poland, a part of which, at least, became free and independent. This independence was certainly limited by the fact that the duchy remained entirely subject to the will of Napoleon, who dictated its constitution, eploited it economically, and even employed a part of its army at the other end of Europe in fighting the Spaniards. Also, the organization of the Duchy of Warsaw departed in many respects from Polish traditions, for example, in imposing upon it an administration of a bureaucratic character on the model of France, as well as the Napoleonic code. But taken as a whole the Constitution of 1807, albeit essentially different from that of 1791, repeated certain of its leading ideas in raising the House of Saxony to the throne in the person of Frederick Augustus, grandson of Augustus III, in strengthening the executive power, and in extending the rights of the third estate and of the peasant class. It went much further than the Act of the Third of May in the provisions which limited the jurisdiction of the Diet and the privileges of the nobility, and which ensured, at least, full liberty of their persons to the peasants. And, in spite of the dissatisfaction that this constitution provoked among the conservatives on one hand and the republicans on the other, in spite even of the mistakes committed by the King of Saxony, the ruler of the duchy, the duchy gave proof of an astonishing vitality, even at such a dangerous moment as that of the campaign of 1809.

Attacked by the Austrians, the Duchy of Warsaw not only succeeded in defending itself and in creating a diversion useful to the Napoleonic army, but, in addition, Prince Joseph Poniatowski, at first obliged to abandon the capital to the enemy, soon took a brilliant revenge, occupying the two Galicias with Lwow and Cracow. The Poles could once more hope that the victory of Napoleon, to which they had contributed useful assistance, would bring them decisive advantages. But the Peace of Vienna, 14th October 1809, was one more disappointment. Its eplanation is to be found, as in 1807, in the equivocal role played by Alexander I, on whom Napoleon counted the more this time, inasmuch as the Russians had been at least formally, his allies. They opposed the project of joining to the Duchy of Warsaw all the territories that Austria had taken from Poland at the first and second partitions. She was only obliged to cede to the duchy her acquisitions of 1795, including Cracow, keeping the Galicia of 1772, of which a frontier district was assigned to Russia, as had been the case with a district of Prussian Poland in 1807.

However, the Polish question, which it was attempted to

solve by half measures, remained one of the essential causes
which made the decisive struggle inevitable between the two
monarchs who were then the most powerful in Europe: the
Emperor and the Tsar of Russia. The latter, while preventing a restoration of Poland by his rival, at the same time was
luring the Poles by promises which surpassed those of Napoleon. A few nobles of the former Grand Duchy of Lithuania allowed themselves to be gained over by the prospect
that Alexander I would, first of all, proclaim the re-establishment of that Grand Duchy, would then reunite it to the
Duchy of Warsaw, and become king of a Poland as great as
Poland before the Partitions. But even Prince Adam Czartoryski no longer placed any trust in the tsar's tortuous
policy, and when the latter attempted to win Joseph Poniatowski, that always loyal soldier repulsed what with good
reason seemed to him a treacherous offer, and hastened to
warn Napoleon of the danger which threatened him from the
side of Russia.

Seeing that it was in vain that he was attempting to conciliate that state, the emperor then envisaged new aggrandize-
ments of the Duchy of Warsaw, and, when war with Alexander I at last broke out in 1812, he did not hesitate to call it
his second Polish campaign. On the other hand, he hesitated
in determining in advance what solution he would give to
the Polish question, and even in encouraging an insurrection
which would have been directed against both Austria and
Prussia, then his allies. All that he permitted was the sum-
moning of an extraordinary Diet in Warsaw, a Diet which
proclaimed the re-establishment of Poland within her historical boundaries, and which, following tradition, formed a
'general confederation' of the nation. He refrained, however,
from officially sanctioning this proceeding when he received
the delegates of the confederation at Wilno. Among vague

promises he imposed upon them the condition that they should wait for the former Polish provinces, which were still under the domination of Alexander I, to adopt a similar attitude.

His distrust, to a certain extent justified in respect of a part of the aristocracy of these provinces, was, on the contrary, by no means justified as regards the great majority of the Poles. As Adam Mickiewicz was later to recall in a magnificent evocation of the Napoleonic legend, in all the regions of the former Republic, and more particularly in that historic Lithuania through which the imperial army passed, the beautiful spring of 1812 had inspired not only hope but wellnigh certainty that the tragic episode of the partitions was nearing its end, and that the country, faithful to the spirit of the Four Years Diet and closely associated with the triumph of the emperor, was about to rise again.

Realizing at last the decision of the Great Diet, the Polish army now numbered a hundred thousand men who had distinguished themselves on every battlefield: at the capture of Smolensk as at Borodino, and even at the tragic crossing of the Beresina. Especially the corps commanded by Joseph Poniatowski sacrificed itself unreservedly, although Napoleon had only entrusted a third of the Polish forces to that leader, who had covered himself with glory, while the rest of those forces had been dispersed among the whole of the Grand Army. He placed, on the contrary, too great confidence in his German allies, which, together with the rash advance in the depth of winter into the interior of Russia, against Poniatowski's advice, contributed to the fatal issue of the campaign.

It was fatal, above all, for the Poles. As might have been foreseen, an alliance was soon effected between the Russians, who occupied Warsaw in the beginning of 1813, and the

Prussians and Austrians who had only marched with Napoleon against their will. Napoleon having hastily returned to Paris, the Poles once more found themselves at the mercy of their reunited enemies. Under these conditions it is not surprising that a mass levy of the whole nation should have proved impossible, and that the Government of the Duchy of Warsaw should have sought its chances of salvation by negotiating with Alexander I. The conduct of the Polish army in remaining faithful to the emperor, even in this last extremity, and fighting under his drooping banners to the end, is all the more meritorious. The Napoleonic epic ended for that army on 19th October 1813, when Prince Poniatowski, who had repulsed all Russia's offers and had been named Marshal of France, perished in the waters of the Elster.

Even after Leipzig, many Poles, attached to the person of the vanquished emperor, followed him to the bitter end. But the fate of the nation was to be decided at the famous Congress of Vienna which, meeting in October 1814, interrupted by Napoleon's return from the Isle of Elba and the campaign of Waterloo, ended in the formation of the Holy Alliance on 26th September 1815.

The Polish question was determined there by a series of treaties which bore the date, rich in memories, of 3rd May. The signing of these had been preceded by thorny negotiations. For it was necessary to find a compromise between the interests of the victors and the principles of right and liberty that they proclaimed, between the desire of re-establishing the state of affairs that Napoleon had just overthrown, and the necessity of taking into account the *faits accomplis* which marked his passage. Among these none was more striking than the abolition of the frontiers drawn up by the partitions of Poland, and the creation of a nucleus of a new and independent Poland with an army which, in spite of recent defeats, still represented a considerable force. Alexander intended to profit by this to resume his programme of a Poland restored under his sceptre and closely bound to Russia, and as he was undeniably the master of the hour, the Prussian project of returning to the conceptions of 1795, though for a moment even supported by England and France, had to be abandoned. But as all the members of the congress opposed a solution which, under the form of a reconstitution, more or less fictitious, of an integral Poland, would have increased inordinately the power of the tsar, his original intentions, which had impressed Czartoryski and even Kosciuszko, underwent essential modifications. He became 'King of Poland,' but of a 'kingdom' which did not even include all the former Duchy of Warsaw. Prussia, who had not succeeded in annexing the whole of Saxony, received by way of compensation the 'Grand Duchy of Posen,' while Cracow became a free city.

These dispositions have often been likened to a fourth partition of Poland. She was, in fact, again cut into pieces by artificial frontiers which persisted, except in the region of Cracow, down to the Great War of 1914. This partition even went further than in 1795, because this time Poland was divided into five parts: the little Republic of Cracow, whose independence was only an illusory symbol as it was placed under the protection of its three powerful neighbours; Austrian Poland, officially called the 'Kingdom of Galicia and Lodomeria'; Prussian Poland, comprising the provinces of Poznania and West Prussia; the 'Kingdom of Poland,' attached to Russia by the person of her sovereign and by a common foreign policy; and, finally, the Lithuanian-Ruthenian 'governments' which remained, as after the partitions, an in-

tegral part of the Russian Empire, although Alexander I long
encouraged the hope of the Poles that he would reunite these
provinces to the 'kingdom.'

The essential and durable difference between the solution
of 1815 and that of 1795 lay in the fact that the partitions of
the eighteenth century had been far more favourable to Poland's German neighbours, who had then secured all the
regions that were purely Polish from the ethnical standpoint, while the part assigned, in one way or another, to
Russia was now a preponderant one. This fact was to influence all the Polish policy of the following century, directing our patriotic aspirations in the first place against the
empire of the tsars.

On the other hand, the decisions of the Congress of Vienna
secured two undeniable advantages to Poland. On the morrow of the partitions her enemies had believed that it was
possible to efface the very name of Poland, and to erect insurmountable barriers between her three sections. In 1815,
Russia, Prussia, and Austria each engaged to guarantee to
their Polish subjects the maintenance and development of
their national individuality by institutions proper to the
purpose. At the same time they recognized the economic
unity of Poland's territory prior to 1772, promising to facilitate communications and transit over the whole extent of
that territory.

Although these promises were not observed, yet they constituted an official and international recognition of Poland's
historical and national rights, a very valuable recognition,
which the Poles owed solely to the events of the Napoleonic
epoch. They likewise owed the full autonomy granted to the
'Kingdom of Poland' to those very recent memories. It was
the constitution of the kingdom, promulgated on 27th November 1815, and based upon the Napoleonic constitution of

the Duchy of Warsaw, that was to differentiate her distinctly from Russia. It even developed the latter constitution in a more liberal sense, enlarged the authority of the Diet, and transformed the regional administration in a direction more in conformity with Polish traditions and with the Constitution of 1791. As in the Duchy of Warsaw, all the public offices were reserved to Poles, and it was a Pole—albeit a bad choice—in the person of General Zajaczek, who was nominated as the emperor-king's viceroy.

Under these conditions one part at least of Poland seemed as though, with its own national institutions and army, it could develop freely. Considerable progress was, in fact, soon effected there, notably in the domain of intellectual and economic life. In 1818 a university was opened in Warsaw; the activities of the Society of Sciences, which had existed there since 1800, took new impetus; literature by its extraordinary development recalled the days of Stanislas Augustus, and, under such an eminent minister of public instruction as Stanislas Potocki, the work of the Commission of National Education, interrupted during the years of crisis and of war, was resumed. Another minister, Prince Xavier Lubecki, energetically carried through the task of placing the finances of the kingdom on a sound footing, and assured her economic prosperity, albeit sacrificing the interests of the peasant population.

But even if the Poles had contented themselves with in tense internal labours under the political tutelage of Russia, they would have had likewise to pay another sacrifice, that of their ideas of independence and of national unity. Those men were rare exceptions who, like Lubecki, resigned them selves to seeing the future of Poland lie in the collaboration of one relatively favoured part of the nation with the Russian power that dominated it. And this prospect was becoming in tolerable in proportion as Russian influence penetrated even into the internal life of the kingdom, threatening the constitution, and inflicting humiliations of an ever-increasingly painful description on the national dignity. This began in the first years of the existence of the Congress Kingdom, preparing Polish minds for a new epoch of armed struggles in the name of the same ideas that had inspired Napoleonic Poland.

21

Romantic Poland: The Insurrections

THE Napoleonic wars which had rekindled the hopes of partitioned Poland and the First World War which realized them are separated by the saddest century in the whole of our history. From its sombre background there stand out the unforgettable scenes of the Polish risings. The November Rising—or rather the Polish-Russian war of 1830–1—the Polish participation in the revolutionary movements of 1848, and, finally, the January Rising of 1863, have each their place in the general history of Europe. The conspiracies and plans of action which filled the intervals between these dates are less known, such as notably the tragic attempt at a general insurrection in 1846. And a particularly interesting revelation in the light of recent researches may be found in the vast network of diplomatic overtures which, emanating from the Polish emigration in Paris, endeavoured at that period to interest the whole of Europe in the Polish question, and to remind it without ceasing of the international character of that question.

Of all our insurrections in the nineteenth century the first had, beyond doubt, the best chance of success. Studying its beginnings, which of themselves explain the causes of its failure, we shall at once grasp the character, the strength, and the weaknesses of all the struggles for Polish independence.

With this object we must revert to the conditions under which, after the Congress of Vienna, the 'kingdom' which it had created developed. We have already drawn attention to the positive aspect: the advantages and the possibilities that the solution of 1815 offered to that central part of Poland. Let us now look at the reverse of the medal.

The idea of a Polish-Russian union, upon which this solution was based, had shown itself to be unrealizable even in those epochs when the partitions of Poland, and the part that Russia had played in them, had not yet dug an abyss between the two countries, and when there had still been a certain equilibrium between the strength of both. To the irreconcilable differences of mentality and culture which resulted from a completely divergent historical evolution were now added the bitterness of the conquered and the conqueror's mistrust. The latter enables us to understand why the Polish army was placed under the command of a brother of Alexander I, the Grand Duke Constantine, well known for his brutality and his incalculable caprices, of whom Russia herself wished to be rid. Owing to this same mistrust a commissary of the Russian Government, the too famous Novosiltsov, was imposed upon the Polish Government. While Constantine himself, morganatically married to a Polish lady, ended by becoming attached to Poland and the soldiers over whom he tyrannized, Novosiltsov was the incarnation of all the hostility of the tsarist bureaucracy against the constitutional liberties of the kingdom.

Fearing lest their influence should make itself felt in the eastern provinces of the former Republic, for whose reunion with the kingdom the Poles hoped in vain, Novosiltsov began by persecutions directed against the University of Wilno. It was then that Mickiewicz and his colleagues were deported to Russia.

However, secret societies were also formed in Warsaw, and the severe sentence upon Lukasinski, who had been at the head of this movement, could not stop it. It is true enough that these conspiracies were encouraged by foreign examples, as the absolutist reaction which had followed the Congress of Vienna was exciting analogous movements at the same moment in nearly every country in Europe. The influence of freemasonry is likewise undeniable. But even this took on an essentially patriotic aspect in Poland, and the revolutionary tendencies which were spreading among the youth of the kingdom were in reality but the echo, still clandestine but all the more violent, of the constitutional struggles of which the Diet had from the outset become the arena.

Alexander I, irritated by the liberal opposition which he met there, had already, above all towards the end of his reign, ceased to respect the constitution which he himself had granted to the Poles. Nicholas I, who succeeded him in 1825 with a very decided conception of autocratic power, took up the course of repression with even greater determination. Accusing the Polish opposition of complicity with the Russian revolutionaries, he was indignant when the tribunal of the Diet treated the Poles who had conspired against his rule with indulgence. The war that the tsar declared against Turkey this same year, 1828, as well as the rivalry with Austria which resulted from it, led him for a moment to seek Polish sympathies. But he lost them finally when, in 1830, it was learned in the kingdom that the Polish army was intended to march with the Russians to crush the Revolution of July in France, and to prevent the Belgians from acquiring their independence.

In the face of this odious prospect, and in the intolerable atmosphere that reigned in Warsaw, the insurrection at last broke out there on the night of 29th November 1830. At the outset it was the work of young enthusiasts, in particular the students of the School of Cadets led by the sub-lieutenant Wysocki. Their attack against the residence of the Grand Duke Constantine aroused the enthusiasm of the populace, and at once gained all the elements of the Left. The Moderates, not less patriotic but more prudent, had the merit of controlling this initiative, a spontaneous and generous one but incalculable in its consequences, and of opposing, through all the duration of the rising, the acts of violence which threatened to compromise it. They had, however, too little faith in final victory and too little firm decision at the critical moments.

This reacted, above all, on the military action of the rising. All the army of the kingdom soon rallied to the insurrection, which extended even to the former Grand Duchy of Lithuania and penetrated into Volhynia. This army was not lacking in courage, a courage often reaching heroism, nor in eminent tacticians who elaborated strategic plans of high value. But the execution of these plans was brought up against the weakness of the supreme command, which passed from hand to hand. Chlopicki and Radziwill, Skrzynecki and Krukowiecki—all these generals were, without any doubt, excellent patriots who freely risked their lives, but none of whom knew how to lead his soldiers to victory. The most important battles remained undecided like that of Grochow, or finished in defeats like that of Ostroleka.

But it was not only on the battlefields, made illustrious, moreover, by acts of gallantry which enabled the resistance of the Poles to last ten months, that the fate of the rising was decided. The Diet in Warsaw sat permanently, and political parties disputed both within and without it. This Diet, which unfortunately did not succeed in solving the question of the complete emancipation of the peasant population, showed itself more resolute in dethroning Nicholas I, on 25th January 1831, and thus repulsing projects of compromise, which served no purpose. It placed at the head of the National Government a personality who possessed a unique experience and an indisputable authority in Poland as well as in Europe— Prince Adam Czartoryski. But even this distinguished diplomat was unable to appease the irresponsible extremists inside the country who were banded together in the Patriotic Society, or to gain for insurgent Poland the support, if only diplomatic, of the foreign Powers. It was in vain that the idea of offering the royal crown to an Austrian archduke or to the Duke of Reichstadt was considered; and neither England nor even France moved any more than Austria.

Under these conditions the overwhelming forces at Russia's disposal, which at the end of the war were commanded by Field Marshal Paskevich, inevitably gained the ascendancy. After a defence which again was signalized by fine examples of devotion, Warsaw capitulated, and in the beginning of October 1831 the remains of the Polish army saw themselves compelled to lay down arms.

European opinion, favourable to the vanquished who had fought for the liberty of all nations, did not prevent Nicholas I, while in certain respects saving appearances, from revenging himself upon them. The amnesty, as a matter of course, excluded the leaders of the insurrection and all the emigrants, who lost their property, as well as the inhabitants of the provinces situated beyond the frontiers of the kingdom. It was then that the brutal Russification of the eastern borderlands of the former Republic began, by confiscation of landed estates, deportations to Russia and, above all, to

Siberia, the persecution of the Uniat Church, carried so far
as its total suppression, and, finally, by the closing of Polish
schools, including the University of Wilno. But scarcely less
severe measures were applied to the kingdom itself, where
the University of Warsaw shared the fate of that of Wilno.
Under the deceitful form of a new 'organic statute' the tsar,
in 1832, suppressed the constitution and replaced it by a fictitious autonomy which no longer provided for a Polish Diet
or army. Paskevich, the victor of 1831, rewarded by the title
of Prince of Warsaw, remained for many years the real master
of the country; and a strong citadel, built at the gates of
Warsaw, became, with its filthy dungeons and its cannon
directed against the town, the symbol of the new rule.

During the whole of the epoch which was thus inaugurated,
the eyes of all Poles were turned to Paris, which then became
the centre, not only of Poland's intellectual life, but also of
her national policy, that of the emigrants. These thousands
of emigrants, among whom the flower of a whole nation was
to be found, had, unfortunately, two rival policies. Under
the impression of the defeat, for which the members of the
Right were held responsible, the Radical Left gained the
upper hand, and it was from its Democratic Society that the
initiative of new revolutionary movements soon started.
Wherever similar movements showed themselves in Europe,
Polish emigrants took an active part in all of them, convinced
that the sacred cause of liberty was common to all nations.
But it goes without saying that the emissaries of the emigration laboured, above all, to prepare a new insurrection in
Poland itself. Many among them attempted to resume a conflict with the Russians and, arrested by the latter, were executed in Warsaw or Wilno. However, during the course of
the years which followed the war of 1830–1, it was to be foreseen that the conflict would be waged also against the other

two Powers which had dismembered Poland: Prussia and Austria.

This is explained, not only by Poland's desire of reuniting the whole of the national territory, but also by the fact that the lot reserved to the Poles in those two States was becoming increasingly hard. The Prussian Government, which, on the morrow of the Congress of Vienna, had shown itself more or less conciliatory, changed its attitude after the November rising. In spite of the sympathy that the insurgents found among the German people, the King of Prussia helped Nicholas I to crush them, and then began an active policy of Germanization. At this epoch President Flottwell employed the same methods in Poznania that Bismarck was to apply later, not even shrinking from a conflict with the Catholic clergy. Moreover, the king, like the tsar in 1833, entered into an understanding with the Emperor of Austria to co-ordinate the repressions directed against their Polish subjects, and shortly afterwards they made an agreement to send garrisons of the three Powers into the free city of Cracow. We must not forget that Austria was then governed by that Prince Metternich who inspired the reactionary policy of all the European monarchies, and whose rule of bureaucracy and police aimed also at stifling the national and liberal aspirations of the Poles in Galicia.

In fact, it was in Galicia that in February 1846 the new Polish insurrection at last broke out, which was to have begun simultaneously in the three sections of Poland. Insufficiently prepared, in spite of long years of propaganda, it was prevented at Poznan by the arrest of Mieroslawski and the other leaders of the conspiracy, and nothing could be attempted in Russian Poland. Cracow alone succeeded in liberating itself from foreign occupation, and the insurrection spread from there into the neighbouring regions of Galicia.

The Austrian Government then struck back by a proceeding which, even in the tragic history of partitioned Poland, remains unique in its horror. This time the insurgents, who were all of very advanced democratic leanings, although for the most part of noble birth, had immediately proclaimed complete freedom for the peasants, to whom they promised full possession of their lands. Before their proclamations were sufficiently known, Austrian officials succeeded in persuading the peasants in certain districts of western Galicia that the insurrection, led only by the nobility, was designed to enslave them. They organized well-paid bands who turned upon the nobles and, by means of hideous massacres, helped the Austrian army to stifle the opening of the insurrection in blood. The insurrection, moreover, served Austria as a pretext to annex the Republic of Cracow, in spite of the protests of France and England.

Yet hardly had this last vestige of a free Poland disappeared when a revolutionary movement, more violent than all those which had preceded it, began in Europe; and the Poles believed they could make use of it to resume, with greater chances of success, their struggle for national independence. In 1848, that year full of enthusiasm and of hope, we see them making their appearance wherever the political order from which they suffered so cruelly was shaken. In Prussia they first of all fraternized with the German revolutionaries who, in March 1848, freed Mieroslawski and the other Poles that had been imprisoned for two years. But the hope that the King of Prussia would see himself forced to grant a large autonomy to his Polish provinces was far from realized. In spite of some successes gained by Mieroslawski, the insurrection which had broken out in Poznania and had even gained Pomerania was easily crushed, and the constitution granted to

Prussia brought no change to the situation in that part of Poland.

The role of the Poles was more considerable in the Austrian revolution. Their representatives participated in the Slav Congress assembled at Prague; others fought against the Hapsburgs under the flag of the King of Sardinia. And when the struggles waged in Cracow and Lwow finished with the bombardment of those two towns, the Poles played a large part in the revolt of the Viennese and, above all, in the Hungarian insurrection. The Polish General Bem, after having directed the defence of Vienna against Windischgrätz, distinguished himself, together with many other Poles, in Kossuth's army. Their appearance in Hungary gave Nicholas I an increasingly plausible argument for Russian intervention, and, in fact, it was Paskevich, the governor of the oppressed 'kingdom,' who, in 1849, put an end to the struggle for Hungarian independence. We know that his victory inaugurated a new period of reaction in all the empire of the Hapsburgs, including, of course, Galicia. In the empire of the tsar no serious revolutionary movement had been able to show itself.

The policy of the Polish Left, which had closely linked the fate of the nation with the cause of European democracy, had, therefore, only led to fresh failures. It remained to be seen whether the Right of the Polish emigration would be more fortunate in its projects. From the beginning it had had at its head the leader of the National Government of 1831, Prince Adam Czartoryski, whom the Polish monarchists were pleased to consider the king *de facto,* and who, indeed, had his diplomatic representatives in different European capitals. The Poles of this group, sceptical and reserved in regard to the revolutionary movement, counted more upon a European war which would place the Polish question, supported, as they hoped, by France and England, once more upon the order of the day. These calculations seemed confirmed when in 1854 these two Powers went to war with Russia, and when at the same time Napoleon III revived the imperial legend, basing his policy on the principle of nationalities, always invoked by the Poles.

Moreover, the Crimean War opened all the more favourable prospects to the latter inasmuch as certain of their military leaders, including General Bem, had found a refuge in Turkey. Hence Czartoryski's chief collaborator, General Ladislas Zamoyski, intended to form a new nucleus there of a national army. It was to remove the difficulties which beset this plan that Adam Mickiewicz went himself to Constantinople, where he died in 1855. But it was already easy at that moment to foresee that the Congress of Paris which was to wind up the Crimean War would not so much as touch on the Polish question. In the course of hostilities, the creation of a Polish State, if only within very reduced limits, was considered, notably in England; but the opposition of Prussia and Austria, whom the allies desired to gain over to their cause, soon brought about the abandonment of this idea, of which there could no longer be any question when it was a case of reconciliation with Russia.

Thus the peace of 1856 only perpetuated the tragic situation of Poland, which seemed more desperate than ever when Czartoryski died in Paris in 1861. Even in 1859, when the principle of nationalities had once more come forward, there was no thought of applying it to our territory, where the following year William I and Francis Joseph met the tsar in Warsaw in order to emphasize the complete understanding between the masters of Poland.

However, the tsar who received them was no longer Nicholas I. His son, Alexander II, who had succeeded him in 1855, warned the Poles against any 'dreams,' but showed himself, nevertheless, less uncompromising than his father. The concessions that he was ready to make on points which were, however, secondary ones, encouraged one of our most vigorous politicians, the Marquis Alexander Wielopolski, to make an attempt at collaboration with the tsarist regime. He actually obtained certain appreciable results. The administration of the 'kingdom' again became Polish; the University of Warsaw was opened under the title of 'Principal School'; he himself was placed, in 1862, at the head of the Government. But his programme of autonomy perpetuated the bond with Russia and seemed to abandon definitely all hope of independence. Also Wielopolski remained isolated. Even the Conservative party—the 'Whites'—with their universally respected leader, Count Andrew Zamoyski, were hardly ever at one with the marquis, who has been erroneously termed 'the last Polish noble.' For, in spite of his aristocratic tendencies which prevented him from solving the agrarian question and encouraging the development of the towns, he had broken with the time-honoured traditions of the Polish nobility, enamoured as it was of freedom and at the same time deeply attached to the national idea.

As a matter of course those on the Left, the 'Reds,' were still more hostile to Wielopolski. The patriotic manifestations that they organized and which, since 1861, had produced sanguinary repressions on the side of the Russians, seemed, with good reason, the prelude to a new insurrection. In the course of the year 1862 this party formed itself into a 'National' Government co-existent with that over which Wielopolski presided, and when the marquis attempted to stifle the movement which was preparing, by allowing the young men who were indicated by the police to be enlisted in the Russian army, the rising broke out openly on 22nd January 1863. It had assuredly no chance of success. Nevertheless, this act of despair has left a memory sacred to every Pole. No sacrifice for the national cause had, in fact, ever been so disinterested and of so moving a nature. Never had such large classes of the population rallied to a movement which, unlike that of 1830, did not possess even the skeleton of a regular army. On the other hand, even the 'Whites,' who at heart disapproved of a conflict undertaken under such conditions, adhered to it as proof of their patriotism. And, as always, Lithuania rose simultaneously with ethnographic Poland.

The January Rising, as it is usually called, lasted even longer than the November Rising. The last insurgent was only executed in 1865. But the fate of Poland was in reality decided when France, England, and Austria, for whose intervention she had hoped, contented themselves in June 1863 with sending diplomatic notes to the tsar in favour of the Poles. Again the latter had universal sympathy, notably that of Napoleon III and Pius IX, but no one in Europe contemplated going to war with Russia, who, on the other hand, found unreserved support from Prussia. Hence Russia succeeded without any difficulty in annihilating, in the course of a number of successive encounters, the forces of the insurrection, which were insufficient, scattered, and badly armed. The last Polish 'dictator,' Romuald Traugutt, died on the scaffold on 5th August 1864.

Examining the situation of Poland on the morrow of this new defeat, we could easily reach the general conclusion that all the armed struggles for Polish independence were nothing but a series of gross political mistakes. But if we would judge that policy fairly, a policy genuinely romantic, and difficult of application to practical realities, we are unable to isolate it from the other manifestations of the national life. The conflicts, apparently useless, which were waged by the Poles at the epoch of the insurrections, only show their true meaning when we consider them in their relations with Polish thought of those same years.

22

Romantic Poland: Her Poets

THREE times in the course of Poland's history her culture
has reached a particularly high level, each time participating
in the powerful currents of European thought. Her role was
never limited to that of passively submitting to western influences, nor even to spreading these in eastern Europe. Each
time also Poland's creative activity in the intellectual sphere
was in close relation to her political situation. In the epoch of
the Renaissance, the first expansion of our national culture,
favoured by the heritage of the last Piast and by the triumphs
of the Jagiellonian dynasty, facilitated, in its turn, the creation of the Royal Republic. Under Stanislas Augustus the
parallel between the progress of the intellectual order and
the work of political reform is entirely obvious. There is, on
the other hand, a striking contrast between the desperate
situation of Poland at the time of the insurrections and the
simultaneous development of her spiritual forces. And, what
is more, this third efflorescence of Polish culture is, beyond
all doubt, the most brilliant and most original.

It is true that again it benefited from an intellectual movement common to all Europe, that of Romanticism. In its

beginning, which was purely literary, Polish Romanticism, reacting as elsewhere against the rigidity of Classicism, followed the model of its foreign inspirers fairly faithfully. To understand how it was subsequently transformed it is enough to recall a symbolic scene from one of the best-known works of Adam Mickiewicz. In the dungeon where he had been thrown by the Russians, the hero, in whose personality that of the poet himself is reflected, inscribes on the walls those often quoted words: 'Obiit Gustavus, natus est Conradus.' Gustavus is the unhappy lover, the Polish Werther; Conrad, the persecuted patriot who suffers for millions of brothers.

But the evolution of Polish Romanticism did not stop at this transition from a personal drama, half imaginary and modelled on many others, to the national tragedy which exalted a cruel reality, unique in the world. The Christian name adopted by the transfigured hero is that of Konrad Wallenrod, in whose person Mickiewicz, on the eve of the November Rising, had glorified a pagan and savage patriotism—to-day we should call it nationalism in the derogatory sense of that term—which does not recoil even before treachery should such a means serve its end. What a difference between this primitive conception of patriotism and that which was to be enunciated by the same poet some ten years later! He will revolt no more against the sufferings of his people which once led him to improvise the most violent of blasphemies. He now believes that, like Christ, Poland suffers for the salvation of the world, to redeem the sins of all the nations so that they may become worthy of freedom.

This, it may be said, was another extreme, not less dangerous and erroneous than the first; another aberration of national idolatry. But if we disengage Polish Messianism from the exaggerations that, like Mickiewicz himself, it owes to Towianski's extravagant mysticism, and essential basis re-

mains which may be summed up in two ideas, both of them
alike true and sublime: that of sacrifice in the Christian sense
and that of the solidarity of the nations. And it is from them
that a light which illuminates the whole political history of
the epoch emerges. When Mickiewicz, while an emigrant in
Paris, wrote his *Books of the Polish Nation and of the Polish
Pilgrims* in biblical style, he was only translating into literary
language what the insurgents of 1830 had dimly felt, what
alone could unite the politicians of the emigration, and what
was to prolong the conspiracies and insurrections of the following generation beyond all possibility of success.

What may seem obscure or pathetic in Mickiewicz's Mes-
sianic visions becomes clear for us, as it did for his contemporaries, thanks to the admirable national epic he has given us,
which constitutes a commentary full of calm and simplicity
upon those visions. The twelve cantos of *Pan Tadeusz* have
been compared to those of Homer. Apart from the purely
literary standpoint this comparison, which may seem a very
daring one, is justified by the fact that in this epic, as in the
Iliad or the Odyssey, the historical tradition of a whole people lives again. In Mickiewicz it is the tradition of a relatively
recent past which already seemed legendary; a few scenes
passing from the daily to the heroic life of the Polish nobility,
of a generation which had still known the free and independent Republic, evoked the whole history of that Poland of
other days, of which the emigrants gathered 'on the Paris
pavement' [1] dreamt with a poignant homesickness.

The historic sense had never been wanting in the Poles.
Hence Mickiewicz was sure of being understood in appealing
to such memories. But what was far more rare in Poland,
even in the epochs of her greatness and among the finest

[1] Translator's note: A quotation from verses intended by Mickiewicz as an
introduction to *Pan Tadeusz*.

minds of the nation, was the philosophic sense. The leading ideas of Polish Messianism, as they had been formulated by this most celebrated of our poets, whose name is familiar even to foreigners, required to be gathered together in a Polish system of the philosophy of history. It was Sigismund Krasinski who took upon himself this task.

With him we reach the most sublime summit to which Polish thought had attained through the centuries. His patriotic exaltation certainly idealizes the past of Poland as no historian would dare to do. But he needed this starting-point as the guarantee, the promise that the risen Poland, whose dawn he foresaw, would fully respond to the ideal which he himself carried in his generous heart and in his conscience of a Christian. This Polish count was, it is true, an aristocrat who turned with horror from the scenes of social revolution that he had depicted in an *Undivine Comedy*. But this is because he foresaw, eighty years before Bolshevism, all the future excesses of the revolutionary movement. This patriot has left us the finest imaginable conception of the universal commonwealth; this man of conservative tendencies, like the greatest Poles of the preceding epochs, only sought the harmonious synthesis of the ideals of justice and liberty.

Like the other Polish poets of his time, Krasinski was from his childhood subject to the influences of western Romanticism, German, English, and French. But he was now to turn back to the Roman origins—classical, therefore, in the proper sense—of European civilization. Like other Polish philosophers with whom he collaborated, he was affected by the so-called idealistic philosophy of Hegel and his disciples. But he transformed this idealism in the light of the Christian doctrine to which he ended by submitting unreservedly. In this manner he was able to work the destiny of Poland, as it appeared to him, into the general plan of providence, being profoundly convinced that each individual nation—instrument of the Divine Will—had its own mission to carry out in the harmonious whole of this plan, to the benefit of all the others.

Krasinski, too, saw in his martyred native country the Messiah of the nations. But even the foreign reader will forgive him as he forgives Mickiewicz for this apotheosis, seeing that its actual work was to encourage all Poles to serve the cause of international society, of a lasting peace, based on justice, liberty, and charity. In union with all the Polish Romantics and Messianists, he firmly believed that this cause, which for him signified the advent of the kingdom of God upon earth, would triumph with the resurrection of Poland, inaugurating a new era in the history of humanity.

Krasinski's prose is full of vigour and poetic inspiration. But he himself suffered from the limitations of his talent as a poet. Such limitations were unknown to Julius Slowacki, the third of the great Polish poets of the epoch of the risings. None of our writers has attained to such perfection of language, which was his obedient instrument in expressing the most subtle emotions in melodious verse. He was in rivalry with Mickiewicz and had differences with Krasinski upon their political opinions. But, agreeing with both in regard to the mystical interpretation of Poland's sufferings, he has transmitted this to us in symbols of incomparable artistic beauty, thereby rendering it more accessible and more beloved to those who had not themselves lived through the experiences of his epoch. Slowacki found these symbols in every epoch of our history. It is sufficient to mention two: one placed by the poet's fancy in the shadows of prehistoric Poland; the other shedding an aureole of the purest beauty on the most appalling miseries in contemporary history. In the first he calls upon us to witness the extermination of a whole innocent nation, as though to imagine an example, if only legendary, of a still more cruel fate than that of modern Poland. In the other he has raised an imperishable monument to that other Polish emigration which, instead of disputing on the banks of the Seine, was slowly dying in its Siberian exile. The idea of expiation by guiltless victims has been expressed in no more moving manner than in *Lilla Weneda* and *Anhelli*. And it is, likewise, their author who has best succeeded in grasping the tormented mental outlook of the first insurgents of 1830.

The three men of genius who were the intellectual leaders of romantic Poland were not isolated. Their prestige, which still reacts on the Pole of to-day, was undisputed among their contemporaries. Nor were they isolated as poets, for we see them surrounded and followed by a whole phalanx of writers who shared their ideas and were subject to their influence. Many of these were not wanting in talent. If we do not attempt to enumerate them it is because it is not our intention to write a bibliographical work, but rathei to set in relief the most representative individualities of the epoch. Yet none of those three inspiring writers was exclusively a poet. Hence the activities of each one of them were also united with other manifestations of Polish intellectual life, upon which they all impressed a poetical stamp.

The epic talent of Mickiewicz was also expressed in his work as historian. His masterly course on the history of Slavonic literature, which attracted so much attention when given at the College de France, is well known. But by the side of Michelet's friend we must hasten to mention the writer who was himself the Polish Michelet. Joachim Lelewel was a professor at the University of Wilno when Mickiewicz was studying there. After playing an important part at the time of the war of 1830–1, he too emigrated, and subsequently worked unweariedly in Brussels and Paris. He was a scholar of

the first rank, who interested himself in questions of method
as well as those of bibliography, in historical geography
as well as the sciences auxiliary to the study of history. Nevertheless, this learned scholar, prudent as he was in analysis,
allowed a large share of poetic imagination to enter into his
attempts at synthesis. Democracy was for this inflexible Republican the supreme ideal that Poland had realized in the
beginnings of her history as well as at the most brilliant moments of her evolution. Because she departed from it she
perished. If she would be reborn she must rally unreservedly
to the democratic and liberal movement of the nineteenth
century. All the political programme of the Polish Left thus
found its theoretical justification in this great historian.

Charles Szajnocha, who held the first place after him
among the Polish historians of the Romantic period, and who
only died on the morrow of the rising of 1863–4, did not follow Lelewel and his school either in their political doctrine
or in their frequently arbitrary interpretation of the past.
The works which he devoted to the most diverse periods of
our history have retained their scientific value to our own
days. No one had surpassed him, especially, in his skilful
reconstruction of the great epoch of Jadwiga of Anjou and
Jagiello. But it was not for nothing that he had begun his
career as a poet. Even in his case, scrupulous though he was
in the examination of texts, intuition now and then ran to
imagination. This is precisely the reason why he has exercised
so great an influence on all Poles, in reviving memories so
different from the miseries of the present hour, with a bril-
liancy heightened by the author's poetical enthusiasm.

In the domain of historical sciences, it was a case of resuming a very ancient tradition reaching from Dlugosz to Naruszewicz. Polish philosophy had to be entirely created by the
generation to which Krasinski belonged. This philosophy

was first developed in close contact with the exact sciences, as we see in another professor of the University of Wilno, John Sniadecki, who surpassed his brother Andrew in the extent of his philosophical conceptions. But even those of our philosophers who, like Hoene-Wronski, started from mathematical problems ended in a doctrine which, in spite of all that distinguished it from that of our poets, was, like theirs, a poetical Messianism.

None of them was so closely associated with the work of Krasinski as his friend Augustus Cieszkowski. Under the form of a vast commentary on the Paternoster, he has left us a philosophy of history which entirely corresponds with the ideas of our romantic poets, determining the mission of Poland within the framework of the Christian universe. It is he who has most clearly predicted the institution of a new international order which, in the third and last period of general history, shall realize the Kingdom of God on earth. But what most interests us is that his theory was essentially a philosophy of action. Nothing is a better proof of this fact than the generous projects of social reform which he propagated as the practical consequence of his speculations. And, in spite of certain points on which his ideas swerved from Catholic orthodoxy, he, like Krasinski, contributed to the religious regeneration of Poland.

The names that we have just cited are not unknown abroad, thanks to the works that these historians and philosophers have written in French or German. Moreover, they, like the poets, wrote such beautiful Polish that their work is distinguished from others by its high artistic value. But at this epoch that was so rich in talent the artistic sense of the Poles was not only exercised in literature. It also saw the birth of a style of Polish painting infinitely superior to that of its modest beginnings in the preceding centuries, when the plastic arts in Poland had been a domain restricted chiefly to foreigners. By the side of the poetic images of a Slowacki, so perfect in form, so vivid in colour, pictures came into being which, for the first time, worthily reproduced every patriotic memory and perpetuated the mental emotions of the time.

Julius Kossak, who so perfectly understood the great Poland of the past, opened the way to John Matejko's magnificent historical pictures, the first of which appeared immediately after the January Rising. This insurrection itself was the subject of two series of pictures by Arthur Grottger, the one entitled *Polonia* and the other *Lithuania*. And let us not forget that this remarkable artist, who died young, devoted another series to *War*, to depict all its horrors, and in this way to send forth in the name of his bloodstained country a desperate appeal for peace on earth.

But the most illustrious Polish artist, inseparable from the great poets who were his contemporaries, is a musician who, in truth, belongs to the whole world: Frederic Chopin. Like the painters, he spoke a language understood by all nations. The sounds which he set vibrating, the echo of which is prolonged unceasingly, have evoked, and still evoke, better than the pictures of the painters, better than the most eloquent verses, all the glories and all the sufferings of Poland. The dream of the Romantics which at times seems no longer to affect the more recent generations when it is embodied in words, or even in pictures, appeals to them without a break as long as the Polonaises of Chopin resound in their ears, accompanied by the same immaterial emotions which once brought strength and comfort to the vanquished heroes of our insurrections.

Hence, is it too bold a claim that these insurrections, and with them the whole of Poland's romantic policy, are only comprehensible if, at the same time, we contemplate the romantic Poland of the poets? Like their heroes, the Poland of that most troubled epoch was a symbol for Europe. She represented all the great ideas which were then revolting in vain against an order based exclusively on force. She was admirably qualified to represent that idea of liberty which had been the leading idea of the whole of her history, and the apparent failure of which, even temporarily, was more painful for her than for any other nation. She was no less qualified to represent the idea of nationality: because by the very fact of her existence she bore witness how false and artificial a thing it is to identify the nation with the all-powerful state, since a nation could survive the destruction of her state and utterly refuse to be amalgamated with the victorious nations who dominated her politically. Finally, Poland was qualified to represent the idea of a new international order based on moral principles, not because she herself had been without reproach, as the Messianists claimed, but because she was expiating in the most terrible manner all the faults that she had committed.

This suggests our reply to the question why the insurrections, in spite of all their disastrous consequences, were indispensable to the history of partitioned Poland, and what their significance is in our historical evolution, taken as a whole. They were, with all the sufferings that they engendered, above all, an expiation, more complete than that for which the Partitions stood: because they were the sacrifice, freely consented to, which redeemed a long series of sins of omission, dictated by individual egoism or by an equally culpable class egoism. Finally, they gave proof that the beautiful language of the poets was by no means a matter of empty phrases, but responded to the sincere convictions of the whole nation, which no longer recoiled before the practical consequences of the principles professed by its finest sons.

23

Organic Work

THE last century of Polish history before the Great War is divided into two halves of an entirely different character. The epoch of insurrections and conspiracies in the course of which the boldest hopes alternated with the most profound disillusions, that epoch when the Polish question incessantly reappeared in international politics, was followed by another, dreary and monotonous, broken by no armed conflict, and which seemed to envelop Poland in the shroud of oblivion. Abroad she was spoken of less and less, and even those she counted as her friends no longer believed in the possibility of her resurrection. From the political point of view each of the three parts of the national territory appeared to be living its life apart; and if one happened to be more fortunate than the others, the separation of their destinies was only the more clearly accentuated. Polish culture remained one and indivisible, conscious of its individuality; but the enthusiasm of Romanticism which had caused it to shine with such splendour was entirely at an end, and the new tendencies which guided it were no longer of a nature to distinguish it from those of other nations.

It would, however, be eminently unjust to pass over the results acquired during these fifty years, and to regard them as something resembling lost time. Such an interpretation would not enable us to understand how the reconstitution of Poland was prepared, indeed assured, in the shadow and silence of that epoch. It is generally termed that of organic work: a happy expression which reveals its secret. Two generations, the sons and grandsons of the insurgents, including those who had themselves fought in their first youth, confined themselves to carrying on practical work day by day. This was an expiation worth that of the wars for independence. No one will ever know how much this apparent resignation cost those who consented to it and even preached it to others. And, moreover, we shall see that this new attitude of prudence and loyalty in regard to the Powers which governed Poland did not spare her fresh persecutions.

But this is not all. Independent Poland had often failed in that spirit of patriotic sacrifice which partitioned Poland practised in the epoch of the insurrections. She had, however, failed still more, and during many years, in patience and continuity in systematic work. Her 'Slav unproductiveness' and her small talent for organization could have been made a reproach against her. In this respect, the years 1864 to 1914 were a valuable school which rendered us capable of providing later the immense effort of organization which a reborn State exacted after a disappearance of more than a hundred years.

Finally—and we cannot insist too strongly on this point—the experience of work in common, and respect for every sort of work which was its consequence, consolidated not only the economic bases of the Polish nation, but also, and above all, her social structure. It is not until this epoch of transition that there disappeared, once for all, the watertight compartments which had too long separated the classes: the nobility, composed of landed proprietors who had formerly believed themselves to represent the whole nation; the bourgeoisie, relatively neither numerous nor influential; and finally, the millions of a poor and ignorant peasant population.

We have seen that each insurrection, beginning with that of Kosciuszko, proposed to remedy this state of things. Each of them had a more democratic character than the preceding one. Unhappily, the very fact of their defeat prevented the insurgents from realizing their programme of social justice. And particularly tragic was the fact that the governments which were fighting against them hastened to forestall them on this delicate ground, and to offer concessions to the masses of the population which were aimed at detaching them from the national cause. This is how the peasants of Russian Poland were finally emancipated by Tsar Alexander II on the morrow of the rising of 1863-4 which had promised them the proprietorship of their lands.

However, in the course of the following years an ever closer collaboration was established between all the Poles. The nobility, always very numerous and active, did not cease to play a predominating part, proving that they could work as well as they could fight. But many of their descendants, impoverished by their participation in the risings and subsequently hit by innumerable confiscations, had lost their estates. They formed the nucleus of a middle class that had hitherto been lacking in Poland: the class of the intellectuals, which, little by little, came to comprise the most gifted sons of the Polish people.

In addition, two other phenomena of capital importance accompanied the social transformations of this epoch. On the one hand, owing to the development of industry and the influx of the rural population, an urban proletariat was formed in the towns which, as everywhere in Europe, was radical in its principles, while interesting itself far more than elsewhere in national claims. On the other hand, the rapid democratization of public life, stimulating the national consciousness of the masses, brought forward the ethnical differences in the midst of the population in the eastern borderlands of former Poland. This grave problem, which had first arisen in Galicia in the middle of the nineteenth century under the form of the Ruthenian question, was to prove still more complex in the vast regions of Russian Poland, from Lithuania to the Ukraine.

It was actually in Russian Poland that the slogan of 'Organic Work' was originally launched. It was a natural reaction against the immediate consequences of the last rising. These were even more terrible than those of the defeat of 1831. In the territory of the former Grand Duchy of Lithuania it was no longer a case of chastising only the insurgents and all those who were suspected of connivance with the culprits, but of exterminating the Polish population there and effacing all the traces of its centuries-old influence in those regions. The Governor-General Muraviev, who carried this programme into execution, was given by the Russians themselves the name of 'Hangman.' The Government went so far as to forbid the use of Polish in any and every public place, finally even in the churches, as well as all teaching, even in private, of that language. In the nine Lithuanian-Ruthenian provinces the Poles were forbidden to acquire landed property; what had been confiscated from the families of insurgents passed into the hands of Russian officers or officials.

But this time these severe measures did not stop at the frontiers of the 'Kingdom of Poland.' It goes without saying that all the concessions that Wielopolski had obtained were immediately withdrawn. But the Russianizers, determined to suppress everything that still distinguished that territory from the rest of the empire of the tsars, did not stop there. The ten provinces of the 'kingdom' lost their very name which recalled the old Poland and which was replaced by that of the 'Vistula Provinces.' Their administration was completely assimilated into that of Russia, from which crowds of officials, hostile to everything that was Polish, streamed into the country. War was waged in the heart itself of Poland against the national language, which was styled a mere dialect, and the Russian Government preferred to lower the level of the whole education of the country rather than tolerate a Polish education. Finally, undeterred by a rupture with the Holy See, it attacked the religious life of all Catholics, and ended, in 1874, by suppressing, with the greatest brutality, the Greek Uniat rite which, prohibited for the last forty years in the eastern provinces, still subsisted in the borderlands of the 'kingdom.'

This persecution, the severest that Poland had ever known, enveloped the whole nation in mourning. Faced with the impossibility of any sort of resistance and under the influence of an understandable discouragement, increasing numbers of voices were to be heard recommending a purely realistic policy. Many Poles, especially in the more well-to-do classes, considered that all that was left to them was at least to profit by the possibilities of economic development that its fusion with Russia offered to the former 'kingdom.' This opened an unlimited outlet to Polish industry, which made rapid progress, especially in the entirely modern town of Lodz. The 'Positivists' who broke with the tradition of the risings believed that by enriching themselves individually they were contributing to the welfare of the nation, and in order to secure modest but tangible advantages for it they followed a policy of compromise with the tsarist rule. Even the recrudescence of autocratic oppression under Alexander

III did not turn them from this course, and the more conciliatory methods that Nicholas II seemed to inaugurate confirmed them in their attitude.

Moreover, this was not entirely dictated by the situation in
which Russian Poland was placed. The policy of the Romantics had always been fed on the illusion that the international situation would prove favourable to the Poles provided that they did not cease to struggle for their independence. No one could now delude himself with such hopes,
since the policy of Bismarck and Prussia's victories in 1864,
1866, and 1870–1 had secured a predominating place in Europe for the new German Empire. From that moment
France, upon whom Poland had so long counted, now herself vanquished, sought for a supporter in Russia. And Prussia, who had helped the latter to suppress all the insurrections, was enabled to resume more methodically than ever
her policy of Germanization which was fundamentally, according to the admission of Bismarck himself, a programme
for the extermination of the Poles under Prussia.

As in Russian Poland, German measures of repression
were directed in the first place against the Polish language.
They were first applied in Upper Silesia and West Prussia,
where its disappearance, as was believed, would be effected
more easily than in Poznania. Facts have proved this belief
to be erroneous. In addition, Bismarck profited by the economic crises through which large properties were passing to
bring about the purchase by Germans of the estates of the
Polish nobility. The chancellor, however, made two mistakes.
One was in wounding the religious feelings of the population. His battle with the Catholic Church at the time of the
Kulturkampf naturally took on a particularly acute character in Polish territory. Mgr Ledochowski, Archbishop of
Poznan and Gniezno, who had opposed the introduction of

the German language into religious instruction, was thrown into prison in 1874, and soon other Polish bishops and priests shared his lot. In 1886 a German succeeded him, and Bismarck, having settled his conflict with the Holy See, believed he had triumphed. But it was precisely at that moment that his second mistake was laid bare. He had imagined that only the Polish nobility was opposed to Germanization. But the religious persecutions had turned the whole oppressed nation into a common front. The Polish population of the towns, as well as the peasants in the country, both admirably organized, showed themselves fully as attached to their nationality as the nobility, and even more unyielding than the latter to any idea of compromise.

Bismarck then ordered, in 1885, the expulsion of thousands of Poles who, though long domiciled in Prussian Poland, were originally Russian or Austrian subjects. The following year a fund of a hundred million marks was created, designed to encourage German colonization in the Polish eastern provinces of Prussia. But in thus supporting 'Hakatism'—as German nationalism was subsequently called after the initials of its leaders—the chancellor only exasperated the antagonism between the two nations, and gradually the Poles began to realize that the Germans were fully as great a menace as the Russians, against whom the principal insurrections had been directed.

The Polish policy in Prussia remained, notwithstanding, a policy of 'organic work,' as that of the Russian Poles had become. No one dreamt of an insurrection, and the most ardent patriots, such as, for example, Father Wawrzyniak, who for some forty years directed the co-operative movement in Poznania, devoted themselves entirely to the economic and social organization of their people, remaining within legal limits. Thanks to them, the Poles under Prussian domination, hardworking and prolific, increasingly conscious of their nationality, were able to resist all the government measures as well as the efforts of the powerful German Association of the Eastern Marches, founded in 1894. Yet the danger grew, for the era of the concessions, very modest as these were, which had followed Bismarck's fall, had not lasted, and it was towards the end of the nineteenth century that the sharpest repressions of the 'Polish-speaking Prussians' began.

This makes the study of the wholly different conditions under which the system of 'organic work' was developed in the third part of Polish territory, Galicia, all the more interesting. As long as the regime of centralizing absolutism was prolonged in Austria, the lot of the Poles there had been in no way less hard than in Prussia or in Russia. However, the defeats which shook the Austria of this reactionary epoch, first in 1859, then in 1866, drove her to seek a new orientation of her policy. After the first of these critical dates the Emperor Francis Joseph, entering the way of reform, appealed to a Pole, nominating Count Agenor Goluchowski Minister of the Interior. His plan of transforming the monarchy of the Hapsburgs into a federated state soon collapsed; but, nevertheless, it was this statesman who inaugurated a new epoch in the history of Galicia, of which he became governor in 1866, on the morrow of Sadowa.

It is true that the constitution adopted the following year by the Austrian Parliament did not realize the hopes of the Poles, nor those of the other Slav nationalities of the empire. Nevertheless, it granted a fairly large autonomy to all the 'countries of the Crown,' of which Galicia was the most extensive. Thus from that moment the latter seems to have become a real 'Piedmont' for the Polish nation, which henceforth was able to develop freely there. While sending her deputies to the central parliament, where they formed a numerous and powerful party, Galicia now had her provincial Diet at Lwow, a local Polish administration, and a vast network of schools, where the teaching was in Polish.

This state of things lasted until the Great War, so that during that half-century the Poles, everywhere else reduced to an absolutely passive political role, in Galicia were able to carry out definite work, not only in the economic and social sphere, but also in public life. Several of them were able to exercise their talents by occupying the highest posts in the central government of the monarchy. We need only mention Agenor Goluchowski's son, well known as Minister of Foreign Affairs for Austria-Hungary. Other Poles have ranked among the best ministers of finance. Moreover, within the limits of the 'Kingdom of Galicia and Lodomeria,' they were able through all those years to govern themselves, enjoying a liberty which was doubly precious at an epoch when Russia and Prussia were implacably persecuting their compatriots.

In certain respects the part that Galicia played on the morrow of the insurrections resembles that of the Congress Kingdom on the eve of those armed struggles. Like that kingdom, she was closely bound to one of the partitioning Powers, but to a Power with a constitutional rule, and which did not represent a homogeneous nation opposed to the Poles. True, the Germans constituted a relative majority among the nationalities of ancient Austria, and occupied a privileged position at the court of the Hapsburgs, in the army, and in the central administration. But in the midst of their incessant rivalries with the other nationalities, they were obliged to reckon seriously with the Poles, who, after the Germans and Magyars of Hungary, were undeniably the most influential. This influence was not strong enough to turn all the external policy of the monarchy in a direction favourable to Poland, nor even to prevent its alliance becoming ever closer with Germany. It was, therefore, impossible to take Galicia as the starting-point from which to liberate the other parts of Poland. Yet for these the Galicia of the constitutional epoch was a rallying centre, to which their souls turned, as in old days to the Paris emigration.

Its attraction was chiefly manifest in the intellectual sphere. The two Galician universities—the very ancient one of Cracow, by the side of which an Academy of Sciences and Arts was founded in 1872, and that of Lwow, dating from the reign of John Casimir, but entirely reorganized—had become Polish once more, at the time when the University of Warsaw was entirely Russianized. They soon became the most important centres of the national culture, where the flower of the whole of Poland's youth came to study. All their faculties were filled by scholars of the highest order. In their faculties of law many Polish officials were trained by the side of eminent theorists as well as politicians, summoned to direct a part, at least, of the partitioned nation. But its most interesting activity, from the point of view with which we are concerned here, is its development of historical science.

In this department, a special one, but typical of the evolution of ideas, a group of scholars who might be called the school of Lwow, and of whom Xavier Liske was the most remarkable, perfected, above all, the method of research, eliminating all political or philosophical view-points. The school of Cracow greatly contributed, on its side, in establishing the documentary bases of the national history; but it is still more famous for the conception which it gave of that history. This conception, held by all its representatives, such as Joseph Szujski and Stanislas Smolka, was conservative, carefully thought out, far removed from that of Lelewel and the Messianists. In certain of its writers, notably Michael

Bobrzynski, both historian and politician, the reaction against the poetical idealization of the past led to extremely severe criticism, levelled chiefly against the institutions of the former Republic.

This historical conception was in strict conformity with the whole political doctrine which inspired the men who had created the new government of Galicia and held power in it. This doctrine had been formulated in 1869 in the famous *Stanczyk Portfolio*, a symbolical name recalling a court fool of Sigismund I. Condemning the revolutionary policy of the insurrections its authors recommended the Poles to work within the sphere of legality, and put them on their guard against all dangerous illusions. Their ideas, carried to extremes, would themselves have been dangerous if they had been taken literally in every part of Poland. In the special conditions which then obtained in Austrian Poland they rendered undeniable services. This they were able to do because, contrary to appearances, the representatives of these highly prudent ideas were far from renouncing the supreme ideal of national independence. It was only the means of attaining it that they debated. This was authoritatively stated by the eminent historian of Polish literature, Stanislas Tarnowski, who was Rector of the Jagiellonian University[1] when it celebrated its five-hundredth anniversary in 1900, and who has devoted very fine pages to our Romantic poets.

But the moment was approaching at the beginning of the twentieth century when the programme of organic work in Galicia, as elsewhere, was no longer sufficient.

[1] Translator's note: The University of Cracow, so called from its renovation under Ladislas Jagiello.

24

Waiting for Freedom

Like the Romantic epoch, that of 'organic work' had its literature. Despite all the Positivist tendencies which dominated it it was not lacking in poets of even high inspiration. We must, at least, mention that woman of exquisite feeling, Maria Konopnicka, and draw attention to, besides her lyrical poems, a new Polish epic which we owe to her, and which glorifies, not the doughty deeds of a noble of historical Poland, but the Odyssey of a poor contemporary peasant emigrant in Brazil. The literary form which best suited the realist epoch was, however, beyond dispute the novel. Since J. I. Kraszewski wrote his innumerable volumes, unequal in merit, devoted either to the national history since its beginning, or to the problems of the hour, the Polish novel had secured an important place for itself in our intellectual life. Two novelists of the highest order made their appearance shortly after Kraszewski: Eliza Orzeszkowa and Boleslas Prus. They were not interested in a distant past and, writing under the Russian censorship, they could not mention the risings except in the form of veiled allusions. But both knew how to invest with all their patriotic significance the demands of organic work; and, true educators of their generation, they guided it to a social progress which was inspired by a very high conception of duty.

It was in this atmosphere that Henryk Sienkiewicz opened his career. This able young follower of Positivism was, however, soon transformed into a true leader of the nation which was aspiring to a better future. From the end of the nineteenth century until the Great War he played a part in Poland that can only be compared to that of Mickiewicz in the Romantic epoch, and, like that poet, the most illustrious of our prose writers became one of the glories of European literature. Like our Romantics he owes his reputation to the universal character of the problems which he has treated. To the tormented soul of the world 'without dogma' [1] of his contemporaries, which he analysed as a penetrating psychologist, Sienkiewicz opposed the faith of the first Christians who, amidst the decadence of the ancient world, found, even at the price of martyrdom, the reply to the eternal question: 'Quo vadis?' Also like our Romantic poets this writer, possessed of an epic talent, was passionately enamoured of Poland's past; but he no longer searched as they did for a mystic explanation of our sufferings, he set himself to find in history that 'strengthening of hearts,' the need of which his generation was experiencing. Therefore, instead of again exalting the persecuted Poland of the nineteenth century, he evoked the heroic Poland of the seventeenth century, then, going still farther back, the triumphant Poland of the fifteenth century. The Trilogy which showed how that Poland of the past, devastated 'with fire and sword,' [2] emerged from 'the deluge'

---

[1] Translator's note: *Without Dogma* is one of Sienkiewicz's few novels of contemporary manners.

[2] Translator's note: The three parts of the Trilogy bear the titles *With Fire and Sword, The Deluge, Pan Wolodyjowski,* the last being the name of the 'little knight' who is its hero.

thanks to 'little knights' without fear and without reproach: those bulky volumes which enraptured thousands of readers mark a turning-point in Polish thought, which passed from resignation to an optimism full of faith in the destiny of the nation. And in recalling the defeat inflicted at the beginning of the fifteenth century upon the Knights of the Cross, Sienkiewicz, who at the beginning of the twentieth century denounced to the world the tragedy of the Polish children in the Prussian school, seemed to foresee an approaching great war the end of which unfortunately he did not live to see.

Happier than he, inasmuch as they died in a free Poland, two other great novelists, Ladislas Reymont and Stephen Zeromski, were apparently more interested in problems of another order: one followed the daily life of the peasant through the four seasons of the year, the other dwelt upon all the miseries of modern life. But both alike formed the link between the preoccupations of the Pole of to-day and the memories of the Pole of the risings, without ever despairing of the new Poland which was soon to be reborn from the 'ashes.' [1]

The young Poles who admired these novelists were also enthusiastic over their poets, more numerous than ever, who seemed to announce a new Romanticism. This Romanticism was less exclusively patriotic than the former one; but its representative, whose glory proved the most enduring, and who was only fully understood after his death by a Poland risen from the dead, in his turn desired, like the Romantics of the past, to solve the enigma of Poland's fate. Only, if Stanislas Wyspianski turned like these to the tombs, to those of our medieval kings as well as to those of our insurgents of yesterday, it was to protest against their hold upon the living, to bring deliverance from the melancholy which had too long

[1] Translator's note: The title of Zeromski's greatest novel.

emanated from the past, and to show in moving symbols that the union of all the classes of the nation must now keep watch until the moment when the long-awaited moment of its liberation should strike.

Wyspianski's heroes speak to us not only from the stage of his dramas, but also in the stained-glass windows that his genius as a painter conceived. They alone would be enough to characterize the new forms that Polish art adopted on the eve of the Great War. But again, as in the Romantic epoch, it is thanks to an outstanding musician, Ignacy Paderewski, that that art which was expressive of so many hopes made the round of the world as though to prepare it for a better understanding of the 'great thing' for which his country stood, which was Freedom. Ready to resume its place among free peoples, the nation found a fresh stimulus in the activity of that generous patriot.

After this brief summary of Poland's state of mind on the threshold of the twentieth century it is time to ask ourselves what justified that very obvious expectation of approaching liberation. With the sensitiveness engendered by suffering the Poles knew better than all others that an armed peace, that peace without justice which the waning nineteenth century wished to perpetuate, could last no longer. What they were awaiting, without intending to provoke it themselves as their fathers had attempted to do, was a political upheaval which would shake the power of their masters. The first of the kind came in 1904 from the Far East.

The Japanese victories proved for the first time the artificial nature of the power of the tsarist empire which held the greater part of Poland under its domination. The revolution which then broke out in Russia was of an essentially social character. But, in any case, this movement, which aroused separatist aspirations among all the nationalities of the empire, seemed to offer a unique opportunity of liberating Russian Poland by a new insurrection, undertaken under far more favourable conditions than any of the preceding risings.

The Polish nation, however, was not prepared for this. The extreme Left fraternized with the Russian revolutionaries, whose methods and doctrinaire internationalism were repugnant to the moderates. Both parties were disposed to content themselves with a programme of autonomy without breaking the link with Russia. Under these conditions it was the undeniable merit of the national wing of Polish Social ism, directed by Joseph Pilsudski, that it clearly proclaimed the principle of independence and fought for it as far as was possible from the outset.

The opposing forces were, however, too unequal. Tsarism, which at first attempted to appease the rebels by concessions proclaimed by the Constitution of October 1905, ended, finally, by crushing all opposition, and, even under the quasiparliamentary government that the Duma of the following year inaugurated, the Polish claims received no satisfaction.

The party of the National Democrats which formulated them also aspired from its beginning to the independence of Poland. But, together with its leader, Roman Dmowski, it considered that the chief obstacle to the realization of this idea, and at the same time the greatest danger of the hour, came from the side of Germany, who held an essential part of Polish ethnographical territory, and who was encouraging the uncompromising attitude of tsarist Russia. What confirmed many Poles in this attitude was the Prussian law of 1908 which authorized the Government to expropriate the Polish landed proprietors. By this Act, contrary to the Prussian Constitution, the Germany of William II and the Chancellor Bulow showed itself still more hostile to the Poles than that of William I and Bismarck. In addition, the use of the Polish language at public meetings was prohibited.

Those who then declared for a compromise with Russia

were also inspired by the sentiment of Slav solidarity against Germanism. In this same year, 1908, Austria-Hungary proceeded to annex Bosnia, provoking lively resentment among the southern Slavs, notably in Serbia, where the nation was counting increasingly on Russia's support. The latter now resumed her old Panslavist programme under a new form, affecting to be willing to respect the independence of the other Slav nations; and hence this 'neo-Slavism' attracted not only the Czechs but also many Poles.

However, a fresh disappointment awaited them. It was precisely at that time that in Russia also repressions began again, more severe than ever. Far from granting any sort of autonomy to the former 'kingdom,' the tsarist Government decided to mutilate it by modifying its frontiers that had been fixed in the past by the Congress of Vienna. It began, in 1909, by creating within these boundaries a new province, the Government of Chelm, and declaring that it was inhabited by members of the Russian Orthodox Church—in reality the Ruthenians, forced to abandon the Greek Uniat Church, formed only a minority there—in 1912 detached it from the 'kingdom' to place it under the Governor-General of Kiev. Accompanied by other rigorous measures which then struck at the Poles, this action, which seemed to be the prelude to a new partition, discouraged even those who had, in the light of the grave events which were preparing in Europe, believed a Polish-Russian reconciliation to be possible.

For it was precisely in 1912 that the war which had been on the point of breaking out on the annexation of Bosnia really began, even though still localized in the Balkans. The war, or rather the two Balkan wars, were a clearer warning than all the preceding crises. The antagonism which was manifested between, on one side, Russia, traditional protectress of the Slav and Orthodox populations of the Near East,

and on the other side Germany and Austria-Hungary, favourable to the Ottoman Empire, rendered a general conflagra-
tion imminent. It was the more so inasmuch as Russia, since
1894 allied with France, had, like the latter, entered into an
understanding with England, so that from 1907 this 'triple
entente' confronted the 'triple alliance' which, since 1882,
had ensured hegemony in Europe to Germany and facilitated her world expansion.

From the point of view of Polish history the immediate
causes of the catastrophe of 1914 matter little, because among
these highly complex causes the Polish question, which had
seemingly disappeared from the international horizon, held
no sort of place. But what concerned all Poles was the fact
that it was precisely those three Powers that had partitioned
their country which were now the most directly engaged in
the conflict that was preparing. And as those Powers were
ranged in two opposite camps it was easy to foresee that from
the outset of the war, which would have to develop on Polish
territory, the Polish question would inevitably come forward,
exploited by each of the belligerent parties to the detriment
of the other.

The rupture of friendship between Russia and Prussia,
which from the epoch of the Partitions had always been fatal
to Poland, therefore opened to the latter the possibility of
her restoration: a possibility only, because, on the other hand,
the fact that there was an inflexible enemy of Poland in each
of the two camps made the situation very delicate for a nation which, in these conditions, could not unreservedly identify itself with one party or the other, and had serious reason
to dread the complete victory of either.

To this difficulty another was added. The ordeal of the
nineteenth century had, by the sufferings of the insurrections
and the experiences of 'organic work,' undoubtedly prepared

the Poles for the reconstitution of their state. And during all this time nothing had been able to break the unity of our nation whose culture had developed in spite of every obstacle, or the continuity of our historical tradition which had become the patrimony of the whole nation. Poland, however, could reappear under two different forms. The reparation of the acts of violence represented by the Partitions required fundamentally the reconstitution pure and simple of the historic Poland of 1772. But the awakening of nationalities that had come into being since then suggested another solution.

On the one hand, Polish populations which had not formed part of the Republic of 1772, the Poles of Silesia in the first place, and to a certain extent those of East Prussia, had become conscious of their origin, and aspired to be reunited with their brothers in race. On the other hand, in the eastern part of the former Republic this same principle of nationality turned against the Poles. We have alluded to this in speaking of the social transformations in the second half of the nineteenth century. From the moment when the map of Europe was bound to change this problem assumed an exceedingly serious political aspect. The Ruthenians, who, in order to be more clearly distinguished from the Russians, had adopted the name of Ukrainians, had fully developed their nationality in eastern Galicia, being, in many respects, encouraged in their growing rivalry with the Poles by the Austrian Government. Their national rebirth had also progressed in the far vaster regions that they inhabited in the empire of the tsars, which in vain disputed the very existence of their nationality. Unfortunately, even in this territory, the common antagonism against Russia had not been able to create a good understanding between the Poles and Ruthenians. Without dilating on the reasons, in great part of a social character, which had impeded it, it is enough to point

out that a similar phenomenon had made its appearance in
the territory of the former Grand Duchy of Lithuania. On
the eve of the war a clearly marked national movement had
already developed among the Lithuanians, who had retained
their ethnical individuality, and a similar movement had set
in even among the White Ruthenians. The latter at present
had no very distinct political physiognomy, but that of the
Lithuanians, while defending itself against the repressions of
the Government, also entered into conflict with the Poles of
those regions, victims of the same persecutions.

The idea of the Jagiellonian union which had been the
basis of our history from the fourteenth century to the Partitions, and the traditions of which had given proof of its vitality, even at the time of the insurrections, thus emerged from
the crisis of the nineteenth century rudely shaken. Hence it
became increasingly doubtful whether the Poland whose liberation was anticipated would be an exact counterpart of
historical Poland. Some considered that while abandoning
none of her ancient territory, and merely adapting her traditions to modern exigencies, it would be enough to give
restored Poland a federal structure. Others preferred to pro-
nounce in favour of an ethnographical Poland, extending
farther to the west and less far to the east than the former
Poland.

Naturally, this ever increasingly discussed problem could
not be determined until the moment came for fixing the
frontiers and the constitution of the new Poland. In the
meanwhile, the most important matter was to solve the fundamental problem of liberation. In spite of all the hesitations justified by the international situation as it presented
itself on the eve of the war, and in spite of the uncertainty as
to which territories would form part of reconstituted Poland,
one thing was certain. The Polish nation could not remain

passive while its fate was being decided on the battlefields of all Europe and in the chancelleries of the great Powers, compelled to reopen the records of the Polish question.

Consequently, the whole nation was agreed upon the necessity of a vast and intense Polish propaganda. Those who most firmly believed that the day of final and full liberation was approaching chose to go farther. During the years which preceded the war that they knew to be inevitable they organized the nucleus of a Polish armed force, military formations reminiscent of those of our insurrections and ready to move as soon as hostilities should begin. This was the work of Joseph Pilsudski and his collaborators.

Given the position in which the three parts of Poland were situated it was evident that this preparatory work could be accomplished on the territory of only one of those parts: Galicia. Hence it was there that in 1914 the new struggle for independence started, to be carried on by every means, until the moment when the voice of Poland made itself heard by the western Powers, her natural allies, when, as under Napoleon, the flag with the white eagle floated by the side of the tricolour, advancing towards the goal of a peace that stood for freedom.

While awaiting that moment millions of Poles were forced to fight and take each other's lives under enemy flags. But they remained convinced that, contrary to all human previsions, they were all dying for one only Poland, and

> That she, never destroyed,
> Would be reborn from their blood.

Part V

NEW POLAND'S TRAGEDY

25

Resurrection

THE resurrection of the Republic, after more than a hundred years of political non-existence, has been the first act of the still unfinished drama which contemporary Poland is living through in the full consciousness of its historical significance and with unshaken faith in its successful solution. This resurrection was effected in three stages: first, the successive defeat in the war of 1914–18 of all the partitioning Powers; second, the decisions of the Peace Conference in 1919; third, the complete establishment of the boundaries of the renewed Polish State, which dragged on until 1923.

When the first World War began, the Polish question, which, as has been pointed out previously, had in no way been instrumental to the breaking out of that war, at once assumed an actual importance. The prospects, however, of that question being resolved in accordance with the claims of the Polish nation to complete independence were not at all promising. It is true that the combatants on either side endeavoured from the outset to conciliate the Poles. Russia, however, who until the fall of tsardom had persisted in treating the Polish cause as an internal question of her own, in the proclamation of her Commander-in-Chief, the Grand Duke Nicholas, of 14th August 1914, only promised autonomy to the Polish territories which were to be united under the sceptre of the tsar; while from the side of the central Powers, among which Germany, who was as opposed as Russia to the real restoration of Poland, had the deciding vote, there only emerged some Austrian promises of a still more general nature.

This alone was certain: that a decisive and long-anticipated change in the lot of Poland would finally ensue, and that in her terrible devastation—as one of the chief theatres of the war—the blood of the unknown Polish soldier, mobilized by the usurpers to a number considerably exceeding three million, would be copiously shed.

At the same time, however, the value and the significance were now made manifest of those preparations for an active share in the threatened war which, as we have seen, had already begun a few years before in the part of the country under Austrian rule.

It is true that in consequence of the diversity of opinion regarding the orientation of Polish policy, unavoidable in the actual situation, Polish volunteer formations appeared on both sides. But in spite of the general sympathy in Poland for the western Powers, France and England, the only real bearing on the situation in the first and longest stage of the war was effected by the Legions which, setting out from Cracow on 6th August under the leadership of Joseph Pilsudski, in the spirit of the never-forgotten traditions of the insurrections began a struggle against Russia, who held in her hands the greater part of the Polish territories.

The heroic share of the legionaries in the campaign, which lasted about two years and drove the Russians almost entirely out of these territories, did not in the least imply solidarity

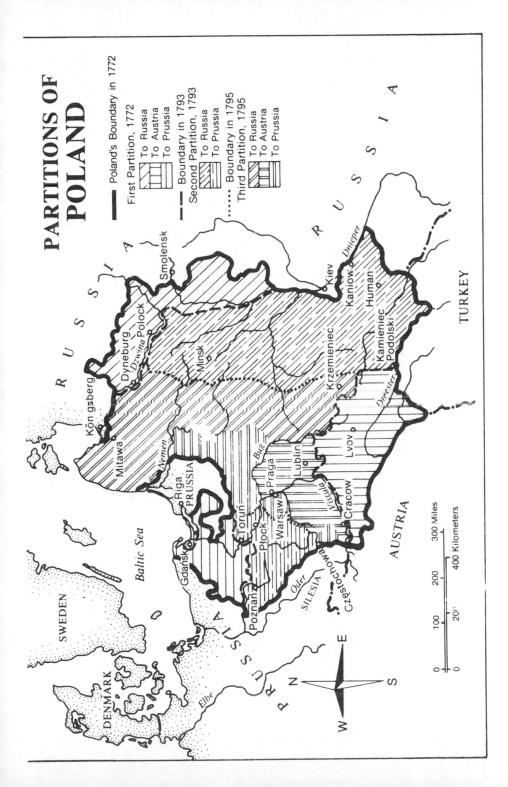

PARTITIONS OF POLAND

Poland's Boundary in 1772

First Partition, 1772
To Russia
To Austria
To Prussia

Boundary in 1793
Second Partition, 1793
To Russia
To Prussia

Boundary in 1795
Third Partition, 1795
To Russia
To Austria
To Prussia

SWEDEN

DENMARK

Baltic Sea

RUSSIA

Königsberg

Mitawa

Riga

Nemen

PRUSSIA

Gdansk

Toruń

Płock

Poznań

Warsaw

Praga

SILESIA

Oder

Elbe

Częstochowa

Vistula

Cracow

Lublin

Bug

Wilno

Minsk

Dynaburg Połock

Dzwina

Smolensk

Kiev

Dnieper

Kaniow

Human

Krzemieniec

Kamieniec Podolski

Dniester

Lvov

AUSTRIA

TURKEY

P R U S S I A

R U S S I A

N
W   E
S

0   100   200   300 Miles

0   200   400 Kilometers

with Austrian, still less with German, policy; Germany and
Austria were not, moreover, in agreement with each other regarding the Polish question and yielded to continual vacilla-
tions. In Galicia, which had been occupied only for a short
time by the Russians nearly as far as Cracow, the Supreme
National Committee, counting on the favourable disposition
of Austria, continued to function; the Congress Kingdom,
however, after the whole of it had been captured by the central Powers, was arbitrarily divided into two occupations,
Austrian and German, the latter of which especially ill-
treated the population, if only by the economic exploitation
of the devastated country.

In their desire to gain, not only the Legions, whose command Pilsudski resigned in September 1916, having failed to
obtain for them an independent standing, but also a Polish
armed force, still more dependent on Germany, by means of
a systematic recruiting in the kingdom, both empires finally
decided to proclaim the restoration of Poland's independence.
But an act to this effect, which was published on 5th November 1916, began by announcing that that State, independent
in appearance only, was to remain in close union with Germany and Austria, especially in military matters, while the
question of the boundaries of the State was left in suspense. It
was clear that those boundaries were not even to include Galicia, since that province was simultaneously granted only a
greater autonomy than hitherto within the structure of the
Hapsburg monarchy; while the German military and political circles were projecting serious mutilations of the kingdom
itself to the profit of the Reich. Thus the proclamation of
November, although not devoid of significance in regard to
the international development of the Polish question, and
enabling the so-called 'activist' element gradually to build up
a Polish state organization even while still under the occupy-

ing Powers, could in no wise satisfy the aspirations of the
Polish nation, and did not give any of the results anticipated
by the Germans in the sphere of military advantages.

On the contrary, an ever greater role was being played in
that sphere by the secret 'Polish Military Organization,' directed against all the usurpers, while the great majority of
the legionaries finally refused the new military oath, aimed at
incorporating them entirely within the German army. This
resulted in severe repressions, and even the imprisonment of
Pilsudski himself in July 1917 in the fortress of Magdeburg.
But by then the great revolutionary upheaval in Russia was
already taking place; the upheaval, which was entirely to
transform the international situation, and, therefore, to
change fundamentally the decisive factors of the Polish question.

The first March revolution in Russia had already freed the
hands of the western allies in this respect, since a new Liberal
Government had acknowledged, in the manifesto of 30th
March, the right of the Polish nation to be an independent
state, only stipulating a 'free military union' between that
new Poland and Russia. This facilitated the diplomatic action of those Polish politicians who, under the leadership of
Roman Dmowski, had for some time previously been so-
journing in the west. In June it was possible to form the
nucleus of a Polish army in France, and in August the Polish
National Committee in Paris, with Dmowski as its president
and with its representatives in London and Rome; while in
the United States Ignacy Paderewski was acting with notably
successful results in the name of the committee. Moreover,
he had already previously influenced President Wilson's declaration in his appeal of 22nd January for the creation of a
united and independent Polish State.

It is true that in the autumn of that same year (1917) the

Bolshevik revolution did great harm to the eastern borderlands of Poland; but, on the other hand, it led to a complete
reversal of alliances. The Soviet Government, not only proclaiming the right of the non-Russian nations to a complete
separation from Russia, but at the same time aiming at an
immediate conclusion of peace, opened negotiations at the
end of the year with the central Powers at Brest-Litovsk.
Those Powers, although they found themselves compelled to
make further concessions to the Poles owing to the development of events, and in October even established a Regency
Council in Warsaw composed of three eminent representatives of the nation, did not admit Poland to a share in the
peace negotiations; moreover, in the first treaty concluded,
on 9th February 1918, with the Ukraine, they included in its
western boundaries the Polish territory of Chelm, and even
secretly promised it a share of Galicia. The final treaty with
the Soviets, on the 3rd March, undertook to maintain German hegemony over the whole of the territories yielded by
Russia.

However, the place of Russia in the coalition was now
taken by the United States; a change the more profitable for
Poland inasmuch as in his famous fourteen points of 8th
January 1918, Wilson devoted the thirteenth to the necessity of creating an independent Polish state, which would embrace all 'the territories inhabited by indisputably Polish
populations' and have 'a free and secure access to the sea.'

The realization of the Polish aims now only needed the
victory of the allies over the Germans. In the months which
assured that victory far-reaching decrees confirming the independence of Poland followed each other in quick succession.
From the 3rd of June Poland was recognized by all the allied
Powers as 'an allied belligerent nation,' and the participation
in the last battles on the western front by a Polish army

under the leadership of General Joseph Haller found a response and a support in the resolute attitude of the whole
country. In Warsaw the Regency Council had already, on
the 7th October, proclaimed the independence of united Poland; in the course again of that same month Galicia separated from Austria; and the memorable day for all the world
on which arms were laid down, the 11th November, was likewise the day on which the ideal of that independence was
completely realized. Pilsudski, who on the eve of that day
had returned to Poland, accepted the rulership from the
hands of the Regency Council, and a few days later became
the first Chief of the restored Polish State.

In consideration of all these facts it was a foregone conclusion that the Peace Conference which was to meet in Paris
would recognize the resurrection of Poland as one of the indisputable results of the World War. It was equally certain
that Poland would be represented at that conference as one
of the victorious allied states. In this respect there existed
one difficulty: that until now the allies had only recognized
the Polish National Committee in Paris as the official representatives of that state, whereas Pilsudski and the Government nominated by him were ruling in the country itself.
The reconciliation of these two hitherto widely differing
trends of political action was in great measure due to Paderewski, who hastened to Warsaw, entered into an understanding with Pilsudski in January 1919, and accepted the post of
Premier and Minister of Foreign Affairs, and then went to
Paris to represent Poland jointly with Dmowski at the Peace
Conference.

There, in the meantime, the work had already begun of
fixing Poland's boundaries, of which, however, eventually
only those in the west, on the German side, were defined in

the Treaty of Versailles. As regards these, the Polish claims were clear and unanimously put forward by the whole nation. It was a matter of repairing the injury of the Partitions and restoring to Poland those parts of Prussia which had belonged to her before 1772. That claim was not founded only on a historical basis: the territories in question, namely Poznania and so-called West Prussia, otherwise the old Polish Pomerania, certainly preserved, in spite of a century of German rule and the policy of Germanization, their ethnically Polish character, excepting only certain strips on the frontiers, insignificant in Poznania, more considerable on the borders of West Prussia. These border regions having been left to Germany, even that latter province possessed—according to the German statistics themselves—such a distinct Polish majority as to fall under Wilson's definition of indisputably Polish territory. Hence the so-called 'Corridor' was by no means an artificial invention of the Treaty of Versailles, departing from Wilson's points, but—as before the Partitions —the natural result of the fact that since the time of the Knights of the Cross, East Prussia had formed but a German enclave on the east of Pomerania.

Consequently, the access to the sea promised to Poland, and realized by the restoration of Pomerania, was not 'free and secure' in reality; the less so, inasmuch as the mouth of the Vistula with Danzig, a town with a population almost entirely German, became, for that very reason, the subject of protracted discussions at the conference. Although the Commission for Polish Affairs unanimously declared for restoring Danzig to Poland, that claim fell to the ground by reason of the stubborn opposition of Great Britain's chief delegate, the Prime Minister, Lloyd George. The intricate solution of the problem of Danzig by which it became a Free City with special rights for Poland in its area, and particularly in its port, was to be the source of unceasing friction and the chief pretext for the outbreak of the present war.

Poland was obliged to consent to a considerable curtailment, especially in this instance, of her historic boundary, from ethnographic considerations, and she anticipated that these considerations would likewise prevail where they turned to her advantage. She therefore claimed the southern part of East Prussia and the eastern part of Silesia, namely Upper Silesia, lands which had been lost by Poland long before her partitions, but were for the greater part inhabited by a Polish population. The conference decided to resolve both these questions by means of plebiscites, although, according to the first peace conditions presented to the Germans in the beginning of May, Upper Silesia was to pass at once to Poland; it was only under the influence of the reply of the German delegation, and again at the request of Lloyd George, that this part of the treaty was changed.

This is surely the best proof that that treaty, as it actually affected the Polish question, was neither a 'dictate' imposed on the Germans without discussion, nor a departure from the Wilsonian principles. At the same time Poland had to sign a special treaty which imposed upon her far-reaching obligations in the matter of the protection of minorities. The idea of protecting any minority was undoubtedly just in principle; moreover, it was entirely in agreement with Polish traditions as with the new Constitution of the Republic that was already being drawn up; but the procedure was humiliating in this respect, that it placed Poland, as well as a few other states unjustly termed 'new,' under international control, which was not provided for as regards Germany. But, in any case, the Versailles Treaty, the first international convention that after the epoch of Poland's bondage solemnly recognized her independence and restored to her the greater part of what Prussia had usurped—the cradle of the Polish State and a strip of the Baltic coast—had, beyond all doubt, an epoch-making significance for the Polish nation.

Its first part, the Covenant of the League of Nations, was also important for Poland. Longing for peace and for international co-operation from which she had been excluded for over a hundred years, she necessarily hailed with satisfaction those two leading tenets of the League, as also the articles by which it solemnly guaranteed the integrity and independence of all the member states. It might, indeed, have appeared that according to the prophecies of the Polish poets an era of international peace and justice was to set in with the resurrection of Poland. Besides those factors springing from fundamental principles and ideals, some concrete enactments of the treaty, especially those which concerned the League's guardianship over Danzig, gave the League an additional and special importance in regard to Poland.

But at the same Peace Conference a further problem absorbed the attention of the Polish delegates: equally with the western frontiers they were occupied with the complicated question how far the restored Republic should stretch to the east. It was a difficult question, not only because it was linked with the whole problem of Russia, who had no official representative in Paris, who was a former ally, and was at the moment plunged into civil war, but also because Polish opinion was not wholly agreed on this weighty point. Linked with the pre-war controversy on historic or ethnographic Poland two points of view clashed. Pilsudski was a resolute advocate of the idea of federation, to which Paderewski also inclined, and which was based on the principle that in the east, as in the west, the historical pre-partition boundaries of the old Republic should be restored, but with the acknowledgment of

the right of self-determination for the non-Polish nationalities in the eastern borderlands, the Lithuanians, White Ruthenians,[1] and Ukrainians, who were expected to join Poland
in a bond of union. On the other hand, Dmowski, who.
thanks to his striking presentment of the Polish cause at the
meeting of the Council of Ten, on 29th January 1919, had
gained great authority at the conference, considered that Poland ought to be a homogeneous national State in which the
part of the eastern borderlands, with a relatively predomi-
nant Polish element, should be immediately incorporated,
while the rest of the White Ruthenian and Ukrainian territories should remain with future Russia.

Uncertainty as to the future of Russia, and the obscure attitude of the conference in regard to Lithuanian and Ukrainian aims for independence, contributed equally to the fact
that the conference reached no final decision regarding the
eastern boundaries of Poland, the drawing up of which, however, the Great Powers reserved to themselves in one of the
articles of the Versailles Treaty. The fate even of Lwow and
Wilno, which was specially troubling the Poles, remained in
suspense, and this in spite of the struggles waged for those
cities during the Paris deliberations.

Ultimately, however, the boundaries of the Republic were
decided not so much by those deliberations as by the hard
fighting which Poland herself, in the hour of her rebirth, was
all at once compelled to engage in with nearly all her neighbours, long after the war in the west was over. Even the actual liberation of the provinces under Prussia was effected
before the opening of the Peace Conference when, at the end

---

[1] It seems advisable to avoid in English the term 'White Russians,' which
leads to confusion. The name 'Blanc-Ruthenes,' used in the French original of
the first four parts of this work, and corresponding to the Slavonic terminology,
makes it quite clear that they do not belong to the Russians in the modern
sense of that word.

of 1918, after the disarmament of the German armies of occupation in the kingdom, a spontaneous uprising broke out with elemental force in Poznania.

Relatively the easier task was to wrest western Galicia with Cracow from Austrian hands, while at the same time, in eastern Galicia, a protracted conflict began in November 1918 with the Ukrainians, who even for a moment occupied Lwow. The heroic defence of the Polish population not only enabled that city to be regained, but became the starting-point for the thrusting back of the Ukrainian armed forces beyond the Zbrucz. But even then, in June 1919, the Peace Conference did not assign that territory to Poland in a definite manner, and at the end of the year it put forth the project of a merely temporary Polish administration of eastern Galicia to last twenty-five years, after which period a plebiscite was to be taken.

Almost simultaneously, on the 8th December, the conference drew an equally temporary frontier, the Curzon line, as it was called later, on the area which Russia had formerly occupied. Up to that line, which corresponded more or less with the frontier gained by Russia after the three partitions of Poland at the end of the eighteenth century, the Polish administration was to be extended from the outset. It was, however, clearly indicated at the time that this line of demarcation did not interfere with the rights of Poland reaching beyond that provisional frontier.

However, the final decision of the centuries-old dispute over the eastern borderlands of Poland depended on the result of the war that had now been waged for nearly a year between Poland and the Soviets, who, in the track of the retreating German armies, were pushing to the west. That war, thrust upon a state only just in the stage of organizing itself, and having at its disposal only a relatively small and newly

organized armed force, indisputably constitutes the most glorious page in the history of the rebuilding of the Republic,
and at the same time the page which was of the greatest importance in world history, because it not only saved Poland
from almost immediate destruction on the morrow of her liberation, but it saved the whole of central Europe from the
Bolshevik inundation which, in the event of the downfall of
the Polish barrier, would have joined the revolutionary
movements in Germany and Hungary.

The first great success in this war was the deliverance, on
19th April 1919, of Wilno, the town in which at the time of
the German occupation a Lithuanian Government had been
created, which, however, had been forced to retreat before
the Russians to Kovno. Three days later Pilsudski published
a proclamation to the population of the former Grand Duchy
of Lithuania promising them the full right of self-determination. But before this federal programme could be realized in
the north-east of the pre-partition Republic, the further
course of the protracted war brought forward in its turn the
Ukrainian question. In April of the following year, when the
negotiations for a truce with the Soviets broke down, Pilsudski concluded a treaty with Hetman Petlura's national
Ukrainian Government, which left eastern Galicia and the
western part of Volhynia to Poland, and, in exchange, promised Polish help in the liberation of Ukraine proper, where
an independent state was to rise, allied with Poland. Despite
the capture of Kiev, on 8th May 1920, this proved to be an
undertaking beyond the power of Poland. The Soviet offensive compelled the Polish armies to retire on the whole eastern front, máking no halt until near Warsaw itself.

In this wellnigh desperate moment help from the west was
completely wanting, with only the exception of the arrival of
a group of French officers under the command of General

Weygand. The latter closely collaborated with the Polish general staff, and Pilsudski's bold strategic plan was carried into execution in the middle of August. It resulted in the rout of the Bolsheviks, thanks also to the gallant defence of the capital by a volunteer army under the command of General Haller, and the co-ordination of the action of all the Polish armed forces, the participation of General Sikorski being especially conspicuous. Defeated again during their retreat through the Niemen basin territory, the Russians were compelled to enter into peace negotiations at Riga. The preliminaries signed there, on 12th October, formed the basis of the treaty of 18th March 1921. That treaty defined a boundary of compromise, corresponding more or less to the Polish-Russian boundary after the second partition in 1793. In spite of her victory, Poland abandoned the claim to her historic boundaries; but, at least, she gained a broad belt of her old eastern borderlands in accordance with the conception which Dmowski had defended at the Peace Conference, a belt ensuring her a certain minimum of safety on that side.

The federal idea, naturally, could not be realized within these frontiers. The greater part of White Ruthenia, as well as the Ukraine beyond the line already drawn in the agreement with Petlura, became Soviet republics whose independence of Moscow was, from the beginning, a theoretical one. Still worse, however, was the fact that in the course of the military operations a conflict ensued with Lithuania who, at the moment of the Polish reverse, in July 1920, attempted to secure Wilno for herself by a treaty with the Bolsheviks.

On the 9th October General Zeligowski took the town, although the Polish plenipotentiaries had quite unnecessarily agreed, two days previously, to a temporary line of demarcation leaving it on the Lithuanian side. The military method of deciding the question, beyond doubt in accordance with the inclinations of the greater part of the population concerned, but drastic in its application, reacted fatally on the future relations between Poland and Lithuania. The conciliatory action of the League of Nations prevented a war between sister nations; but Lithuania would never consent to acknowledge the incorporation of the Wilno district in the Republic of Poland, which, however, followed in March 1922, after the elections in all the disputed territory, at the request of the Wilno Diet. A year later, on the 15th March 1923, the Conference of the Ambassadors of the western Powers definitely recognized the eastern boundary of Poland in all its extent, including Wilno and Lwow.

The difficult position of Poland in the summer of 1920, caused by the war for the eastern frontier, also reacted drastically on the fixing of those portions of the boundary in the west that were still disputed. It was in July of that year that the Conference of Ambassadors decided the dispute which unfortunately had broken out between Poland and the Czechs immediately after the dissolution of Austria, and which antagonized for a long time those two nations who had so many interests in common. This decision, taken without the plebiscite requested by Poland, divided the disputed Cieszyn Silesia in a rather unfortunate manner, and likewise assigned to Poland only small strips of Orava and Spisz. It is not surprising, either, that the plebiscite held at that critical moment in the ethnographically Polish part of East Prussia yielded results unfavourable for the Republic, which was just then overrun by the Soviet armies.

The still more important plebiscite in Upper Silesia was, in the meantime, being deferred amidst insurrectionary movements of the Polish population in protest against the German terror. When the voting was finally carried out, on 20th March 1921, the dispute on the interpretation of its results led to a dangerous tension which evoked not only a third rising under the leadership of Wojciech Korfanty, but also a conflict between the Powers which were to carry out the division of Upper Silesia on the basis of the plebiscite. Only France favoured the Polish claims, while England and Italy wished to assign only two agricultural districts to Poland. In the end, the question was solved in the manner most consonant with international justice. It was referred to the League of Nations, which proposed a boundary line, subsequently accepted by the Powers; and in its halls the Polish and German delegates, presided over by a Swiss statesman, drew up the Convention of 15th May 1922, regulating in detail the carrying out of the division with regard to the economic necessities of the population. In this way Poland also obtained a considerable part of the rich industrial districts, and the Treaty of Versailles was completed in one of its most important points by means of an agreement reached by arbitration, the highest international authority acting as the mediator. The voivodeship of Silesia, subsequently created out of the parts of Upper Silesia and of Cieszyn Silesia assigned to Poland, was the sole, small part of the restored Republic which overstepped her pre-partition frontiers, and in exchange for her resignation of the rebuilding of the Poland of the Jagiellos, it restored to the Polish nation a part of the immemorial, early lost, apanage of the Piasts.

26

Reconstruction

WITHOUT waiting for the end of the war, which as we have seen lasted nearly two years longer for Poland than for the western States, or for the settlement of the boundaries of the Republic which dragged on still longer, the Polish nation proceeded at once to the constructive work in the regained country. Furthermore, she started on that work while still under foreign occupation, at least in those spheres of life where it proved possible. But in every department a veritable mountain of tasks awaited her, calculated to last for many years. The profound tragedy of contemporary Poland consists in the fact that she experienced so few years of peace; no one foresaw that there would be scarcely twenty of them! To-day, when amidst the new whirl of war we cast a glance at the terribly interrupted creative effort of those twenty years, we can affirm that in that time a great deal was effected on the road of progress, a fact which struck every foreigner who visited Poland at intervals, however short.

Progress was visible, above all, in the department of culture, material and spiritual alike. Here, independent Poland could link up with the no less fruitful work which partitioned Poland carried through in the preceding century. The possession of her own state organization and the absence of foreign oppression which hitherto had so seriously hampered even cultural development, created incomparably more favourable conditions; but, on the other hand, she had to overcome the terrible results of the destruction caused by the war. The nation could at last be mistress of her own free land, but she received that land in a desperate condition of impoverishment, and that at the moment when the whole of Europe was suffering from the economic effects of the war epoch. Poland was obliged at the very outset to carry on a struggle against famine and the contagious diseases disseminated by the war.

The rebuilding of the country in the literal sense after the ravages committed up to the last moment, demanded gigantic financial means. In the meantime, however, the collapse of the currency rendered all rational economic policy impossible. The so-called Polish mark, a legacy from the German occupation, began falling with increasing rapidity, and though inflation did not reach such catastrophic dimensions in Poland as in neighbouring Germany, yet it followed in the track of the fall of the German mark. A radical restoration to health, in this case especially urgent, could not ensue before the restoration of complete peace within settled frontiers. Thus the first attempts at remedying the evil by further drastic measures of economy had no effect, and it was not until the year 1924 that a great financial reform, linked with the name of the Prime Minister and Minister of Finance, Ladislas Grabski, brought about a decided turn for the better. Although in the following year it became clear that the value of the unit of the new Polish currency, the zloty, was at first fixed too high, namely, on a par with the Swiss gold franc, it was very soon established at a slightly lower level and kept a stable position; and the maintenance of a balanced national budget remained the leading principle of the Polish treasury policy. Thus the economic policy of the State not only profited by the favourable economic opportunities of the years 1926–30, but it also held out through the serious general European crisis of the following years.

This was the more difficult, since, on the one hand, the dangerous political situation of Poland demanded enormous expenditure for military purposes, and, on the other, the country was not only devastated, but generally poor, the standard of life of the great majority of its inhabitants being very low, especially that of the agrarian population which constituted almost two-thirds of the whole. To assist this large section of the population, it was indispensable that there should be a comprehensive agrarian reform, involving the parcelling out of the great landed properties. This difficult problem, which after the war confronted all the countries of central and eastern Europe, Poland endeavoured to solve without excessive radicalism, and therefore avoided expropriation without adequate compensation; the maximum area of a private landed property was fixed at 180 hectares, and in the eastern borderland 400 hectares, with the object of not weakening to a too great extent the Polish possession of land there. Directed by a special department, the agrarian reform proceeded steadily forward, and having carried through about two-thirds of its programme, it contributed in a marked degree to the diminution of the social differences that were until then so considerable.

The democratization of the commonwealth and the removal of differences between the relatively better developed western part of the state and the eastern borderlands, which were especially backward after the long Russian rule, were helped by efforts towards a progressive development of in-

dustrialism. Besides Silesian coal-fields which, contrary to anticipations, were operating quite normally under Polish rule,
and in addition to the old industrial centres of Warsaw and
Lodz, in the years immediately preceding the new war the so-
called Central Industrial District was created in the very middle, seemingly the safest section, of the Republic, on the
borders of her western and eastern parts, round the region
of Sandomierz. But the most conspicuous result of Polish efforts to raise the economic condition of the country, to develop her commerce, and to establish trade relations with the
whole world, was the creation of a port at Gdynia. From the
obscure fishing village which Poland inherited on the small
strip of Baltic coast that had been given back to her, there
arose at a positively American tempo a great commercial and
industrial town and a splendid port which not only out-
stripped Danzig, and in great measure made Poland independent of that city, but after scarcely fifteen years occupied
the first place among the Baltic ports, and was among the
chief ports of the world. The building of a Polish fleet, both
naval and mercantile, proceeded no less rapidly, step by step
with the steadily growing interest of the whole nation in the
sea and even in colonial problems.

Without adding further examples from the sphere of material development, we must lay a still greater emphasis on
the development of social and intellectual life in reborn Poland.

Playing an important part in the activity of the International Labour Organization, she proved anxious to apply to
her national life the leading principles of social progress discussed and recommended at Geneva. The eight-hour working day, inspection of working conditions with the view of
protecting especially women and juveniles, arbitration between employers and employees—all these were steadily in-

troduced into the social legislation of the Republic. The
system of social insurance in Poland was in advance of most
of the other countries, and so was public assistance, which
without excluding private charity supplemented it most effectively, particularly in the difficult post-war period and in
the years of the general economic depression. One of the
typical features of the Polish assistance system was its respect
for both individual dignity and family life. Hence the great
development of 'home relief,' including the rule of placing
poor children and orphans in families rather than in public
institutions. In protecting the children, half a million of
whom were born every year, special care was taken of the
workers in the cities, but the seasonal children's camps in
the country were hardly less useful to the peasant population.

The democratic trend in the evolution of contemporary
Poland was giving to all classes, through educational progress,
a chance of participating in the development of national culture.

Beyond all doubt, the most urgent necessity was the enlarging and building up of an elementary school system, and
the spreading of adult education, again especially in the
former Russian provinces which had been neglected in that
respect; the result achieved was that even in Polesia the
illiteracy, which Poland found there to an alarming extent,
was quickly disappearing. The general number of schools
remained always insufficient; but we must remember that at
the same time it was indispensable to organize the Polish secondary education, which hitherto had been developed only in
the former Austrian provinces, and which everywhere required co-ordination and many essential reforms. It was also
necessary to restore, after long suppression, Polish university
life. On the eve of the Great War it existed only in Galicia,
thanks to the Universities of Cracow and Lwow. The Uni-

versity of Warsaw, long since Russianized, became the metropolitan university of Poland, even under the German occupation, and developed in the following years into one of the greatest of European seats of learning; in the first year of independence also the ancient University of Wilno was at once restored to life, and two entirely new universities were founded, in Poznan and Lublin, the last of a Catholic character. The total number of academic schools had risen at the end of twenty years to well over twenty, with almost one hundred faculties.

Under such conditions research work in all the arts and sciences was able to progress favourably in spite of great material obstacles, which it was attempted to remedy by the creation of the Fund of National Culture, distributing scholarships, and facilitating the printing of scholarly publications. The same course was taken by the increasingly active learned societies, with the Polish Academy of Arts and Sciences at their head. In addition to existing collections of books a magnificent National Library arose in Warsaw, in great part composed of the books and manuscripts carried away by Russia at the time of the Partitions and subsequently returned in accordance with the Treaty of Riga. In keeping with the tradition of the preceding century, literature and the fine arts likewise developed; although not producing such famous masterpieces as those which the bondage of the nineteenth century had inspired, they brought forth after the death of the masters of the past a succession of new and promising writers, especially in the department of fiction. Finally, there followed the rebirth and deepening of religious life, on the immemorial foundations of Catholic tradition, which was of great importance in its effects on national culture and characterized by a deep concern in social problems; in all of which Poland's youth took a prominent part.

Two entirely new problems resulting from the regaining
of an independent status were linked both with Poland's cultural life and with her internal policy. One of them, which
at first seemed disquieting, namely the unification of the
three parts of dismembered Poland into a homogeneous national and state organism, was solved with surprising rapidity and smoothness. The reason for this was simple: the
Polish nation, in spite of all the minor differences between
the three divisions, had never lost the feeling of unity, and
the creation of a Polish state administration was considerably
facilitated by the circumstance that at least one of those divisions, Galicia, had been autonomous for half a century and
provided the first ranks of civil servants for the whole restored
State. The problem of national minorities was, however, less
successfully handled during that score of years.

Because of the mixture of nationalities in this part of
Europe, and also because of the difficulties of harmonizing
the conceptions of historic and ethnographic Poland, a considerable number of national minorities were necessarily to
be found in the new Republic. Nor must we forget that a
large number of Poles, about two and a half millions, not
counting the Americans of Polish descent, had found themselves beyond her frontiers, especially in Germany, and in the
Soviet Union, and also in Lithuania, Latvia, and Czechoslovakia. But against this almost one-third of the population of
the Polish State, which altogether numbered over thirty-five
millions, belonged to other nationalities. The number of
Lithuanians and Russians was negligible, the national sentiment of the White Ruthenians feebly developed, but this
gave all the greater significance to the question of the German, Jewish, and Ukrainian minorities.

The first of the last-mentioned proved to be the most dangerous, although the number of the Germans amounted to hardly more than three-quarters of a million and nowhere were they living in a compact mass; against that, however, they enjoyed support in the neighbouring Reich, who, although she oppressed her Polish minority, complained continually of the condition of the Germans in Poland, which was an incomparably better one. The Jewish question became particularly acute before the present war; it was, indeed, a very considerable one, having regard to the fact that over three million Jews—almost ten per cent of the entire population—were living scattered all over the country, constituting a far higher percentage still among the populations of the towns, in trade and industry, and in certain professions, and that only an insignificant number of them were really assimilated. Under these conditions the rise of an anti-Semitic movement on economic, rather than racial, grounds, was unfortunately almost inevitable. It did not, however, assume such violent proportions as in a number of other European countries, and on the part of the Polish Government it was steadily suppressed. The question of the Ukrainian minority was in reality far more important, and, generally speaking, not properly appreciated; it was the most numerous group, for it numbered about five millions, occupying a compact area in the south-east of the state, and, in contradistinction to the Germans and the Jews, it was composed, not of immigrants, but of immemorial inhabitants of these lands. The territorial autonomy that had been announced was very difficult to carry through, for it was precisely where the Ukrainian population was highest in culture and national consciousness, namely, in the former eastern Galicia, that it was most mingled with the Polish population. In spite of this, it is to be regretted that neither successive governments nor the Polish nation achieved in regard to the Ukrainians a consistent programme which might have reconciled them to the Republic.

We speak of successive governments, for the system of internal policy yielded in the course of twenty years of independence to far-reaching changes, of which the most important was the *coup d'état* of May 1926. In the period preceding that May the nature of the Republic's government was purely democratic, with a strong predominance of the legislative authority, with often sharp party quarrels, and frequent changes of Cabinets. After the *coup d'état* of Marshal Pilsudski, who for several years had retired from political life, a gradual restriction of the role of the Diet and of the significance of political parties succeeded, until finally Pilsudski effected a formal change of the Constitution. In contradistinction to the Constitution of 17th March 1921, the Constitution of 23rd April 1935 notably strengthened the position of the President and of the Government, and while retaining the Parliament, greatly restricted its power.

From the historical perspective it is apparent that in contrasting the periods before and after May 1926, of which the adherents of Pilsudski have condemned the first and exalted the second, while his adversaries have appraised these two periods in reverse fashion, there has been a good deal of exaggeration, entirely comprehensible in the fire of political rivalry. To-day we must acknowledge that the gigantic progress of the whole country briefly characterized above was the result of both these epochs and the common merit of various political camps, each of which strove to serve its country to the best of its ability. In the first period the unavoidable party antagonisms only once led to a really critical situation, when, in December 1922, after Pilsudski's resignation from the position of Chief of the State and the

election of the first President in the person of Gabriel Narutowicz, the latter was assassinated by a fanatic who acted on
his own initiative. At that moment, however, after the election of Stanislas Wojciechowski as President, the Government of General Sikorski immediately restored peace and
order. The parliamentary crisis in 1926 might certainly have
been overcome in a less violent manner and one less liable to
undermine respect for legality than that which Pilsudski had
chosen in May. He endeavoured, however, after his victory
in a fratricidal battle in the streets of Warsaw, to legalize the
coup. He did not accept his election as President, to which
post Professor Ignacy Moscicki succeeded at his suggestion,
although in reality everything henceforth depended on the
decision of Pilsudski. In the further course of the dispute
with the opposition of the Diet he once more took violent
measures, condemning its leaders to a cruel imprisonment at
Brzesc in the autumn of 1930, thereby arousing universal indignation. Yet he did not proceed to a system of totalitarian
government, which would never have taken root in Poland;
he strove rather to create such peculiar constitutional forms
as could permit the Polish State to develop a middle course
between the greatly prized, though often excessive, tradition
of freedom, and the strengthening of the executive that was
necessary in its dangerous position.

It was beyond doubt the tragedy of the first Marshal of
Poland that, uncritically idolized by some, passionately opposed by others, he was not able to create a harmonious national unity. The dispute about his personality was not
silenced even by his death, on 12th May 1935. The collaboration of all political parties was, however, doubly necessary
when the leader who had gained such a strong position in
Europe for Poland and for himself was no longer there. President Moscicki, re-elected in 1933 for another period of

seven years, and General Rydz-Smigly, who after Pilsudski's
death received the dignity of Marshal and to whom—outside
the Constitution—was assigned the position of the 'second
person' in the State, declared themselves for this political
collaboration. The so-called 'Non-Party Group of Co-operation with the Government' which, under the leadership of
the most extreme partisans of the regime called the 'Colo-
nels,' excluded, strictly speaking, every other political group
from any influence on the fate of the State, was dissolved,
and an organization came into being, the very name of
which, 'Camp of National Unity,' seemed to sum up a programme worthy of recognition. But unfortunately it remained a dead letter, as the two contending sides attached
completely different meanings to 'unity.' An additional difficulty resulted from the fact that neither of the two was by
any means homogeneous. Among the followers of Pilsudski
ever wider divergences appeared, and the opposition was
divided into a right and left wing, so that the ruling group
was in a position to approach one or the other alternately.
But all these regrettable frictions in internal politics were no
worse than similar manifestations in other states not reduced
to uniformity by totalitarianism, and in the midst of these
frictions certain leading principles were becoming clearer
and were increasingly acknowledged by all. As to internal
affairs, one of these principles was the necessity of a return to
more democratic parliamentary forms by the alteration of
the rules which, after the passing of the new Constitution
and the death of Pilsudski, had given a merely fictitious character to the elections to the legislative bodies. The second
principle was the maintenance of unity between all Poles in
the face of the growing external danger.

In spite of the differences of opinion on the methods to be
applied in the foreign policy of the State, never, before 1926

or after it, neither during the life of Joseph Pilsudski nor after his death, was there the least doubt in the nation that its external situation demanded the closest vigilance to ensure peace and the safety of the Republic that had only been rebuilt with such effort. The nation also succeeded in avoiding the two chief errors of pre-partition Poland, namely, the admission of foreign intervention in internal conflicts, and the lack of sacrifice in the defence of the country. As to the latter, it is enough to point out that although the army was in the hands of the adherents of Pilsudski and his regime, it is a fact that the whole nation rallied round it, not excepting the extreme opposition, grudging no sacrifice for armaments, which was often criticized abroad as a manifestation of Polish militarism or imperialism and which, in fact, as the occasion proved, was always insufficient. As to foreign policy, it can be treated as almost independent of all the changes in internal affairs, since through the twenty years of reborn Poland it was fraught with the same major problem which through the centuries had weighed upon the development of the old Republic, namely, the twofold, mortal danger threatening her without a break from the two inexorably hostile neighbours who had risen to power in the west and the east.

We have seen that the resurrection of Poland was made possible through the conflict between these two Powers, and the successive defeat of each of them. But even the years of their greatest weakness, after the upheaval of war and revolution, brought Poland no real respite; they only allowed her to thrust back the Bolshevik invasion in the dawn of her independence, without fear of a simultaneous attack from the side of Germany. The latter, however, already at that time sympathized with Poland's eastern adversary, and scarcely a year after the Peace of Riga entered into an alliance with him by the treaty concluded at Rapallo, a treaty which remained undisturbed through all the changes of the external and internal policy of Germany and Russia in the following years. This treaty was the clearest reminder that when Germany and Russia re-entered the group of great Powers determining the fate of Europe—and that re-entrance was actually beginning at the Genoa Conference in 1922—Poland was again confronted with the spectre of their renewed collaboration to destroy her as in the eighteenth century.

Already a year before this, Poland endeavoured to avert the danger by the conclusion of a close alliance with France which should ensure the safety of both contracting parties against German revenge, and which became the main foundation of Polish foreign policy; and, in addition, by an alliance with Rumania with the object of a common defence of the eastern frontiers of both states against the Soviets. It was obvious, however, how desirable was the extension of that system of alliances by still wider regional agreements. The alliance with France exacted an agreement with all the French allies in Central Europe, not only with Rumania, but also with the other members of the Little Entente. The danger in the east could only be met by a common front, not only with Rumania in the south, but also with the whole group of Baltic States, including Finland, in the north.

Unfortunately, both these conceptions met with insurmountable obstacles. The strained relations with Czechoslovakia, an unfortunate result of the territorial dispute at the moment of the liberation of both nations, as well as the well-nigh exclusively anti-Hungarian attitude of the Little Entente, prevented Poland from acceding to it, and even from closer collaboration with it. The no less regrettable Polish-Lithuanian dispute, despite a series of highly promising Baltic conferences. made the formation of a strong Baltic Entente with the participation of Poland impossible. In the place of this, however, it might have appeared through several years that a still broader conception would be realized, a system of collective security of all the European States which belonged to the League of Nations, and which should be faithful to its principles of peaceful collaboration.

The realization of this idea seemed nearest in 1924, when, in the atmosphere of general relief from the political strain, the Assembly of the League unanimously accepted the Geneva Protocol. When this project came to nothing with Great Britain's refusal to ratify the protocol and when, in the following year, the Locarno Treaties, concluded outside the League between Germany and her neighbours, superseded it, there was a great disillusionment for Poland because a notable discrimination between the western and eastern boundaries of Germany had been made, and only the former were recognized as immovable and guaranteed by all the contracting parties. Although in the east peace was ensured only by a Polish-German treaty of arbitration, and the strengthening of the Polish-French alliance, the Republic, whose Minister of Foreign Affairs in those years of transition was Count Alexander Skrzynski, did not retire from participation at Locarno, and only made it her aim that after the anticipated entrance of Germany into the League not only that nation, but also Poland, should gain a permanent seat in its council. Finally, in September 1926, Poland had to be satisfied with a semi-permanent seat; but thenceforward, with Augustus Zaleski as the new director of her foreign policy, she remained faithful to the principle of strengthening her security by collective treaties, and took an active share in all efforts to maintain universal peace. The Polish proposition, condemning all aggressive warfare, accepted by the Assembly of the League in 1927, paved the way to the Paris Pact in the following year, the so-called Kellogg Pact which solemnly outlawed war. In her negotiations with Soviet Russia, Poland endeavoured to hasten the coming into force of that pact as far as eastern Europe was concerned, and both sides accepted a definition of aggression which was more precise than any previous definition.

The conclusion by Poland of a special treaty of non-aggression with the Soviets in 1932 appeared to be a further step in this direction. At the same time it was the first sign of a change in her foreign policy. That year, in which the Disarmament Conference convoked at Geneva proved to be condemned to failure, undermined the belief in collective security, and Poland, who still brought forward at this conference the highly interesting project of moral disarmament, entered with Colonel Joseph Beck as new Minister of Foreign Affairs upon the road of so-called bilateral pacts. The most important of these appeared to be the treaty of non-aggression which, in January 1934, was concluded for ten years with the German Reich. It was preceded by a seeming relaxation of the strain in their mutual relations, which followed, wholly beyond expectations, after the taking over of the government by Hitler. Before its rise to power, the National Socialist movement had taken up a specially hostile attitude to Poland, an attitude which, however, in principle differed not at all from the general unchangeable position of Germany, who, from the moment of the Versailles Treaty, had not ceased to claim the revision of her territorial dispositions in the east; that one-sided demand was repeatedly brought forward by Germany, although it was obvious that Poland could never agree to it, but would resist the curtailment of her only just regained territories and would especially oppose being cut off from the sea. In the treaty of 1934, it is true, Hitler did not distinctly acknowledge Poland's frontiers; but from that time he was not sparing in assurances to her of his friendship, which appeared to postpone disputed questions to a far future, and, in any case, to safeguard Poland for the period of ten years.

Besides being natural on her part, if only because she had no aggressive intentions whatsoever towards Germany, the chief explanation of Poland's signing this treaty was that she had lost hope in effective assistance from the western States, who, in 1933, had agreed to Mussolini's suggestion of concluding a Four-Power Pact with him and with Hitler. After the evaporation of that illusive, and for Poland highly dangerous, conception of a European 'order,' collective security was to be strengthened by an understanding with the Soviets, who were admitted to the League of Nations in the autumn of 1934. Under such conditions Poland might well be inclined to attempts at safeguarding herself by direct independent treaties with both her neighbours, and the unreadiness of the democracies to stop Hitler in 1936 when Poland declared to be ready to oppose the violation of the Locarno treaty, seemed to justify these attempts. For Hitler, on the other hand, who from easily understood motives, some geographical and others bound up with the general disposition of forces in Europe, was anxious to postpone his reckoning with Poland until the period after the incorporation of Austria and the conquest of Czechoslovakia, the isolation of Poland and her subjection to the will of Germany was an object only too greatly desired.

He did not entirely gain that object. Although, unfortunately, the policy of Beck through several years played into his hands, and these apparently friendly relations exposed Poland to German influences, and especially to a methodical system of spying, the relations of Poland with the west, above all her alliance with France, remained unshaken, in spite of a certain cooling. Moreover, Poland always refused to participate in any German aggression against Russia. On the other hand, the Polish Minister of Foreign Affairs endeavoured to establish closer bonds between Poland and the whole group of states lying between Germany and Russia, stretching as far as Scandinavia and not excluding even Lithuania, whom immediately after the fall of Austria he finally persuaded to enter into normal diplomatic relations with Poland. Before, however, these extensive and difficult processes were able to create a compact group of those states possessing so many obvious interests in common, the catastrophe of Czechoslovakia ensued and Beck's policy made use of it to regain the part of the Silesian borderland that had for so long been the subject of dispute. This most regrettable step weighed little in the scale of events, which the Munich policy of the Great Powers had decided; but on Poland it was notably avenged, because almost on the morrow of this small and illusive success, Hitler brought forward his claims in the matter of Danzig and the Corridor which, after the total absorption of the Czech State in March 1939, he presented to Poland in the form of a direct threat.

27

Destruction

It would be superfluous to demonstrate why Poland could not accept the conditions dictated to her by Hitler in the spring of 1939, the final draft of which, going so much further than the earlier claims, he would not even communicate to her by the ordinary diplomatic channels, in the critical days and hours at the end of August. To-day we clearly perceive that all the questions which had been brought forward by Hitler up to that time were regarded by him as only secondary; they were only pretexts to attain, either by the total capitulation of the Polish Government or else by the war that had been secretly prepared for years, the actual aim of German policy in regard to Poland: a fresh destruction of the Polish State, this time final, which should encompass the destruction of the whole nation.

For the first time Hitler met with the resolute resistance of the intended victim. But for the first time also Europe reacted against the very intention of the new outrage. Even the British Government, which under Chamberlain was so strenuously aiming to preserve peace, confronted with the fresh example of Hitler's broken promises in regard of Czechoslovakia, immediately after the March ultimatum gave Poland a guarantee of full support in the event of German aggression. After Beck's visit to London this promise was succeeded by a mutual Polish-British guarantee, linked with the strengthening of the alliance with France. Although Hitler took advantage of this purely defensive treaty to denounce the Polish-German pact of non-aggression, it could be anticipated that in face of the attitude of the western Powers he would hesitate before declaring a war which was bound to become a European war, and for Germany a war on two fronts. All his hesitations were cut short, however, by the treaty which his Minister of Foreign Affairs, Ribbentrop, signed with the Soviets in Moscow on 23rd August.

This pact was equally unexpected by those who saw in Hitler and National Socialism the bulwark against the danger of Communism, as by those who saw in the Soviet Union the desired ally of democracy in the fight with Nazism and Fascism. In spite of the simultaneous negotiations by which the representatives of England and France were misled in Moscow, the natural solidarity of all the revolutionary totalitarian systems now became manifest, together with the immemorial German-Russian solidarity in the project of destroying Poland, broken only for a short while in the former World War. The final signing of the Polish-British treaty two days later could not now preserve peace, nor did the appeals of Pope Pius XII, President Roosevelt, the King of the Belgians, and the Queen of the Netherlands. While diplomatic negotiations were still being carried on through British mediation, Hitler, without a declaration of war, on the morning of 1st September, flung all his forces against Poland.

These forces were so overwhelming, especially in the field of aviation and in the motorized panzer divisions, that it was totally impossible for the Republic to check them by her own means, as was confirmed later by the experience of a series of other states stronger in that respect than Poland. But she was obliged to wage that desperate September campaign literally alone. England and France, who, in fulfilment of their obligations, declared war against Germany after two days' delay, were unprepared for it, and practically had to restrict themselves to military activities that were hardly more than spectacular demonstrations. Nevertheless, the heroic resistance of the Polish armies, outflanked from the beginning by attacks from the west, from East Prussia, and across German-dominated Slovakia, was prolonged until the beginning of October; the long battle in the region of Kutno was acknowledged by the Germans themselves to be one of the bloodiest in history, and at the end of the campaign some of their divisions were still suffering severe defeats. Therefore, the German assertion that the campaign lasted only three weeks, or even only eighteen days, is false. False, but in two respects highly characteristic.

It proves, in the first instance, that in their own view the decisive moment of the campaign was reached immediately after the 17th September. We know that precisely on that day Poland fell a victim to another entirely unprovoked attack. Under flimsy pretexts Soviet Russia broke the second of the bilateral pacts by which Poland had desired to maintain peaceful relations with her neighbours, and with the fresh forces she had been long assembling she invaded the Republic's eastern territories. It was only that stab in the back that made the Polish resistance, which had just at that moment begun to stiffen, indeed hopeless.

Nevertheless, it was continued in many places, and, above all, in Warsaw, under the inspiring leadership of the mayor, Stephen Starzynski. The city only surrendered when the Germans, who from the first hours of the war, against Hitler's solemn declarations, employed their powerful air force in the most savage manner by bombarding open towns and villages, peasants working in the fields, and refugees on the roads, and by terrorizing the entire population, women and children, crowned this barbarous work of destruction by turning Poland's capital into ruins. The bombardment of Warsaw actually began on the first day of the war; but it was when the Germans considered the campaign finished, and the fall of the capital was, in fact, inevitable, that the aerial attack was let loose in all its fury against the unhappy city. Combined with the simultaneous artillery fire, these air raids systematically reduced whole streets to rubble and ashes, started innumerable unquenchable fires, after the destruction of the water supply, destroyed churches during Sunday services, and found only too often for their targets the historical monuments, including the Royal Castle, as well as hospitals overflowing with wounded. The martyrdom of Warsaw, frankly designed as a punishment because the capital did not instantly submit to the invader, will remain, together with the similar fate of a number of other towns, as, for instance, Siedlce, which was levelled to the ground, a disgrace to the Germans, the greater because they could not even gloss over their barbarity with the pretext of 'retaliation'. Not one Polish bomb fell on Germany.

The day after the capitulation of the ruins of Warsaw, 28th September, a German-Soviet treaty was concluded effecting the division of the Polish territories between the aggressors. Most of the inhabitants, especially the major part of the purely Polish population, fell under the German yoke; the Russians appropriated more than one-half of the territory of the Republic. It is entirely erroneous to maintain that they only took the lands inhabited by White Ruthenians and Ukrainians, as far as the Curzon line. On the contrary, besides eastern Galicia with Lwow, which the provisional demarcation in 1919 did not actually affect, they arrogated to themselves a strip of purely Polish land west of that line as far as the Pisa and Narew Rivers, and at least five million Poles on both sides of the Curzon line passed under the rule of the Soviets. Nearly four times as many Poles found themselves under the German occupation, which besides the districts occupied by Prussia prior to 1914, held the greater part of the Congress Kingdom and all western Galicia.

Among the Poles not even the smallest political group could be found to recognize the conquest of the country, or to show any willingness to 'collaborate' with the invaders. No state in the world formally acknowledged the 'liquidation' of Poland, although Mussolini made use of that phrase in an occasional address, and the war between Poland and the temporary occupiers of the country continued to be carried on, and in two different forms.

One of these was the protracted martyrdom of that overwhelming majority of the population which remained in the country. This was clearly not a war in the common sense of a struggle between two armies. The September campaign itself was in great measure an extermination of the civil population. After its conclusion there started on the one hand a persecution of the Poles, so cruel that the most terrible experiences of the past pale before it, and on the other hand a resistance, so consistent and widespread that it gives the lie to the popular belief in the seeming Polish want of concord; so heroic that no military action could be more worthy of praise or more fraught with sacrifice.

This common characteristic extends to the whole of the Polish territories. Obviously, in details there appeared to be notable differences between the German and the Soviet occupations, and, within the frontiers of the first-named, between the territories 'incorporated' into Germany and the so-called 'General Government.' In glaring violation of

international law, Hitler, without waiting for the end of the
war and the treaty of peace, not long after the 'regulation' of
frontiers with the Soviets, drew up yet another boundary line.
This was intended to be the 'final' eastern frontier of Germany
in the strict meaning of the word. By it she annexed not only
the Free City of Danzig and the Corridor — the ostensible
subject of the conflict — not only all beyond it that belonged to
Prussia in 1914, that is Poznania and Upper Silesia, but, in
addition, a considerable part of the former Congress
Kingdom, and even a slice of the former Galicia almost as far
as Cracow — altogether 35,700 square miles, with a Polish
population of more than nine millions. The district of Suwalki,
cut off from the rest of the Reich's Polish conquest by the
Soviet occupation, was joined to East Prussia; a broad belt of
territory reaching nearly to Warsaw, including Lodz, which
received the name of 'Litzmannstadt,' was incorporated partly
into East Prussia and partly into 'Wartegau,' as Great Poland
was named.

In this 'annexed' area the persecution was undoubtedly the
most brutal, openly aiming at the total extirpation of the
Polish element. The Germanizing methods of former Prussia
which National Socialism officially renounced in the name of
the purity of race, but which, in case of necessity, it did not
disdain to apply, were not sufficient here. It employed,
therefore, other methods, far more ruthless still; having at the
outset removed the leaders of the nation by numberless
executions, it proceeded to the mass eviction of the Poles, and
this under the most inhuman conditions, with the result that a
large number, especially children, died on the road. This
proceeding was carried out most systematically in Pomerania,
where for example, the whole population was removed from
Gdynia, a town created solely by Polish efforts and now named
Gotenhafen. But thousands of Poles were expelled equally

from Poznan and the other towns of Great Poland; one street after another was cleared of its inhabitants, and the unhappy occupants were compelled to leave all their property for use of Germans brought from the Reich or the Baltic countries, and placed in their homes. Even those deportations of more than one million and a half victims could not drive out all the eight and a half millions of the Polish population. Therefore, those elements, economically the weakest, which remained on the spot were the more oppressed, as was the only refuge left to them, the Catholic Church.

A part of the Poles who were driven out from the 'annexed' provinces were transferred to forced labour in Germany, which was also the lot of many thousands of youths from central Poland. The rest of the expropriated were literally flung on the pavement in that central part of the Republic which Hitler assigned to the Polish nation as a sort of 'reservation.' But even regarding the 'General Government' with its capital in Cracow and divided into four areas, Cracow, Warsaw, Radom, and Lublin, every opportunity was taken to proclaim officially that it was to belong to the Reich 'for all time.' In this manner an indefinable, purely artificial creation had arisen, to which even the name of protectorate was not applied. It was to be simply a German colony which, although situated in the middle of Europe and inhabited by indisputable 'Aryans' — with the exception of the Jews now starving behind the ghetto walls — was to be exploited in the same way as, if not worse than, some African colony.

An inexorable persecution of the Polish intelligentsia was waged, denying the Poles the right to their own culture. Its most notorious manifestation was the insidious arrest in November 1939 of nearly all the professors of Cracow University for the sole reason that that university had been for more than five hundred years a bulwark of all that is Polish;

the professors were interned in a concentration camp, not
excepting scholars of world-wide fame and old men over
seventy years of age. Eighteen of them, exactly a tenth part,
died as the result of ill-treatment; and in spite of the gradual
release of the majority, other scholars were among the
innumerable victims of Oranienburg. Dachau, or the worst of
all the concentration camps, established at Oswiecim. Not
only the University of Cracow, but all the Polish universities,
indeed all educational establishments from and including
secondary schools, were closed 'for ever,' and all Polish art
treasures, public or private, confiscated by an order of 16th
December 1939. Other regulations aimed at the systematic
destruction of Polish industry, and the giving over of all
material resources of the country to Germany's use. After the
extermination of its leading classes the rest of the population,
those who would survive starvation and disease, were to be
used as the slaves of the Reich.

At the same time, in the eastern part of Poland which was
under Soviet occupation for twenty-one months, the Russians
also started persecuting the Polish population. Deportations to
hard labour in Siberia, once the severest punishment,
exceeded only by that of death, for political offenders, were
now administered to about one million and a half, not
excepting women and children, against whom nothing could
be charged except that they were Poles. It would be
superfluous to stress that to the systematic, hurried
Sovietization of the occupied areas was added — as in the
German occupation — a specially intensive war against
traditional Polish culture and, obviously, against all religion,
and the reduction of the population to abject misery. The
comedy of the 'elections' carried through immediately after the
invasion naturally led to the 'voluntary' accession of the
northern part of the usurped territory, including the purely

Polish region of Lomza and the prevailing Polish region of Bialystok, to the Soviet White Russian Republic, and of the southern part, together with Polish Lwow, to the Soviet Ukraine. However, the independence of these republics was always purely fictitious. Under Stalin's dictatorship Communism harmonized perfectly with Russian nationalism, which wished to profit, as in the preceding historical epochs, from its alliance with German nationalism and to seize the Lithuanian-Ruthenian territories which for so many centuries have been a subject of dispute, blotting out from them every vestige of Poland's cultural influences. Moreover, in its aim at a complete extinction of Poland, it took advantage of the opportunity thus offered to reach even into the very depth of her ethnical territory.

Speaking of the Soviet occupation, special mention should be made of Wilno and its district. A fortnight after its capture the Bolsheviks magnanimously gave it to Lithuania. The Polish inhabitants at first hailed with relief the entrance of the Lithuanians, who unfortunately, in great measure destroyed their expectations, closing, on 15th December 1939, the Wilno University, and imposing various repressions on the Poles. Soon, however, the fundamental error of the Lithuanian policy in the course of the last twenty years — its distrust of Poland, and its neglect of the German and Soviet peril — was bitterly avenged. Half a year before the catastrophe of Poland, who desired nothing from her except normal neighbourly relations, Lithuania lost Klajpeda to the German Reich. After that catastrophe she regained temporarily one disputed town, but only to experience at once a serious limitation of her sovereignty and, nine months later, together with the other Baltic States, to lose it entirely. The transformation of independent Lithuania into a Soviet Republic, subject, like all the others, to Moscow, was at the same time a blow for that section of Polish people then living there, who were in a better position than those under the yoke of the Germans and Bolsheviks in Poland proper.

In the mute daily warfare waged by the whole Polish nation against the invaders, none of the Poles faltered. A certain number of Poles succeeded in crossing the frontiers of the Republic before they were closed, or, albeit at the gravest risks, in extricating themselves out of that twofold concentration camp into which a recently happy country had suddenly changed. Their history is not only a sad Odyssey of fugitives who, driven from one country to another, often only found in the other hemisphere a temporary shelter. It shows at the same time another form of Poland's unceasing war with her enemies, war in the full significance of that word, carried on by an independent government, by arms and diplomacy, with profound faith in final victory.

This proved possible owing to two circumstances. President Moscicki, before he crossed the Rumanian frontier with the whole Government, laid down his office, and, in conformity with the constitution, Ladislas Raczkiewicz, a man with great experience in politics, moderate in judgment, and universally respected, was named his successor. In the place of the old Government, which was interned in Rumania and unable to fulfil its functions, he immediately formed in Paris on 1st October 1939, a new Government composed of prominent politicians who had succeeded in getting through to France, with General Ladislas Sikorski as Prime Minister, and August Zaleski as Minister of Foreign Affairs, replaced in 1941 by Count Edward Raczynski. In this manner the continuity of the only lawful Polish State authority was assured, under the charge of personages enjoying the full confidence alike of the nation and of her western allies. This Government, with the gold reserve of the State at its disposal, which fortunately had been successfully transported to France, moved together with the President, to an exterritorial seat which the French Government assigned to it at Angers; it completed its composition steadily, as more political leaders found their way to France. Among others these included General Sosnkowski, who had played a distinguished part in the September campaign, and whom the President nominated as his eventual successor. A National Council by the side of the Government was formed in January 1940, named by the President from the representatives of every political opinion, filling the place of Parliament for the duration of the war, and giving every guarantee that in agreement with the declarations of the new Government the structure of post-war Poland would be founded on genuine democratic principles of legality and social justice. The most internationally famous Polish citizen, Ignacy Paderewski, who inaugurated its work by a notable speech setting forth its programme, was chosen as the head of the Council and occupied this position until his untimely death on 29th June 1941.

General Sikorski not only accepted the portfolio of military affairs, which later, in 1942, was given to the noted historian General Marian Kukiel, but also became the Commander-in-Chief of the reorganized Polish army. This was possible owing to the second favourable circumstance that part of the Polish army which, after the September campaign, passed into Hungary and Rumania, especially many officers and airmen, succeeded, in spite of having been interned, in again assembling in France, where their ranks were swelled by mobilization among the pre-war Polish emigrants in that country, who numbered almost half a million. Thanks to the indefatigable efforts of its leader, the Polish army, numbering nearly 100,000 and admirably trained, was ready for battle by the spring of 1940, when the war at last blazed on the western front. Some of its units had already distinguished themselves in the distant Norwegian expedition of the allies, especially in the battle for Narvik; but the Polish soldier covered himself with fresh glory, in the share he took in the defence of France.

The collapse of France was likewise a heavy blow for Poland. It did not, however, break her spirit. In spite of fresh losses and the capitulation of one of the allies, the Poles did not even dream of ceasing to fight. About 15,000 who had heroically protected the retreat of one of the French armies, had to cross into Switzerland, where they were received with extraordinary warmth, but naturally had to be interned. The greater part, however, of the Polish army was successfully transported to England, by whose side the remains of the Polish navy had been already fighting from the beginning of the war, and where now, at the end of June 1940, the Polish Government together with the President and the National Council transferred themselves. The Polish troops, quartered chiefly in Scotland, undertook the defence of a certain part of the British coast, the Polish airmen began increasingly to distinguish themselves, acting with the Royal Air Force, and a little later Polish soldiers dispersed through the world, as of old in the Napoleonic wars, appeared in Palestine and on the fields of the Egyptian-Libyan battles, while Polish volunteers were not absent even from the Greek front.

In addition to the Balkan campaign, the year of 1941 brought two other momentous changes in the political and military situation which were of the greatest possible importance for the Polish nation and proved decisive for the issue of the whole war.

Nothing was more striking than the break between Hitler and Stalin, between Nazism and Communism, whose joint action against Poland has been described above. The German-Russian war, starting on Polish soil, brought still more devastation and hardship to an already inhumanly suffering country, and confronted the exiled Polish Government and the whole nation with a difficult decision. Taking into consideration the foremost necessity of defeating Germany, who now occupied and oppressed the whole of Poland, the common interests of all the allies, and the cruel aggression whose victim after so many others had become the Russian nation — Poland not only agreed to make peace with Russia on 30th July 1941, a few weeks after the German invasion, but concluded with her a close alliance on 4th December of the same year and decided effectively to co-operate with the Russians.

The same Polish soldiers who had suffered for nearly two years in Soviet prisons immediately started forming a new army ready to pour out their blood for the liberty of all allied peoples. They had a right to expect, with all the other Poles wherever they were, that the Soviet Union, having annulled her treaty with Germany of 1939, would respect the Polish-Russian frontier fixed by mutual agreement in 1921, the full independence of Poland, and the democratic constitution of a nation which was always opposed to Communism.

Poland's hope for the complete restitution of her freedom and integrity received the strongest possible support by the second great event of 1941: by America's entry into the war after the aggression of Pearl Harbor on 7th December. Foreshadowed by the Atlantic Charter, the participation of the world's greatest democracy in the second World War and in the making of the future peace, seemed to the Poles another guarantee — just like the alliance with Great Britain — that their ordeal would not be forgotten when the United Nations established their new European order.

In opposition to the so-called 'New Order' which the totalitarian Powers desired to impose upon Europe, Poland was already preparing agreements with other allied nations whose exiled governments had gathered on English soil, in the conviction that the new, truly just, and permanent order of Europe and the world must be founded on the principles of independence, security, and legal equality of all the countries, great and small, each of which must have its living space. The declaration given out in common by the Polish and Czechoslovakian Governments at the end of the year 1940, on the memorable anniversary of the 11th of November, proved that Poland had a full comprehension of the necessity of these independent states joining into federal unions, and that she was conscious of her share of responsibility for precisely such a settlement in that most threatened part of Europe between Germany and Russia, in which the central key position has for centuries fallen to Poland. The promise of a closer Polish-Czechoslovakian collaboration towards that object had a deep significance, removing the unfortunate misunderstanding between these two nations, and at the same time offering a distinct encouragement to other nations of that region to join, obviously on the principle of equality for all, the projected federal system. Moreover, at the International Labour Conference held in Washington one year later, these two nations decided closely to co-operate with two others, Yugoslavia and Greece, which concluded a similar agreement.

In any case, Poland's place, as well as that of the other Central European allies, in the post-war world seemed secure, provided only that Hitler would be decisively defeated. At the beginning of 1942 when the United Nations Declaration of 1st January solemnly confirmed the principles of the Atlantic Charter, such a victory still seemed far away, but the war situation definitely turned to the better in the fall of the same year, thanks to the battles of El Alamein in Egypt and of Stalingrad in Russia. Unfortunately it soon became obvious that the promised restoration of 'sovereign rights and self-government' to the liberated peoples, including Poland, depended not only 'the final destruction of the Nazi tyranny' but also on the post-war policy of Soviet Russia, whose relations with Poland deteriorated again very rapidly.

We know today that the real cause of the misunderstandings which appeared almost immediately after the agreements of 1941 was the Russian plan to set up Communist puppets who had been trained in Moscow in opposition to the legitimate Polish Government with whom these agreements had been concluded. The Polish forces which were organized in Russia after their release from prison camps had to be transferred to the Near East, while the fate of most of their officers who did not reappear after the so-called 'amnesty,' remained unexplained. Suddenly, in April 1943, the Germans announced that they had discovered the mass-graves of these thousands of Polish officers in the forest of Katyn near Smolensk where they obviously had been shot. When the Polish Government requested an investigation by the International Red Cross of that unprecedented crime, Soviet Russia broke off diplomatic relations with that Government which, in the midst of that alarming crisis lost its leader, General Sikorski, in an airplane crash, on 4th July 1943.

As Commander-in-Chief Sikorski was replaced by General Sosnkowski and as Prime Minister by the peasant leader Stanislaw Mikolajczyk who for almost a year and a half tried hard to re-establish friendly relations with the Russians. However, President Roosevelt and Winston Churchill, who exercised a strong pressure upon him, already at the Teheran Conference in the fall of 1943 tacitly admitted Stalin's claim to the eastern half of Poland as far as the badly misinterpreted Curzon line. They hoped that if she achieved satisfaction in that territorial issue, Soviet Russia would at least respect the real independence of the remaining part of Poland: as a matter of fact, a Communist 'Committee of National Liberation' was already prepared to seize control of the country as soon as the Red Army crossed the Curzon line.

These Russian agents, under Boleslaw Bierut, were indeed formally established in Lublin following their manifesto of 22nd July 1944. Before and after that happened the real Polish patriots made their two most outstanding and bloody contributions to the Allied war effort, one of them being a splendid victory of the regular Polish army in Italy, the other one ending in an especially glorious defeat of the underground forces on Polish soil.

When allied armies from various lands failed to take the stronghold which the Germans had established next to the Monastery of Monte Cassino thus blocking the way to Rome, the Polish corps under the command of General Wladyslaw Anders started another attack on 11th May and after eight days of desperate fighting, suffering the heaviest losses, finally broke the German resistance, and in a well-deserved triumph planted the Polish flag on the ruins of the monastery. That same corps, though decimated and without reserves, continued to fight on during the whole Italian campaign, liberating, among others, Bologna and Ancona, in spite of the disappointing news which was arriving from their country.

They knew only too well that the eastern part of Poland from which so many of them were coming, instead of being liberated, simply passed from the German occupation to the Russian. But in the heart of the country the underground forces, organized as a 'Home Army' under the command of General Tadeusz Bor-Komorowski, were still at the disposal of the secret authorities of the 'Underground State,' loyal to the exiled government in London. In spite of the systematic resistance with which these forces, supported by the whole population, opposed the Germans, conducting sabotage activities on the largest possible scale, they were blamed by Russian propaganda for not being active enough and called upon by repeated broadcasts openly to revolt against the Nazis when the Red Army reached the outskirts of Warsaw at the end of July 1944. When the Polish authorities really ordered such a general uprising on the fateful day of 1st August, the Russians first denied its importance and then, considering it contrary to their own plans, not only remained passive on the other side of the Vistula, but created the greatest difficulties when the Western Allies tried to assist, as least from the air, the Polish forces which had temporarily liberated a large part of the city.

Nevertheless, heroic street-fighting with the participation of the whole population continued for sixty-three days. What remained of the Home Army in the Polish capital, which thus sacrificed itself for the second time in the war, capitulated only when all supplies were completely exhausted, and even the enemies promised to spare the people of the city whom Hitler in his fury wanted to exterminate. These people were, however, expelled and deported in the most inhuman conditions and the buildings which were still standing after the bombardment of 1939, the annihilation of the Jewish ghetto in 1943, and the struggles of the uprising itself, suffered systematic destruction long after the cease-fire, with a view to removing all traces of Polish culture.

That work of destruction, truly symbolic of the fate of Poland in World War II, was being completed while Prime Minister Mikolajczyk and some of his colleagues had to negotiate in Moscow, both in August and October 1944, not only with the Soviet Government, but also with the Communist agents whom Stalin pretended to be the real 'government' of the 'liberated' country. Being exposed again to the pressure of

the Western Allies who still had far-reaching illusions as to
Stalin's intentions, Mikolajczyk became inclined to a compromise, but on his return to London had to resign in view of
the opposition of the majority of the Government. On 29th
November, the socialist leader, Tomasz Arciszewski, became
Prime Minister, and though practically without any allied
support, the Polish Government-in-Exile remained fully loyal
to the Allied cause until the end of the war against Germany.
This was best evidenced by the fact that the Polish forces,
which had participated from the outset in the invasion of the
Continent and distinguished themselves in France, particularly
at Falaise, played their part also in the liberation of Belgium
and Holland where they suffered serious losses at Arnhem, and
simultaneously with the last struggles of their comrades in
Italy, a Polish panzer division entered Germany from the west.

In doing so these soldiers could no longer hope to reach the
inspiring goal of their long campaign in foreign lands: a truly
free Poland. For from the east, from the devastated homeland
which had merely changed its conquerors, other Polish forces
were advancing as far as Berlin, not, however, as free men but
under Russian control and subject to Communist indoctri-
nation. Their fate was symbolic of another destruction which,
after the material ruins left behind by the German invaders,
was now threatening their country: the destruction of its spirit
and of its tradition by the same neighbour who had
participated in Hitler's aggression at the beginning of the war
and now, at its end, had gained even more than the German
dictator had offered him in the planned partition of
Poland — the complete control of that country, the annexation
of its eastern part being accompanied by an indirect
subjugation of the rest.

This had been decided some months before the struggle
against Germany was over at a conference which was held

amidst the continuing war-time destruction, but still must be considered the basic peace conference which settled the European problems of World War II: at Yalta. It was there that the third act of New Poland's tragedy was practically concluded by what has been so well called 'defeat in victory,' and that a curtain, soon to be called 'the Iron Curtain,' descended upon the scene of that tragedy, though the fourth act was already starting.

28

Ten Years of Trial

At Yalta the Polish question was only part of much larger issues. Yet no other problem was discussed at such length and in no other matter were the Russians less inclined to make any concession. For them the annexation of Eastern Poland was the final implementation of the historical process of 'collecting' all what they considered 'Russian lands,' a process which had started in the Middle Ages. And making Poland in its restricted boundaries a Russian satellite was a basic objective of Russian policy from the days of Peter the Great. In achieving this, Stalin was more successful than Catherine II had been, whose policy of partitioning Poland with the Germans he had been obliged to follow in 1939. Now, in 1945, he was even more successful than Alexander I in 1815, because this time no Polish territory was left outside the new Poland 'restored' by, and connected with Russia, and also because at the Crimean Conference — Russia's revenge for her setback in the Crimean War of ninety years before — the western powers accepted the Russian solution of the Polish question with even less opposition and misgivings than at the Congress of Vienna.

Their readiness to compromise at the expense of Poland—this time the most loyal ally—was the more surprising, because that Russian solution was also the Communist solution of the Polish problem, which made Poland, on whose conquest the control of all East Central Europe depended, the open gateway for Communist expansion toward the West. In 1920, a similar attempt had failed at the gates of Warsaw. When on 17th January 1945, that same heroic city was taken from the Germans not by the Polish underground forces, sacrificed a few months before, but by the Red Army which, in the two weeks preceding the Crimean Conference, occupied Western Poland also, 'a new situation' had been created indeed, as the Yalta Conference decision rightly pointed out. But neither President Roosevelt, deadly ill and badly advised, nor even Winston Churchill who knew Bolshevism so well, seemed to realize that this situation, far from being a 'liberation' of Poland, was a terrible threat to Europe. They did not realize either that the Red Army was no longer needed to defeat Germany whose last offensive, not long before Yalta, had seemed so alarming, nor to win the war against Japan whose remaining power of resistance was equally overrated. Without challenging any of Stalin's spurious arguments, they confirmed him in the possession of Eastern Poland including even Lwow which President Roosevelt tried in vain to save, and accepted a formula regarding the government of Poland which, though it seemed open to different interpretations, was, as a matter of fact, just another surrender to the Russian claims. For not only was the very existence of the legitimate Polish Government, an allied government still recognized by all powers except the Soviet Union, simply ignored, but instead of creating an entirely new government, according to the original intentions of the western negotiators, it was decided 'to reorganize on a broader democratic basis,' that is merely to enlarge, 'the provisional government which is now functioning in Poland,' viz. the group of Communist agents which Russia had put in power.

Speaking in that connection about 'democracy' was as misleading as the whole usual Soviet terminology in similar matters, since all these basic decisions were taken without even hearing any Polish representatives; the 'reorganization of the present (i.e. Communist-imposed) government' was entrusted to a commission composed of Molotov and the American and British ambassadors to the Soviet Union who would only 'consult' in Moscow some 'Polish Democratic leaders' obviously chosen by these three foreign diplomats; and last but not least, the Government thus enlarged was to be recognized by the western powers without waiting for the 'free and unfettered elections' which were promised without fixing any date nor providing any guarantees of real freedom.

The difficulties of carrying out even that most unfortunate agreement, in particular of choosing the 'democratic leaders' from Poland and abroad, became apparent immediately. President Roosevelt died deeply disillusioned as to the possibility of peaceful co-operation with Soviet Russia in this and many other questions, and his successor, President Truman, had to open the San Francisco Conference of the United Nations with the Polish chair left empty. A few days later Molotov admitted that the most qualified 'democratic leaders' from inside Poland, the leaders of the underground resistance against the Nazis, had been brought to Moscow not for consultation but for trial as war criminals, after a treacherous 'invitation.' In spite of initial American and British protests against such a 'kidnapping' of Polish patriots, both western powers continued to negotiate with that same Molotov as to the invitation of a few others, including also representatives of the Poles in exile, and insisting particularly on the participation of Mikolajczyk. This inclusion was the only concession which Harry Hopkins, when sent to Moscow by President Truman, was able to obtain from Stalin. He understood only too well that the presence of a former Polish Prime Minister who, contrary to the solemn protests of his government, had publicly approved the Yalta decision, would create the misleading illusion that, after all, there was a 'merger' of two Polish governments with appearances of legality.

Besides Mikolajczyk only one more of the three invited 'London Poles,' now another private citizen, agreed to come to Moscow at the time when the sixteen underground leaders were sentenced, and to join, along with two politicians picked up in occupied Poland, the sixteen Communist tools in what was accepted by the Molotov Commission as the 'Polish Government of National Unity.' Proclaimed in Moscow on 23rd June that 'government' was recognized on 5th July by the United States and the United Kingdom, who at the same time withdrew recognition from the constitutional Government of Poland, their faithful war-time ally. This was, for the time being, the end of Polish independence and a clear evidence that the trial, not of a few leaders only but of the whole Polish nation, would continue indefinitely without any assistance from the outside world. The Soviets had started this trial immediately after expelling the German invaders. Gradually most countries established diplomatic relations with the new Warsaw regime, and only the Vatican, Ireland, Spain, Lebanon, and a few Latin American republics continued to recognize the legal Polish authorities which remained in exile in London. So did, scattered all over the world, most of the Poles who had escaped from their Nazi occupied country, including the overwhelming majority of those who had fought on the Allied side to the bitter end.

The Potsdam Conference, which on 1st August of the same
tragic year of 1945 announced that the Polish government in
London had 'ceased to exist,' had to consider another aspect of
the Polish problem which at Yalta had been left in suspense. It
had been recognized there 'that Poland must receive
substantial accession of territory in the north and west.'
Already then the Oder-Neisse line had been considered as the
Polish-German boundary and now, at Potsdam, the territories
east of that line were placed under Polish administration.
While, however, the northern part of East Prussia with
Koenigsberg was definitely attributed to Soviet Russia, the
final delimitation of the lands which were supposed to
compensate Poland for her extensive losses in the east was left
again to the future peace conference. In spite of that vague
reservation which was to encourage German revisionism, the
Polish authorities were permitted to continue, in an orderly
fashion, to remove the German population of these regions
which, to a large extent had already fled or was expelled
during the advance of the Red Army. These mass migrations
resulted, of course, in great hardships though not greater than
those suffered by the Poles who were being transferred from
Soviet annexed Eastern Poland to these western territories. In
any case, the Poles could only interpret as permanent the
attribution of these lands which they called 'recovered'
territories, because all of them from Pomerania with Szczecin
(the German Stettin) at the mouth of the Oder to the whole of
Silesia with its capital Wroclaw (Breslau), had once belonged
to medieval Poland.

Having also gained the full control of Gdansk (Danzig) and
the southern part of East Prussia, the new Poland acquired
indeed a much better western frontier than after World War I
and also lands which in the past had been richer than most of
those she lost in the east. At the given moment, however, they

were completely ruined and devastated, and therefore required a special effort of reconstruction. Furthermore, even with these accessions, the area of Poland was about 20 per cent smaller than in 1939—121 thousand square miles—and her total population reduced to about two-thirds, the cruel extermination of almost three million Jews by the Nazis being about one-third of that terrific loss. Under these conditions, the determination to retain at least the partial compensation in the west soon became the unanimous attitude of all Poles including those in exile, though at Potsdam only representatives of the new regime were consulted in that vital matter.

That regime, though obviously imposed by Soviet Russia and subservient to her, was not yet exclusively composed of Communists. Mikolajczyk was made second Vice-Premier and Minister of Agriculture and the two members from inside Poland who were added to the original group belonged to the Peasant Party. Like the other Pole from London, who was made Minister of Labor, the Prime Minister himself, Edward Osobka-Morawski, and a few other ministers, these men were members of the Socialist party. A few minor parties also had representatives in the 'Government of National Unity,' which soon ceased to call itself 'Provisional.' But all these temporarily tolerated parties, even before the planned 'mergers,' had to conform to the Moscow-dictated directives of the 'Polish Workers' Party,' as the Communists called themselves. This leading party contained the 'President of the National Council' and as such temporary Head of the State, Boleslaw Bierut, the first Vice-Premier, Wladyslaw Gomulka, other ministers in key positions like the Minister of Public Security and dreaded chief of the secret police, Stanislaw Radkiewicz, and the power behind the scene,' Under-Secretary Jakob Berman.

The remainder of the Home Army and in general all those who having been well trained in the underground resistance

against the German occupation, could have played a similar
role in opposing Russian occupation and Communist rule,
were rapidly liquidated, some of them after continued
resistance 'in the woods.' New concentration camps, called
labour camps, replaced those which the retreating Germans
had left behind, and considerable forces of the Red Army
which were stationed in Poland, allegedly to protect the
communication lines with the Russian forces in Germany,
helped to keep under strictest control the Polish people who,
cut off from the free world, were squeezed between the Soviet
Union and the Russian zone of occupation in Germany.

Under such conditions any resistance movement soon
became entirely hopeless and would have been simply suicidal.
Furthermore, the Communists, benefiting from some natural
feeling of relief after the ordeal of open persecution by the
Nazis, were wise enough not to proceed immediately and
violently to the complete Sovietization of the country. They
even tolerated some kind of 'loyal opposition' practised by the
Peasant Party, but postponed as long as possible the pledged
elections in which that party could expect to have the support
of all those opposed to Communism, that is of the tremendous
majority of the nation. In preparation for these elections and
with a view of confusing public opinion, the government
decided at last, not before the spring of 1946, to hold a
'referendum' in which three specific question were to be
answered by a 'yes' or 'no.' One of these questions: whether the
new western frontier ought to be permanent, was uncontro-
versial and the expected, quasi-unanimous affirmative vote
was to be a first test in favour of those in power. Another
question concerned the permanence of the nationalization of
basic industries and of the land reform which the Communists
had introduced immediately after seizing control and which
they wanted to be included in the Constitution. Since the

Manifesto of 22nd July 1944 had already decided that all estates of more than 50 hectares should be distributed to landless peasants and since that drastic reform which did not even leave those 50 hectares to owners of larger estates but expropriated them completely had been carried out in the greatest hurry, it would have been hardly possible to annul all that had happened. There remained, therefore, only one question which the opposition had a chance to make a test against the regime: the question of whether or not the Senate should be abolished. Since an affirmative answer was to imply an important change in the democratic Constitution of 1921 which the regime pretended to respect, it was only natural for all those who wanted to prevent the Sovietization of Poland, to vote 'No.' So indeed did a very large majority on the day of the referendum, 30th June 1946, in spite of the strongest pressure and even terror of the authorities, which, however, did not hesitate to falsify the counting and reporting of the ballots and to announce officially that even on that decisive question the government had won. It now felt safe to hold the long-delayed elections half a year later, on 19 January 1947.

The only possibility of controlling these elections which the Yalta agreement had given to the western powers was to have them observed by their diplomatic missions in Poland. All reports thus received, and in particular those of the American Ambassador, Arthur Bliss Lane, stressed most emphatically that the elections, far from being 'free and unfettered,' were preceded and accompanied by another wave of terror and fraudulent procedure, directed especially against Mikolajczyk's Peasant Party, leading the opposition. That party received, therefore, only 28 out of 444 seats in the new, unicameral Diet and no representation at all in the government which nevertheless continued to be recognized by the democratic powers. Bierut was now formally elected 'President' of the

Republic and the so-called 'Little Constitution' created a 'State Council' under his chairmanship which was to exercise full power when the Diet was not in session.

This was indeed a first step toward the enforcement of an entirely new constitution following the Soviet pattern, and in order to crush any possible opposition, an almost uninterrupted series of political trials was being staged which all ended in severe, frequently death, sentences against alleged 'spies and foreign agents.' Mikolajczyk, who felt personally threatened, succeeded in escaping from Poland at the end of October 1947 and through London went to Washington. He organized there his own political movement based on the experience that any co-operation with the Communist regime was impossible, but unfortunately, instead of co-operating with the legitimate Polish authorities in exile, he created a split in the Polish emigration. Its majority, however, remained loyal to the constitutional Government and to the President whose office, after the death of W. Raczkiewicz, on 6th June 1947, was now held by August Zaleski, the former Minister of Foreign Affairs in the years 1926-32 and 1939-41.

About the same time, in July 1947, Poland was forced by Moscow to reject any participation in the Marshall Plan which would have been so helpful in the task of post-war reconstruction, much more difficult than after World War I. That nevertheless so much was accomplished in this field, particularly with regard to the rebuilding of the capital and the rehabilitation of the formerly German provinces, must be attributed to the strenuous efforts of the Polish people, while its present masters were 'planning' even their economic policy, including the industrialization of the country and the development of trade relations, strictly on the Soviet pattern.

The opposition between the natural trends and interests of the nation and the orders coming from Moscow became even more striking in the field of cultural reconstruction. In the first years after the defeat of the Germans who had tried to suppress any cultural life in Poland, the possibility of reopening at last all Polish educational institutions and of publishing what had been secretly written under the German occupation was welcomed indeed, and what was left of Poland's intellectual leaders tried hard to revive the national tradition in learning and literature. The lost universities of Lwow and Wilno were replaced by those of Wroclaw, where the German university was taken over, and Torun, where an entirely new university was founded. New universities were founded at Lodz and at Lublin, in addition to the old Catholic university there. But the only too well-known principle of the nationalities policy of the Soviet Union was gradually and with increasing vigour applied also to the national culture of the allegedly 'free and sovereign' Poles: they were free again to write and to teach in their own language, though a subtle process of Russification was soon to start, but in that 'free form' the ideological 'content' of culture was supposed to become more and more identical with that in Soviet Russia. Nothing could be more typical in that respect than the systematically promoted process of re-writing Polish history, and nothing more symbolic than the enforced liquidation, at a mass-congress of scholars held in Warsaw in the summer of 1951, of the Polish Academy and its replacement by a new Academy of Science entirely similar to the Russian, with its headquarters in a gigantic palace erected as a 'gift' of the Soviet Union in the very heart of the capital.

Only a few months after the formal establishment of that Academy, on 22nd July 1952, the anniversary of the Manifesto of 1944, now the official 'national' holiday, the new Constitution of the Polish 'People's Republic' came into force after long preparatory studies with appearances of 'free' public discussion. Year after year careful steps had been taken leading to that momentous turning point in the Sovietization of the country. At the end of 1948, the Polish Socialist Party was forced to merge with the Communists in the 'United Polish Workers' Party,' and in that merger the preponderance of the Communist element was so complete that it mattered very little that another former Socialist, Josef Cyrankiewicz, succeeded Osobka-Morawski as Prime Minister. Much more important and profoundly shocking was, in November 1949, the appointment of a Soviet Marshal, apparently of Polish origin, Constantine Rokossovsky, as Minister of Defence and Commander-in-Chief of the Polish army, where all higher positions were given to Russion officers. Next came, in 1950, the replacement of the old civil administration by 'People's Councils' on all levels, practically identical with the Russian 'Soviets' and completely under Communist control. That hierarchy of Councils, following the Soviet pattern, was to become a striking feature of the new 1952 Constitution, through which the National Council at the top of the ladder, composed of sixteen members, received almost dictatorial powers; since its chairman, chosen in the person of a well-known Communist, Alexander Zawadzki, was to be the Head of the State, the office of President of the Republic was completely abolished, Bierut taking over the premiership.

That in March 1954, one year after Stalin's death which hardly affected conditions in Poland, Bierut was shifted to the post of First Secretary of the Central Committee of the Communist Party and replaced in turn by Cyrankiewicz, seems to have been only one of the secondary personal changes in the regime. Highly significant is, on the contrary, the interpretation of the 'Socialist' Constitution as a preparation for, and transition to, a fully-fledged Communist system, the main difference being that private ownership of land is still admitted. However, the collectivization of agriculture is strongly encouraged and the number of collective farms, identical with the Russian 'Kolkhozy,' steadily growing.

For that very reason the Polish peasants, very individualistic and badly disappointed in their hope that the land reform would favour private enterprise, are one of the most determined elements of opposition against the whole foreign imposed regime, so alien to the national tradition. Disappointed, too, are the workers who have to labour harder than ever before and suffer, along with the intellectuals, from entirely inadequate wages, without the right to seek improvements through strikes, and fully aware that the Communist leaders are forming a new privileged class to the disadvantage of all others. But in all classes of society the opposition to the present conditions, unbroken though silenced, is far from being animated exclusively or even predominantly, by material motives. The materialistic ideology itself, so contrary to the Polish mind and to the dignity of the human person, dear to all Poles precisely because foreign oppression so frequently violated their inalienable human rights, is rejected by a majority of the nation which is still so overwhelming that, according to the most reliable estimates, hardly 5 per cent have been really won over to Communism. The deep religious revival which had already started during the sufferings of Nazi rule, continued with truly remarkable ardour in defiance of the most intense Communist propaganda. Therefore the Catholic Church, to which almost all Poles belong and which represents both the heritage of their past and their intimate connection with the western world, became the most powerful stronghold of moral and spiritual resistance in their present trial.

Even the Communists and their Russian masters were so well aware of this that they avoided the mistake of directly attacking and openly persecuting the Catholic Church, particularly during the first post-war years. It was highly significant, however, that they decided at once to denounce the Concordat which free Poland had concluded with the Holy See in 1925, and to start a campaign of slander against the Vatican accusing Pius XII himself, who had given so many proofs of sympathy with the Poles, of favouring the Germans and serving American imperialism. Nevertheless, the Primate of Poland, Cardinal Hlond, was permitted to return and to reside in Warsaw, uniting this archbishopric with his traditional See of Gniezno. Until the death of this outstanding religious leader on 22nd October 1948, his unique authority remained unchallenged, and so was that of Archbishop Sapieha of Cracow who had played a truly heroic role during the German occupation and soon after the war was also made a cardinal. However, when he, too, died on 23rd July 1951, the situation of the Church in Poland, unshaken in its loyalty to Rome, was already extremely critical, in spite of an agreement with the state which had been signed on 14th April 1950.

The hierarchy including the new Primate Archbishop Stefan Wyszynski, though deeply disturbed by the recent suppressions of the Catholic charities organization which was taken over by the State, accepted that agreement, because it formally recognized the supreme authority of the Holy See in all religious matters and seemed to guarantee for the time being the existence of what remained of Catholic education, including the University of Lublin, and of Catholic publications. But it soon became apparent that the Communist regime was ready to seize every pretext for accusing the Church of not respecting the agreement, for instance in the matter of the Soviet sponsored peace campaign, while the administration violated systematically the promises made to the hierarchy. Particularly dangerous proved the ever-

growing diversionist inteventions which tried to oppose to the
bishops the so-called 'patriotic priests' and groups of Catholic
laymen co-operating with the regime. Even so, the plan of
creating a schismatic 'national' church did not succeed: on the
contrary, even the delicate problem of the ecclesiastical
administration of the formerly German Western territories was
settled in spite of the obvious provocations of the regime which
not only attacked the Vatican in that matter but wrongly
accused the hierarchy of lack of loyalty to their country.

Such charges continued to be made, on different grounds,
against individual members of the clergy who were tried and
sentenced for 'spying' or treason, and even against several
bishops who were put in jail or at least interned. When
Primate Wyszynski was made a cardinal at the end of 1952 he
did not find it possible to come to Rome for the Consistory in
January of the following year. But even so the recognition
which he received from the Holy See was answered on 9th
February 1953 by a decree which made all ecclesiastical
positions in Poland entirely dependent on the administration,
an interference which was contrary to the very principle of
separation between Church and State as stressed in the new
constitution. This decree was, however, only one item of the
long list of violations of the 1950 agreement by the State and of
the repressions directed against Poland's religious life which
the hierarchy, headed by Cardinal Wyszynski, denounced in a
long memorandum sent to Bierut on 8th May the feast of St.
Stanislaus, the patron of Catholic Poland canonized 700 years
before.

In no other case has the 'Church of Silence' — as Pius XII
called the Catholic Church in the Communist-controlled
countries — broken that enforced silence so courageously as did
the Polish bishops on that memorable occasion. Without
entering into politics, they openly opposed atheistic materialism

with its ruthless and malicious methods and eloquently defended the nation's religious tradition as well as the person of the Pope, so that their protest and their declaration of 'non possumus' was the most energetic and at the same time the most dignified challenge of Communist rule in Poland—a truly historic testimony in Poland's contemporary trial.

The reaction was quick to come. After one more spurious trial of a bishop who was sentenced to twelve years of jail, the Primate himself was brutally arrested on 26th September on the pretext of not having condemned an alleged American spy among the hierarchy. He was removed to some unknown place and prevented from exercising his authority, while the episcopate was obliged to elect another temporary head. That arbitrary act of violence against the worthy successor of those who in old Poland replaced the person of the king in the interval between two reigns, did not succeed in disorganizing the Catholic Church of Poland nor in separating it from Rome. It was, however, another mortal blow inflicted upon the Polish people and a stern warning that nobody was safe any longer in the unhappy country.

Coming after similar actions against the Primates of Croatia and Hungary, two other Cardinals under Communist power, the fate of Archbishop Wyszynski deeply shocked the free world, where it raised a wave of solemn protests. This certainly was a comfort to the people of Poland who, though behind the so-called 'Iron Curtain'—a rather misleading expression—are reached by the voice of the outside world. They resent the fact that usually their own situation is not sufficiently understood by so many foreign peoples, who are inclined to identify Poland and the Poles with the Soviet-controlled regime which was forced upon them in 1945. This being so, it must be strongly emphasized that it is impossible to speak, with reference to the period which started that year, of any 'Polish' foreign policy. The history of Poland throughout the present years of trial is nothing but the sad story of her internal Sovietization and of her misrepresentation in all external relations by Communist agents who in practically every matter take and must take an attitude completely contrary to that of the Polish people and to their real interests.

There is only one important exception in that respect, and it concerns Poland's western frontier. Without being reconciled at all with the enormous territorial losses in the east, the Poles are indeed determined to keep what they have recovered, resettled and rebuilt in the west. They are, therefore, alarmed whenever their definite possession of these lands is questioned by the western powers, and this is the only point where Russian and Communist propaganda has any chances of influencing them. Nevertheless, they realize that even in that matter the support which is being received from the Soviet Union and shrewdly discounted by her agents is dictated by mere expediency and depends entirely on Russia's German policy. The Poles know, too, that if the Government of East Germany, which is as dependent on Moscow as is the Warsaw regime, makes statements and even signs agreements—in 1950 and 1951—recognizing the Oder-Neisse line as permanent, this does not mean an acceptance of that boundary by the German people. Furthermore, being fully aware that an agreement with the Germans in this and other matters, desirable and even necessary as it is, will not be easy to reach after liberation, the Poles are also impressed by the Russian arguments against the rearmament of Western Germany, though they are hardly misled by similar propaganda against any integration of Europe on federal lines.

They know only too well that the trend toward federalism, which during the war was so strong among all Poles, including those in exile and the underground leaders, was and is opposed by Soviet Russia even as far as any free co-operation among the so-called 'satellite' countries is concerned. Just because they are supposed to be and to remain satellites, they are not permitted, even under their present Communist regimes, to join in any federal unions which would make them stronger with respect to the Soviet Union. Only bilateral agreements, especially in the economic and cultural field, between Poland and the other enslaved countries are encouraged, and all of them, Poland even more than any other, are supposed individually to tighten their relations with Soviet Russia, in order to build up a solid monolithic bloc under the absolute control of that overwhelmingly stronger power.

To serve the interests of that bloc under Russian leadership is the only task of the diplomats, by now practically all Communists, who are supposed to represent Poland in the free countries and in those international organizations which she is permitted to join, particularly in the United Nations, where the place due the legitimate allied Polish Government was taken soon after the San Francisco Conference by such Communist, Russian-controlled agents. Their attitude, especially when they were elected, as 'Polish' delegates, to the Security Council or the Economic and Social Council, offered the most convincing evidence that they were simply adding their vote to that of the Soviet republics and supporting the Russian policy directed against the western, democratic powers and in particular against the United States. That attitude found its clearest expression during the war in Korea, and therefore the participation of 'Poland' as a 'neutral' country in the armistice negotiations was just another painful fiction. The same must be said of the 'Polish' participation in the settlement of the problems of Indo-China, in the Moscow Conference at the end of 1954 which was supposed to oppose the whole Soviet bloc to the North Atlantic Treaty

Organization and in the treaty signed in Warsaw, in May of 1955, with a view to consolidating the military co-operation of all Soviet-controlled countries.

On several other occasions, patriotic Poles, who inadvertently had been included among the representatives of the regime, seized the first opportunity to escape, to ask for asylum in the free world and to confirm that under Communist control they had not been able to represent the Polish people. They confirmed, too, that these people, in spite of the disappointment of 1945 and of the anti-American propaganda to which they have been subject ever since with increasing intensity, continued to look upon the United States and its leading role in world affairs as their only hope for a better future. Though they do not know when and how liberation will be achieved, they are convinced that it must come as part of the liberation of all nations which in 1945 shared Poland's fate. The unity of the whole region between Germany and Russia, between the Baltic and the Mediterranean, is indeed becoming evident more than ever before in history, and equally evident is Poland's key position once more in that region whose freedom is vital for the peace of Europe, hence for world peace and for the United States of America, desirous to see that peace solidly established.

Once more the Polish question, apparently a source of trouble, is, as a matter of fact, a real test case, and the issue of her present trial, like the issue of her ordeal in the nineteenth century, will have a deep significance for all mankind. Much more than then, or during World War I and even during World War II in which from June 1941 totalitarian, imperialistic powers were fighting on either side, the conflict of which Poland is the most typical victim is a conflict between freedom and tyranny, human rights and their negation, the

Christian conception of a peaceful world under God and a mechanistic mass organization by atheistic materialsim.

No historian can even begin to predict how long Poland's present trial is going to last. But looking upon Polish history as a whole, it is easy to find out that this trial, the fourth act of new Poland's tragedy, cannot be the last one. The story of that new Poland which started with World War I, is indeed, like that of her heroic army in World War II, a story still 'without the last chapter.' Millions of Poles at home and in exile hope and pray that this last chapter may be written as a glorious conclusion of Poland's millennium which is to be celebrated in a few years, recalling the greatness of the Piast Kingdom, the Jagiellonian Union, and the Royal Republic. In our time, in that twentieth century so different from the tenth when Polish history started at the extreme border of western, Christian civilization, in that new period of general history when the destinies of all nations are so closely interrelated, such a conclusion does certainly not depend on the Poles alone, even less than when they tried so hard to save their old Commonwealth from partition. But their own responsibility which they share with their equally suffering neighbours and sister nations, some of which had once been connected with that Commonwealth, is heavy enough, heavier perhaps than during the partition period. For that great majority which continues to live in the homeland, it is the responsibility of going through an unprecedented trial with a spirit unbroken and faithful to the principles on which Poland's greatness was founded in the past. For those in exile it is the responsibility of remaining united in dedication to the cause of Poland's independence and of raising the voice of free Poland in the free world. And both of them have to wait for human justice and Divine mercy.

29

The Rise and Fall of Gomulka

The rigid Stalinist system established in Poland between 1949 and 1953 did not long outlast the death of Stalin in March 1953. Yet the process by which it was dismantled proved initially to be somewhat slower than parallel developments in Hungary and Czechoslovakia. Indeed, the high point in the conflict between the Church and the Communist authorities, the arrest of the Primate, Cardinal Wyszynski and his confinement in a monastery took place as late as September 1953. Similarly, in spite of some concessions to the 'New Course' adopted by Malenkov in the USSR in August 1953, the second congress of the Polish United Workers Party in March 1954 still upheld without major modification the basic Stalinist economic policies of rapid industrialization, stress on heavy industry and further collectivization in agriculture. A number of factors explain the relative lack of movement in Polish politics in the year after Stalin's death. In the first place, the process of Stalinization had not been as ruthlessly pursued in Poland as elsewhere in Eastern Europe. As late as 1955, for instance, agriculture was dominated by private production, with state farms controlling only 14 per cent of arable land and

collectives 9 per cent. A significant private industrial sector
and class of artisans had also managed to survive in spite of
punitive taxation. Though Wladyslaw Gomulka and a number
of his associates had been purged from the party and
imprisoned, the party leadership had rejected all pressures
from Moscow to make them the victims of a show trial similar
to those taking place elsewhere in Eastern Europe.
Furthermore, Boleslaw Bierut, the Party First Secretary, never
enjoyed the unchallenged political ascendancy of Stalin and
some of his other protégés. It is also characteristic that Poland
was the one country in Eastern Europe where a monument to
Stalin was not erected. In addition, though church-state
relations had deteriorated drastically, so that by 1954 nine
bishops and several hundred priests were under arrest, the
regime failed to mount a show trial against Cardinal
Wyszynski. The Catholic University of Lublin continued to
function and provided a haven for both staff and students who
found access to higher education elsewhere difficult on social
or political grounds.

Change was also inhibited by the fact that by 1953, the
Party, though still enjoying minimal support in Poland, had
become a vast and privileged bureaucracy numbering over one
million members. The main interest of a large proportion of
the Party functionaries, many of whom were poorly educated
and owed their advance to the purges of 1949-52 in which at
least 30 per cent of the Party members were expelled, was to
avoid any changes which would endanger their position.
Moreover, the regime was well aware of its weakness and
isolation. Most of those in prison were supporters of the
pre-war regime or the government-in-exile, while any change
of agricultural policy could only strengthen the peasantry who
were also regarded as hostile. There was a real fear that any
modification of the rigid political model imposed on Poland

might lead to incalculable consequences. Finally, western support for West Germany seemed to many Poles to call into doubt Poland's hold on her newly acquired western and northern territories and thus dictated some accommodation with the existing regime which could at least guarantee Soviet protection.

Nevertheless, pressures for change soon began to build up. These were the result both of the impact of events in the Soviet Union and of demands in Poland itself for the modification of the Stalinist system. Stalin's rule by personal terror did not survive him, and his death was followed by the establishment of the principle of collective leadership and the repudiation of the principle of the cult of the individual. At the same time, the fall of Beria, head of the HVD, in 1953 led to a drastic weakening of the security apparatus. These changes were bound to initiate demands for similar reforms in the countries of Eastern Europe. The 'New Course' initiated by Malenkov in August 1953 and not seriously modified by Khrushchev after the establishment of his personal ascendancy in May 1955 also seemed to have implications for the Soviet Union's satellites. This policy called for greater stress on consumer goods, aid to agriculture, a diminution of the power of the security apparatus and greater freedom in the arts. The new softer line in Soviet foreign policy towards the west made the rigours of Stalinism more difficult to justify, while Khrushchev's rapprochement with Yugoslavia from May 1955 seemed to legitimize the concept of 'separate roads to socialism' the very deviation for which Gomulka had been expelled from the Polish United Workers Party. Finally, the obvious policy divisions within the Soviet leadership stimulated those in the Polish party who wanted greater autonomy in Polish affairs.

In Poland, calls for change became increasingly vocal. Writers and intellectuals called for an end to the crude rigidities of Stalinism in the cultural field. Under their pressure, the weekly press became notably freer in highlighting the social problems which had been created in Poland by rapid industrialization and which had been ignored previously since official dogma had denied they could exist under socialism. In April 1954, the Minister of Culture, Wlodzimierz Sokorski, even admitted that 'stagnation' and 'deterioration' had occurred in the artistic field as a result of the 'false interpretation' of the doctrine of socialist realism. Censorship of the arts was now somewhat relaxed, and the crudities of the official Marxist line in history and sociology subjected to scathing criticism. Party attempts at re-establishing discipline over the writers and intellectuals in late 1955 were completely unsuccessful and were in fact repudiated by the party theoretical journal *Nowe Drogi* in January 1956. The intelligentsia was again taking on its traditional role of spokesman for the Polish nation. Its mood, and particularly that of its younger members, was summed up in an article in the student newspaper *Po Prostu*, which proclaimed 'We are people who cannot stop meddling with all that happens around us. We are a group of the discontented; we want more things, wiser things, better things.'

Within the United Workers Party, many members were disillusioned with the way the country was being governed and, in particular, at the way in which its interests were being subordinated to those of the Soviet Union. Their dissatisfaction was greatly increased when the defection in December 1954 of a senior official of the security apparatus, Jozef Swiatlo, revealed that Bierut, probably under Soviet pressure, had established in 1952 a special department to watch over the loyalty of the top Party leadership. As a result, Bierut was strongly criticized in the Politbureau in December 1954. A number of political prisoners, including Gomulka himself, were released, Radkiewicz, the head of the security police was demoted and the separate status of the Ministry of Public Security was abolished. In general, the power of the secret police was now drastically cut down. The divisions between reformers and Stalinists in the Party emerged clearly at the Third Plenum of Central Committee in January 1955. On this occasion, the majority favoured further changes to reduce the power of the security apparatus, to increase the scope for free discussion in the Party and to modify the planning system so as to make it more responsive to initiatives from the shop-floor. Yet the strength of the conservatives on the Politbureau was sufficient largely to frustrate the introduction of these reforms.

At the same time, many economists were demanding a more flexible economic system, less based on the Soviet experience of the 1930s and more responsive to Polish conditions. The Six-Year Plan adopted in 1950 had been largely successful in its main goal, the tripling of the index of producer goods between 1950 and 1955 and the increase of non-agricultural employment by over 60 per cent (according to the official figures). But these gains had been achieved by investing what was officially estimated at 25 per cent, but was probably nearer 30 per cent of the national income mostly in heavy industrial projects. Agriculture, consumer goods, housing and social services had all been neglected, the system had proved wasteful and over-centralized and the living standards of the workers had almost certainly fallen. Moreover criticism was raised not only against the conception of the plan but at the way in which, in order to justify its implementation, statistics had been juggled with and even falsified.

It was in 1956 that the pace of change began to accelerate startlingly. At the Twentieth Congress of the Soviet Communist Party, the concept of separate national roads to socialism was given clear legitimization, while Khrushchev's secret speech, with its revelation of the horrors which had accompanied Stalin's rule, seriously undermined the authority of local Stalinists in Poland. So too did the public announcement during the Congress that Stalin's dissolution of the Communist Party of Poland in mid-1938 and the subsequent deaths of most of its leaders in Soviet camps had been the result of accusations 'based on materials which were falsified by subsequently exposed provocateurs.' These revelations would almost certainly have led to Bierut's fall and probably hastened his death on 12th March 1956. He was succeeded by Edward Ochab, who in spite of his Stalinist past was by now committed to moderate reforms. In April, he told a meeting of Party activists that 'democratization' would continue and announced the release of Gomulka and the restoration of his Party rights and those of a number of his associates. In the same month a wider amnesty led to the release of some 28,000 political prisoners. Further barriers to change were removed by the dismissal in April of Sokorski, the unpopular Minister of Culture, and in May of Jakob Berman, a vice-premier and the leading Stalinist ideologist in Poland. At the same time Khrushchev's secret speech was released to Party members in a fairly large edition. Its contents soon became widely known and increased the political ferment. Pressure for further democratization was centred above all in the various writers' circles, among students and in the press.

The Party itself remained divided on how to react to demands for change, for, while the Party Secretariat now had a reformist majority, conservatives were strongly entrenched in the Central Committee. These divisions were seriously widened by an outbreak of labour unrest at the ZISPO engineering works in Poznan, the largest industrial establishment in Poland, at the end of June. The workers, who had originally limited their demands to economic questions soon began to call for political changes. Matters took an ugly turn when the army began to use firearms to restore order. Over fifty workers were killed and several hundred wounded.

The rioting in Poznan was interpreted by the conservatives in the Polish Party and also by the Soviet leadership as proof that the process of democratization was being exploited by hostile forces in the west to undermine socialism in Poland. To the liberals however, it was, in Ochab's phrase, the result of the 'immense wrongs' which the working class had suffered during the Six-Year Plan and demonstrated the urgent need for continuing the policy of liberalization. These divisions were clearly evident at the Seventh Plenum of the Central Committee at the end of July. Here the liberals, sometimes referred to as the Pulawy faction, from the street in Warsaw where they met, were able to secure the adoption of a resolution calling for further democratization. The hardliners, also known as the Natolin group from an estate outside Warsaw where they gathered were, however, able to add a series of qualifying clauses stressing the dangers in the democratization process which could play into the hands of 'the class enemy and alien imperialist agents.' This resolution represented the first open disagreement between the Polish Party and the Soviets and it was adopted in spite of the presence at the Plenum of a large Soviet delegation.

Throughout the summer, the fate of the reform programme hung in the balance. Conservatives in the Party, aware of the divisions in the Central Committee and the opposition of the Soviet Union, did all they could to oppose further changes. At the same time, considerable pressure for liberalization began to build up from below. The reformists controlled the Party organization in Warsaw and in several other cities and enjoyed considerable support in the Party youth organization, among the intelligentsia and in the radio and some sections of the

press. A new and more liberal head of the State Planning
Commission was appointed, while the previously docile
parliament (Sejm) began to display an unwonted degree of
independence. Only light sentences were imposed on the
workers tried for their participation in the Poznan riots, while
in a number of factories reformist workers councils began to
spring up.

Clearly by now the divisions were so deep that they could
only be resolved by the establishment of a new Politbureau and
Central Committee in which one or other faction would be
dominant. Another key issue was the terms on which
Gomulka, who was being courted by both groups but who
inclined towards the liberals, would be incorporated into the
Party leadership. Gomulka, for his part, refused to accept high
office unless a number of his principal opponents were
removed from their positions, above all Hilary Minc, who had
dominated Polish economic planning since 1949, and Marshal
Rokossovsky, the symbol of Soviet hegemony in Poland.

The decisive meeting of the Central Committee Plenum was
scheduled for the end of October. Already by this time, the
political balance was swinging in favour of the reformists. In
August Zenon Kliszko, who had been purged along with
Gomulka in 1949, was appointed Deputy Minister of Justice,
while another of Gomulka's associates, General Waclaw
Komar, was placed in command of the paramilitary Internal
Security Corps. In early October Minc was deprived of his
position. The Plenum met between 19 and 21 October and
immediately co-opted Gomulka to the Central Committee. In
spite of strong pressure on behalf of the conservatives from a
Soviet delegation headed by Khrushchev, which even
threatened military intervention, the liberals triumphed. This
threat was certainly not an idle one, for the Soviets had
mobilized a large number of their own troops both within

Poland and on its eastern and western borders, but they were deterred both by the firm resistance of the liberal majority on the Plenum, led by Gomulka himself, and by Gomulka's assurances that Poland would not pursue an anti-Soviet policy. Moreover, it soon became clear that the loyalty of the Polish Army could not be relied on, that the Internal Security Corps commanded by General Komar would intervene on the side of the Plenum majority and that the various workers' councils were also mobilizing in its defence. Gomulka made a strong speech in the Plenum attacking the economic policies which had been pursued since 1949, and also the cult of the personality, and stressed the need for equality and independence in Polish-Soviet relations; he was elected First Secretary of the Central Committee. A new Politbureau dominated by Gomulka's supporters was created, from which the most intransigent Stalinists as well as Marshal Rokossovsky were excluded. General Spychalski, closely linked with Gomulka, was placed in charge of the Polish army, while the independence of the Committee of Public Security was finally abolished and its functions shared out among the various ministries, above all the Ministry of the Interior.

Paradoxically, Gomulka's position was significantly strengthened by the impact of the Polish changes in Hungary. Here a smooth transition from Stalinism proved impossible to arrange and a revolution occurred which took an increasingly anti-Soviet character and was bloodily repressed by the Soviets in early November. These developments discredited the Stalinist faction in Poland, who had been prepared to risk Soviet intervention to maintain their positions. They also seemed to many Poles, mindful of the enormous sacrifices of the Second World War, to justify Gomulka's policies of moderate reform and to underline the dangers of pushing the Soviets too far.

It was perhaps inevitable that Gomulka should have disappointed the high hopes raised by his return to power. The overwhelming majority of Poles gave him their wholehearted support, as they clearly demonstrated in the elections of January 1957, which were transformed into a plebiscite on the events of the 'Polish October' which had brought Gomulka back to high office. Yet they did so because they believed that, in his calls for a 'Polish road to socialism', Gomulka envisaged far-reaching measures of internal democratization and a large degree of independence from the Soviet Union. Their goal, in the words of the student newspaper *Po Prostu*, was to 'bring about a radical transformation of the Stalinist model of socialism to a Polish model, genuinely socialist.' The changes they demanded lay in a widening of cultural and religious freedom, the establishment of institutional checks to safeguard the rule of law and prevent a return to arbitrary rule and the transformation of parliament into a body which could exercise some control over the administration. In addition they called for a reduction of the power of the bureaucracy, the granting of greater autonomy to local government bodies and the development of the rights of voluntary association.

It was never either within Gomulka's power or, indeed, part of his intentions to introduce changes of this type. In the first place, Soviet actions in Hungary and the still unresolved power struggle in the USSR seemed to him to demonstrate the severe limitations imposed on Polish freedom of action. As he bluntly warned in his election address, a failure to support him could well result in the 'crossing out of Poland from the map of European states.' In addition, although a number of the more extreme Stalinists were purged, the bulk of Party officials regarded both the events of October in Poland and developments in Hungary as an indication of the dangers inherent in reform. They had no desire to embark on a radical policy of democratization.

Nor, for his part had Gomulka. A man of strong conviction, he had demonstrated his personal courage both after 1949, when he had refused to co-operate in the various attempts to brand him as a national deviationist, and in standing up to Khrushchev in October 1956. He was also not interested in material advantages for himself, and threw away in disgust a gold cigarette case embellished with diamonds given to him by Tito on a state visit to Yugoslavia. At the same time, he was a man with little formal education, who had escaped Stalin's purge of the Polish Communist leadership because he occupied too insignificant a role in the Polish Communist Party for the Soviets to seek by exchange his release from jail in Poland in the 1930s. He strongly distrusted intellectuals, whom he described as people 'who produce neither steel nor bread but only chitchat,' and as his regime became more established, he showed an increasing unwillingness to listen to advice which did not accord with his view of the world. His health too, began to deteriorate and increased his general political inflexibility.

Politically, his views have been described as Leninism applied to Polish conditions. A deeply committed and rather dogmatic Marxist-Leninist, he was convinced that the Poles would be reconciled to Communism if only it were clear that the Polish regime was fully autonomous. As he stressed in an article in *Pravda* in November 1957, intended to justify the Polish position to the Soviets, 'The most characteristic feature of the Polish nation, which is a consequence of its history, is its sensitivity to its independence.' At the same time, he was a strong believer in close ties with the Soviet Union, both in the interests of the world Communist movement and because the

USSR constituted the principal guarantor of Poland's western
and northern territories.

Within the Party, he favoured a measure of democratization,
but already in his speech at the Eighth Plenum of the Central
Committee in October 1956 he warned that this process should
not be allowed to become a pretext for undermining socialism.
He certainly had no intention of limiting to any significant
extent the Communist monopoly of power in Poland. He was
still more explicit in his views in his speech at the Tenth
Central Committee Plenum in October 1957, when he
attacked the 'revisionists', who, he claimed, were demanding a
'second stage of the Polish October.' He argued that they were
a far more serious danger to Poland than the Stalinists,
comparing the former to tuberculosis and the latter to mere
influenza. 'Influenza,' he argued, 'even in its most serious form
cannot be cured by contracting tuberculosis. Dogmatism
cannot be cured by revisionism. Revisionist tuberculosis can
only strengthen dogmatic influenza. . . . The revisionist must
be expelled from the party.'

He was, however, for fairly pragmatic policies. Central
industrial planning was to be maintained, but the excessive
targets of the period 1950-6 were to be avoided. There would
be greater consultation with the shop-floor which, he believed,
would release a surge of enthusiasm, enabling rapid industrial
growth to be maintained. In agriculture, forced collectivization
was to be abandoned, individual farmers encouraged, the
compulsory delivery of farm produce reduced and the break
up of collectives permitted. Gomulka also, largely for tactical
reasons, was prepared to seek a *modus vivendi* with the
Catholic Church. The party, he argued, could not ignore the
existence of a large mass of Catholics, and in its policy should
'not apply administrative methods towards the believers,

ignoring the fact that the old quarrel with the church had repelled millions of people from socialism.'

Yet, in spite of the gulf between his views and those of the majority of Poles, Gomulka enjoyed a fair measure of success in his first years in power. People welcomed the relaxation of tension after the continual political crises which had affected Poland since 1939 and were grateful for the degree of liberalization which was introduced. Thus the period from 1957 to about 1964 has come to be referred to as that of the 'little stablization,' in contrast to the difficulties and upheavals of Gomulka's last years. Gomulka's greatest achievement was probably in the establishment of a far more satisfactory relationship with the Soviet Union. In November 1956, a Polish delegation travelled to Moscow and, after four days of talks, an understanding on the most difficult points dividing the two sides was reached. The Soviets now accepted that relations between the two countries were to be conducted 'on the basis of complete equality, respect for territorial integrity, national independence and sovereignty and non-intervention in internal affairs.' In recompense for the artificially low price at which Polish coal had been supplied to the USSR and the failure of the Soviets to pay for the cost of maintaining Soviet troops in Poland, the Soviets cancelled all Polish debts to the Soviet Union, amounting to $500 million. Grain was to be supplied to Poland on credit and a new long-term loan arranged. The cost of stationing Soviet troops in Poland was now to be borne by the Soviet Union and the conditions of their presence was to be regulated by treaty. Finally, those Poles still in the Soviet Union who wished to return to Poland were to be allowed to do so.

The two sides still remained mistrustful of each other, but relations became increasingly warm as a result both of Gomulka's increasing hostility to the revisionists in Poland and the defeat of Khrushchev's hard-line opponents in the Soviet Union in June 1957. This new closeness was cemented by Gomulka's visits to the Soviet Union in November 1957 and October and November 1958. At the same time a close personal relationship was established between Gomulka and Khrushchev, who in his turn visited Poland in July 1959. As the Sino-Soviet dispute grew in bitterness and as the Polish regime became increasingly orthodox, Khrushchev came more and more to rely on Gomulka, the leader of the largest Communist state loyal to the Soviet Union. Indeed, it was partly as a result of Gomulka's insistence that Khrushchev abandoned his plan for the creation of a new Communist international organization. Relations with the other socialist countries of Eastern Europe, above all Czechoslovakia and the German Democratic Republic improved, and Polish economic co-operation with these countries was greatly intensified. But of course this new closeness was bought at the cost of any real independence in foreign affairs. From 1958, Polish foreign policy closely followed that of the Soviet Union, Gomulka supporting the Soviets in their new dispute with Yugoslavia and condoning the execution of the Hungarian leader Imre Nagy and his associates in June 1958.

In relation to the peasantry, Gomulka kept his promise to allow the re-establishment of private agriculture. Between October and December 1956, over 80 per cent of the existing collective farms dissolved themselves, so that by early 1957 only about 2,000 remained, accounting for barely 1.3 per cent of agricultural production. Further assurances were given to the peasantry in a joint statement of the Polish United Workers Party and the United Peasant Party in early December. This affirmed that compulsory grain deliveries would be reduced by a third and the prices paid by the state increased, while credits would be extended to 'all groups of farmers.' In addition, communal machine tractor stations would be disbanded and the equipment sold to individual farmers. Yet the Government's agricultural policy did not prove entirely successful. Many farmers found it difficult to obtain loans, while the state policy of discouraging the emergence of larger farms also preserved the inefficiency inherent in the small peasant plot. The Government did attempt from 1959 to foster the establishment of 'agricultural circles' which would enable peasants to make collective use of agricultural equipment provided by the State. By and large, however, the peasants refused to participate in these circles, seeing them as a new and underhand means of introducing collectivization, a fear given substance by Gomulka's reference to them as the first stage in the establishment of socialism in the countryside. The backwardness of agriculture thus remained a severe brake on Polish economic progress.

One of the main factors which had led to Gomulka's return to power had been dissatisfaction with the rigid and overcentralized system of economic planning which had been in operation between 1949 and 1956. Some attempts were now made to establish a more flexible economic model. In October 1956, the State Planning Commission, which had exercised far-reaching control over the whole economy, was abolished and was replaced by a smaller planning commission under the direct control of the Cabinet. Its authority was restricted and it was to concentrate on general, overall long-range planning.' There was also to be more emphasis on housing and consumer goods when economic priorities were assessed. In order to provide a greater degree of economic expertise, an Economic Advisory Council headed by the eminent economist, Oskar Lange, was set up to report to the Commission and the Cabinet. At the same time, the workers' councils which had sprung up in the autumn of 1956 were given official recognition, while encouragement was given to the expansion of handicrafts, private trade and services and small-scale industry.

There were hopes for even more wide spread changes. In May 1957 the Economic Advisory Council issued a report calling for a far-reaching economic decentralization with autonomy for individual enterprises, the introduction of a profit system and a high degree of dependence on the market in determining wages and prices. Each enterprise was to be run by a State-appointed director, but in co-operation with an elected workers' council. Reforms of this type were unacceptable to Gomulka on both political and economic grounds. Thus from early 1958, the autonomy of the workers' councils was undermined and they were eventually deprived of all significance by being merged with the Party committees and trade union workers' councils in individual factories. The proposals of the Commission for granting independence to factory managers were rejected in early 1958 and a new body, the 'group of enterprises,' was established to occupy a place between the planning commission and individual factories. In practice this meant the maintenance of the centralized planning system. Central controls were further tightened in autumn 1959, when the conservatives, Eugeniusz Szyr and Julian Tokarski, became Deputy Premiers with responsibility for the economy. Private enterprise was also now discouraged and in general rates of growth remained disappointing, and living standards failed to rise as fast as expected. The recommendations of the Advisory Council were consistently ignored and in 1963 it was finally abolished.

A limited *modus vivendi* was also established with the Church. Late in October, Cardinal Wyszynski and a large number of other priests and bishops were released from confinement and resumed their functions. In December a

Church-State agreement was reached. Religious education was again to be allowed in the schools and Government control over ecclesiastical appointments was restricted to a veto over candidates nominated by the Church. Two Catholic journals, the weekly *Tygodnik Powszechny* and the monthly *Znak*, were revived and five members of their editorial boards were allowed to stand for parliament. In return, the hierarchy undertook to support the Government, and accordingly Wyszynski exhorted Catholics to vote for the Government candidates in the election of January 1957.

The regime did not enter into this agreement with any enthusiasm. Indeed, it continued to regard the Church as one of its main ideological opponents and was determined to cut down its power. Gomulka thus took no action to curtail the influence of the now discredited Boleslaw Piasecki, who had collaborated with the Government in the Stalinist period in its attempts to split the Church, and continued to sponsor various pro-Government Catholic factions set up between 1949 and 1956. In addition, in 1957 an Association of Atheists and Freethinkers was established to combat the Church's influence, while a Society for Secular Schooling was set up to campaign for the ending of religious education in the schools. Religious instruction was increasingly hedged about with restrictions and was eventually abolished in schools, while fairly irksome controls were established over instruction in church premises. The Government also took other actions against the Church. The tax exemption of ecclesiastical institutions was abolished, and though the full rigour of the tax laws was not always implemented, the fear of punitive taxation remained a potent threat. Permission to found new churches was refused on a number of occasions, the rights of chaplains in the army, prisons and hospitals were restricted and the holding of some church pilgrimages and processions obstructed. Strict

censorship was imposed on the Catholic press, whose
circulation was also restricted by the allocation of inadequate
supplies of newsprint.

Yet both sides were aware of the limits to which they could
push the conflict, and from 1961 relations eased somewhat,
aided by the relaxation of the international climate and the
election of Pope John XXIII. In April 1963 a meeting between
Gomulka and Wyszynski was arranged, while in April and May
negotiations between the Papacy and the Polish Government
were also initiated. The improvement in relations did not
prove lasting, however, and by late 1963 Church-State
relations were again tense, Gomulka attacking Wyszynski as an
opponent of Church reform and an ally of reactionaries both
in Poland and abroad. The Cardinal responded in kind asking
in a sermon in January 1964 'How long do we have to work
until a man becomes a citizen in his own country, not a slave,
not a prisoner constantly suspected and shadowed and
followed even in his innermost thoughts?'

The area where the Gomulka regime proved to be most
disappointing was that of intellectual freedom. Gomulka had
little sympathy either for intellectuals or for liberals, as shown
by his attacks on 'revisionism' and his praise of the security
forces in November 1956, who were indispensable for the
defence of socialism in Poland against 'international reaction'
and 'attempts aimed at resisting the political line mapped out
by the party leadership.' Thus efforts were soon made to clamp
down on the intellectual ferment unleashed by the
destalinization process in Poland. In October 1957 the
principal reformist weekly *Po Prostu* was banned and its
editors expelled from the Party, while in January 1958 there
was a drastic purge of the editorial board of the weekly *Nowa
Kultura*. At the Third Congress of the Polish United Workers'
Party in March 1959, Gomulka attacked the Polish Writers

Union for tolerating books which 'smear socialism' and in the summer of that year, Leszek Kolakowski, a leading revisionist, was dismissed as editor of *Studia Filozoficzne*. In October, a prominent liberal, Wladyslaw Bienkowski, lost his position as Minister of Higher Education, while in December, the outspoken Antoni Slonimski was replaced as Chairman of the Polish Writers' Union by the more orthodox Wladyslaw Iwaszkiewicz. The pressure on unorthodox opinions was maintained in the early 1960s, with the closing in February 1962 of the 'Club of the Crooked Circle,' an important centre for political discussion, and the merger in June 1963 of the two main literary weeklies *Nowa Kultura* and *Przeglad Kulturalny*. The principal function of *Kultura*, the journal which replaced them, was declared to be 'the struggle against reactionary ideology.' The worsening cultural climate aroused growing opposition from intellectuals, which culminated in the publication in March 1964 of an open letter from thirty-four leading writers protesting against measures which were creating 'a situation endangering the growth of Polish national culture.'

These developments were closely linked with the evolution of the Polish United Workers' Party in this period. When Gomulka had returned to power, there had been four main factions within it, the Pulawy group of moderate reformers, the Natolin hard-liners, a small number of personal followers of Gomulka of whom the most important were Zenon Kliszko and Marian Spychalski, and the out-and-out revisionists. The revisionists soon lost all influence, and Gomulka, not wanting to be too dependent on any one faction and concerned for Party unity, began increasingly to balance between the various groups. His willingness to appoint hard-liners to positions of authority was, moreover, increased by his hostility to revisionism. Thus, by the Third Party Congress in March

1959, the conservatives had regained considerable influence. The security apparatus was strengthened and expanded and General Kazimierz Wilaszewski, one of Gomulka's main opponents in October 1956, was appointed head of the Party's Administrative Department, in which capacity he exercized control over all Party appointments. The failure to democratize the Party had important consequences. It meant the abandonment of any hope for radical reform of the economy or political system. In addition it created a promotion block for the younger, ambitious Party members, which was to have far-reaching effects in the late 1960s.

From 1964 things began to go seriously wrong for the Gomulka regime. Gomulka himself, plagued by worsening health, became increasingly rigid and inflexible and tended to fly into rages if his views were contradicted. He was also considerably taken aback by Khrushchev's approaches to the West Germans in 1964, which he seems to have feared would endanger the security of Poland and might even lead to territorial changes on the Polish western border. Khrushchev's fall further increased his feeling of political isolation though he did quickly establish close relations with his successors Brezhnev and Kosygin.

The economic situation, too, became increasingly unsatisfactory. The half-measures of economic reform which had been introduced since 1956 did not stimulate a high rate of growth, which was all the more necessary because of the rapid population growth in Poland. It is true that the rate of natural increase of the population fell from 18.5 per thousand in 1956 to 9.4 in 1966, but the high birth-rate of the 1950s meant that there was a large number of young people coming on to the labour market in the early 1960s for whom it was difficult to provide jobs. Some attempts were made to introduce further reforms of the economic system in 1964 and 1965, but little progress was made, although the need for allowing individual factories to establish their own investment policies was recognized. As a result standards of living remained low by west European standards. As late as 1968 the average monthly wage was still only 4,200 zloties (£21 at the official exchange rate).

Relations with the Church also deteriorated. A major conflict was precipitated by the Church's desire to commemorate the thousandth anniversary of the introduction of Christianity into Poland in 966. The State authorities bitterly resented the Church's appropriation of the millennium celebrations, since, in an effort to provide itself with a degree of legitimacy, it wished to stress that Peoples' Poland was 'the crowning point of our present historical process and the custodian of the great progressive traditions of our nation and state.' An appeal of the Polish episcopate in November 1965 to its German counterpart asking forgiveness for all Polish wrongs to the Germans was thus seized upon to attack the Church for craven appeasement of the hereditary national enemy. The conflict escalated throughout 1966, with a ban on Polish bishops travelling abroad and a refusal to allow Pope Paul VI to attend the millennium celebrations at the Jasna Gora monastery in Czestochowa. The Church was able successfully to withstand Government pressure and in the summer half a million people attended the meeting at Jasna Gora, where the empty papal throne bore eloquent witness to the depth of the conflict. Yet, as before, both sides were unwilling to push the clash beyond certain limits, and from December 1966 the bitterness began to subside somewhat. In May 1967, a number of new Church appointments were made and four apostolic administrators replaced the Vicar-General in the western territories, a tacit acceptance by the Vatican of the Oder-Neisse frontier. However, the Church continued to complain of restrictions on its activities and censorship and an atmosphere of mutual suspicion persisted.

The Government was also not able to heal its breach with the intellectual community. It responded to the letter of the thirty-four writers attacking its cultural policy by launching a strong counter-offensive. Not very successful attempts were made to obtain signatures for a declaration of support for the regime, while publication of the works of the letters' authors was discontinued in a number of cases. In autumn 1964, one of the signatories of the letter, Melchior Wankowicz, was even sentenced to three years' imprisonment for criticizing the rulers of Peoples' Poland in a private letter to his family in the U.S. His sentence was, however, never carried out. Efforts were stepped up to impose the Party line on the writers, who were accused of being 'out of step with the rest of the nation.' These proved largely unsuccessful and Warsaw University in particular became one of the main centres of opposition to the regime. In 1965, for instance, the Government arrested two young lecturers, Jacek Kuron and Karol Modzielewski, for circulating what was in effect a Trotskyite critique of the regime for betraying the interest of the workers. More significant was the expulsion from the Party of a leading revisionist, Leszek Kolakowski, for a speech on the tenth anniversary of the Polish October in which he contrasted the high hopes raised by Gomulka's return to power with the grim reality of life in People's Poland. The crudity of the regime's cultural policy was well exemplified by the speech of Zenon Kliszko, its principal exponent, in a speech at the 1957 Plenum of the Party Central Committee. The Party, he affirmed, 'would not allow criticism which is destructive and which blackens our reality by a one-sided concentration on negative phenomena.'

Gomulka's own position within the Party also came under fire. The increasing difficulties of the regime and the feeling of immobility aroused by Gomulka's unimaginative policies stimulated the growth of the new faction within the Party composed mainly of people who had spent the war years in the communist underground in Poland. The Partisans, as this group came to be known, were bitterly opposed to those Communists, many of whom were of Jewish origin, who had spent the war in the Soviet Union. In addition, they called for more authoritarian policies *vis-à-vis* the Church and the intellectuals and a greater stress on Polish nationalism. They were led by Mieczyslaw Moczar, who had served as head of the security police in Lodz after the war and who became Minister of the Interior in 1964. Moczar, a primitive populist who sought popularity by stressing that 'he who is not against us is with us,' soon built up the veterans' organization, the Union of Fighters for Freedom and Democracy (ZBOWID), into a formidable political base, providing valuable privileges for its 250,000 members. The Partisans first emerged as a significant force at the Fourth Party Congress in June 1964 when one of their supporters Ryszard Strzelecki became a candidate member of the Politbureau, which he entered as a full member at the end of the year. Moczar was able to establish his followers in powerful positions in the police force (militia), the security apparatus and the army. He also won the support of a number of intellectuals, above all in the journals *Kultura, Stolica* and *Zolnierz Wolnosci*, who were attracted by his assertive Polish nationalism.

All the pent-up forces in Polish society came to the surface in 1968. The Israeli victory in the Middle East war of June 1967, which was generally welcomed by the Poles, was seized upon by the Partisans as a means of getting rid of their Jewish opponents. They took as their pretext a speech of Gomulka shortly after the war in which he attacked 'Zionist circles of Jews who are Polish citizens' and who constituted a 'fifth column' in Poland. As a result, in the second half of 1967 a large number of Jewish Party officials, including many in the army and journalism, lost their posts. They included Leon Kasman, editor-in-chief of the Party daily *Trybuna Ludu*, Leopold Unger, *de facto* editor of *Zycie Warszawy* and Jerzy Zarzycki, Chairman of the Warsaw National Council.

At the same time, events in Czechoslovakia, where the conservative Antonin Novotny had been overthrown in December 1967 and a new reformist regime set up under Alexander Dubcek, stimulated demands by students and intellectuals for similar changes in Poland. 'Poland is waiting for its Dubcek' (*Polska czeka na swego Dubceka*) became a popular slogan. The banning under Soviet pressure of the production of a Polish classic by Mickiewicz in late January 1968, in which critical remarks about Russians were loudly applauded, led to growing unrest. This culminated in the outbreak of a large number of student demonstrations between 8th and 23rd March. Considerable police violence was used against the demonstrators and altogether over a thousand students were arrested.

These riots, in which *agents provocateurs* may have played some role, were seen by the Partisans as a way of further strengthening their position and perhaps also of challenging that of Gomulka. Liberal university lecturers were held responsible for the unrest and dismissed. More important, the Partisans and their adherents seized upon the fact that among the protestors were a number of children of leading Communists, many of them of Jewish origin. They included Andrzej Duracz, whose father was a hero of the war-time Communist resistance, and who was now senior editor of a leading Polish publishing house, Adam Michnik, whose father had played an important part in the pre-war Communist Party and Antoni Zambrowski, son of the former leader of the

Pulawy faction, Roman Zambrowski. Articles in the press underlined the Zionist character of the disturbances, stressing the original names of Jews who had adopted more Polish names after the war and a climate of anti-semitism was created which enabled the Partisans to obtain the dismissal of many of their opponents.

The extent to which the campaign, which now claimed that the demonstrations were the product of a 'West German-Israeli conspiracy,' was directed against the position of Gomulka became clearer when the First Secretary delivered a speech to Party activists on 19th March. He refused to associate himself fully with the anti-zionist campaign, which was vociferously supported by a Partisan claque in the audience and stressed that 'It would be a misunderstanding to see in Zionism a danger to socialism or to the existing socio-political system.' At the same time, his rejection of anti-semitism was less than categoric. He divided Jews into three categories: 'patriotic Jews,' 'Zionists' and those who were neither Jews nor Poles but 'cosmopolitans' and who should 'avoid those fields of work where the affirmation of nationality is indispensable.' He also made a strong attack on the liberals and the intelligentsia, whom he held responsible for the March disturbances.

Gomulka's speech did not end the campaign to oust Jews and liberals from positions of authority. A large number of university teachers lost their posts, including ninety-nine at Warsaw University, while in the foreign ministry it had been estimated that about 40 per cent of those in senior and middle positions were dismissed. Altogether some 9,000 people lost their positions, while the large majority of the remaining 30,000 Jews in Poland left the country for Israel, Western Europe and North America. Gomulka himself made little attempt to reinstate those dismissed and this tactic of swimming along with the tide meant that by July he was in a much stronger position in the Party. At the same time Moczar also gained in strength, becoming an alternate member of the Politbureau, responsible for military and security affairs.

The First Secretary's position was further buttressed by the growing Soviet unease at the development of the situation in Czechoslovakia, which culminated in the invasion of that country by Warsaw pact troops in August. Gomulka had consistently opposed the reformists' plans in Czechoslovakia and had been a strong protagonist of Soviet military intervention which took place mainly from Polish territory. In the aftermath of the invasion, he was able to count on Soviet support for his loyalty, the more so since the Soviets were extremely unwilling to countenance any further changes which could affect their position in Eastern Europe. Thus, at the Fifth Congress of the Polish United Workers' Party in November 1968, Gomulka was able to assert his firm control over the party. Moczar remained only a candidate member for the Politbureau and though the liberals lost almost all their remaining positions on the Central Committee, they were not replaced by supporters of the Partisans. For the first time since 1956, Gomulka now had a clear majority of his own adherents in the Politbureau and Central Committee. Only in the Party Secretariat were the Partisans able to gain a significant foothold. At the same time, Edward Gierek the technocratic First Secretary of the highly industralized area of Upper Silesia, also increased his authority.

Gomulka's personal ascendancy now seemed unchallenge-able. His position was further strengthened by a major triumph in foreign policy. The new Social-Democratic Government in West Germany had been attempting from 1969 to pursue a more flexible policy towards the Soviet Union and Eastern Europe. Thus following an agreement with the USSR, the West Germans declared their willingness to sign a treaty with the Poles in effect recognizing the Oder and western Neisse rivers as the western frontier of Poland. At the same time it was hoped that credits from West Germany would help revive the flagging Polish economy. Willy Brandt, the West German Chancellor, journeyed to Poland in December 1970 to sign the treaty and by this act of personal reconciliation seemed further to underpin Gomulka's undisputed position in Poland. In fact, by removing the threat from a 'revanchist' West Germany the agreement significantly weakened the First Secretary's hold on the Polish population, particularly in the areas which had previously been claimed by West Germany.

What finally undid Gomulka was the persistence of the economic crisis. Although economic problems had been discussed at the Fifth Party Congress, little had been done to deal with the pressing problems of the economy. The campaign against 'revisionists' and 'zionists' had meant that many of the ablest economists in the country had been dismissed, while Boleslaw Jaszczuk, the Party Secretary appointed by Gomulka to take charge of the economy, was both erratic in his judgments and lacking in any real understanding of the principal problems facing the country. The rigid centralization of the economic system was thus not modified, while the policies of increasing the indices of economic growth without any real regard for consumer preferences or the standard of living of the population was maintained. The percentage of the GNP invested rose from 24.2 in 1960 to 29.7 in 1969 with results similar to the period 1949-55: the neglect of housing, services and the standard of living. Even according to official figures real wages rose by less than 10 per cent in the years 1965-70. In discussions of this problem after Gomulka's fall, it was admitted that there were some groups of workers who actually suffered a decline in their real wages. Yet although the rate of investment was higher than that of all the other socialist countries of Eastern Europe, the rate of growth remained very unsatisfactory, because of poor productivity and the growing technological gap between Poland and the rest of the industrialized world.

The negative effects of this policy were further exacerbated by the need to import western machinery to bridge the technological gap. In order to meet the growing trade deficit, the export of Polish agricultural products, above all meat, was stepped up with obvious effects on the domestic market. According to a Warsaw wit, Gomulka's policy was to create a 'meatless zone in Central Europe.' The shortage of food products was made still worse by a drought and poor harvest in 1969. The First Secretary's response to criticism of his economic policy was to claim that the country was 'living beyond its means' and to call for a further cut in consumption. Already in November 1968 a series of price increases was introduced and a further set was decreed in early 1970 in terms of which the price of some basic foodstuffs would be raised by as much as 30 per cent. In compensation the prices of some consumer durables were to be lowered. A modification of the wage system was also proposed, which was seen by better-paid workers as a threat to their lucrative bonuses.

This economic package proved the last straw. Mass strikes and demonstrations broke out among shipyard workers in the three northern cities of Gdansk, Gdynia and Szczecin which were brutally suppressed between 14th and 19th December. At least 500 people lost their lives and civil war seemed near. Gomulka appealed vainly for Soviet support, but it was clear that he was losing his grip politically. At the Politbureau meeting of 18th December, he suffered a minor stroke, and the majority of that body now swung to support Gomulka's main opponents, Gierek, Moczar and Piotr Jaroszewicz, Deputy Premier and Poland's representative on the Comecon executive committee. On 19th December Gomulka was asked for his resignation as First Secretary and suspended from the Central Committee. Kliszko and Spychalski also lost their positions. On the following day Gierek was appointed First Secretary. Thus Gomulka, whose rise to power had been the direct consequence of a workers' demonstration in Poznan, was in turn overthrown fourteen years later by a new set of demonstrations.

30

Poland under Gierek:
The Failure of Consumer Communism

Edward Gierek was a very different sort of man from Gomulka. The son of a miner, he was born in 1913 in Porabka, a town in that part of the Silesian coal basin which before 1914 had been ruled by Russia. Following the death of his father in a mine accident, he emigrated with his mother to France where he too became a miner at the age of thirteen. Active in trade union affairs, he joined the French Communist Party in 1931 and was expelled from France in 1934 for his part in a miners' strike. He returned to Poland but emigrated again in 1937, this time to Belgium, where he also worked as a miner and became a member of the Belgian Communist Party and of the war-time resistance movement. He returned to Poland only in 1948, with the consequence that he speaks better French than Russian. He rose rapidly within the Polish United Workers Party and from 1957 was First Secretary of the Party in the province of Upper Silesia where he won considerable renown for the skill and efficiency with which he ran this highly industralized province.

He was sometimes described as a technocrat, concerned above all with the establishment of an efficiently functioning

Polish economy. This was not strictly accurate. Gierek was certainly concerned to modernize Polish industry, not so much by economic decentralization as by increasing trade with the west so as to make possible the large-scale importation of western machinery. In this respect, his concept of how to make the economy work was totally different from the pennypinching and cautious approach of Gomulka. Yet he was also a convinced Marxist-Leninist. As a former Party member who knew him well wrote: 'Edward Gierek is an old fashioned communist, but without fanaticism or zealousness. . . . He believes profoundly in the leading role that history conferred upon Communist parties, and lives by the maxim that a government should be strong and rule unshakeably.' He himself, characteristically, in a speech to Party activists in September 1971, described the Party's several functions as being 'dialectically related': it was to achieve a higher rate of growth and at the same time significantly raise living standards; the socialist state was to be strengthened while socialist democracy would be further developed; the leading role of the Party was to be raised to a higher level while the participation of non-party men in social and political life would be expanded. His years in power increasingly demonstrated the difficulty of pursuing these various aims simultaneously.

His first task was to re-establish a semblance of order in the country. On 23rd December, he announced in Parliament that his Government would drastically revise the economic policies of its predecessor, redrafting the Five-Year Plan for the period 1971-5 to make greater provision for agriculture, consumer goods and housing. In addition, he stated that prices would be frozen at their 1970 level for two years and promised a wage increase for lower-paid workers and a rise in pensions and child welfare benefits. These concessions did not appease the workers and a wave of strikes swept the country, accompanied by many meetings in which radical changes in the economic and political system were demanded, as well as the punishment of those responsible for the loss of life in the December unrest.

Gierek himself, accompanied by the new Prime Minister Jaroszewicz, had two mammoth discussions with the shipyard workers of Szczecin and Gdansk as a result of which they were able to persuade them to go back to work in return for abandoning the new wage scheme which had been proposed by Jaszczuk. This agreement constituted a 25 per cent wage rise for dockyard and shipyard workers. Further wage increases were granted by the Central Committee Plenum in early February, but even these did not end the strikes which spread in mid-February to the textile factories of Lodz, where pay levels were among the lowest in Poland. Following a traumatic meeting with hysterical women workers, the Prime Minister announced on television on 15th February that the December increases in food prices would be annulled. The strike wave, unprecedented in any Communist country, thus compelled the Government to make concessions in wages, prices and welfare benefits worth 60,000 million zloties. It also gave the working class a quite unwonted sense of its own power. As one of the shipyard workers told Gierek to his face at a mass meeting in January,

> We must give Comrade Gierek a chance. . . . We must have confidence in him as we had confidence in Gomulka. Except that the latter failed us. . . . We have to give the Government a chance for a year or two . . . we must do it. If in a year or two, there is no improvement, then we will say: Comrades, we were deceived.

This awareness of the workers' power was also shared by the Party, and the Politbureau report to the February Central

Committee Plenum stressed that the Party 'must always in the future aim at preventing conflicts with the working class.' For his part, Gierek was extremely conscious of the precarious nature of his authority and he moved skilfully and swiftly to introduce a new economic policy. The first area where major changes were implemented was agriculture. The 1971-5 plan had envisaged a 35 per cent increase in food supply, and an increase in agricultural production was made even more urgent by the wage increases granted between December 1970 and February 1971, since the average Polish family spent 50 per cent of its income on food and was now likely significantly to increase its consumption. In order to achieve the necessary increases, Gierek was prepared to give far greater incentives to the private farmer than Gomulka had been. Most limitations on the sale and inheritance of land were abolished, while about 1 million farmers whose title to their land was unconfirmed were given clear rights of ownership. Private farmers were also for the first time included in the State health scheme. At the same time, a number of measures were taken aimed at improving the efficiency of agriculture. Gierek abandoned any attempt at making Poland self-sufficient in grain, thus making possible a greater concentration on livestock production, for which much of Polish land was more suitable. Compulsory deliveries were abolished from January 1972 and higher prices paid to the peasants. In addition the tax system was made more favourable to farmers, while credit was to become more readily available. In order to create larger and more viable farms (by 1970, 30 per cent of all farms were smaller than 3 hectares) a generous pension scheme was introduced to persuade older farmers to sell up their holdings. These would be used either to create collectives or would be sold to individuals. In practice, most of the land acquired in this way was retained by the State and this enabled Gierek to claim that his policy would ultimately lead to the introduction of a greater measure of socialism in the countryside. Between 1970 and 1975, the percentage of land held by State and co-operative farms increased from 17.9 to 22.7. The new policy was also initially successful in increasing agricultural production, and by late 1971 it was possible to reduce the high level of food imports. The farming population as a whole benefited considerably and farmers' incomes now equalled and probably surpassed those of the population of the towns.

In the industrial sphere, Gierek ruled out a radical decentralization of the economy and the use of the market to determine a significant proportion of prices on the lines of the 'New Economic Mechanism' introduced in Hungary after 1965. The attempt by Gomulka to bring in a major economic reform had after all led to his overthrow and such a change was in addition anathema to the Soviets. Indeed, the crisis significantly increased Gierek's dependence on the USSR, which agreed in early January to sell the Poles 2 million metric tons of grain (later increased to 2½ million) and subsequently also agreed to grant Poland a substantial loan, partly in hard currency, and to furnish other agricultural produce. Economic assistance was also provided by Czechoslovakia and the German Democratic Republic. Thus it was not surprising that at the Congress of the Communist Party of the Soviet Union in March 1971 Gierek reaffirmed his support for a centrally planned economy.

The essence of his economic policy was to make use of the increasing commitment of the Soviet Union to *détente* in order to improve relations with a number of western countries. This would enable Poland to acquire western machinery on easy credit terms in order to modernize her industry. The debts incurred in this manner would be repaid by a vastly increased export of Polish goods to the West, the result of the increase in production which the new factories would make possible. As a result, Poland embarked with some success on a policy of increasing her links with France, the Scandinavian countries, Britain, Italy and several other countries in Western Europe. Relations with the United States also improved as did, after many difficulties, those with West Germany, to which Gierek made a State visit in June 1976. With the relaxation of tension came a major increase in trade and credits. By 1975 West Germany had become Poland's fourth trading partner, with France and Britain in the fifth and sixth positons. Trade with Comecon countries has also grown, but not nearly so rapidly. Between 1970 and 1974, for instance, the share of Polish trade with capitalist countries rose from 27 per cent to 44.3 per cent while that with Comecon countries fell from 63.2 per cent to 47 per cent.

Some degree of institutional change was also introduced through the 'small economic reform.' This maintained and even extended the control of the central planning apparatus over the economy, but also gave greater scope for independent action by specified large industrial enterprises. By mid-1974 those firms to whom this new freedom of manoeuvre had been granted produced nearly half of Poland's industrial goods. In addition, a number of firms were allowed to borrow hard currency directly from Poland's Commercial Bank, thus bypassing the Ministry of Foreign Trade. These loans could be used at the discretion of the firm's management to modernize production techniques. The only condition imposed was that sufficient foreign currency should be generated by the expenditure of goods and services to repay the loan in hard currency. This arrangement did a great deal to stimulate entrepreneurial talent. In the years 1971 to 1975, to take one example, the food-processing industry, one of Poland's main exporters, trebled its investments in comparison with the previous five years and also greatly modernized its plant by the importation of western equipment.

Initially, this bold and rather risky policy enjoyed a substantial measure of success. During the 1971-5 Five-Year Plan, national income increased by approximately 60 per cent, while industrial production rose by over 70 per cent. At the same time, foreign loans and a high level of investment made possible a substantial renovation of Polish industry. By 1976, nearly 54 per cent of the industrial machinery in Poland was less than five years old. Living standards also rose significantly. In contrast to the stagnation of Gomulka's later years, real wages rose, according to the official figures, at 11.9 per cent per annum between 1971 and 1975 while State-controlled food prices remained frozen (though not those at private peasant markets). This increase was the highest in the Comecon countries and one of the highest in the world. The supply of consumer goods, both produced at home and imported, improved significantly and the target of one million new flats which had been proposed by the revised Five-Year Plan was slightly over-fulfilled. At the same time, old age and invalid pensions as well as sickness and family benefits were significantly increased. Gierek's boast that he would create a 'second Poland' by doubling the country's national income began to appear well-founded.

In the political field, Gierek initially displayed a degree of flexibility. He attempted to win over the intellectuals, alienated by the policies of Gomulka's last years, promising them a relaxation of censorship and a greater say in the running of the country. For the moment, there was a palpable liberalization of the cultural scene, although the continued presence on the Politbureau of two principal instigators of the purge which had followed the events of March 1968, General Moczar and Jozef Kepa, made it clear that this freedom had definite limits. Gierek also promised a more open style of government, engaging in frequent 'consultations' with groups of workers at which political and economic problems were freely discussed. He did not however give way to demands that the trade unions be given a more autonomous role, though he did allow a fair number of unpopular trade union officials to be dismissed.

The tone of radio and particularly television also became less hectoring and more concerned to reflect the people's problems and aspirations. Ministers now appeared in question-and-answer sessions and an attempt was made to provide more accurate and detailed coverage of political affairs. Short bulletins were issued after the weekly Politbureau meetings, while the First Secretary himself established a regular off-the-record briefing session for leading Polish journalists. Though the power of parliament was not significantly increased and the number of non-affiliated and independent Catholic members fell as a result of the election of March 1972, some attempts were made to widen the scope of parliamentary activity and involve non-Party individuals in it. An independent member was made deputy speaker, while the National Unity Front appointed a man with no political affiliations to the chairmanship of its Praesidium. The patriotic enthusiasm of the country was aroused by the decision to rebuild the Royal Palace in Warsaw, destroyed by the Germans in 1944, something Gomulka had never been prepared to consider. Also popular was the new support which the Government gave to increasing the country's links with the Polish communities outside Poland mostly in Western Europe and North and South America, which now numbered about 10 million people.

Further, Gierek made a new attempt to improve relations with the Church. In March 1971 the new Prime Minister, Jaroszewicz, met Cardinal Wyszynski, the first meeting of this type for nearly ten years. Although no response was made to many of the Church's complaints, the regime did agree to grant legal title to Church property in the western and northern

territories, thus restoring to the Church some 7,000 ecclesiastical buildings which had been seized by the State. Permission
was also granted to build 130 churches in new localities, including one in the steel town of Nowa Huta, where permission had
previously always been refused. Yet not all requests for the
construction of new churches were acceded to and the State
continued its policy of demolishing churches built without
authorization. The limits of the regime's willingness to make
concessions were further demonstrated by the appointment to
the Council of State of Boleslaw Piasecki, the discredited leader
of the pro-Government Catholic organization Pax. Relations
with the Vatican improved as well, partly reflecting the government's desire to reach an agreement with the Pope over the
head of the Church in Poland. Following the establishment of
diplomatic relations between Poland and West Germany in
June 1972, the Vatican agreed to appoint six Polish bishops to
the western and northern territories. In November 1973, the
Polish Foreign Minister paid a formal visit to Pope Paul VI and
from 1974 contact with the Vatican has been maintained by a
special group of diplomats in the Polish embassy in Rome.

Throughout the early period of his rule, Gierek's main
political preoccupation was to establish firm control over the
Party. He acted first against Moczar, with whose help he had
come to power and whose followers still retained an important
hold on parts of the bureaucracy. In May 1971, Moczar over-
played his hand and seems to have made some sort of attempt
to overthrow the First Secretary. Gierek responded by dismissing a number of Moczar's supporters from their positions
and then appointing Moczar himself in June 1971 to the largely
powerless post of Chairman of the Supreme Control Council.
He then proceeded to place his own adherents in key positions.
By December 1971, he had replaced thirteen of the nineteen
provincial Secretaries and he consolidated his position by a

purge of the Party, as a result of which 100,000 people were expelled in 1971. At the Sixth Party Conference in December 1971 he further tightened his grip, obtaining the dismissal from the Politbureau of Moczar, who was subsequently forced to resign from the Secretariat as well, and also of two survivors from the Gomulka era, Stefan Jedrychowski and Jozef Cyrankiewicz. The Politbureau was now dominated by men with close links with the First Secretary. One consequence was that it was now a significantly younger and better-educated group.

In 1974, Gierek further increased his power by forcing the removal from the Politbureau and the post of Minister of the Interior of another potential rival, Franciszek Szlachcic. Szlachcic, who had helped Gierek consolidate his position against Moczar in 1971, had cultivated a relatively liberal image and had also called for greater independence from the Soviet Union while building up his own faction within the Party. The other members of the inner leadership, Edward Babiuch, Jan Szydlak, Stanislaw Kania and the Prime Minister, Piotr Jaroszewicz, were all clearly dependent on Gierek, who further buttressed his own authority by enlarging both the Central Committee and the Politbureau and filling them with his own adherents. In addition, between 1973 and 1975 Gierek introduced a major reform of local government, replacing the three-tier system (village, district and province) by a two-tier system (commune and province) and increasing the number of provinces from seventeen to forty-six. The reform could certainly be justified on the grounds that it would increase administrative efficiency, but it also made it possible for Gierek to get rid of much dead wood in the bureaucracy and to limit significantly the autonomy enjoyed by Party Secretaries in the industrial provinces. The First Secretary's unchallenged control of the Party was clearly demonstrated at the Seventh Party Congress in December 1975, where his leadership was given a personal endorsement by the presence of Brezhnev himself.

Having entrenched himself in power, Gierek embarked on an attempt to tighten ideological controls in the country as a whole. This campaign partly reflected his own view that the rising standard of living in Poland should not lead to an erosion of Marxist-Leninist principles, but it was also the result of pressure from the Soviet Union and some other socialist countries, notably Czechoslovakia. Already in 1971 the First Secretary had reorganized and expanded the Higher School of the Social Sciences attached to the Central Committee which was responsible for training Party cadres. More political education was also insisted upon at lower levels of the Party. In May 1971 special directives were issued by the Secretariat on ideological training, and new textbooks and courses were developed. The handling of this problem by the Secretariat and not, as previously, by the Central Committee Ideological Commission was an indication of the importance attached to it by Gierek. By December 1971 of 125,000 Party members in Warsaw alone, 80,000 were undergoing part-time ideological training.

In December 1973, shortly after a conference in Moscow of East European Party Secretaries responsible for ideological affairs, an 'ideological offensive' was launched in Poland. To advance it, an Institute for the Study of the Basic Problems of Marxism-Leninism was established in February 1974 under the aegis of the Central Committee. Its head was Andrzej Werblan, who had played a highly discreditable role in the anti-zionist campaign of 1968. In the following month a national conference of Party activists was held in Warsaw. On this occasion, Jan Szydlak, a prominent member of the Politbureau, argued that the policy of peaceful coexistence did not mean 'the end of the class struggle either now or in the future.' The main ideological tasks of the Party were to stress the unbreakable nature of the ties between Poland and the Soviet Union and to expose the inevitable 'advancing crisis' of capitalism. Indeed, a constant note in the regime's propaganda, perhaps intended to reassure the Soviet leadership that the growing trade with the West had no political implications, was the stress on the immutable character of Poland's link with the USSR. Szydlak also bitterly attacked the Church as 'the only centre of social right-wing forces which has at its disposal a coherent philosophic outlook, a strong organizational base and numerous cadres.'

Another aspect of the tightening of ideological controls was the amalgamation of the five principal youth organizations in the country into a single body, the Federation of Socialist Youth Organizations in April 1973. In this way the regime hoped to increase its influence over young people whose participation in the student unrest of 1968 and the strike wave of 1970-1 had considerably discomfited Party officials. This was also one of the aims of the major educational reform introduced in October 1973, although with its provision of a universal ten-year schooling system it could also be justified on educational grounds.

Inevitably the 'ideological offensive' led to a clash with the intelligentsia. Already at the end of 1974 fifteen prominent intellectuals, headed by Antoni Slonimski, wrote an open letter to the relatively liberal Minister of Culture, Jozef Tejchma, complaining of the restrictions on the cultural life of the more than 1 million Poles who still lived in the Soviet Union, mostly in areas which had been part of Poland before 1939. The failure to seek redress for their grievances was, it was implied, the result of the regime's servile dependence on the USSR. The increasing vigour with which historical writings were being censored was strongly criticized by a well-known Catholic publicist, Stefan Kisielewski, in a letter reprinted in an emigré

journal in September 1975. Kisielewski, who had always advocated a policy of compromise with the regime, concluded
bitterly, 'The speciality of our system, as Orwell envisaged it,
is history in the service of politics, adjusted and transmitted
backwards.'

The Church, too, was not slow to express its discontent.
Throughout 1974 Cardinal Wyszynski attacked the Government in his sermons for failing to allow the establishment of
new churches, for its educational reforms, which made more
difficult the provision of religious instruction after school
hours, and for its creation of a single youth movement. He also
stressed the need for the Government to respect basic democratic principles, 'the right of free association, as well as the
rights to freedom of the press, expression of opinion and
unrestrained scientific research.'

What brought the conflict to a head was the regime's attempt
in late 1975 to introduce a new constitution which would
underline the socialist character of the Polish State, based as it
was, in the official phraseology, on 'the same class-
revolutionary principles which originally triumphed in the
Great October Socialist Revolution.' The intelligentsia and the
Church particularly resented the attempt to write into the new
constitution clauses upholding the 'unshakeable fraternal bond
with the Soviet Union' and the leading role of the Communist
Party and also the claim in the draft proposal that citizens'
rights were dependent on the fulfilment of their obligations. A
storm of protest was unleashed which clearly surprised the
Government, and some gestures to appease public opinion
were made. The phrases describing the relationship between
Poland and the Soviet Union and that making citizens' rights
contingent on their fulfilling their duties were abandoned.
These rather grudging concessions did not satisfy the opposition. In April 1976 the episcopate issued a statement calling for

respect for human rights and national self-determination as guaranteed by the Helsinki agreement, while the regime's subservience to the Soviet Union was attacked by the veteran socialist, Edward Lipinski, and the former Communist Minister, Wladyslaw Bienkowski. Lipinski concluded his open letter to Gierek,

> There is no more important goal for Poland than the reassertion of its sovereignty. Only after regaining political independence will it be possible to undertake systematic economic reform and to restructure the political and social system so as to release the creative potential of the nation.

Gierek might well have been able to contain the opposition of the intellectuals had the economic situation not also turned against him. His ambitious policy of modernizing Polish industry to make possible export-led growth had been embarked on just as the western world was experiencing its most severe economic downturn since 1929. Polish trade thus moved sharply into deficit, the negative balance of payments rising from 662 million zloties in 1971 to 9,935 million during the first nine months of 1975. By September the total deficit amounted to 24,000 million zloties, five-sixths of which was with the capitalist world. In addition, there was the need to repay Western loans, which at the end of 1975 totalled over $6,000 million. In that year, for instance, a quarter of Polish exports to the West had to be used for debt repayment. The screw was further tightened by the impact of the oil crisis, which led the Soviets to raise the price of oil to Poland by 130 per cent in January 1975 and by an additional 8 per cent in January 1976.

There were also other reasons for Poland's economic difficulties. The import of western machinery did not, in fact, solve the problem of increasing productivity and improving quality control. In 1975 machinery still made up only 13 per cent of Polish exports to the West. Moreover, in order to boost productivity in industries crucial to the export drive the regime was forced to offer substantial increases in pay. In 1974, to take one example, Silesian coal miners received two wage rises, one of 12 per cent and another of 30 per cent. By 1977 wages as a whole had risen by 40 per cent instead of the 18 per cent planned at the sixth Party Congress in December 1971. Yet as wages went up, consumer goods and above all food became ever more difficult to obtain. In addition, because of the impact of the high birth-rate of the 1950s, the problem of acquiring a flat had not become significantly easier. As a result, in spite of the substantial building programmes, in 1976 there were still 1½ million families without their own homes. Rising expectations had been created by the boom of the early 1970s and by the regime's rather grandiose boosting of its own achievements. Popular disillusionment when the increase in the standard of living began to tail off was therefore all the more marked. In the summer of 1974 there were strikes among dockyard workers in Gdynia, while in the spring of 1975 housewives, enraged by the difficulty of obtaining meat, set fire to a grocery store in Warsaw.

The shortage of food and particularly meat was not the result of a failure of the agricultural sector, whose output increased by about a quarter between 1971 and 1975, a very creditable performance, particularly given the droughts of 1974 and 1975. Rather it was caused by a rise in demand at home, coupled with the regime's growing dependence on food exports to bridge the balance of payments gap. Moreover, Poland now had to import ever-larger quantities of grain as agriculture became more diversified, and much of this had to be paid for in hard currency. Gierek's agricultural policy had bizarre consequences. The price of subsidized bread made with imported grain was so low that farmers fed it to their pigs; the pigs were in due course exported as ham for hard currency to pay for the grain. The regime was thus in a cleft stick. It could not force the peasants to reduce prices because they would then cut production. This became clear in 1975, when farmers forced the Government to raise pig prices by keeping their livestock off the market in the previous year. Yet the cost of maintaining the freeze on food prices was proving increasingly hard to bear. By 1976 the State was having to spend a staggering 12 per cent of the country's gross domestic product in order to keep prices stable.

This was not a situation which could continue indefinitely. In the new Five-Year Plan for 1976-80, targets were significantly scaled down and the regime stressed that wages could only rise half as fast as they did between 1971 and 1975. In June 1976 it finally screwed up the courage to raise food prices by around 60 per cent. At the same time, the peasants were to be forced to pay considerably more for raw materials. This, it was hoped, would both soak up the extra profit accruing to farmers and also significantly reduce the profitability of small farms, thus accelerating the transfer of land from individual to collective ownership. The result was another major outbreak of working-class unrest. Workers went on strike in the Baltic towns, and at the Ursus tractor factory near Warsaw railway lines were ripped up to prevent trains reaching the capital; in Radom there was a virtual general strike and widespread rioting. Within two days, the Prime Minister appeared on television to announce the withdrawal of the price rises.

Having yielded on this issue, the government attempted as in 1970 to buy off the workers with further economic concessions. The large industrial concentrations established under the economic reforms of the early 1970s had been granted a good deal of autonomy and many of them now proceeded to

offer additional increases in wages, in most cases not matched
by any significant increase in productivity. At the same time,
the authorities tried to cow the workers by arresting hundreds
of the strikers, many of whom were summarily sentenced to
imprisonment or dismissed from their jobs. In addition, stage-
managed meetings were convened all over Poland at which the
'wreckers' were condemned.

This attempt at repression only succeeded in driving
together the workers and the discontented intellectuals. In September 1976 a Workers Defence Committee (Komitet Obrony
Robotników—KOR) was set up, headed by a well-respected
Polish writer Jerzy Andrzeiewski and including a number of
prominent members of the intellectual opposition. It was
careful to stress that it wished to act in accordance with the law
and organized legal help and financial assistance to workers
and their families who were affected by the government's
repression. In addition it sought to win support for the strikers
by publishing accounts of their trials, and soon widened its
activity to involve the defence of all those who could argue that
the government was violating their human rights.

Gierek, himself a relatively tolerant and easy-going individual, was disinclined to undertake a thorough-going
repression of the growing unrest. His economic strategy was,
moreover, dependent on continued access to western loans
which would certainly become more difficult to obtain should a
harder line in domestic policy be introduced. The conclusion in
1975 of the Helsinki agreement, affirming the obligation of its
signatories to uphold basic civil and political liberties, was a
further brake on his freedom of action, as was his own desire to
preserve good relations with Western leaders, several of whom,
including Helmut Schmidt, the German Chancellor, and
President Carter, were due to visit Poland in 1977. The result
was that the policy of repression was only fitfully carried out. In

May 1977, after large-scale public demonstrations in Kraków sparked off by the suspicious death of a student, a number of the leading figures in KOR were arrested. But they, along with the overwhelming majority of those taken into custody in the aftermath of the strikes in 1976, were released as part of a large-scale amnesty in July 1977.

The amnesty acted as a tremendous fillip to the opposition which grew rapidly in strength and confidence. This opposition was very different from earlier political movements in Poland and the other socialist countries. These had all attempted to reform the Communist system from within by advancing their ideas through the various Communist or Workers' parties. Drawing from the experience of the Czechoslovak reformers in 1968, the Polish opposition, many of whose leaders had played a prominent part in the student unrest in Poland in that year, came to the conclusion that the Polish United Workers Party was incapable of reform and that the Soviet Union would anyway use all its influence to prevent any undermining of the principles of communist orthodoxy, above all the principle that the Communist Party should be the leading political force in Poland and that its internal organization should be based on 'democratic centralism', in accordance with which factions within the party were not to be tolerated and party policy was to be determined by the Politbureau and handed down to the rest of the party apparatus. The opposition accordingly concluded that the Communist Party should be left to rule.

The role of the opposition was to create the foundations of a plural society in Poland which could then put pressure on the authorities to behave in a more responsible way and take into account divergent social and political ideas. In advancing these principles a whole range of organizations outside party control was set up ranging from an unofficial or 'flying' university, taking its name from a similar organization in Tsarist times, which challenged the official monopoly over knowledge and raised many taboo subjects, to a series of unofficial publishing houses producing books and newspapers which contained opinions not acceptable to the censorship. From the events of 1970 and 1976, the opposition also drew the conclusion that the official government-controlled trade unions could not be counted on to defend the interests of the workers and that what was required was the establishment of independent unions with the right to strike. The growing link between the intellectual and workers' movements was one of the principal strengths of the opposition. By the late 1970s, unofficial newspapers were circulating on the Baltic coast in editions of up to 100,000 copies.

Moreover, in spite of the opposition's belief that the party itself was unreformable, political ferment was also soon to make itself felt within the PZPR. It is true that there was little sign that the party leadership had any realization of the seriousness of the crisis. Prime Minister Jaroszewicz retained his post in spite of having been the principal architect of the ill-fated price increases, while the resignation in December 1977 of Kazimierz Barcikowski, the Minister of Agriculture, and in January 1978 of Józef Tejchma, the Minister of Culture, saw the removal of two of the remaining relatively liberal members of the government. But at a lower level discontent became increasingly evident within the party. In November 1978 an 'Experience and the Future' discussion group was set up to act as a forum where party members and intellectuals could discuss the increasingly pressing social and political crisis. Its criticisms of current policy were so severe that the government stepped in and prevented its meeting after the middle of 1979. It was able to put together two analyses of the situation. *The Report on the State of the Republic* and *Which Way Out?* which showed clearly the isolation and unpopularity of the party leadership and the weaknesses of the increasingly insensitive and immobile governmental apparatus.

Gierek also attempted to defuse the crisis by improving relations with the Church. The Church had played a relatively moderate role in June 1976, supporting the strikers' basic demands but at the same time appealing for calm and opposing violence. This stance was reiterated in a letter submitted by Cardinal Wyszyński and the episcopate to the government in July. Though it called for the release of the arrested strikers, respect for civil rights and a real dialogue with society, it also underlined the Church's conviction that violent protest was fraught with incalculable consequences and that progress could only be achieved in conditions of peace and stability. The government responded favourably to this appeal for co-operation and in September 1976 Gierek affirmed that Church and State were not in conflict in Poland and that there were many areas in which they could work together. The Primate and the First Secretary duly met for the first time in the following month and the government further relaxed its policy on granting permission to build churches so that nearly 100 new parishes were now established in urban areas. The government was not, however, prepared to see in the Church a genuine political partner. It thus failed to modify its unwilling-ness to allow practising Catholics to hold political office and still pursued an ideological attack on religious belief which offended the sensibilities of many Catholics, so that Church-State relations were still marked by considerable mutual suspicion and coolness.

Indeed, the political ferment was now further increased by a largely unforeseen development, the elevation of Karol Wojtyla, the archbishop of Krakow, to the Papacy in October 1978. This event had an electrifying effect on the Poles. They had long thought of themselves as the stepchildren of Europe,

the exponents of Western beliefs and values in a difficult
geographic situation who had been let down in 1939 and abandoned by the West in 1944-5. Now for one of the principal
institutions of the Western world (for many Poles *the* principal
institution) to elect a Pole as its first non-Italian head for nearly
450 years, seemed to most Poles an unprecedented act of
reparation for all they had suffered and a clear legitimation of
their own view of their historical role. National self-confidence
increased dramatically as did the belief that major political
change was now inevitable. In the summer of 1978 Pope John
Paul II visited his homeland amid scenes of almost hysterical
rejoicing. Over 1½ million poeple attended an open-air mass
at the national shrine, the Jasna Góra monastery in Częstochowa. For the two weeks of the Pope's visit, it was as if the
communist authorities had ceased to exist. A submerged
Poland, Catholic, national and self-assertive, showed itself and
clearly demonstrated that it had the support of the overwhelming majority of the nation. It is possible that Gierek
could have harnessed the new mood by a spectacular act of
national reconciliation, a renewed appeal to the nation to co-
operate, coupled with a real attempt to open up the political
system. Such an appeal was, however, beyond his rather
limited political horizons and the chance to defuse the growing
social tensions was lost.

Moreover these tensions were being fuelled by the increasing
seriousness of the economic crisis. The failure to increase prices
in June 1976, coupled with the wage increases which followed,
increased the inflationary pressures on the economy. State sub-
sidization of consumer goods, above all food, was thus an
increasing burden on the state budget. By the end of the decade
it was estimated that nearly one-third of the state budget was
consumed by subsidies: the state was paying nearly 70 per cent
of the price of basic foodstuffs. This policy was adopted to

defuse social tensions, but from the mid-1970s, because of the excess purchasing power in the hands of the consumers, it led to the socialist equivalent of a runaway inflation, a runaway shortage. Goods disappeared from the shops, the black market increased and as queues lengthened so frustration grew. The government which had loudly trumpeted its initial economic achievements was now held responsible for the economic crisis.

Its own measures to deal with the situation proved half-hearted and lacking in coherence. Some attempts were made from 1976 to curtail investment so that more resources could be released to satisfy consumer demand, while the emphasis of economic planning was shifted from expensive major projects which had proved wasteful to modernizing existing plant. However, the over-bureaucratic and cumbersome planning apparatus was not modified and very high and completely unrealistic hopes were placed on an increase in exports to the West as a means of extricating Poland from her difficulties.

In order to improve the supply of basic foodstuffs, a major effort was undertaken to encourage private farmers, thus reversing Gierek's earlier encouragement of the State sector in agriculture. Investment in agriculture was greatly increased, with much more money now earmarked for the private farmers who still owned three-quarters of Poland's agricultural land. In addition efforts were made to persuade the farmers that the government had abandoned collectivization as a long-term goal. In February 1977, private farmers were given the right to buy or lease land from the State and given financial incentives to specialize on specific crops. At the end of the year, farmers were given the right to join the state pension plan while still being entitled to pass on their land to their heirs, thus removing a long-standing grievance. The aim of the government was to create a prosperous private agricultural sector in which there would be a large number of medium-sized farms of 20-30 hectares. This was a laudable long-term goal, and a recognition of the obvious fact that in a situation where nine-tenths of the farms in the country were smaller than 10 hectares, the private sector was unlikely ever to be able to feed the country. But the immediate impact of these measures was small and was partly undermined by the suspicion of the farming community and the lack of goods which farmers might want to buy which diminished their willingness to produce for the market. Not surprisingly therefore food and meat production barely increased between 1976 and 1980.

Under these conditions, the government tried to borrow its way out of the crisis. Hard currency indebtedness rose from over $6,000 million at the end of 1975, to $21,000 million by mid-1980. A major part of this borrowing was short term and the repayment of interest and capital became an increasingly heavy charge on the economy. Moreover, much of the investment was poorly planned and poorly implemented with little thought for the country's real needs. For example, a huge Massey-Ferguson tractor factory was built outside Warsaw. Lack of preparation meant that expensive machinery could not be installed and waited in the open to rust, while the fact that the new machines were based on imperial not metric measurements made them incompatible with existing plant. Even more serious, the plant produced massive tractors which could only be used on collective farms or exported, rather than the small tractors suitable for individual farmers for which there was a crying need.

Another effect of the policy of borrowing from the West was an enormous increase in corruption. Gierek himself was probably not a venal man nor one who cared much for personal possessions, but as a result of his trips to the West, he became convinced that the Western system worked well because of the way it rewarded its wealth-creators. He thus turned a blind eye and indeed sometimes even encouraged the efforts of his subordinates to enrich themselves and obtain private villas, cars and Western consumer goods, frequently at state expense. The gross excesses of these new 'bosses' (*prominenci*) were widely resented particularly at a time when shortages had become almost universal and queueing a way of life for ordinary people who had no access to special party shops or hospitals.

By the summer of 1980 the economic crisis had become so serious that in spite of its fears of provoking unrest, the government could no longer postpone the introduction of a new austerity programme. As on earlier occasions, there was inadequate consultation with the population and when on 1st June the price of meat was more than doubled, protest strikes began in Warsaw and Lublin and soon spread widely. On 14th August, the workers in the Lenin shipyard in Gdańsk came out on strike. Originally their demands had no clear political character; they called for the reinstatement of two former strike-leaders, one of them Lech Wałęsa, an electrician who had been fired for his attempt to organize a Free Trade Union on the Baltic Coast, the erection of monuments to the victims of December 1970, an increase in wages and family benefits and mass media coverage of the strike. Very quickly, however, the effect of the political agitation and the growth of political sophistication which had characterized the years since 1976 made themselves felt. The workers in Gdańsk now formulated a series of 21 economic and political demands. These included the establishment of independent trade unions with the right to strike, the acceptance by the state that Mass would be broadcast on radio and television, and the restriction of censorship to state secrets of a military or economic character. The policy of radio, TV, press and publications was also to be modified to make possible 'the expression of a heterogeneity of ideas, views

and opinions.' In addition a programme of economic reform
should be initiated by the government 'to bring the country out
of the state of crisis', while managerial appointments were in
future to be made on the basis of qualifications and not political
allegiance. The strike soon spread to Szczecin where similar
demands were made. A decisive factor in its success was the
appearance at the shipyard on 14th August of Lech Wałęsa
himself, a man with remarkable oratorical skills and an ability
to negotiate who was able to give the strike a political direction
and yet undertake to compromise with the authorities. With his
indomitable humour, his Catholicism and his Pilsudski-like
moustache, he seemed to many Poles to embody their demands
and aspirations. A colourful, charismatic figure, he could not
have made a greater contrast with the grey and sombre
communist officials with whom he had to negotiate.

These negotiations were to prove long and difficult and often
seemed near to collapse. They were marked by threats by the
Soviet Union to intervene and by calls from the Catholic hierarchy to the workers to compromise. Initially the government
tried to win over the workers by costly economic concessions
and by sacrificing some of the most discredited of its members,
most notably Prime Minister Jaroszewicz, but in the end it
gave way and agreement was reached on 31st August on all the
strikers' demands. The chief government negotiator, Mieczyslaw Jagielski, affirmed that 'We have spoken as Poles to Poles
. . . There are no victors or vanquished.'

One man who was vanquished, however, was Gierek himself. His policies had ended in disaster in the most serious crisis
of communism in Poland since its establishment and in a rejection of the communist system by those it claimed to represent
whose only parallel was the Kronstadt insurrection of 1921. He
lost office in early September and the Polish communist
authorities have sought to blame him for the crisis, even

threatening to put him on trial. This is too harsh a judgment. Gierek's ambitious economic plans could perhaps have succeeded had they been better implemented and had the general economic climate been more propitious. Equally he would have had more success in introducing austerity measures had he not so grossly exaggerated the economic successes of the early 1970s and had he been more prepared to consult with the population as a whole He was caught in a vicious circle. Not a repressive man himself, he was not willing to broaden the base of communist rule significantly for fear of upsetting the Soviet Union and his own hardliners. Fear of popular unrest led him to postpone long-overdue economic reforms and to try to borrow his way out of the crisis. The consumer boom which he had engineered to defuse political dissent was financed by other people's money. When the debts came home to roost, the prosperity he had created was shown to be illusory. Not surprisingly, when the incompetence and cynicism of the government became public knowledge, it provoked a profound popular disillusionment which made extremely difficult any satisfactory resolution of the crisis.

31

From Kania to Jaruzelski

The agreements reached with the shipyards workers at Gdańsk
and Szczecin and with the miners at Jastrzębie defused a very
dangerous situation. There was widespread relief that a peaceful solution had been reached by negotiation, a relief which was
articulated by Lech Wałęsa. 'We have shown', he declared at
the end of the Gdańsk strike, 'that Poles can always come to an
agreement if they want to. . . . My gratitude goes to all those
who have enabled this conflict to be resolved without the use of
force.' He had principally in mind the Minister of Defence,
General Jaruzelski, who had held this post since 1968, and
Stanislaw Kania who succeeded Gierek as First Secretary of the
Polish United Workers Party (PZPR) and who had previously
been responsible for security, the military and for religious
affairs on the Central Committee Secretariat. Both these men
were widely reputed to have refused to implement Gierek's
orders to dislodge the strikers by force, Jaruzelski allegedly
claiming, 'I will not send my army against four hundred fortresses', while Kania affirmed that while the party was confronted with 'counter-revolution', it would have to 'deal with it
by political means'.

In the succeeding weeks, free trade unions were established all over the country, leading to the setting up of a nation-wide organization, 'Solidarity'. It claimed a membership of nearly 10 million and although its principal strongholds were the two dozen or so great industrial concentrations, it was also powerful in smaller enterprises and in provincial centres. In its ranks it united supporters of widely differing political orientations— members of the various opposition groups which had developed since 1976, above all the Workers' Defence Committee (KOR), often disillusioned communists whose views now resembled those of West European Social Democrats, adherents of the political orientation of the Catholic Church and some followers of more radical and nationalist groups like the Confederation for an Independent Poland (KPN). One million of the 3 million members of the PZPR also joined Solidarity, some on instructions from the party to penetrate the organization but most out of support for the aims and objectives of the union.

Indeed, the establishment of Solidarity and the shock which the workers' revolt had administered to the communist system led to a new climate of hope which was shared by the reformers and moderates within the PZPR. They believed that they could channel the pressure for change generated by the crisis and use it to compel the party to introduce long-overdue social and economic reforms and undertake a genuine dialogue with the nation. There was always an element of unreality in these hopes. Although Kania was a relatively well-intentioned and undogmatic individual, he lacked dynamism and the ability to generate enthusiasm, giving the impression of merely responding to events without pursuing any clear objective. Moreover, for all his willingness to negotiate, his characterization of the strike movement as 'counter-revolution' did not bode well for the establishment of a fruitful relationship between the party and Solidarity. The hardliners within the party apparatus never regarded the concessions which they had been forced to make as more than tactical; as in all communist regimes, they were particularly strongly entrenched in the coercive apparatus and the army. General Jaruzelski, for all his fine words, had been quite prepared to use the army against strikers in 1970. The view that everything possible should be done to limit the scope of the concessions already made was also strongly held by the governments of the DDR and Czechoslovakia and above all of the Soviet Union. Events in Hungary in 1956 and Czechoslovakia in 1968 had shown how the institutional rigidity of communist systems makes peaceful reform difficult to achieve and that demands for change tend to spiral out of control. In these conditions, it was always unlikely that the PZPR would be able to produce the bold and innovative policies which were necessary if it was to master the crisis.

Moreover, this crisis was a particularly acute one. After the failure of both Gomulka and Gierek to achieve significant changes in the system, there was little inclination on the part of the Polish people, largely anti-communist and anti-Russian in their attitudes, to give this government the benefit of the doubt. A generation had passed since the catastrophic crushing of the Warsaw uprising, and romantic and insurrectionary views had a much more favourable hearing than voices calling for caution and compromise. In this context it should be pointed out that the bulk of the leadership of Solidarity was relatively young, with 36-year-old Wałęsa one of the most senior individuals. The leadership was often to find its views too moderate for its own radical supporters.

The economic crisis further undermined political stability and it was exacerbated by the rash concessions made by the government in its attempt to avoid giving way to the strikers' political demands during the Gdańsk negotiations. These included a blanket assurance that wages would be raised 'for all working groups, especially the lowest paid', as well as a promise that pensions would be raised, the health service and child care facilities improved and that a plan to phase out Saturday working would be introduced by the end of the year. As a consequence, whereas national income fell by 2.3 per cent in 1979, it was to fall a further 6 per cent in 1980 and another 12.1 per cent in 1981. It should have been possible to trade off political concessions by the government in return for the acceptance by Solidarity of a programme of economic stabilization and austerity. This was never achieved largely because of the lack of a willingness on the part of the government to introduce significant reforms, although it is true that Solidarity would have had difficulties in persuading its adherents of the need for such a programme.

It should not, however, be assumed from the start that the breakdown of relations between the government and Solidarity was inevitable. Polish communism had already demonstrated its ability to deviate from Marxist-Leninist orthodoxy in the maintenance of private agriculture and in the special position enjoyed by the Catholic church. In the first months after August the economic situation had still not deteriorated as catastrophically as it was later to do, and there was still a willingness on the part of the moderate leadership of Solidarity, above all Lech Wałęsa, to accept a lead from the government. At this time Wałęsa stressed that the aim of his movement was only to defend the interests of working people and that it had no political goals. Yet these months, when some sort of partnership could have been achieved, were wasted in fruitless wrangling. It began almost immediately when the government insisted that as a precondition of its registration, Solidarity should add to the first paragraph of its statutes a passage explicitly recognizing the 'leading role' of the PZPR and

Poland's established system of international alliances. This the
Union refused to accept on the grounds that its statutes had
declared an adherence to the constitution of the Polish Peoples'
Republic which contained an article upholding the leading role
of the party. There was more than mere legalistic hair-splitting
to this dispute which delayed the recognition of the union until
November when the authorities finally yielded. The government at this stage was determined to co-opt Solidarity into the
existing system of control, whereas the union, learning from
the way the government had emasculated demands for change
after 1956 and 1970, resisted incorporation of this sort. Indeed,
throughout these months the government seemed more concerned to reassure its own hardliners and the Soviet Union of
its ability to contain the union and assert its authority in the
country than to establish a working relationship with the union
or press ahead with reforms. Throughout this period the hostility of the more conservative elements in the party to the
changes occasioned by Solidarity was made clear and it was
intensified by their alarm at the fact that on every occasion
when the authorities attempted to stand firm in the face of the
demands of the union, they were in the end compelled to give
way. The hardliners' sense of being an embattled force was
strengthened by the large-scale personnel change which
occurred at this time. By the end of 1980 only 7 of the 19
members of the Politbureau in August still held office, while of
the 8 members of the Secretariat only 1 remained. Similar
changes occurred at the provincial level: by the end of 1980, 22
of the 46 party secretaries had been removed.

Under these conditions, with the pent-up demands for
change in the provinces arousing strong resistance and in the
absence of other methods of putting pressure on the government, the strike became a political weapon and was freely used
in local and regional conflicts. January 1981 was thus marked

by strikes and occupations in many towns which resulted in the dismissal of unpopular officials and the handing over to local communities of facilities whose use had previously been restricted to Party officials or members of the security apparatus. These local clashes were over-shadowed by a major conflict over Saturday working, whose abolition had been promised by the Gdańsk agreement. By now the radicals in Solidarity were convinced that the authorities only made concessions under the threat of force and were determined to hold the government to the letter of the agreement. Wałęsa was eager for a compromise since it was apparent that the country could not afford to end Saturday working. The maladroitness of the government made this impossible and in early February the authorities again gave way. In an attempt to strengthen his position, Kania now appointed General Jaruzelski as Prime Minister and for a time the atmosphere improved, with the government calling for social dialogue and an understanding with the Church.

How explosive the situation remained was soon demonstrated. On 20th March, while Kania was in Hungary and General Jaruzelski was on Warsaw Pact manoeuvres, the hard-liners tried to precipitate a confrontation with Solidarity which would enable a state of emergency to be introduced. After a meeting in the western Polish town of Bydgoszcz, three Solidarity activists were beaten up by the security police. Solidarity saw this as a frontal assault on its position and responded by calling for those responsible to be brought to justice. If not, it would declare a general strike. A majority of the Politbureau seems to have supported a hard line, but Kania, supported by General Jaruzelski, was able to maintain his policy of negotiation by shifting the focus of the decision to the larger central committee where he commanded a majority and by seeking the backing of the reformist PZPR branches in some of the large factories. Several days of very tense negotiations followed, in which a key mediating role was played by the Church. Agreement was eventually reached, to the relief of both Walęsa and his negotiating partner, the Deputy Prime Minister Mieczyslaw Rakowski, an agreement which was strongly criticized both by Party hardliners and by some of the radicals in Solidarity. The government promised to investigate the Bydgoszcz incident and also agreed to the formation of an independent union for farmers, Rural Solidarity. This concession had been strongly resisted by the party on the grounds that it breached the principle that only the PZPR could be a nationwide organization, with branches both in the town and country.

The Bydgoszcz crisis strengthened the hands of those in the party who favoured a policy of conciliation. On the day the agreement was reached, one of their number, the Chairman of the Polish Journalists Association, Stefan Bratkowski, circulated an Open Letter to the Party in which he called for an end to confrontation provoked by the hardliners and affirmed that the Bydgoszcz incident constituted 'the last chance crisis for those who wanted to turn our party back from the road of social understanding and to guide our state in this manner on to the path of an unavoidable catastrophe.' His views were widely shared by ordinary party members. Indeed, Kania's decision to mobilize PZPR branches in the large factories in his support acted as a tremendous fillip to the rank-and-file movement which had begun to emerge in the party from the turn of the year. This 'horizontal' movement, so-called because it sought to establish 'horizontal' links between party branches, thus bypassing the need for contact through the party hierarchy, sought to democratize the party and was a reflection of the political ferment pervading Polish society. It advocated more open methods of running the party, calling for the rotation of senior officials and their election by secret ballot. 'Horizontalist' influence was particularly strongly felt in the run-up to the extraordinary party conference which was now scheduled for mid-July, where the movement's supporters hoped to consolidate their position and place the party firmly at the head of the political and social transformation taking place in the country.

This development was anathema to the party hardliners who had also bitterly opposed the Bydgoszcz concessions. They still retained powerful positions in the party, above all in the security apparatus and the army and the most extreme among them now began to form political clubs, calling for the abandonment of conciliation and the crushing of opposition. One of these groups, the Katowice forum, on 28th May, went so far as to claim that 'the threat of a revisionist *coup d'état* in the party has been growing as a result of the passive posture of PZPR leadership, which has in fact consented to this course of events.'

This group and others which were only slightly less extreme certainly received the support and encouragement of the Soviet Union. Here too the failure of the party to stand firm over the Bydgoszcz incident was seen as fundamentally misguided. The Soviet leaders were even more alarmed by the rank-and-file movement in the PZPR which seemed to them to threaten the fundamental Marxist-Leninist principle of 'democratic centralism', the idea that decisions should be taken by the Politbureau and the central committee and transmitted down to the rest of the party. It seemed too to breach the rule that independent 'factions' were not to be permitted in the party and aroused uncomfortable memories of the ferment in the Czechoslovak Communist Party in 1968. Soviet dissatisfaction was made brutally plain in a letter from the Central Committee of the Soviet Communist Party to that of the PZPR on 5th June. Kania and Jaruzelski were criticized for failing to abandon a policy of 'concession and compromise', which had aroused 'profound anxiety for the future of socialism in Poland . . .' It went on:

> Only a month is left before the Polish Party Congress yet forces hostile to Socialism are increasingly setting the tone of the election campaign. It cannot be excluded that during the Congress itself an attempt could be made to strike a decisive blow against Marxist-Leninist forces within the party and in fact to liquidate it.

This was almost certainly a call to the PZPR Central Committee to replace Kania by a firmer and more resolute opponent of Solidarity. In the event at the 10th Plenum of the Central Committee held a few days later on 10th June, Kania was able to fight off the challenge to his position. But he now began to pay much more attention to Soviet and hardline views. He intervened to damp down unrest in the party and to prevent the 'horizontal' movement, many of whose members were also alarmed by the Soviet letter, from playing a major role in selecting delegates to the conference. Indeed, he went out of his way to ensure that his two principal hardline opponents, Tadeusz Grabski and Stefan Olszowski, were granted representation at the conference. In addition, since the Soviet letter had asserted that 'the class enemy had gained control of the mass media', Kania now compelled the relatively liberal head of the Central Committee media department, Jozef Klasa, to resign and replaced him by a close associate of Olszowski. A new hard line in the media was quickly evident, above all in television news coverage which, as in the West, was the most widely disseminated source of information in Poland. Bitterness over 'falsification of the news' in violation of the Gdańsk agreement grew within Solidarity and dissipated the improvement in the political atmosphere which had followed the agreement to end the Bydgoszcz confrontation.

In these circumstances, although there was a major turnover of personalities and many new faces were seen at the party conference held between 14th and 20th July, radical voices were few. The proceedings were characterized by great frankness of debate and secret balloting, but in the end resulted in the election of a centrist rather than reformist Central Committee and Politbureau. The fact that so many of the members of these bodies were now political novices strengthened the hand of the more experienced members and the hierarchy, while of the new members of the Politbureau, there were two prominent hardliners, General Milewski, head of the police, and Albin Siwak. Even more important, though the new party programme contained many radical proposals and calls for renovation, it made no serious attempt to grant to Solidarity a significant place in the political system.

The failure of the PZPR to put itself at the head of the pressure for change emanating from Polish society probably averted direct Soviet military intervention but it had the result of creating a political vacuum, with the party increasingly paralysed and incapable of a decisive initiative. Under these conditions, Solidarity, which had up to now ostensibly sought to avoid a directly political role, found itself sucked into the vacuum. It responded by the formulation of its own programme for the resolution of the crisis, which involved fundamental economic, social and political reforms, including workers' control over management in industry and whose ultimate goal was the establishment of a plural society, although one in which the leading role of the communist party would be retained in form if not in substance.

The inertia of the party was rendered still more threatening by the serious deterioration of the economic situation from the summer. The shortage of hard currency necessary to buy spare parts and raw materials for the factories bought in the West during the Gierek era, as well as grain, which had been one of the factors which had made necessary the ill-fated austerity programme of the summer of 1980, was exacerbated by the fall in exports, above all of coal, which had been caused by the ending of Saturday working and the hated four-shift system in the mines. Further wage increases since August 1980 only increased the already inflated demand for low-priced subsidized goods, principally basic foods, many of which effectively disappeared from the shops.

The summer was accordingly marked by street demonstrations and hunger marches which the Solidarity leadership tried vainly to channel in a constructive direction. Significant sections of its supporters were now strongly radicalized and the influence of previously unimportant groups like the nationalist Confederation for an Independent Poland (KPN) grew. The increasingly hostile tone of the media towards Solidarity fuelled mutual distrust, and although some talks were initiated with the aim of reaching agreement between union and government on a joint approach to the economic crisis, they were broken off without agreement in early August. In addition, the death in May of the revered primate, Cardinal Wyszyński, removed another factor working for political stability. His successor, Archbishop Glemp, had been close to him and his policies, but inevitably lacked his charisma and authority.

The political and economic situation was thus already critical when Solidarity's national conference took place in September. This event, preceded by a solemn mass celebrated by Archbishop Glemp in Oliwa cathedral, was quite without precedent in Eastern Europe since the establishment of communist rule. It proved to be protracted, difficult to control, intensely democratic and marked by a determination to allow every viewpoint to be fully heard. The conference was highly critical of the government's half-hearted attempts to deal with the crisis. Its mood of opposition was intensified by the government's announcement on 2nd September that it was dropping the investigation into the Bydgoszcz incident and by a dispute over radio and television coverage of the proceedings. Political tension was further heightened by the simultaneous holding of major Soviet land and naval exercises in the western USSR and the Baltic.

As a result, the first part of the conference was marked by the adoption of radical proposals, with calls for free national elections, a referendum on workers' self-management and a declaration of support for workers elsewhere in Eastern Europe 'who have decided to undertake the hard struggle for a free trade union movement'. These resolutions, and particularly the last, roused the Soviet leadership to a new pitch of fury and provoked the sternest warning thus far to the Polish authorities, calling on them 'immediately to take determined and radical steps to cut short malicious anti-Soviet propaganda and actions hostile towards the Soviet Union', while *Pravda* openly accused Solidarity of making a 'grab for power'. The response of the PZPR Politbureau was only slightly more restrained, claiming that Solidarity had unilaterally violated the agreements which had brought it into being. 'The resolutions', it continued, 'have raised to the level of an official programme for the whole organization . . . adventurist tendencies which had appeared to be only extremist undercurrents.' Solidarity's programme was now one of 'political opposition, striking at the vital interests of the Polish nation'.

Faced with what appeared to be the prelude to a concerted effort to crush Solidarity, Wałęsa and his associates made a determined and successful attempt during the second half of the conference to pull the organization back on to a more moderate course. Wałęsa himself convincingly defeated his

opponents in the elections for the union leader and succeeded
in negotiating an agreement with the government on the vexed
question of workers' control in factories. Above all, he induced
the union to accept what he described as a 'new social
contract', in which political power would be shared. Final decisions would remain with the government but it would first
discuss all important matters of policy with Solidarity and the
Church. This was more than the centrist elements controlling
the party, Kania himself and General Jaruzelski, were prepared to accept: they were willing to go quite far to consult
Solidarity, the Church and other social forces in Poland, but
they were not prepared to erode in any meaningful way the
political monopoly of the Communist Party. Moreover, they
were under increasing pressure both from the hardliners in
Poland and the Soviet leadership to abandon conciliation
altogether and to use force to crush opposition. Torn between
those who favoured outright repression and the advocates of
more far-reaching concessions, Kania lost control of the Central Committee and was voted out of office by an incongruous
coalition of moderates and exponents of a tough line.

He was succeeded as First Secretary by General Jaruzelski,
who still retained the posts of Prime Minister and Minister of
Defence. General Jaruzelski's appointment did not constitute
the final abandonment of conciliation and a decision to resort
to force. Rather, the General hoped to use the considerable
prestige of the armed forces in Poland to persuade Solidarity to
moderate its demands for a share of power and to agree to
accept a consultative role. His aim was in this way to co-opt
Solidarity so that it could be induced to persuade its members
to accede to the government's austerity plans for dealing with
the country's economic collapse. Had something like this been
offered a year previously, it would have gone far to resolving
the political crisis. By now, however, the Solidarity leadership

was not prepared to undertake the thankless task of selling the government's cuts in consumption to the population without being conceded a larger say in the running of the country. In these circumstances, the trilateral talks initiated by General Jaruzelski in mid-November between the Church, Solidarity and the government had little chance of success, particularly since the General made Solidarity's acceptance of his terms dependent on the union's renouncing the right to strike, its only effective means of putting pressure on the government. The administration's proposals were rendered still less attractive to Solidarity by its insistence that the discussions on economic reform be broadened to include other groups, above all the discredited pre-1980 trade unions and youth movements in a transparent attempt to dilute Solidarity's influence. Conversely, the pressure on the government to take tough action was intensified by the obvious inability of the Solidarity leadership to control local disputes, which continued to erupt, ranging from industrial disturbances to sit-ins of students and farmers.

The two sides tried fitfully to reach agreement, but there was no longer any real common ground. In retrospect the government's strategy in these weeks is clear—to hem in Solidarity by offering very circumscribed co-operation of a type calculated to divide the union, while initiating a campaign to discredit it in the eyes of the population by presenting its leaders as dangerous and irresponsible firebrands. The radicals in Solidarity played into the government's hands. They were now convinced that the weakness of the authorities would compel them to yield to their principal demands. Faced with the government's use of riot police, backed by the army, to dislodge striking fire cadets occupying the Fire Academy, they adopted a militant stance which Wałęsa and his allies were unable to moderate. Calls for preparedness in the face of the inevitable showdown were voiced by the union's executive in a secret meeting at Radom, whose proceedings were recorded and publicized by the authorities. At the meeting of the union's 100-strong national commission in Gdańsk on 13th December, proposals were adopted calling for a national referendum on the maintenance of the existing government and for a redefinition of the country's military relationship with the USSR. These resolutions were subsequently to be used by the government as the reason for suppressing the union, but they were in fact irrelevant except in the battle for public opinion since the authorities had already effectively decided on repression and were only waiting for the appropriate moment to strike.

This came almost immediately on the night of 13th December when martial law was duly proclaimed, trade unions and other organizations were suspended, all kinds of activity were subjected to severe restrictions and nearly 6,000 people were arrested, including the whole leadership of Solidarity, who were conveniently in Gdańsk for the meeting. So heavy was the blow that hopes of paralysing the country by a general strike failed and resistance to the police and army was only sporadic.

In introducing martial law under the Military Council of National Salvation, General Jaruzelski aimed at bringing under control a threat to communist power in Poland, which he believed could only provoke Soviet intervention. As he put it in his speech to the nation, 'Poland was not days but hours from catastrophe.' He hoped to employ the minimum of force so that he would be able to reach agreement with the more moderate elements in Solidarity and the country, and continue those aspects of the policy of reform which he considered would not undermine the authority of the government. 'There can be no return,' he asserted in his first speech, 'to the faulty methods and practices of the period prior to August 1980 just as there can be no retreat from socialism. The steps we have taken today have as their goal the preservation of the basic requisites of socialist renewal. All major reforms will be continued under conditions of order, substantial discussion and discipline.'

In addition, General Jaruzelski hoped to make use of the powers conferred on him by martial law to introduce a drastic economic stabilization plan, and he believed that this would induce Western governments and bankers to overlook the repressive side of his actions and furnish new credits and economic assistance to Poland. Indeed, the new government placed high hopes in the new economic policy which it intended to implement. Speaking slightly later, one of Jaruzelski's closest advisers, Captain Wieslaw Górnicki, justified the intro-duction of martial law on the grounds that 'it has made possible economic reform which to speak frankly, is the most far-reaching transformation in any socialist country since the Second World War. It goes further than the Hungarian reforms. . . .' Indeed, the example of Hungary was very much in the minds of the men around General Jaruzelski. They often described their objective as 'Kadarization'—that is to say, they hoped to accomplish what they believed First Secretary Janos Kadar had achieved in Hungary since the brutal crushing of the uprising of 1956. There would be a period of political repression, but it would be accompanied by a far-reaching decentralization of the economy and the use of the market mechanism rather than central planning to regulate economic policy. This would encourage initiative, create an economic revival and make possible a degree of political liberalization but under the firm control of a reorganized Communist Party.

The government's success in achieving these goals has been at best partial. The actual imposition of martial law was meticulously planned and carried through without too much difficulty. The strategy of using the politically reliable riot police (ZOMO) to break strikes and factory occupations, while employing the largely conscript army to hold the ring and act as a back-up force proved successful. Fears that the apparatus of coercion at the disposal of the authorities would prove inadequate and that a clampdown would precipitate a collapse of the government proved misplaced, although it should also be pointed out that the awareness of the population that a successful revolution of this type could only provoke Soviet intervention acted as a damper on resistance.

It has proved far more difficult to undertake positive initiatives. The decision to establish martial law was as much a defeat for the party as for Solidarity. The principal organs of party rule, the Politbureau and the Central Committee, were not formally consulted about the decision and have been largely elbowed aside since. The language used to justify the establishment of the Military Council of National Salvation avoided Marxist-Leninist phraseology and appealed rather to patriotic sentiments in a manner redolent of the Pilsudski era. Justifying the establishment of martial law, for instance, General Jaruzelski embarked on a panegyric of military virtues:

'The Polish soldier,' he claimed, 'has faithfully served and still serves his country. He is always in the front line of every social necessity. Today, too, he will perform his duty with honour. Our soldier has clean hands, he does not know the word selfishness, only hard service. He has no other aim but the good of the nation.'

Army officers have taken a key role in the administration both of the country and of the economy and they are clearly not going to be dislodged easily. One of its members has even described this government as one made up of 'military men and technocrats'. Under these conditions, attempts to revive the party so that it could again play a leading role in the country's political life have had little success. General Jaruzelski has shown some skill in outmanoeuvring the hardline elements within the PZPR who could pose a threat to his position, which at present seems almost unassailable. But he has also felt compelled to undertake a purge of moderates and liberals within the party which has robbed it of many of its most dynamic members. In the eyes of Polish society as a whole the party lacks credibility and its re-emergence as an effective force seems a long way off, in spite of exhortations from the General for it to go on an 'ideological offensive'.

Perhaps more important, it has proved impossible for the government to establish an effective dialogue with society. Although the introduction of martial law went fairly smoothly, it was accompanied by considerable violence and brutality. According to official estimates, 10 people were killed while unofficial sources put the figure at anything from 25 to 60. Many people were injured when occupation strikes were broken, while those interned were often held under extremely harsh conditions. As a consequence, the government's hopes of reaching agreement with the more moderate elements in Solidarity, above all with Lech Wałęsa himself, proved incapable of achievement. Some soundings did take place between January and March, but Wałęsa refused to co-operate unless the rest of the Solidarity leadership was released and consequently little progress was made.

The government had more success with the Church. The Church hierarchy, and particularly the Primate, Cardinal Glemp, feared that the government would be unable to master the situation and would be replaced by more hardline elements, perhaps after a Soviet invasion, which would undermine the very real gains the Church had made since 1956. The authorities, for their part, went out of their way to woo the Church, specifically excluding church services from the ban on meetings under the emergency measures. As a result, Archbishop Glemp issued a strongly worded appeal for calm on the day after the establishment of martial law. 'The Church,' he affirmed, 'will be unyielding when it comes to defending human life. It does not matter if the church is accused of cowardice . . . it will call for peace . . . I shall plead even if I must on my knees: Do not start a fight between Poles. Do not give your lives away, brother workers, because the price of human life will be low.'

In the spring, the Church renewed its attempt to play the role of mediator, hoping to persuade the government to release the internees and acquiesce in the re-establishment of a Solidarity shorn of its political objectives and its more radical advisers. Alarmed by the revival of unrest from March onwards, General Jaruzelski was not prepared to yield on these issues, and by the summer it was clear that the mediation attempt had failed. As a result popular frustration fuelled by the very limited relaxation of martial law announced in July in spite of earlier hints of major concessions erupted in large-scale demonstrations in July and August, particularly on the second anniversary of the signing of the Gdańsk agreement. From these the government drew the conclusion that it could not afford to compromise with Solidarity and the organization was duly banned in October. However, it was clear that repression alone could not resolve the country's problems. The government thus also made contact with the Church and an agreement was reached that Wałęsa was to be released, martial law brought to an end and the Pope allowed to visit Poland in the summer of 1983. A new trade union law was passed providing for the establishment of ostensibly independent unions which would have the right to strike under very restricted conditions. For the moment, they were to be limited to individual factories where only one union was to be allowed, but ultimately a nation-wide organization would be established.

At the time, there were high hopes that these developments

presaged the adoption by the government of a far-reaching policy of conciliation. The new trade unions would be granted real autonomy and some place would be found in the political system for Wałęsa and the Solidarity moderates. In the event more cautious counsels have prevailed. Martial law was suspended, though not abolished, on the first anniversary of its introduction. But the government has not been prepared to engage in any sort of dialogue with Wałęsa and while most of those interned have been released, no general amnesty has been proclaimed for the more than 2,000 people sentenced for political offences under martial law regulations. Indeed the government seems determined to mount show trials both of the leaders of KOR and of the more radical figures in Solidarity. Its strategy seems clear—to grind down society and lower its political expectations by holding out and then dashing hopes for major political concessions, while carrying out a limited and controlled but nevertheless far-reaching campaign of repression. This has, in effect, led to a political stalemate. The opposition knows that it cannot by demonstrations induce the government to change course. Indeed, if too successful, these risk rather putting into power more hardline elements. Equally the government has been unable to overcome the hostility and indifference of the population. Its attempt to widen the basis of its support by setting up ostensibly non-party organizations such as the Patriotic Movement for National Rebirth (PRON) has clearly failed, largely because the Church has refused to take part. Equally, the opposition's campaign to persuade the workers to boycott the new unions has proved largely successful and they have succeeded in recruiting only about one and three-quarter million members from the total labour force of over 12 million.

This political stalemate would, under normal conditions, be tolerable to the government. The authorities are clearly reconciled to ruling without popular support and they have demonstrated their willingness to use force to maintain themselves in power. What makes it dangerous is the persistence of the economic crisis, with its attendant frustrations, which means that there is always a danger of the situation exploding, as has been frankly conceded by General Jaruzelski. In late February 1983, for instance, he admitted that 'today it is easy to exercise anti-socialist demagogy on the economic plane, since it is here that the well-known burdens and weaknesses are most painfully felt.'

It is true that some successes have been achieved in placing the economy on a more satisfactory footing. The re-introduction of Saturday working and a substantial increase in wages have led to a revival of mining output, above all in the coalmines. This has produced a large supply of coal for export, although the cost has been high in terms of the neglect of safety precautions, and the military commissar in charge of mining has warned that the increase in coal output may soon tail off because of the need to devote more attention to maintenance and the repair of equipment. The expected boost to the economy in terms of hard currency has also been less than was anticipated, since the recession has meant that demand for coal on the international markets has been low.

Martial law has also made possible the introduction of long-overdue price increases. In early 1982 the cost of electricity was doubled and that of gas tripled. Threefold increases were also introduced in the price of sugar, milk, bacon, pork, ham and sausage, while the cost of cheese and sirloin went up fivefold. These and other increases, which led to a rise in the cost of living index of 105 per cent in 1982 have not proved sufficient to restore equilibrium, partly because their effect has been mitigated by the palliatives introduced by the government to make them more acceptable. Bank savings were revalued upwards by 20 per cent, annual bonuses were paid to all workers in the administration, in State-owned enterprises and in co-operatives, and in addition many other workers were able to obtain significant increases in wages. Further increases in prices are clearly necessary, but the government has hesitated to introduce more than very marginal changes because of its fears of social upheaval.

The core of the economic reform was its attempt to use the discipline of the market to replace rigid central planning. The central planners' function was to be reduced to that of setting general goals, while the great industrial cartels so favoured by Gierek would be broken up and individual enterprises would be given far-reaching freedom to determine the levels of production, wages and prices. Those firms unable to produce at a profit would accordingly be compelled to modify their policies in response to market forces. This, it was believed, would stimulate managers to greater efficiency while labour discipline would be improved by incentive schemes and by the introduction of a wide measure of worker self-management in the factories which would give individual workers a stake in the profitability of their firms.

This ambitious programme has not yet borne significant fruits. In the first place, it has not yet been possible to introduce any significant measure of worker self-management, and the work-force, for the most part still loyal to Solidarity, has given only the most half-hearted and grudging support to the reform. The plan was, moreover, introduced at the height of an unprecedented slump in the Polish economy. Between 1979 and 1981 national income fell by over one-fifth and it continued to fall in 1982. This made impossible the full implementation of a rigorous socialist version of monetarism, which anyway ran counter to the *dirigiste* assumptions of many of the military men running the economy. Since resources were very scarce, the government introduced 'operational programmes' and 'state contracts' under which firms are obliged to supply key goods which are difficult to obtain. This privileged sector comprises some 30 per cent of industrial production and its establishment has meant that every factory manager's principle has been to have his enterprise placed on a priority programme with corresponding damage to the remaining 70 per cent of industry. Free competition has been difficult to establish, given the habits ingrained in managers from nearly four decades of central planning, and large industrial associations have continued to dominate the economy, causing the deputy minister responsible for economic reform, Professor Zdzislaw Sadowski, to threaten anti-cartel legislation. In addition, incentive schemes for workers involving higher wages have had relatively little attraction given the severe shortage of consumer goods. One bright spot on the industrial scene has been the encouragement of Poles abroad to establish small private firms under very favourable conditions, which have plugged some of the more glaring holes in the economy. These have, however, come under increasing fire because of their private character and the way they have threatened the monopoly of the great cartels.

Another reason for the lack of impact of the economic reform has been the unwillingness of the government to accept the logic of its position. Firms were supposed to show themselves profitable or go to the wall. Yet of the 900 or so enterprises which found themselves in serious financial difficulties in 1982, only one was allowed to go bankrupt while the remainder were bailed out either by bank loans or ministerial subsidies. As before 1980, individual firms and the government as a whole have not been loath to buy social peace with costly economic concessions. Thus in a situation in which individual firms are able to decide wage levels, it is perhaps not surprising that in

1982 wages and disbursements rose by 70 per cent without any significant increases in productivity, undermining the effect of the price increases and fuelling a new inflationary surge. Similarly, though theoretically firms have the right to discharge workers, they have hesitated to tackle the serious problem of overmanning for fear of social disturbances. This, coupled with the fact that many people have taken advantage of government schemes enabling them to retire early, has created a severe shortage of labour.

The government has also continued earlier policies of wooing the private farmers. Although Rural Solidarity was banned, farmers have been granted the right to form associations, while their right to own land and pass it on to their heirs has been guaranteed. In addition, the authorities have had to improve the grain supply situation and make it more attractive to farmers to sell grain by introducing a scheme for grain loan bonds under which farmers delivering grain would receive bonds which could be redeemed in 1983-5 at the prices then obtaining. This has not, however, overcome the distrust of the private farmers and their unwillingness to sell grain in a situation where little is available for them to purchase with the money they receive. Farm production fell by 4.5 per cent in 1982 and widespread grain hoarding occurred, leading to estimates that at least 100,000 tons of grain had gone mouldy. A classic scissors crisis has occurred, with the farmers having little incentive to produce for the market. In spite of some threats to re-introduce compulsory deliveries of agricultural produce, the authorities have hesitated to confront the farmers, partly because this would also lead to a serious deterioration in Church-State relations. As a consequence the supply of food in the towns remains unsatisfactory and a source of tension.

Under these conditions, the economic reform seems to be

running out of steam, with national income falling another 8 per cent in 1982 and official estimates conceding that the country can only hope in favourable conditions to achieve again the levels of consumption of the late 1970s in 1990. The authorities have been compelled increasingly to resort to moral exhortations rather than to the discipline of the market. Above all the government underestimated the degree to which the economy had become dependent in the Gierek period on hard currency to buy raw materials and spare parts. Western sanctions have had relatively little effect on the Polish economy though in some areas, as in the American stopping of supplies of chicken feed, they have been palpable. Far more important has been the inability to borrow more money on world markets. Western private banks did agree to reschedule their Polish debts, under relatively favourable conditions, in 1982 but sanctions have meant a freeze on the re-negotiation of government debt. Though this has afforded the government some immediate relief in that interest payments no longer had to be paid, it has effectively stopped new borrowing.

The first year of martial law dispelled hopes that the Soviet Union and her partners could make good this shortfall of hard currency estimated at a minimum of 2 billion dollars. Thus, while in the longer term the Polish government can probably reorient the country's economy towards the Comecon bloc, though at the cost of falling further behind the West in technology and quality control, on a shorter time-scale a real recovery is dependent on Western economic assistance. This has been openly admitted by the weekly *Polityka* and it has clear political implications. 'It would seem therefore to be essential', the paper commented, 'that steps be taken to ease the restrictions on obtaining credits from the capitalist states. These steps should include both international and internal political action aimed at achieving national accord and removing the causes which led to sanctions . . .'

Poland's leaders thus find themselves at a crossroads. They certainly possess the power politically to keep the lid on for some years, but it will be at the cost of continuing economic stagnation and the frustration of the hopes expressed by General Jaruzelski when he took power. This could create a dangerous situation. The crises of 1956 and 1970 led to the establishment of a more satisfactory relationship between rulers and ruled although on both occasions the authorities eventually dissipated the goodwill they had created. The crisis of 1980-2, on the contrary, has led to an increase in tension— society, as a whole, is probably more alienated from the government now than at any time since the establishment of Communist rule. In addition, the stakes have been raised. On previous occasions strikes and demonstrations have been taken as a sign that the government has lost its mandate and have been followed by changes of both policies and personnel. With the establishment of martial law and the subsequent repression the authorities have made it clear that they will not shirk from the use of force to hold on to power. But equally, in spite of the danger of repression, the opposition now has less reason to hold back on its own measures of protest if the moment should seem propitious. This is a recipe for conflict which could have reper- cussions far beyond Poland's borders. Only a major act of con- ciliation by the government can break the vicious circle, and create the conditions which will make possible the successful implementation of economic reform and establish the stability, political understanding and economic well-being for which all Poles crave.

Part VI

TOWARD THE ''GRAND FAILURE''
OF COMMUNISM IN POLAND

32

Poland under Jaruzelski

The martial law declared by General Wojciech Jaruzelski on December 13, 1981 did not, in the long run, save Communism in Poland. In fact, the outrage it produced only accelerated the process which Zbigniew Brzezinski described as an "organic rejection of Communism." Ultimately, it brought about its own "grand failure" before the end of the 1980s not only in Poland but throughout Eastern Europe as well.

Uncharacteristically, the Polish nation did not put up any significant active resistance to Jaruzelski's forces. Even if they had, severe winter conditions, the surprise arrest of approximately five thousand Solidarity leaders and activists, as well as the complete cut-off of national and international telephone and telegraph communications, would have made resistance difficult. But since only peaceful, non-violent methods of struggle had been accepted by Polish workers during the turbulent strikes of August 1980, there was not much choice: Solidarity leaders and supporters understood that an armed society had no chance against a well-armed police and army.

Some Solidarity leaders initially thought of radical forms of resistance such as a general strike, but Zbigniew Bujak, who escaped imprisonment, vehemently opposed it, saying that "it was a call to send thousands of people to their graves." The Primate of Poland, Archbishop Józef (later Cardinal) Glemp, added his voice by openly pleading to avoid bloodshed and civil war in which Poles would fight against other Poles.

In the end, the very few Solidarity leaders who were not arrested worked to organize an underground network, urging passive resistance. On April 22, 1982 a few Solidarity leaders managed to organize the TKK (Provisional Coordinating Commission of Solidarity), headed by Bujak. Solidarity was kept alive and remained a powerful symbol of freedom for Poles and freedom-loving people everywhere. But Solidarity was in disarray and no longer an organized force. This became apparent when TKK, after much confusion and indecision, called for a one-day national strike on November 10, 1982 which ended in failure.

The sense of outrage expressed by the United States and Western Europe—and the political and economic sanctions that followed—gave some psychological comfort to the Poles. Jaruzelski was put on notice that only an end to martial law, the release of political prisoners, and the start of genuine dialogue with Solidarity and the Catholic Church would end the harmful sanctions. General Jaruzelski realized that his martial law coup created an abnormal situation that widened the gap between his regime and society as never before, and that eventually something would have to be done to bring about a normalization and reconciliation. He began by making promises that he would not return "to the erroneous methods and practices that were used before August 1980," but would instead follow "socialist renewal and economic reforms." In March 1982, two new articles were placed in Poland's 1952 Communist Constitution. The first created a Constitutional Tribunal that reviewed the constitutionality of parliamentary statutes and executive decrees. The second established a Tribunal of State, a sort of impeachment court designed to hold Party officials accountable for violations of the constitution and laws. (The need for such a tribunal became evident during the later Solidarity period, when abuses of power by Party officials were being uncovered.)

To further show that he was serious about reform, Jaruzelski pressed the Party Commission to complete its investigation on the causes for political crises that had plagued Communist Poland during its past forty years. Headed by the liberal professor and Politburo Secretary in Charge of Cultural Affairs Hieronim Kubiak, this Commission, created in September 1981 (before the martial law crackdown), finally reported to the Party's Politburo on July 1982. Much of the report was not made public, but Kubiak's conclusions—which condemned the Party's centralized system of authority for reacting with brute force to the protests of the working class—were found unacceptable and resulted in his dismissal from the Politburo. Yet General Jaruzelski and his Party comrades could not so easily dismiss other parts of the report, such as those that blamed Party officials for ignoring public opinion and discouraging local initiatives for independent action and reforms.

Although some Polish citizens had been induced to cooperate with the regime through such government-sponsored organizations as the Patriotic Front for National Renewal (PRON) and new trade-union organizations, most of Polish society remained either passively unresponsive or openly hostile to Jaruzelski's regime. This was especially true for the intelligentsia and the young people, who considered the Communist establishment to be fundamentally untrustworthy and Jaruzelski's program to be lacking credibility.

The government was well aware of such sentiments. In March 1983, Minister of Internal Affairs and Justice General Czeslaw Kiszczak had announced to the Sejm that the "process of states' disintegration had been arrested" and "the anarchy that paralyzed the economy has been overcome." Nevertheless, the political system had been defended and stabilization achieved at a great price: Kiszczak openly admitted that society "hates the government and is more distrustful and apathetic toward it than at any other time before."

Some Poles lost hope and opted to leave the country, via Austria, either for Western Europe or the United States. Most, however, turned to the Catholic Church as the only institution to remain untainted and where Polish national values (such as were stressed by Solidarity) were preserved. Little wonder that the Church became the center of a wide range of cultural and welfare activities. These activities established an unofficial culture with a genuine political life throughout Poland.

The Church was naturally opposed to the martial law, but its hierarchy tended to have a conciliatory attitude toward the government, not wishing to exacerbate a situation that might lead to massive repression or Soviet intervention. For this reason, the Church was praised by the regime for its "realism," given access to the media, and permitted to construct hundreds of churches during a time of severe housing shortages. There was a growing rapprochement between Jaruzelski's regime and the Catholic Church, and it was strengthened by an agreement, made in November 1982, for Pope John Paul II's second papal visit to Poland in June 1983.

Also in November 1982, Lech Walesa was released from detention. This was an event celebrated in the United States and other Western countries. From the moment of his release, Walesa acted publicly as the symbol of the Polish resistance. Walesa would go on to win the Nobel Peace Prize two years later—an event that further elated the Polish People and friends of Poland everywhere.

Upon his arrival in Poland in June 1983, John Paul II was placed in a difficult position, as he was a guest of the government.

He did his best, however, to lift the morale of the people, while being careful to counsel restraint. Shortly after, in July 1983, martial law was formally removed.

Jaruzelski was determined to demonstrate that he had learned a lesson and was now embarking on a policy of "socialist pluralism" and renewal. Two days before martial law was formally lifted (July 20, 1983), the electoral system was changed by the Sejm to permit a limited multi-party system. The United Peasant Party and the Democratic Party were now allowed to officially engage in the political life of the country.

By the summer of 1983, General Jaruzelski had been able to achieve pacification and stabilization but certainly not normalization. Coercive measures, taken during martial law, had produced diminished returns. The Jaruzelski regime knew it had to convince the public that the government was working in its interest, so that people would trust the government and work hard to improve Poland's economy. Without an effective consumerism of the type introduced earlier in Hungary by Kadar, it was clear that the Communist system in Poland was in deep peril.

Jaruzelski could not count on aid from his discredited and emasculated party or from any government-sponsored organization. The only means by which he could reach out to society at large was through the Catholic Church. Jaruzelski, therefore, saw the Church as the essential mediator between the government and society.

It was evident, however, that the Church endorsed Solidarity. During the heyday of Solidarity, many local parish priests were completely involved in the political concerns of their flock; and it was no secret that Pope John Paul II, a native Pole and now head of the Roman Catholic Church—and the Polish hierarchy as well—supported the aspirations of the Solidarity movement.

Thus, a serious step toward reconciliation was reached when

General Jaruzelski announced a far-reaching amnesty which freed most Solidarity leaders and advisers. Bodgan Lis and Piotr Mierzewski, prominent underground leaders, were released in early December 1984.

But the Church-State rapprochement had strong opposition from important hard-liners in the Party and the police, which were responsible for two crises in 1984. The first was the so-called "Battle of the Crosses," which began in the spring of 1984 when a principal in Garwolin removed a cross hanging illegally in the classroom. In the ensuing dispute the government found itself unable to publicly abandon the principle of secularism. The second, more serious incident was the murder of Reverend Jerzy Popieluszko, in October 1984, a priest well known for his anti-government sermons during the martial-law period.

Reverend Popieluszko was immediately hailed as a martyr; his burial place outside his Warsaw Church became a national shrine. General Jaruzelski and his government reacted quickly to disassociate themselves from his murder; the policemen and one of their superiors who had defied official policy were brought quickly to trial in early 1985, convicted of murder, and given sentences of up to twenty-five years.

Jaruzelski and the moderate wing of the Party were serious about working out an arrangement with society with the help of the Catholic Church and they would not have allowed themselves to be deterred. Without such an agreement there could neither be economic reform nor vital assistance from the West. A change in the atheistic Communist philosophy was seen to be taking place when a prominent Communist journal proposed that "a religious world outlook is favorable to socialism."

In the summer of 1985, General Jaruzelski began appearing at official functions in civilian clothes, thus signaling that he, at least, considered normalization to have been achieved. His optimistic view was further strengthened by the elections to the Sejm in October 1985 in which, despite Solidarity's call for a boycott, over seventy per cent of the voters participated. Following the election in November 1985, a general shakeup occurred which resulted in General Jaruzelski becoming the head of state (Chairman of the State Council), while Zbigniew Messner, an economics professor, replaced him as Prime Minister. Other changes included Marian Orzechowski, replacing hard-liner Olszowski (who was also removed from the Politburo) as Foreign Minister. Mieczyslaw Rakowski, a well-known enemy of Solidarity, was forced to resign from his post as Deputy Prime Minister.

In reality, Jaruzelski did not have much reason to be overjoyed. The political impasse of the last five years had worsened Poland's economic problems and made them almost unsolvable. Economically, Poland was much worse off at the end of 1985 than it had been in 1980. The economic stagnation that started with martial law had not been reversed. Poland's hard currency debt climbed to over $30 billion, its standard of living had dropped to startling low levels. The entire infrastructure was breaking down. The Polish people were living in great misery, with their real income dropping by an astounding twenty-five per cent.

Real, meaningful economic reform was still politically stymied. If there was one message that Solidarity delivered not only to the Polish Communists, but to the entire Communist world, it was that political reform was a precondition of a successful economic reform. People would only make the sacrifices called for by the government if they first could participate fully and democratically in the political process. The limited legal freedom offered so far by Jaruzelski and his moderates was insufficient to win society's support. But even these moderate measures of "self-regulating pluralism" that were always insisted on in the guiding role of the Party were opposed by hard-line party leaders and most of the Communist bureaucracy and managers of state enterprises. Post-martial law Poland continued to develop into two societies: the official society, composed of the regime establishment, with a good number of people willingly or unwillingly cooperating with it; and the alternative society—with heavy participation by the youth—"with its own media, literature, cultural and educational activities," well-organized and self-sufficient "receiving strong moral and material support from the West." This latter society, according to Brzezinski, eventually made possible "a rebirth of genuine political life in Poland signaling the end of totalitarian rule."

33

Gorbachev's Impact

The economic crisis described above was not confined to Poland alone. According to Lawrence Goodwyn, "It pervaded the entire Eastern bloc and nowhere was it more pronounced than in the Soviet Union. Its cause was a structural breakdown of the Leninist system of production." The appearance of Mikhail Gorbachev as top Soviet leader in March 1985 produced, in time, a fundamental shift that made a big difference not only for Poland, but for all of Eastern Europe.

Gorbachev had concluded that to save socialism in the Soviet Union, badly needed economic reforms had to be introduced. But he became frustrated when he saw economic reforms blocked by the Party's economic managerial apparatus and the Central Committee. Influenced by the Solidarity experience, Gorbachev became convinced that political reforms were needed first to make economic reforms work. Thus he advanced the line of glasnost as well as democratization.

Jaruzelski benefitted from the spectacular shifts in Moscow. At the Tenth Party Congress of the Polish Communist Party (formally known as the Polish United Workers Party), in June-July 1986, he received enthusiastic endorsement from

Gorbachev. He became Moscow's favorite son and was given the widest possible latitude to do what he deemed was necessary, including instituting new forms of political participation and competitive elections. (Of course, Jaruzelski reciprocated by fully backing Gorbachev's reform policies.) Emboldened by support from Moscow, the Jaruzelski regime took a daring step. On September 11, 1986 Interior Minister General Kiszczak announced the unconditional release of the remaining two hundred twenty-five political prisoners, "in the interest of strengthening the process of national accord." Now all Solidarity leaders were free, including Zbigniew Bujak, the TKK leader who had been captured only two months previously after four-and-a-half years in hiding. This was followed up in December 1986 by the creation of a Social Consultative Council to help increase societal participation in public life. Impressed with these developments, the United States responded by lifting its remaining sanctions in February 1987.

Solidarity circles seemed unprepared for the amnesty announcement. But it could not be lightly dismissed since, as Jacek Kuron pointed out, the regime had fulfilled the primary preconditions for talks. Solidarity, however, was no longer the mass-trade union it once was. Now it was largely symbolized by Lech Walesa and his hand-picked advisers and colleagues. On September 19, 1986 Walesa decided to create a new leadership body that was called the Provisional Council of Solidarity (TRS) which would act openly and legally and prepare Solidarity's eventual return to legality. At the same time, the underground TKK network was to continue with regional organizations given the option of remaining underground or coming out into the open.

The existence of several Solidarity structures caused confusion and disorganization, as well as exacerbating personal animosities and conflicts. Eventually, Walesa and his colleagues would scrap both the TRS and TKK and create a National Executive Commission (KKW) made up of ten regional representatives. Jacek Kuron was prompted to remark jokingly that "Walesa deserves another Nobel Peace Prize for his work in trying to reconcile differences within Solidarity."

Most of the Solidarity leaders were now in agreement that the focus should be on systemic political reform rather than trade union activity. In addition, they adopted a pro-market position in April 1987, calling for extensive privatization of Poland's economy. With Solidarity leadership demanding economic reforms, the regime and Solidarity were converging. This convergence led twenty-two members of the 1981 Solidarity National Commission to complain to Walesa that there was now hardly any concern for the "social and standard of living problems" of the workers.

The policy of reaching out to society through the Church was continued with even more vigor throughout 1987. In January, Jaruzelski had made a State visit to Italy. At the same time, he made an official visit to Vatican City, where he had talks with the Pope. In June, John Paul II made his third papal visit to Poland during which time he spoke of the need for more freedom while recognizing the limitations of Poland's geopolitical situation. A month later, Church and government officials agreed on a way to support Poland's private farmers with United States financial aid. In 1987, Jaruzelski and other high party officials learned that the Soviets had decided to retrench from Eastern Europe. In a secret memorandum in mid-1987, Mieczyslaw Rakowski further informed Jaruzelski that the Soviets would no longer protect or save Party rule in Poland. To save itself, Rakowski argued, "the Party must learn to persuade and compete in a democratic system." This confidential information must have influenced Jaruzelski's decision to place in referendum on November 19, 1987, an elaborate radical economic package that would require steep price increases and short-term austerity, but would also commit the government to "deep democratization."

Walesa and his close colleagues were faced with a dilemma. They were in favor of both economic reform and democratization, but if the voters gave the government a "yes vote," the government would receive a vote of confidence without Solidarity getting something in return. So, Walesa advised the voters to boycott or at least ignore the referendum. The public response was sufficient to deprive the government of victory. The voters were not willing to make the necessary sacrifices without political concessions that would assure genuine political pluralism and legalization of Solidarity.

The referendum, however, was not totally fruitless. It encouraged some leaders to bring together the reform elements of the Communist Party with Solidarity. In early 1988, pleas were published in leading official newspapers urging that the government open up talks with Walesa and the opposition so as to save the country from impending disaster. Jerzy Holzer wrote about the prospect of "Wojciech Jaruzelski and Lech Walesa signing an historic pact," while Bronislaw Geremek proposed an "anti-crisis" pact between the government and Solidarity.

Such proposals could now be made, since many Solidarity leaders had become convinced that the government was interested in genuine reform. They were impressed that freedom of the press in Poland was virtually complete by 1988. It also appeared that all parties had learned a great deal from the last eight years, so perhaps it was not unrealistic to expect a grand accord between the government and the opposition. The latter would help provide social peace while the former would recognize society's right to organize itself. But it took the strike wave of April–May 1988 in the Gdansk shipyards to finally bring the two forces together.

The young radical workers reacted strongly to the skyrocketing inflation. They were unwilling to follow Solidarity's leadership, and Walesa barely managed to control them at the price of joining them. The strike ended in May, only to break out again in August. These events proved that the party could not govern without the participation of independent representatives of the opposition. Therefore, something drastic had to be done. Jaruzelski decided to act by authorizing Interior Minister General Kiszczak to open up discussions with Walesa. These negotiations started in August 31, 1988 on the eighth anniversary of the signing of the famous Gdansk Accord. For the first time after martial law, the regime and Solidarity sat down for negotiations. Thus, Solidarity won formal recognition for itself. Walesa was satisfied that this was sufficient basis for ending the strike, but he had great difficulties in persuading the angry young strikers to do so.

The four-hour August 31 meeting was designed to lead to a general "Round Table" discussion between the Party and the opposition. However, this did not happen immediately. The Party was sharply divided into reform and anti-reform factions, and these resisted compromise. It took Rakowski's arguments "that there is no other choice but to devolve power" and Jaruzelski's threats to resign before the party agreed to begin "Round Table" discussions. Solidarity was not ready either, since it had to find a way of maintaining its new political role without giving up its trade-union status. The formula for this was found on December 18, 1988 when, at the personal invitation of Lech Walesa, one hundred twenty-eight prominent intellectuals and activists gathered at a meeting in Warsaw and announced the formation of the Solidarity Citizens Committee. Its presiding officer was the veteran KOR and Solidarity activist, Henry Wujec, and its members included such well-known names as Bronisaw Geremek, Tadeusz Mazowiecki, and Andrzej Stelmachowski.

This committee was criticized for not being representative enough and for being dominated by Warsaw intellectuals, and Wujec was forced to expand the committee to two hundred thirty-two members. But criticisms—such as Solidarity's National Coordinating Commission, with its strong ties to the working class, being bypassed—continued. Nevertheless, the Citizens Committee became the political arm of Solidarity, ready to serve as a negotiating group and receiving considerable attention in the official media.

The conditions for an agreement seemed favorable. The Communist government needed a partner to share responsibility for unpleasant measures necessary to improve the economy and Solidarity needed the government to prevent anarchy and vengeance. Thus it was in this context that the historic "Round Table" negotiations began on February 6, 1989.

The two sides at the "Round Table," which referred to themselves as a "government coalition" and "Solidarity opposition," quickly appointed representatives to a number of committees and sub-committees that were mandated to work out agreements on various issues such as economic policy, political reform, trade-union pluralism, health, education, housing, etc. But the most important decisions were by the small "Magda-lenka Group" made up of Walesa, General Kiszczak and their closest advisers, with a Church representative in attendance as neutral observer, stepping in as an arbiter whenever necessary. The "Grand Coalition" of Solidarity, the government authorities, and the Church proposed earlier in November 1981 by Ryszard Reiff, leader of the historically pro-regime PAX organization, seemed to be in the making.

On April 5, 1989 an accord was reached which included an agreement for new elections. Very soon after, the Sejm lifted the ban on the Solidarity movement, giving it full legal status.

The elections, held on June 4, 1989 produced spectacular,

unanticipated victories for Solidarity candidates. In the newly created Senate, Solidarity won ninety-two of the one hundred seats, with the remaining eight unfilled because no candidate had received the required fifty per cent. In the Sejm, it won one hundred sixty out of the one hundred sixty-one seats allotted. Of the remaining two hundred ninety-nine seats allotted to the Communists and their allies, only five were won since voters crossed out the Communists from the ballots, and they could not secure the necessary fifty per cent. In the end, the Communists and their allies claimed two hundred ninety-four seats. On July 19, 1989, in accordance with the "Round Table" compromise, Jaruzelski was grudgingly elected President by the Sejm with wide powers in foreign policy and as Commander in Chief of the armed forces.

Originally the Solidarity victors were determined to become a tough opposition, but they had no intention of assuming power at a time of economic crisis. They would have preferred to accept Jaruzelski's nominee for prime minister, but when General Kiszczak was asked to form the government, public opinion was shocked and offended. Walesa, responding intuitively to public opinion, went into action. He informed Jaruzelski that Solidarity could not accept Kiszczak, whose ministry during martial law was in charge of the police. Then, in a surprise move, he worked out an alliance with once-subservient parties, the United Peasant Party and the Democratic Party. With this alliance, Solidarity could take over and organize a new government headed by Walesa's hand-picked candidate, Tadeusz Mazowiecki. President Jaruzelski obliged and on August 19, 1989, he asked Mazowiecki, the Catholic journalist with strong ties to the Catholic hierarchy (and Walesa's closest adviser) to form a government.

Some Polish Communist leaders, such as First Party Secretary Rakowski, expressed reservation about cooperating with a prospective Solidarity government. It was then that Gorbachev himself telephoned Rakowski and, informing him that he was ready to accept a Polish government with a Communist minority, urged him to accept it also.

The August 1989 developments in Poland were sensational and considered by some to be miraculous. One historian observed, "All across Eastern Europe, extending to be the Soviet Union itself, aspiring reformers watched Poland with hope, trepidation, and increasingly genuine exultation." A political system had been completely changed without violence. It was truly a remarkable change that soon facilitated the emancipation of all Eastern Europe from Communist totalitarianism before the end of the year.

34

Post-Communist Poland:
Mazowiecki's Government

Tadeusz Mazowiecki was sworn in on September 12, 1989. Immediately he was faced with enormous social and economic difficulties. The economy was bankrupt and inoperative; the industries outdated and mismanaged; work force demoralized; agriculture ruined; the police corrupted. The preceding "caretaker," Prime Minister Rakowski, had introduced reform measures that resulted in runaway inflation reaching two thousand per cent and leaving a huge budget deficit. The Solidarity Prime Minister did have a majority in the Sejm and the newly created Senate, but the Communists still had the Presidency, control of the army and security forces, and the foreign ministry. The Party apparatus remained strong in the various ministries at all administrative levels.

With his unquestioned integrity and hard work, Mazowiecki at first won the respect and admiration in Poland as well as in Europe and America. His efforts to lay the foundations for a modern democratic state with a prosperous free-market economy were recognized and applauded. Solidarity leaders such as Bronisaw Geremek (leader of Solidarity's Parliamentary Club), also saw that the future of democracy in Poland was dependent on

445

its economic success. Therefore, it would be necessary for Solidarity to work diligently to prove that the free-market system it advocated was superior to the Communist system it would replace.

Mazowiecki placed the highest priority on economic reconstruction, but at the same time believed in gradual political change and the rule of law. Taking the high ground, he did not order wholesale purges of the government bureaucracy which many expected, insisting instead that everyone be given an opportunity to prove his professional abilities and loyalty to the new government. Problems were created, however, when his "no witch hunt" policy was seen as accommodating the Communist Party apparatus without sufficient explanation to those who had sought change. Mazowiecki's "honeymoon" period did not last long. It became clear that Polish society—which was roughly divided into groups of workers, peasants, white collar bureaucrats, and intelligentsia—was deeply divided on what methods would achieve a modern, democratic, prosperous Poland. While most Poles understood that painful, austere measures would be necessary to deal with the economic crisis, they wanted the pain to be fairly distributed. Peasant farmers and workers, watching their standard of living fall precipitously, chafed at the sight of Communist bureaucrats and others benefiting from the introduced changes. Class tensions were on the rise, and Mazowiecki's government could not escape the political responsibility for the inevitable pain that accompanied the transition to a democratic, free-market economy.

More welcome were the constitutional and symbolic changes that began to take place during Mazowiecki's tenure. As a result of a bill of amendments passed by the Sejm and Senate in December 1989, Poland was no longer a "socialist state" with the Communist Party guaranteed a leading role in the governance of Poland; instead, it became a democratic legal state, with the original name of "Republic of Poland" restored. Supreme authority resided in the nation rather than in the working people.

The task of writing a new democratic constitution was given to a Constitutional Commission chosen by the Sejm. The Commission included forty-six deputies from the Sejm representing a variety of political groups and parties. A system of genuine local self-government was introduced with fiscal autonomy and responsibility for providing local services. These efforts culminated in May 1990, with the first free elections held to select local officials. Local governments, however, experienced difficulties because of insufficient funding.

Generally, consensus was achieved in foreign policy matters which were in the capable hands of Foreign Minister Krzystof Skubiszewski, formerly a well-known scholar in international law. Skubiszewski based Poland's foreign policy on the fundamental principles of external sovereignty and internal independence. After the swift and surprising unification of the two Germanies, Skubiszewski demanded that the existing Oder-Neisse border be confirmed by an internationally binding treaty. This demand was fulfilled and, on November 14, 1990 a united Germany and Poland signed a treaty recognizing the finality of their borders and renouncing claims to former German territories. As far as the Soviet Union was concerned, Poland began lobbying for the dissolution of the Warsaw Pact which did occur on July 1, 1991. Poland started negotiations in August 1990 for the withdrawal of Soviet troops from Polish soil. Hitherto taboo subjects, such as the massacre of Polish officers in the Katyn forest, deportation of Polish citizens to the Soviet Union during World War II, and the plight of the Polish minority in the USSR, were broached with some positive results. Poland gave every indication that it saw its future with Europe and was interested in eventually being admitted to the existing Western European institutions.

More controversial was the economic reform designed by Mazowiecki's Financial Minister, Leszek Balcerowicz. The program, which went into effect on January 11, 1990, was based on a proposal from Harvard economist Jeffrey Sachs and supported by the International Monetary Fund. The plan called for a "shock therapy" approach that acknowledged sharp pain, but presumably would make possible a "quick leap" into a market economy. The plan signaled the abandonment of the command-type socio-economic planning that characterized the Communist economic system and beginning of free economic activity. Within five months, Balcerowicz's plan reduced the inflation rate from forty to five per cent; the *zloty* was made fully convertible and stabilized at 9,500 *zlotys* to the dollar; food and consumer goods were readily available (albeit at much higher prices); and the budget was balanced.

Balcerowicz then concentrated his attention on the privatization of the large, state-owned "dinosaur" enterprises that were generally inefficient and unprofitable. He was determined they should no longer receive government subsidies. These large firms were the greatest obstacle to the development of healthy market mechanisms. Lacking the flexible response to demands and fluctuations in the market, their only solution was to cut back on production, which in turn only deepened the recession and increased unemployment-hitherto unknown in Communist Poland.

Privatization, however, was stalled by the Sejm, which questioned some provisions in Balcerowicz's draft legislation; and by the workers' self-management lobby, who opposed privatization and demanded special privileges for workers in privatized industries. Privatization was also attacked because many Communist-installed managers had shrewdly transformed their enterprises into private companies buying up assets at undervalued prices; this precipitated an outcry from the population to curb such takeovers.

In addition, workers (whose purchasing power was reduced by the fight against inflation) and farmers also challenged Balcerowicz's program. They claimed they would be ruined before the benefits of the free market could be felt. Farmers demanded, in contradiction to Balcerowicz's economic program, that they be guaranteed sales and prices for their agricultural goods and preferential credits, in a similar manner that West European governments provided for their farmers. In spite of strong lobbying by the Polish Peasant Party; Mazowiecki did not wish to make any exceptions to the rule, and soon the Mazowiecki government was being portrayed by the Polish farmers as anti-farmer, anti-peasant. Indeed, the Polish Peasant Party withdrew its support from the Mazowiecki government and Czeslaw Janicki, Minister of Agriculture, resigned.

But controversial economic policies were not the only factor that made Mazowiecki's government increasingly unpopular. It was felt that, in the political arena, the Mazowiecki government had allowed itself to be overtaken by events. In November 1989 the entire world was electrified by the sight of the Berlin Wall tumbling, and new political parties and movements appeared in Hungary, Czechoslovakia, East Germany, Bulgaria, and Romania before the end of the year. These unexpected developments produced more dramatic changes than the ones being made in Poland where the East European revolution began.

Not many tears were shed when, in January 1990, the Polish Communist Party collapsed and dissolved itself, ending the era of totalitarian rule in Poland. (The Communist Party would later reorganize itself along Social Democratic lines.) Many Poles, however, became exasperated and thought that the "Round Table" agreement, which gave the Presidency to General Wojciech Jaruzelski and guaranteed to the Communists and their allies sixty-five per cent of the seats in the Sejm, should no longer be honored. By February 1990, strong voices were heard calling for fully free elections and the replacement of Jaruzelski by a new president who would be elected directly by the people.

Soon Lech Walesa began identifying himself with these sentiments. Walesa had been overshadowed by the high profiles of Prime Minister Mazowiecki and the Solidarity parliamentary leader, Bronisaw Geremek; and he had been generally left outside the new power structure. In the spring of 1990, Lech Walesa began to present himself as the person who could provide the necessary impetus to bring about Poland's democratic transformation. Strong hints were given that he was interested in running for the presidency. He started to criticize Mazowiecki for making his government too elitist and allowing too many former Communist administrators to remain in influential positions.

As early as February 1990, Walesa appointed Zdzislaw Najder, a literary scholar and political writer, head of Solidarity's Citizen's Committee with the mandate for making it more pluralistic. This was followed by loosening ties with the left-of-center group; e.g., Henry Wujec was removed as Secretary of the Citizen's Committee and Adam Michnik was not supported for the editorship of *Gazeta Wyborcza*. Walesa's position was that "two strong political orientations, left- and right-of-center, were needed in Poland."

Mazowiecki, on the other hand, argued that the "Round Table" agreement was still functional and should be continued to assure stability and consistency, and to allow for the gradual completion of political and economic reforms. If changes were to be introduced, they should be made only with the agreement of all parties concerned and with a clear timetable for implementation.

Differences on issues and strategy exposed a sorry spectacle of the once-unified Solidarity camp falling apart into factions and turning against its own leadership. Further complicating matters was the estrangement between Lech Walesa and Tadeusz Mazowiecki, once close friends. According to Bronisaw Geremek, Walesa and Mazowiecki had been engaged in a "more or less silent war" since the establishment of a Solidarity-sponsored government. It appeared that Walesa was offended when Mazowiecki failed to consult him about the composition of his government in August-September 1989, and by his exclusion from politics and government in general.

Mazowiecki's response to Walesa's criticism was not very gracious. He was angered by efforts to stir up opposition to his government and accused Walesa of "demagogucry, populism, sloganeering without proposing specific programs for change." The idea that Walesa should become President was strongly rejected by him.

Differences between Mazowiecki and Walesa continued to widen in spite of mediation efforts. On May 31, 1990, Walesa's supporters organized themselves into a political group called the Center Alliance, which urged the swift election of Walesa as President to take charge of the government and accelerate changes. On June 30 and July 1, 1990, Walesa won support from the Solidarity's Citizens Committee, whose representatives came to Warsaw from all parts of Poland. The program of "pluralism and acceleration" was accepted, but the call was for a "renewed" government, not a new government.

Nevertheless, there was no doubt that Walesa was the victor. Following the July meeting, Mazowiecki supporters established the Citizen's Movement for Democratic Action, emphasizing deliberate evolutionary changes without any "witch hunts." The entire Polish nation became aware of the deep differences between the two much-admired men when they delivered their speeches in Gdansk on August 31, 1990, on the tenth anniversary of the famous agreement between Solidarity and the Communist authorities. The unity of the Solidarity camp had ended and a full-blown political power struggle had begun.

General Jaruzelski was now under pressure to give up the Presidency. He had kept a low profile and had cooperated with the Mazowiecki government, but he remained an unpopular politician identified with martial law. As a symbol and a relic of the hated past, his presence in the Belweder Presidential Palace was considered intolerable by most Poles. Jaruzelski, sensing all of this, wrote a letter to the Sejm on July 28, 1990, expressing his readiness to retire before the end of his term (1995) if and when it authorized a new presidential election.

Soon after, in early August 1990, Walesa formally announced his candidacy for the presidency and appointed a campaign advisory body which was oriented toward Catholic and conservative political traditions.

In October, just a month before the presidential elections, Tadeusz Mazowiecki decided to challenge Walesa, thus assuring that there would be neither cooperation nor reconciliation between the two leading political personalities in Poland.

During the presidential campaign, the Polish people realized that the new institution of the presidency might have a decisive influence on the evolution of their political system. The presidency was a new institution created by constitutional amendment in April 1989 as part of the "Round Table" agreement, but it had extensive powers; e.g., power to dissolve Parliament, influence foreign policy, and control the armed forces. The new constitution, in preparation since December 1989, could not be completed before the November 1990 election, but it was expected to be in place on May 3, 1991, in time for the bicentennial of the Constitution. The voters, therefore, were faced with an anomalous situation since they would be voting directly for a president, without knowing exactly what his future powers would be. So during the heated campaign, the hottest issue was the scope of presidential powers. Walesa supporters favored a strong chief executive modeled after the American or

French presidency, while his opponents vociferously opposed a strong presidency. Adam Michnik openly opposed Walesa and his idea of a strong presidency since he feared that he would set up an authoritarian dictatorship, following the example of Jozef Pilsudski in 1926.

Lech Walesa, the charismatic leader of humble social origins, was elected President of Poland on December 9, 1990. He was certainly not the choice of the intelligentsia, many of whom considered him a "coarse proletarian," and unfit to be President; but he was the favorite of the workers and farmers, a man with whom they could identify. Walesa's victory did not come easily. It came after a most unedifying and even embarrassing campaign and required two rounds of voting.

The entry of a complete unknown and outsider, Stanislaw Tyminski, a Polish emigre businessman from Canada and Peru, complicated the election. The first round resulted in forty per cent of the popular vote for Walesa, less than the fifty per cent needed. But the unknown Tyminski had humiliated Mazowiecki by receiving twenty-three per cent of the vote, while nineteen per cent for Mazowiecki had put him in third place. This was interpreted by many as a "no-confidence" vote for Mazowiecki's government policies.

The second round of voting gave Walesa an overwhelming seventy-four per cent of the popular vote and the rest to Tyminski. But the latter's relatively strong showing convinced Walesa that there was a need to "sew back together the forces associated with Solidarity." In spite of pressures to break with the past, Walesa chose continuity and reconciliation with the Mazowiecki group.

Only two days after the election, Walesa traveled to the National Shrine in Czestochowa and entrusted his presidency and the fate of Poland to the Black Madonna, "Our Lady of Czestochowa," who had been revered as the Queen of Poland since the seventeenth century. This was good politics, as it endeared him to Poland's heavily Catholic population, but it was also something that reflected his genuine Catholic faith. Poles would not forget that throughout the troubled decade of the 1980s, Walesa kept the image of the Black Madonna ostentatiously placed on his lapel.

The formal inauguration ceremonies for Lech Walesa took place on December 11, 1990 and ended with a thanksgiving mass celebrated by the Primate of Poland, Cardinal Jozef Glemp, at St. John's Cathedral in Warsaw. Significantly, Leszek Balcerowicz agreed to stay on as Finance Minister; Foreign Minister Skubiszewski remained as well. In fact, fifteen of the twenty-five incumbents from the previous government remained at their ministerial posts.

A week later, Jan Krzysztof Bielecki, a thirty-nine year old liberal businessman from Gdansk, was nominated Prime Minister. It was Bielecki's policy to create a team of specialists who would lead a program of economic growth and rapid privatization while preserving the fiscal stability achieved by Mazowiecki. Walesa planned to center politics and important decision-making in the Belweder (the Presidential Palace, equivalent to America's White House.) The organic rejection of Communism had been finally accomplished and Poland was beginning its long, difficult journey toward a pluralist democracy.

Postscript

The artificial and forcible separation of Poland and other Eastern European nations from Western Europe and the United States (the Atlantic Community) by the Communist Iron Curtain in the post-World War II Cold War period was regarded as a great tragedy and injustice by Oscar Halecki, but it did not shake his Christian faith. He never lost hope that "peace and freedom" would come to the nations of East Central Europe, not as a result "of the inhuman price of another world war," but as a result of moral power and peaceful methods. It is incredible that—at the height of the Cold War in the early 1960s when the two superpowers verged on nuclear holocaust—Halecki was able to envision "a truly Christian Europe, including a converted Russia" that would emerge as the year 2000 approached (*The Millennium of Europe*, University of Notre Dame Press, 1963, p. 394).

The astonishing peaceful revolution of 1989 in East Central Europe that ended the Cold War and began the process of emancipation in a region of nearly 200 million people of different ethnic groups—Poles, Czechs, Slovaks, Hungarians, Croats, Serbs, Slovenes, Romanians, Byelorussians, Lithuanians,

455

Estonians, Latvians, and Ukrainians—would have delighted him but not have caused him to gloat. However, the role played by the united Polish nation in initiating the transition from Communist totalitarianism to pluralist democracy, would certainly have given him additional satisfaction.

Halecki, although a strong Polish patriot, was first a Christian European, loyal to the larger European community and thus keenly interested in supra-national federal organizations. No doubt, he would insist that Jadwiga's message of peace and the prospects of a federal system advanced by her—based on the respect, equality, and freedom of its members in the ''Borderlands of Europe''—is still vital and relevant today.

Led by its creative moral leaders, Pope John Paul II and Lech Walesa, the Polish nation exposed the moral bankruptcy of Marxist-Leninist, materialistic and atheistic ideology and pointed the road to peace, justice and freedom, based on the enduring Western Judeo-Christian values and traditions. Humanity was urged to abandon violence and terror, to embrace instead love, non-violence, pluralism, truth, and morality. Queen Jadwiga's heritage has thus survived in Poland.

Thaddeus V. Gromada

1992

Index

Academy of Sciences and Arts,
  Polish, 261, 295, 335
Adalbert, St, 16
Adriatic Sea, 97
Akkerman, 100, 102
Albert of Brandenburg, Duke of
  Prussia, 108 ff., 119 f., 149
Albrecht of Austria, 87 ff.
Alexander I, 217, 220 ff., 230, 326
Alexander II, 239, 254
Alexander III, 256
Alexander of Poland, 102 ff., 107
Alexis, Tsar of Moscow, 157
Altmark, Treaty of, 149
Altranstadt, Treaty of, 181
America, 195, 205, 296, 319, 328 f.,
  333, 338, 340, 342 f., 379
Anabaptists, 123
Ancona, 322
Anders, Wlad., General, 322
Andruszow, Truce of, 162
Andrzejewski, Jerzy, 390
Angers, 317
Arciszewski, Tomasz, 324
Arians, 123 f., 183
Arnhem, 324
Association of Atheists and
  Freethinkers, 361

Atlantic Charter, 319 ff.
Augustus II, the Strong, 179,
  181 ff.
Augustus III, 179, 187 ff., 190
Austria, Austrians, 40, 109, 111,
  139, 149 f., 160, 166 ff., 170, 175,
  180, 187, 193 f., 205, 208 f., 212,
  215, 221 ff., 231 ff., 237, 259 ff.,
  268 f., 270, 276 f., 285, 305 f.
——, House of. See Hapsburgs
Austrian Succession, War of the,
  186
Avignon, 49, 56

Babenbergs, 40
Babiuch, Edward, 383
Balkans, 151, 268, 318
Baltic Sea, 12 f., 69, 75, 92 f., 120 f.,
  149 f., 157, 168 f., 283, 293, 343
Bar, Confederation of, 194 f.
Barbara Radziwill, wife of
  Sigismund Augustus, 117
Basil II, 99
Basil III, 108 ff.
Basil IV (Shuisky), 147
Basle, Council of, 86 f.
Bathory, Stephen. See Stephen
  Bathory

457

Batu Khan, 37
Bautzen, Peace of, 15
Beck, Colonel Joseph, 304 ff.
Belgians, Belgium, 231, 324
Bem, General, 237 f.
Beresina, passage of the, 223
Beresteczko, battle of, 157
Beria, 347
Berlin, 149, 324
Berman, Jakob, 331, 350
Bialystok, 315
Bienkowski, Wladyslaw, 363, 387
Bierut, Boleslaw, 322, 331, 333, 336, 339, 346, 348, 350
Bismarck, 235, 257 f., 267
Black Sea, 5, 59, 67 f., 73, 92, 100 f., 103, 151, 154, 173 f.
Bobrzynski, Michael, 262
Bogorja, Jaroslaw, archbishop, 59
Bohemia, 5, 10 f., 16, 40, 45, 47, 49, 53, 82, 87 ff., 96 ff., 102, 109 f., 111, 133
Bohemian Brethren, 123
Boleslas I, the Great or Brave, 13 ff., 52
Boleslas II, the Bold, 18 ff., 37, 43
Boleslas III, the Crooked-mouthed, 21 ff.
Boleslas IV, 24
Boleslas V, the Chaste or Pious, 31, 39, 45 f.
Boleslas of Masovia, 90
Bologna, 322
Bona Sforza, wife of Sigismund I, 114, 117, 141
Boniface VIII, Pope, 47
Bor-Komorowski, T., General, 322
Boris Godunov, Tsar, 145 f.
Bosnia, 268
Braclaw, 125, 154, 161
Brandenburg, 45, 60, 82
——, Electors of, 110, 149
——, House of, 120
——, margraves of, 40, 47 ff.
Brandt, Willy, 371
Bratkowski, Stefan, 406

Brest Litovsk (Brzesc Litewski), Treaties of, 279. *See also* Brzesc
Brezhnev, 364, 384
Bruhl, Count von, 186
Bruno, St, 16
Brussels, 247
Brzesc, 299, *See also* Brest Litovsk
——, Synod of, 139
Buda, 68, 112
Bug, river, 13, 27, 80, 208
Bukovina, 103 f.
Bulgaria, 89
Bulow, Chancellor, 267
Byczyna, battle of, 137
Bydgoszcz incident, 405–7, 411
Byzantium, 4, 9, 16

Calvin, 123
'Camp of National Unity,' 300
Campo Formio, Peace of, 219
Canossa, 19
Carinthia, 20
Carlovingian Empire, Carlovingians, 4, 6, 8
Carter, J. 390
Casimir I, the Restorer, 18
Casimir II, the Just, 24 ff.
Casimir III, the Great, 50, 52–61, 65 ff., 74, 94
Casimir IV, son of Jagiello, 87, 90–102, 108
Casimir, St, son of Casimir IV, 97, 104
Casimir of Stettin, 60
Catherine, daughter of Louis of Anjou, 66
Catherine of Austria, wife of Sigismund Augustus, 125
Catherine II of Russia, 187 f., 192 ff., 196, 203 ff., 207, 217, 326
Catholicism, Catholics, 29, 38 f., 55, 68 ff., 97 f., 111, 124 f., 136, 139, 144, 146, 178 f., 184, 235, 249, 256 f., 295, 314, 338 ff., 345, 356, 360 ff., 365 ff., 381 f., 385 ff., 390

Cecora, battle of, 148, 166
Central Industrial District, 293
Cesarini, Julian, papal legate, 89 f.
Chamberlain, Neville, 307
Charles IV, Emperor, 56 f., 66
Charles V, Emperor, 109 f., 115
Charles VI, Emperor, 183
Charles V of France, 66
Charles IX of France, 134
Charles IX of Sweden, 140, 146, 148
Charles X of Sweden. *See* Charles Gustavus
Charles XII of Sweden, 180 f., 183 f.
Charles Gustavus, 157 f., 160
Charles of Lorraine, Prince, 171
Charles of Luxemburg. *See* Charles IV
Charles Robert of Anjou, King of Hungary, 49, 53, 56
Chelm, Government of, 268, 279
Chelmno, 35, 53, 78, 94
China, 358
Chlopicki, General, 232
Chmielnicki, Bohdan, 155 ff., 161 f.
Chmielnicki, George, 161 f.
Chmielnik, battle of, 37
Chocim, battle of (1621), 148; (1673), 166
Chodkiewicz, John Charles, 140, 148
Chojnice, battle of, 93
Chopin, Frederick, 250
Christianity, spread of, 3, 9, 17 f., 23, 38, 55
Churchill, Winston, 321, 327
Cieszkowski, Augustus, 249
Cieszyn (Teschen) Silesia, 288
Clement XIV, Pope, 198
Club of the Crooked Circle, 363
Colloquium Charitativum, 150
Commission of National Education, 198, 227
Commission for Polish Affairs, 281
Conde, Prince de, 163

Conference of Ambassadors, 288
Congress Kingdom, 228, 277, 311 f.
Conrad II, Emperor, 17 f.
Conrad III, Emperor, 25
Conrad of Masovia, 28, 31, 33 f., 39, 44, 167
Constance, Council of, 79 f., 82, 86
Constantine, Grand Duke, 230, 232
Constantinople (Stambul), 55, 88, 90, 139, 238
Constitution of the Third of May 1791, 200 ff., 221, 227
—— of 1807, 220
—— of 1815, 226
—— of October 1905, 267
—— of March 1921, 298
—— of May 1935, 298
—— of July 1952, 335
Conti, Prince Francois Louis de, 179 f.
Convention of 15th May 1922, 289
Copernicus, Nicolas, 115
Corridor, Polish, 281, 306, 312
Corvinus, Matthias. *See* Matthias
Cossacks, Ukrainian, 140, 147 f., 152 ff., 166, 173, 181, 212
Council Permanent, 197
Courland (Kurland), 120, 207
Cracow, 7, 19, 24 ff., 39, 42 ff., 56 f., 68 ff., 74, 79, 81, 85, 88, 90, 110 f., 115, 134, 142, 144, 158, 181, 198, 206 ff., 221, 225, 235 ff., 261 f., 276, 285, 294, 312 ff., 338
——, Congress of, 56 f.
——, University of, 57, 74, 79, 115, 198, 261 f., 294, 313 f.
Crecy, battle of, 56
Crimea, 100, 104, 112 f., 151, 154, 156, 173 f., 203
Crimean War, 238, 326
Croatia, 340
Crusades, 26, 32, 57, 88, 151
Curzon Line, 285, 311, 321
Cyrankiewicz, J., 336, 383
Czarniecki, Stephen, 159

Czartoryski, Prince Adam, 193
Czartoryski, Prince Adam George,
  217, 222, 225, 233, 237 f.
Czartoryskis, 184, 187 f., 191 ff.
Czechoslovakia, 296, 302, 305 f.,
  307, 320, 345, 358, 368, 370,
  378, 384
Czechs, 16, 18, 57, 77, 83, 268,
  288, 306
Czernihow, 147, 161 f.
Czestochowa, monastery, 158, 195,
  365

Dabrowski, General, 207, 219 f.
Dachau, 314
Danes, Denmark, 12, 57, 82, 96,
  121, 160, 180
Daniel, King of Halicz and
  Volhynia, 29, 38 f., 54, 69
Danticus, John, 115
Danube, river, 100, 173
Danzig, 48, 78, 93, 111, 134, 167,
  180, 185, 196, 203, 205, 207, 220,
  281, 283, 293, 306, 312, 330.
  See also Gdansk
——, Pomerania, 35 f., 45, 47 ff.,
  53, 76, 78, 92, 94, 281, 313
—— ——, Duke of, 29, 35 f., 45
——, Treaty of, 167
Demetrius, the false, 145 f.
Democratic Society, 234
Deputies, House of, 101, 118, 126
Diet of Convocation, 192
——, Dumb, 182
——, Four Years, or Great, 199 ff.,
  203 f., 211, 223
——, Galician, 260
—— of Grodno, 206
—— of Investigation, 138
——, Lithuanian, 122
—— of Lublin, 118
—— of Pacification, 180
—— of Warsaw, 222, 232
—— of Wilno, 288
Dietines, 101
Diets, 101 f., 113, 118, 122 f.,

125 f., 199 ff., 352, 381
——, regional, 76
Directory, French, 219
Disarmament Conference, 304
Dissidents, 178, 183
Dlugosz, John, 85, 106, 248
Dmowski, Roman, 267, 278, 280,
  284, 287
Dnieper, river, 14, 92, 100, 154,
  162, 173, 196
Dniester, river, 92, 100, 173
Dobrzyn, 50, 53, 73, 76 f.
Doroszenko, Cossack leader, 166
Dubcek, Alexander, 368
Dubravka, wife of Mieszko I, 10
Duma of 1906, 267
Duracz, Andrzej, 368
Dvina, river, 36, 149, 162, 196
Dzikow, Confederation of, 186

East Prussia, 93 f., 110, 120, 148,
  158, 161, 167, 169, 196, 270,
  281, 282, 288, 309, 312, 330
Egypt, 318, 320
El Alamein, 320
Elba, island, 224
Elbe, river, 5, 14 f.
Elbing, 94
Elizabeth of Austria, wife of
  Casimir IV, 95
Elizabeth of Bosnia, queen mother
  of Hungary, 66
Elizabeth, daughter of Ladislas the
  Short, 49
Elizabeth of Luxemburg, queen
  dowager of Hungary, 88
Elster, river, 15, 224
Enghien, Duc d', 163
England, 72, 82, 104, 170, 183,
  225, 233, 236, 238, 240, 245,
  269, 276, 289, 307 ff., 318, 320
Eric XIV of Sweden, 121
Ermeland. *See* Varmia
Ernest, Archduke, 138
Estonia, 121, 140
Eugenius IV, Pope, 88 f.

'Execution of laws' policy, 118, 122 f.

Falaise, 324

'Family, the,' 184, 187 f.

Federation of Socialist Youth Organizations, 385

Feodor I, 145

Feodor III, 168

Ferdinand I, of Austria, 109, 111

Ferdinand II, 150

Ferdinand III, 151

Finland, 302

Flemming, Field Marshal, 182

Fleury, Cardinal, 185

Florence, Union of, 88 f., 139

Flottwell, President, 235

France, French, 21, 32, 53, 68, 72, 79, 82, 90, 96, 104, 112, 132 ff., 149 ff., 163 f., 167 f., 169 f., 173, 175, 178 ff., 185, 188, 193, 195, 198, 205 f., 208, 218 ff., 227 f., 231, 233, 236, 238, 240, 245, 247, 249, 257, 269, 276, 278, 286, 289, 302 f., 305, 308 f., 316 ff., 324, 379

Francis Joseph, Emperor of Austria, 238, 259

Frederick I (Barbarossa), Emperor, 25, 32

Frederick I of Prussia, 180

Frederick II, Emperor, 25, 32, 35, 37

Frederick II of Prussia, 187, 192 ff., 196, 203

Frederick III, Emperor, 95 f., 98

Frederick of Brandenburg, 90

Frederick, son of Casimir IV, Cardinal, 104

Frederick of Saxony, Grand Master of Teutonic Order, 104, 108

Frederick Augustus I, Elector of Saxony. *See* Augustus II

Frederick Augustus II, Elector of Saxony. *See* Augustus III

Frederick Augustus, King of

Saxony, Duke of Warsaw, 221

Frederick William, Elector of Brandenburg (the Great Elector), 157 f., 167 f.

Frederick William II of Prussia, 203

Frederick William III of Prussia, 235

Frederick William IV of Prussia, 236

Fund of National Culture, 295

Gabriel Bethlen, 148

Gailhard de Carces, papal nuncio, 53

Galicia (Halicz), 27, 38, 54 ff., 71, 204, 208, 221, 225, 235 ff., 255, 259 ff., 270, 272, 277, 279 ff., 285 f., 296 f., 310 f.

Gasztold, John, Palatine of Wilno, 91, 101

Gasztold family, 118

Gdansk, 372, 376, 389. *See also* Danzig

Gdynia, 293, 312, 372, 388 f.

Gedymin, Grand Duke of Lithuania, 49, 54 f., 67 f., 70, 81

'General Government' territory, 311

Geneva, 293, 304

Geneva, Protocol, 303

Genoa, Conference of, 302

George of Podiebrad, 96 f.

German Association of the Eastern Marches, 259

German Democratic Republic, 358, 378

German Knights. *See* Teutonic Order

Germany, German Empire, Germans, 4 ff., *et passim*

Gero, margrave, 8

Gheri family, 100, 113

Gierek, Edward, 370, 372 ff., 380 ff., 387, 389 ff.

Glemp, Archbishop, 410, 417–18

Glinski, Prince Michael, 108

Glogow, 23
Gniezno, 7 f., 15 f., 42, 45 f., 257, 338
——, Congress of, 14
Godunov. *See* Boris Godunov
Golden Horde, 100, 103
Goluchowski, Agenor, 259 f.
Gomulka, Wladyslaw, 331, 346 ff., 352 ff., 366 ff., 377, 380 f., 391
Górnicki, Wieslaw, 415
Grabski, Ladislas, 291
Grabski, Tadeusz, 408
Great Britain, 281, 303, 319, 328 f., 379. *See also* England
Great Elector. *See* Frederick William, Elector
Great Poland, 7, 24 f., 36, 40, 45, 47 f., 57 f., 67, 91, 123, 136, 158, 196, 205, 207, 312
Great Russia, Great Russians, 68, 157
Great War, 225, 229, 260, 264, 266, 275, 280, 294, 308, 320
Greece, Greeks, 3, 82, 88, 318, 320
Gregory VII, Pope, 19
Grochow, battle of, 232
Grodno, 206, 208
Grottger, Arthur, 250
Grunwald, battle of, 75, 77 ff., 82, 84, 93
Guillaume de Machault, 56
Gustavus Adolphus, 148 f., 162

Hadziacz, Union of, 161
'Hakatism,' 258
Halicz (principality). *See* Galicia
Haller, General Joseph, 280, 287
Hapsburg, 87, 89, 95, 98 f., 104, 109, 112, 118 f., 132, 135, 138, 148 f., 151, 160, 169, 173, 237, 259 f.
Hegel, 245
Helsinki agreement, 387
Henri de Valois, 132 ff.
Henry I, of Silesia, the Bearded, 31, 36 f.

Henry II, Emperor, 15 ff.
Henry II, the Pious, 37 ff.
Henry III, Emperor, 18
Henry IV, of Breslau, 44 ff.
Henry IV, Emperor, 19
Henry IV, of France, 142, 149
Henry V, Emperor, 23
Henry VI, Emperor, 32
Henry, son of Boleslas III, 24
Henry of Glogow, 45, 47 f.
Henry von Plauen, 78
Hertzberg, Count von, 203
Hitler, 304 ff., 312, 314, 318, 320, 323 f.
Hlond, Cardinal, 338
Hoene-Wronski, 249
Hohenzollern-Ansbach, 108
Hohenzollerns, 110, 120, 149, 168
Holland, 324
Holy Alliance, 227
Holy League, 172, 174
Holy See. *See* Papacy
Hopkins, Harry, 329
Horodlo, Union of, 75, 80 ff., 84
Hosius, bishop, 124
Hundred Years War, 178
Hungary, Hungarians, 13, 19, 29, 34, 40, 47, 49, 53, 56 f., 59, 65 ff., 71, 73, 82, 87 ff., 95 ff., 101 ff., 109, 111 f., 119, 133 ff., 148, 167, 170, 172 f., 237, 260, 286, 302, 317, 340, 345, 353 f., 358, 378
Hunyadi, John, 89 f., 96
Huss, Hussites, 83, 87, 96, 123
Indo-China, 33, 342
Innocent III, Pope, 28 f.
Innocent IV, Pope, 38
International Labour Organization, 293
Ireland, 329
Israel, 367, 369
Italy, 32, 57, 115, 217, 219, 322, 379
Ivan III, the Severe, 99, 101, 103 f.

Ivan IV, the Terrible, 110, 119, 121, 133 ff., 145
Iwaszkiewicz, Wladyslaw, 363

Jadwiga of Anjou, 65–74, 76, 80, 248
Jagiello (Ladislas II), 67–87, 94, 248
Jagiellonian University. *See* Cracow, University of
Jagiellos, Jagiellonian system, 61, 84, 85 ff., 97 f., 100, 104, 108, 114, 120 ff., 144, 344
January Rising, 229, 240, 250
Japan, 266, 327
Jaroszewicz, Piotr, 372, 376, 381 ff., 390
Jaruzelski, General, 400–20 *passim*, 425
Jasinski, General, 207
Jaszczuk, Boleslaw, 371, 376
Jedrychowski, Stefan, 383
Jesuits, 125, 136, 144, 184, 198
Jews, 58, 155, 296 f., 313, 323, 331, 367 ff.
John Albert (John I), 97, 101 ff.
John Casimir (John II), 155 ff., 163, 166, 261
John of Luxemburg, King of Bohemia, 49 f., 53
John Paul II, Pope, 394, 418
John Sobieski (John III), 166–175, 176, 178, 180 f.
John III of Sweden, 121, 140
John XXII, Pope, 49
John XXIII, Pope, 362
John Zapolya, King of Hungary, 112
Jungingen, Ulric von, 77

Kador, Janos, 415
Kaffa, 100, 103
Kalisz Treaty of, 53
Kamieniec, 166, 168, 173, 180
Kania, Stan., 383
Kaniow, 203

Kara, Mustapha, 170
Karlowitz, Peace of, 180
Karpinski, Francis, 198
Kasman, Leon, 368
Katyn, 321
Kellogg Pact. *See* Paris, Pact of
Kepa, Jozef, 380
Kettler, Gothard, 120
Krakow, 391
Krushchev, Nikita, 347, 349 ff., 352, 355, 358, 364
Kiejstut of Lithuania, 67 f., 72
Kietlicz, Henry, archbishop, 29
Kiev, 13, 15 ff., 19 f., 27, 37, 67, 103, 126, 150, 154, 157, 161 f., 174, 268, 286
Kilia, 100, 102
Kilinski, John, 207
Kipchak, Khan of, 38
Kirkholm, battle of, 140
Kisielewski, Stefan, 386
Klajpeda, 315. *See also* Memel
Kliszko, Zenon, 352, 363, 366, 373
Kluszyn, battle of, 146
Kochanowski, John, 125
Kolakowski, Leszek, 363, 366
Kollataj, Hugo, 199
Komar, General Waclaw, 352 f.
Komorowski. *See* Bor
Konarski, Father Stanislas, 191
Koniecpolski, Stanislas, 149, 151
Konigsberg, 94, 149, 330
Konopnicka, Maria, 263
Kordecki, Father Augustine, 158
Korea, 342
Korfanty, Wojciech, 289
Kosciuszko, Thaddeus, 250 ff., 219, 225, 254
Kossak, Julius, 250
Kossuth, Louis, 237
Kosygin, 364
Koszyce (Kassa), Compact of, 66
Kovno, 286
Krasicki, Ignatius, 198
Krasinski, Sigismund, 245 f., 248 f.
Krasinskis, the, 195

Kraszewski, J. I., 263
Kremlin, 147
Krewo, Treaty of, 69, 92
Krukowiecki, General, 232
Kujavia, 44, 50, 53
Kukiel, General, 317
Kultura, 363, 367
Kuron, Jacek, 366
Kutno, battle of, 309

Ladislas I. *See* Ladislas the Short
Ladislas II. *See* Jagiello
Ladislas III, 85, 87 ff.
Ladislas IV, 142, 146 f., 149 ff.,
  155, 163
Ladislas, King of Bohemia and
  Hungary, 96 ff., 101 ff., 109, 111
Ladislas, son of Boleslas III, 24
Ladislas, Herman, 20 ff.
Ladislas of Opole, 73, 76
Ladislas, the Posthumous, King of
  Bohemia and Hungary, 95 f.
Ladislas the Short, 46 ff.. 52 f.
Ladislas, Tsar, 146
Lane, Bliss, A., 333
Lange, Oskar, 359
Laski, John, archbishop, 107
Laski, John, the younger, 124
Lateran Council, 34
Latin America, 329
Latvia, 296
League of Nations, 283, 288 f., 303,
  305
Lebanon, 329
Ledochowski, Mgr. archbishop, 257
Leipzig, battle of, 224
Lelewel, Joachim, 247 f., 261
Leliwa, House of, 67
Lenczyca, 27, 44
Leopold I, Emperor, 170, 172
Leopold II, King of the Belgians,
  308
Leopold III, Duke of Austria, 67
Leszczynska, Maria, 185
Leszczynski, Stanislas (Stanislas I),
  181, 185 f., 190

Leszek, the Black, 44, 46
Leszek, the White, 28 f., 31, 38
Liberum veto, 163, 200
Libya, 318
Lignica, battle of, 37, 41, 44
Lipinski, Edward, 387
Liske, Xavier, 201
Lithuania, Lithuanians, 7, 36,
  38 f., 49, 54 ff., 67 ff., *et passim*
Little Entente, 302
Little Poland, 7, 26, 28, 31, 37,
  44 f., 47, 58, 66 f., 91, 136
Little Russia, 126, 157. *See also*
  Ukraine
Livonia, 36, 71, 76, 93, 103, 120,
  127, 134 f., 140, 148 f., 162, 180
Lloyd George, 281 f.
Locarno treaties, 303, 305
Lodomeria, 225, 260
Lodz, 256, 293, 312, 335, 367, 376
Lomza, 315
London, 191, 278, 323 f., 329 f.,
  330, 334
Lothair II, Emperor, 23
Louis II of Bohemia and Hungary,
  111
Louis IX (St Louis), 41, 69
Louis XIV, 167 f., 174 f.
Louis XV, 185
Louis of Anjou, King of Hungary
  and Poland, 55, 57, 59 f., 65 f.,
  71, 73, 88
Louis, the Bavarian, Emperor, 49
Louis of Orleans, 66, 69
Louise Marie e Gonzague, 151,
  163, 167
Low Countries, 170
Lubecki, Prince Xavier, 227
Lublin, 118, 131, 145, 161, 295,
  313, 322, 335
——, Union of, 118, 131, 145, 161
——, University of, 295, 338, 346
Lubomirski, George, 163 f.
Luck, Congress of, 82 f.
Lukasinski, conspirator, 231
Luneville, 190, 219

——, Peace of, 219
Lusatia, 15, 18
Lutheran movement, 110 f., 123 ff.
Lwow, 54, 71, 159, 168, 174, 221, 237, 260 f., 287 ff., 310, 315, 327, 335
——, University of, 261, 294

Maciejowice, battle of, 207
Magdeburg, 278
Mahomet IV, Sultan, 166
Malachowski, Stanislas, 201
Malenkov, 345, 347
Maria, daughter of Louis of Anjou, 66, 68
Maria Casimira, wife of John Sobieski, 167, 175
Maria, Theresa, 196
Marienburg, 49, 78, 93 f.
Marini, Antoine, 96
Marshall Plan, 334
Martin, V., Pope, 79
Masovia, Masovians, 7 f., 18, 24, 26 f., 28, 31, 33 f., 39, 44, 50, 54, 67, 72, 96, 111, 126, 205
Matejko, John, 250
Matthias, Corvinus, 96 ff.
Maximilian I, 98, 108 f., 114
Maximilian II, 134
Maximilian, Archduke, 137 f.
Mazarin, Cardinal, 163
Mazeppa, 181
Mediterranean, 343
Melsztyn, lords of, 67
Memel, 93. *See also* Klajpeda
Mendog, King of Lithuania, 38 f., 69
Mengli Gherai, Khan of the Crimea, 100, 103
Messianists, 243 ff., 249, 251, 261
Metternich, 235
Michael Romanov, Tsar, 147
Michael Wisniowiecki, King, 165 f.
Michelet, Jules, 247
Michnik, Adam, 368

Mickiewicz, Adam, 223, 231, 238, 243 f., 246 f., 264, 368
Microslawski, L., 235 f.
Mieszko, I, 8 ff., 18, 28
Mieszko II, 17 f.
Mieszko, the Old, 24 ff., 28, 36
Mikolajczyk, Stan., 321, 323 f., 329, 331, 333
Milewski, Gen., 409
Minc, Hilary, 352
Mniszech, son-in-law of Count Bruhl, 186
Mniszech, George, 145
Mniszech, Marina, 146
Moczar, Mieczyslaw, 367, 370, 372, 380, 382 ff.
Modrzewski, Andrew Frycz, 125
Modzielewski, Karol, 366
Moghila, Peter, 150
Moghila family, 147
Mohacs, battle of, 111 f., 171
Moldavia, 56, 71, 100, 103, 113, 119, 139, 147, 150, 173 f.
Molotov, V., 328 f.
Mongols, 37 f., 68, 154
Monte Cassino, 322
Moravia, 5 f., 15, 18, 97
Morsztyn, Andrew, 169
Moscicki, Ignacy, President, 299, 316
Moscow, 27, 38, 68, 70, 82, 97, 99 ff., 103, 107, 109, 112, 120, 127, 135, 139, 141, 145 ff., 151, 157, 161 f., 168, 174, 287, 308, 316, 320, 321, 323, 328 f., 331, 334 f., 341, 323
Movement for the Defence of the Human and Civil Rights of Man, 390
Munich, 306
Murad, II 89
Muraviev, Count, 255
Mussolini, 305, 311

Nagy, Imre, 358
Naples, Kingdom of, 66

Napoleon I, 218 ff.
Napoleon III, 238, 240
Narew, river, 311
Naruszewicz, Adam, bishop, 198, 248
Narutowicz, Gabriel, President, 299
Narvik, 318
National Commission of Education, 198
National Council, 318 f.
National Democrats, 267
National Library, 275
National Socialism, Socialists, 304, 308, 313, 318
Natolin group, 351, 363
Neisse, river, 330
Nevers, Abbey of, 164
New March, 60
Nicholas I, Tsar, 231, 233, 235, 237 f.
Nicholas II, Tsar, 257
Nicholas, Grand Duke, 276
Nicholas, Palatine of Cracow, 28
Niemen, river, 35, 78, 92
——, basin, 287
Nikopoli, battle of, 90
Nimeguen, Peace of, 169
Non-aggression treaty with Germany, 304, 308
Non-aggression treaty with Soviet Russia, 304
Non-Party Group, 300
Norsemen, 5 f., 12
North Atlantic Treaty, 342 f.
November Rising, 229, 232, 235, 240, 243
Novgorod, Republic of, 71, 82, 99
Novosiltsov, Count, 230
Novotny, Antonin, 368
Nowa Huta, 382
Nowa Kultura, 362 f.
Nowe Drogi, 348
Nystadt, Peace of, 183

Ochab, Edward, 350 f.

Oder, river, 5, 12, 15, 26, 29, 40, 330
Oder-Neisse line, 330, 341, 365, 371
Olesnicki Zbigniew, bishop, 85 ff., 91, 101
Olgierd, Grand Duke of Lithuania, 67 f.
Oliva, Treaty of, 162, 180
Olszowski, Stefan, 408
Opalinski, Palatine, 158
Oranienburg, 314
Orava, 288
Organic Work, 255
Orsza, battle of, 108
Orthodox Church, 55, 68, 70, 87, 108, 119, 139 f., 146, 150, 155 f., 173, 183 f., 194, 268
Orwell, George, 386
Orzeszkowa, Eliza, 263
Osman II, Sultan, 148
Osobka-Morawski, Edward, 331, 336
Ossolinski, George, 151, 155
Ostrogski, Prince Constantine, 108, 141
Ostroleka, battle of, 232
Ostrow, 72
Oswiecim, 314
Otto I, Emperor, 9, 11, 14
Otto II, Emperor, 11
Otto III, Emperor, 12, 14 ff.
Ottokar II of Bohemia, 40
Ottoman Empire. *See* Turkey

Pacta Conventa, 133
Paderewski, Ignacy, 266, 278, 280, 283, 317
Palcogi, the, 99
Palestine, 151, 318
Panin, Count, 196
Panslavism, 268
Papacy, 4, 12 f., 17, 19, 28 f., 32, 35, 37 ff., 42, 46, 48 f., 53, 56, 59, 83, 88, 96, 135, 151, 170, 172, 256, 258, 362, 365

Paris, 79, 134, 142, 191, 224, 247, 261, 283 f., 316
——, Congress of, 238
——, Pact of, 303
——, University of, 79
Partisan faction, 367 ff.
Pasek, John Chrysostom, 161
Paskevich, Field Marshal, 233 f., 237
Patriotic Society, 233
Paul I, Tsar, 217
Paul II, Pope, 96
Paul VI, Pope, 365, 382
Paul, son of Vladimir, 79
Pax, 382
Peace Conference of 1919, 273, 280, 283 ff., 287
Pearl Harbor, 319
Perejaslaw, Treaty of, 157
Petchenegs, 17
Peter III, 187
Peter, the Great, 180 ff., 326
Petersburg, 192, 204
Petit, Jean, 79
Pethura, Symon, 286 f.
Philip of Burgundy, 89
Piarist Order, 191
Piasecki, Boleslaw, 361, 382
Piasts, 7–61, passim, 66, 69, 72 f., 111, 344
Pierre de Lusignan, King of Cyprus, 57
Pilica, river, 208
Pilsudski, Joseph, 267, 272, 276 f., 278, 280, 283, 286 f., 298 ff.
Piramowicz, Gregory, abbe, 198
Pisa, river, 311
Pius II, Pope, 86
Pius IX, Pope, 240
Pius XII, Pope, 308, 338 f.
Plelo, Comte de, 185
Plowce, battle of, 50
Po Prostu, 348, 354, 362
Podlasie, 27, 126
Podolia, 55, 84, 90 f., 168, 173, 180, 205

Polaniec, Manifesto of, 207
Polesia, 294
Polians, 6 f.
Polish Academy of Sciences and Arts. See Academy
Polish Legions, 219, 276 f.
Polish Military organization, 278
Polish National Committee (Paris), 278, 280
Polish Writers' Union, 363
Polock, 121, 135
Poltava, battle of, 181
Pomerania, Pomeranians, 12, 17, 23 f., 29, 35 f., 40, 45, 47 ff., 53, 60, 76, 78, 92, 94, 236, 281, 312, 330. See also Danzig Pomerania
Poniatowski, Prince Joseph, 205, 221 ff.
Poniatowski, Stanislas, 184, 191
Poniatowski, Stanislas Augustus. See Stanislas Augustus
Posen, Grand Duchy of, 225. See also Poznan
Positivists, 256
Possevino, Antonio, 135
Potocki, Ignatius, 203
Potocki, Stanislas, 227
Potockis, the, 147, 184, 187
Potsdam Conference, 330 f.
Poznan (Posen), 7, 45, 205, 235, 257, 295, 313, 350 f., 352
——, University of, 295
Poznania, 225, 235 f., 257 f., 281, 284, 312
Praga, sack of, 208
Prague, 15 f., 57, 59, 74, 96, 237
Premyslides, 48
Presburg, 109
Protestants, 110 f., 123 ff., 133, 139, 144, 150, 178, 179, 183 f., 194. See also Lutheran movement
Prus, Boleslas, 263
Prussia, Prussians, 7, 16, 26, 34 ff., 68, 72, 76, 78, 86, 92 ff., 98, 107, 109 f., 119 f., 148 f., 157 f.,

175, *et passim*
Prussian League, 92 f.
Przeglad Kulturalmy, 363
Przemysl, 13
Przemysl, King, 45 ff.
Pskov, siege of, 135
Pulaski, Casimir, 195
Pulawy faction, 351, 363, 369
Raclawice, battle of, 207
Raczkiewicz, Ladislas, President, 316, 334
Raczynski, Edward, 316
Radkiewicz, Stan., 331, 349
Radom, 313, 389
——, Confederation of, 194
Radziejowski, vice-chancellor, 158
Radziwill, Barbara. *See* Barbara Radziwill
Radziwill, Princes Boguslas and Janusz, 157
Radziwill, Michael, 232
Radziwill, Nicholas, the Black, 118, 122
Radziwill, Nicholas, the Red, 118, 122
Radziwills, the, 102
Rakoczy, George, Prince of Transylvania, 160
Rakowski, Mieczyslaw, 406
Rapallo, Treaty of, 301
Reformation, the, 110 f., 123 ff.
Regency Council, 279 f.
Reichstadt, Duke of, 233
Repnin, Prince, 194
Republican Commonwealth, 126 f. *See also* Royal Republic
Rey, Nicholas, 125
Reymont, Ladislas, 265
Reytan, Thaddeus, 197
Ribbentrop, 308
Richelieu, Cardinal, 150
Riga, 56, 120, 148, 287
——, Treaty of, 295, 301
Rokossovsky, Marshal, 352 f.
Roman Church. *See* Papacy *and* Catholicism

Roman of Volhynia and Halicz, 29, 38
Romanticism, Romantics, 243 ff., 262, 264 f.
Rome, Romans, 3 f., 13, 15, 38, 42, 45, 56, 99, 124, 139, 170, 278, 322, 340
Ronsard, 125
Roosevelt, President, 308, 321, 327 f.
Royal Air Force, 319
Royal Prussia. *See* West Prussia
Royal Republic, 136, 143, 172, 175, 177, 179, 189, 199, 201, 208, 211, 213, 242. *See also* Republican Commonwealth
Rudolf I, Emperor, 40, 45 f.
Rudolf II, Emperor, 137
Rugen, 23
Rumania, 302, 316 f.
Ruriks, the, 27, 145
Russia, 5, 15 f., *et passim*
Ruthenia, Ruthenians, 13, 16 ff., 27, 29, 38 f., 54 f., 68 ff., *et passim*. *See also* Ukranians *and* White Ruthenians
Rydz-Smigly, General, 300
Sadowski, Zdzislaw, 422
Sadova, battle of, 259
Saint-Germain-des-Pres, 164
Salza, Hermann von, 34
Samogitia, Samogitians, 36, 76 ff., 92 f.
San, river, 13
Sandomierz, 24 f., 39, 293
San Domingo, 219
San Francisco Conference, 328, 342
Sapieha family, 175
Sapieha, Adam, Cardinal, 338
Sapieha, Paul, 159
Sarai, 38
Saxons, 19
Saxony, 177, 179, 181, 184, 185 ff., 193, 201, 220, 225
——, House of, 177, 185, 193, 220

Scandinavia, Scandinavians, 4, 13, 56, 121, 306, 379
Schmidt, H., 390
School of Cadets, Warsaw, 232
Scotland, 318
Sejm. *See* Diets
Sempach, battle of, 70
Senate, 101 f.
Serbia, 89, 268
Seven Years War, 186
Shuiski. *See* Basil IV
Siberia, 234, 314
Sicinski, deputy, 163
Sieciech, Palatine, 22 f.
Siedlce, 310
Sienkiewicz, Henryk, 264 f.
Sieradz, 44
Sievers, Baron, 206
Sigismund I, the Old, 104, 106–119, 123, 141, 262
Sigismund II. *See* Sigismund Augustus
Sigismund III, 131, 137–149, 151, 162
Sigismund Augustus, 117–127, 131, 134, 136, 140, 149, 154
Sigismund, Grand Duke of Lithuania, 84, 87, 90 f.
Sigismund of Luxemburg, King of Hungary, German Emperor, 66, 69, 73, 82 f., 87 f.
Sikorski, General, 287, 299, 316, 321
Silesia, Silesians, 7 f., 18, 23 ff., 31, 36, 39 f., 42, 44, 46, 50, 53 f., 73, 87, 97, 148, 158, 167, 187, 257, 270, 282, 288 f., 293, 306, 312
Silvester II, Pope, 14
Siwak, Albin, 409
Skarga, Father Peter, 141
Skrzynecki, General, 232
Skrzynski, Count Alexander, 303
Slav Congress, 237
Slavs, 4 ff., 9, 12, 15 f., 40, 60, 83, 88, 237, 247, 253, 259, 268

Slonimski, Antoni, 363, 385
Slovakia, 15, 309
Slowacki, Julius, 246 f., 250
Smolensk, 70, 73, 108, 110, 121, 147, 157, 162, 223, 321
——, Grand Duke of, 70
Smolka, Stanislas, 261
Sniadecki, Andrew, 249
Sniadecki, John, 249
Sobieski, Alexander, 175
Sobieski, James, 175
Sobieski, John. *See* John Sobieski
Socialists, 267
Society for Secular Schooling, 361
Society of Sciences, Warsaw, 227
Sokorski, Wlodzimierz, 348, 350
Solidarity, 401–23 *passim*
Soliman I, the Magnificent, 111
Sorbonne, 74
Sosnkowski, General, 317, 321
Spain, Spaniards, 220
Spisz, 288
Spychalski, Marian, 353, 363, 373
Stackelberg, Count, 197
Stalin, 316, 318, 321, 323, 326 f., 329, 336, 345 ff., 355
Stalingrad, 320
Stambul. *See* Constantinople
Stanczyk Portfolio, 262
Stanislas I. *See* Leszczynski, Stanislas
Stanislas Augustus (Stanislas II), 189 ff., 197 f., 201, 203, 205, 212, 217, 227, 242
Stanislas, St, Bishop of Cracow, 20, 43 f., 340
Starza, House of, 67
Starzynski, Stephen, 309
Staszic, Stanislas, 199
Stephen Batory, 132, 134 ff., 138, 141, 145, 154
Stephen, the Great, of Moldavia, 100, 103
Stettin, 60, 330. *See also* Szczecin
——, Congress of, 121
Stolica, 367

Strzelecki, Ryszard, 367
Studia Filozoficzne, 363
Suchywilk, John, 59
Supreme National Committee, 277
Suvorov, Field Marshal, 208
Suwalki, 312
Sweden, Swedes, 121, 132, 137,
    140, 147, 149, 151 f., 157 f.,
    160 ff., 167, 180 f., 183
Swiatlo, Josef, 348
Swidrygiello, Grand Duke of
    Lithuania, 84, 86
Swienca family, 48
Swientopelk, Duke of Danzig
    Pomerania, 29, 35 f., 45
Swinka, James, archbishop, 46 f.
Switzerland, Swiss, the, 70, 123,
    289, 318
Sword Bearers, Order of the, 36,
    120
Szajnocha, Charles, 248
Szczecin, 372, 376. *See also* Stettin
Szczekociny, battle of, 207
Szeged, 89
Szlachcic, Franciszek, 383
Szujski, Joseph, 261
Szydlak, Jan, 383, 385
Szydlowiecki, Christopher, 107
Szyr, Engeniusz, 360

Tamerlane, 68, 73
Tannenberg, 77
Targowica, Confederation of,
    204 f., 212
Tarnogrod, Confederation of, 182
Tarnow, lords of, 67
Tarnowski, John, 113
Tarnowski, Stanislas, 262
Tartars, 37 ff., 54 f., 68, 71, 73,
    77, 82, 94, 100 f., 103, 112, 119,
    127, 142, 148, 151, 153 f., 156,
    162, 171, 173 f., 203
Teheran Conference, 321
Tejchma, Josef, 385
Tenczyn, lords of, 67

Teutonic Order (German Knights,
    Knights of the Cross), 34 ff.,
    38 f., 48 ff., 60, 67 f., 70, 72 f.,
    76 ff., 82, 84, 86, 92 f., 96, 98,
    104, 108 ff., 120, 281
Thirty Years War, 147, 150, 158,
    178
Thorn. *See* Torun
Tilsit, Peace of, 220
Tito, 355
Tokarski, Julian, 360
Tokoly, Imre, 170
Tomicki, Peter, 107
Torun, 34, 78, 94, 96, 98, 104,
    108, 150, 184, 196, 203, 205,
    335
——, Peace of, 78, 94, 96, 98, 104,
    108
Towianski, Andrzej, 243
Transylvania, 119, 134, 137, 148,
    160
——, Prince of. *See* Stephen
    Bathory
Traugutt, Romuald, 240
Trebizond, 147
Trembecki, Stanislas, 198
Trent, 124, 136, 142
——, Council of, 124, 136
Triple Alliance (1882), 269
Triple Entente (1907), 269
Troki, 72
Truman, H. S. President, 328 f.
Turkey, Turks, 82, 88 f., 94,
    100 ff., 103, 112 f., 119, 135,
    139, 142, 147 f., 151, 154, 156,
    162, 166 ff., 171 ff., 180 ff., 186,
    195, 203, 231, 238, 269
Tygodnik Powszechny, 361
Tyszowce, Confederation of, 158
Tyzenhaus, Anthony, 197

Ukraine, 126, 148, 153 ff., 161 f.,
    166, 131 f., 195, 205, 212, 255,
    279, 286 f., 315
——, Soviet, 287, 315
Ukrainian Cossacks. *See* Cossacks

Ukrainians (Ruthenians), 270, 284 f., 286, 296 ff., 310
Unger, Leopold, 368
Uniat Church, 150, 173, 234, 256, 268
Union of Fighters for Freedom and Democracy (ZBOWID), 367
United Nations, 319 ff., 328, 342
United States. *See* America
Ursus factory, 389
Utraquists, 96

Valdemar Atterdag of Denmark, 56
Varmia (Ermeland), 94
Varna, battle of, 85, 90, 92, 95, 151, 171
Vasas, the, 131, 140, 149
Vatican, 329, 338 f., 382
Vavel, Cathedral, 43 f., 46, 69, 90, 115, 134, 208
Venceslas II, of Bohemia, 45 ff.
Venceslas III, 48
Venice, Venetians, 89, 151, 170, 172
Versailles, Treaty of, 281 f., 284, 289, 304, 313
Vienna, 70, 107, 109, 148, 167, 170 f., 172, 175, 191, 224 ff., 230 f., 235, 237, 268
——, Congress of, 109 f., 112 ff., 224 ff., 230 f., 235, 268, 326
——, Peace of, 186, 221
Virgin Mary, cult of the, 159
Visegrad, Congress of, 53, 57
Vistula, river, 7, 29, 34 f., 78, 92, 196, 256, 281, 323
——, Provinces, 256
Vitold, 68, 70 ff., 80 ff., 91 f., 100
Vladimir, the Great, of Kiev, 13
Volga, river, 27, 38, 100
——, Tartars of the. *See* Golden Horde
Volhynia, 27, 54, 82, 84, 90 f., 126, 205, 208, 232, 286

Walachia, 139, 173
Wałęsa, Lech, 397-8, 400, 402-3, 405, 411-19 *passim*
Wankowicz, Melchior, 366
War of the Austrian Succession, 186
War of the Polish Succession, 186
Warsaw, 53, 134, 142, 146, 158, 160, 193, 205 ff., 220 ff., 227, 231 ff., 238 f., 261, 279 f., 286, 293, 295, 299, 309, 313 f., 323, 327, 329, 335, 338, 341, 343, 388 f.
——, Confederation of, 133 f.
——, Duchy of, 218, 220 ff., 224 f., 227
——, University of, 227, 234, 239, 261, 295, 366, 369
Warta, river, 40
Washington, 320, 334
Werblan, Andrzej, 384-5
Westphalia, Treaty of, 152
Waterloo, battle or, 224
Wawrzyniak, Father, 258
Wehlau, Treaty of, 161
West Prussia (Polish of Royal Prussia), 94, 111, 148, 161, 196, 225, 257, 281
Weygand, General, 287
White Ruthenia, Ruthenians, 121, 127, 157, 271, 284, 287, 296, 310 315
Wieliczka, salt mines, 59
Wielopolski, Alexander, 239, 255
Wienerwald, 171
Wilaszewski, Kazimierz, 364
Wilhelmina, Queen of the Netherlands, 308
William I, of Germany, 238, 267
William II, of Germany, 267
William of Hapsburg, 67, 69 f.
Wilno (Vilna), 70, 72, 91, 136, 157, 198, 207, 218, 222, 231, 234, 248 f., 284, 286 ff., 295, 315, 335
——, University of, 136, 198, 217 f..

231, 234, 248 f., 295, 316
Wilson, President, 278 f., 281 f.
Windischgraetz, Field Marshal,
  237
Wisniowiecki, Prince Jeremy, 156,
  165
Wisniowiecki, Michael. *See*
  Michael Wisniowiecki
Wittelsbach, House of, 49
Wojciechowski, Stanislas, President,
  299
Wojtyla, Karol, 393
Workers' Defence Committee, 390
Worskla, battle of the, 73
Wroclaw (Breslau), 330
Wyhowski, John, 161
Wysocki, Peter, 232
Wyspianski, Stanislas, 265 f.
Wyszynski, Stefan, Cardinal,
  339 f., 345 f., 360 f., 382, 386

Yalta Conference, 325–327, 329 f.,
  333
Yatvegians, 26, 39
Yugoslavia, 320, 347, 358

Zajaczek, General, 227
Zaleski, Augustus, 303, 316, 334

Zaluski, J. A., bishop, 199
Zambrowski, Antoni, 368
Zambrowski, Roman, 369
Zamosc, University of, 141
Zamoyski, Andrew, 193, 197, 239
Zamoyski, John, 132 f., 135 ff.,
  143 ff.
Zamoyski, Ladislas, General, 238
Zapolya, John. *See* John Zapolya
Zapolyas, the, 118
Zarzycki, Jerzy, 368
Zawadzki, Alexander, 336
Zbaraz, siege of, 156
Zbigniew, son of Ladislas Herman,
  22 f.
Zborowski, Samuel, 137
Zborowskis, the, 137
Zbrucz, river, 285
Zebrzydowski, Nicholas, Palatine,
  144, 146
Zeligowski, General, 287
Zeromski, Stefan, 265
Ziemovit of Masovia, 67
Znak, 361
Zolkiewski, Stanislas, 144, 146 f.,
  166
Zolnierz Wolnosci, 367